Agora Paperback Editions

GENERAL EDITOR: ALLAN BLOOM

The Roots of Political Philosophy

D1571145

Agora Paperback Editions

GENERAL EDITOR: ALLAN BLOOM

Jean-Jacques Rousseau, *Politics and the Arts: Letters to M. d'Alembert on the Theatre*. Translated by Allan Bloom.

Leo Strauss, *On Tyranny*.

Leo Strauss, *Xenophon's Socratic Discourse: An Interpretation of the "Oeconomicus."* With a translation of the *Oeconomicus* by Carnes Lord.

Medieval Political Philosophy: A Sourcebook. Edited by Ralph Lerner and Muhsin Mahdi.

Averroes on Plato's "Republic." Translated by Ralph Lerner.

Alexandre Kojève, *Introduction to the Reading of Hegel. Lectures on the "Phenomenonology of Spirit."* Assembled by Raymond Queneau. Edited by Allan Bloom. Translated by James H. Nichols, Jr.

The Roots of Political Philosophy: Ten Forgotten Socratic Dialogues. Translated, with Interpretive Studies. Edited by Thomas L. Pangle.

THE ROOTS OF
Political Philosophy

Ten Forgotten Socratic Dialogues

Translated, with Interpretive Studies

EDITED BY

Thomas L. Pangle

Cornell University Press

ITHACA AND LONDON

First published 1987 by Cornell University Press.

First printing, Agora Paperback Editions,
Cornell Paperbacks, 1987.

Library of Congress Cataloging-in-Publication Data

Plato.
  The roots of political philosophy.

  (Agora paperback editions)
  Includes index.
  1. Plato—Political and social views. 2. Socrates—Political and social views.
3. Political science. I. Pangle, Thomas L. II. Title.
JC71.P2213 1987   320'.01   87-47550
ISBN 0-8014-1986-7
ISBN 0-8014-9465-6 (pbk.)

Printed in the United States of America

To the memory of our friend and colleague

J A M E S   L E A K E

CONTENTS

vii

viii   Contents

CONTRIBUTORS

ALLAN BLOOM is Professor in the Committee on Social Thought at the University of Chicago. His publications include *The Republic of Plato*, translated, with an interpretive essay (New York: Basic Books, 1968).

CHRISTOPHER BRUELL is Associate Professor of Political Science at Boston College. He has published studies of Thucydides, Plato, and Xenophon.

STEVEN FORDE is Assistant Professor of Political Science at North Texas State University. His publications include *The Ambition to Rule: Alcibiades and the Politics of Imperialism in Thucydides* (Ithaca: Cornell University Press, forthcoming).

JAMES LEAKE, prior to his death, taught at Kenyon College and the University of Chicago. His doctoral dissertation, on the political thought of Tacitus, won the American Political Science Association's Leo Strauss Award for the best dissertation in political philosophy in 1981.

CARNES LORD is Senior Defense Analyst at the National Institute for Public Policy. His publications include *Education and Culture in the Political Thought of Aristotle* (Ithaca: Cornell University Press, 1982) and a translation of Aristotle's *Politics* (Chicago: University of Chicago Press, 1984).

JAMES H. NICHOLS, JR., is Associate Professor of Political Science at Claremount-McKenna College. His publications include *Epicurean Political Philosophy* (Ithaca: Cornell University Press, 1976).

CLIFFORD ORWIN is Associate Professor of Political Science and Fellow of St. Michael's College at the University of Toronto. He is the author of articles on Aeschylus, Plato, and Thucydides and is completing a book on Thucydides' political philosophy.

THOMAS L. PANGLE is Professor of Political Science and Fellow of St. Michael's College at the University of Toronto. His publications include *The Laws of Plato,* translated, with an interpretive essay (New York: Basic Books, 1980).

LEO STRAUSS, the late Robert Maynard Hutchins Distinguished Service Professor of Political Science at the University of Chicago, was the reviver in the twentieth century of authentic Socratic political philosophy. His many books include three volumes in the Agora series published by Cornell University Press: *On Tyranny, Xenophon's Socratic Discourse,* and *Xenophon's Socrates.*

DAVID R. SWEET is Assistant Professor of Classics and Director of the Graduate Program in Humanities at the University of Dallas. He is the author of articles on Juvenal and Catullus.

The Roots of Political Philosophy

EDITOR'S INTRODUCTION

This volume brings together ten Socratic dialogues that are for the most part little known in our time. Partly because these miniature works are so unfamiliar, but mainly because of their intrinsically paradoxical character, they convey with unrivaled force the most puzzling or unexpected, and hence liberating, dimensions of Platonic political philosophizing. To confront, to take seriously, to become captivated by, these shorter dialogues is to discover a Socrates who shakes the foundations of many of our conventional assumptions about what and how Socrates or Plato might have thought. We hope that by assembling these gems, and by presenting them in literal translations, we will help ourselves and others understand better the dialectical and relentless but productive questioning that we believe lies at the heart of the Platonic enterprise.

Our effort is premised on a rejection of the currently fashionable opinion according to which the dialogues presented here are at best preliminary sketches from an "early" Plato. Nor are we satisfied to regard them as merely sparks and fragments that might have flown from the Platonic chisel as the great works such as the *Symposium* were sculpted. The interpretive essays are intended to substantiate our judgment that each of the lesser dialogues presented here is a polished achievement worthy of the mature Plato and probably written by him. We contend that each of these dialogues conveys an investigation that has been executed in a manner that seems perfectly to suit the requirements of the theme or questions at issue. In some instances the question pursued is of the utmost significance and is thematically treated, as a question, nowhere else in the Platonic corpus (e.g., the question "What is law?" in the *Minos*). In other cases themes that appear over and over in other Platonic dialogues finally cease to be secondary and become the cynosure of the drama and argument (e.g., Socrates' "demonic voice," in the *Theages*). Each of the dialogues presented here can be seen to take its unique place in the Platonic cosmos. But each provides a new and irreplaceable perspective on that cosmos and thereby on the nature of things as Plato understands and reveals it. The implication is that in meditating on each of these short dramas we must sooner or later compare it with the more famous works. Yet the opposite also holds: those more famous dialogues will not disclose their full meaning until they are read in the light shed by these neglected or less brilliant beacons. In our own reading we have tried to approach these and all the dialogues with the fewest possible preconceptions and in the hope that we can bring to the surface, and bring into question, even those preconceptions with which we cannot dispense. Thus far, as our essays will reveal, what we have discovered has been frequently surprising and sometimes disturbing. Certainly our probing of these works has nurtured the conviction that many of the generally accepted accounts of the meaning or teaching of Plato, as well as many of our own previous notions, need drastic revision.

The *Theages,* for example, leads one to reconsider the relation between Socrates' famous "demonic voice" and his equally famous "eroticism." In the *Cleitophon* we encounter a Plato who presents doubts or questions about the civic success of Socratic moral exhortation and teaching. The *Hipparchus* compels us to adopt a much more austere conception of the Platonic evaluation of moral indignation. The *Minos* prompts a thorough reexamination of the Socratic estimation of the rule of law. The *Lovers* sheds unexpected light on Socrates' own way of conceptualizing the relation between his political philosophizing and the pre-Socratics' natural-scientific investigations.

As is obvious by now, we question the widespread (but often poorly thought out or casually accepted) view according to which some of the dialogues here translated were not in fact written by Plato. Although few scholars would today deny the authenticity of the *Laches, Lesser Hippias,* and *Ion,* the case is otherwise—sometimes drastically so—when it comes to the remaining dialogues in our selection. The present volume is intended primarily for students, teachers, and scholars who do not read Greek, and it would be out of place to undertake in this context a detailed sifting of the arguments that have been advanced to impugn or defend the genuineness of each dialogue. We must therefore confine ourselves to a few provocative and necessarily controversial reflections. These preliminary remarks cannot, of course, be conclusive, but they can challenge the prejudices that may obstruct a candid reconsideration of the fascinating dramas that follow.[1]

We begin from the observation that every one of the dialogues included here seems to have been accepted in antiquity as a genuine Platonic work.[2] That is, all were recognized as authentic, for centuries after Plato, by scholars who knew the language with an intimacy we can never hope to rival and who had at their disposal a vast body of Greek literature irretrievably lost to us—including perhaps letters and memorabilia belonging to Plato himself as well as to his immediate students and contemporaries.[3] Our principal source in this matter, Diogenes Laertius (ca. A.D. 225), reports a generally or unanimously accepted scholarly listing of genuine Platonic dialogues as opposed to spurious ones (*Lives of Eminent Philosophers* III 62). There

[1] A selected and annotated bibliography of some of the writings pertinent to the question of authenticity is appended; all citations in the Introduction refer to the editions designated in the Bibliography.

[2] Scattered idiosyncratic doubts, to be sure, were expressed about many of Plato's dialogues. Aristoxenus and Favorinus both claimed, apparently, that the *Republic* was written mostly by Protagoras (Diog. Laer. III 37–38, 57). "Some" seem to have claimed that the *Epinomis* was written by Plato's close student Philip of Opus (ibid., III 37). A remark of Thrasyllus reported by Diogenes Laertius (IX 37) indicates that Thrasyllus at least knew of doubts about the *Lovers,* whether or not he shared them (earlier, however, Diogenes speaks as if Thrasyllus agreed with the consensus that did not treat the *Lovers* as a spurious work: ibid., III 56–61). Panaetius, the great Athenian Stoic philosopher, rejected the *Phaedo* on the grounds that it was unworthy of a true philosopher like Plato to write seriously in defense of so childish a notion as the immortality of the soul. "This verdict of Panaetius," George Grote remarks, "is the earliest example handed down to us of a Platonic dialogue disallowed on internal grounds—that is, because it appeared to the critic unworthy of Plato" (1867:158). Aelian (*Various History* VIII 1–2) doubted the *Hipparchus;* if anything, it is surprising, Guido Calogero suggests (1938:18–19), that we do not find more such doubts voiced by late, moralistic Platonists or by neo-Platonists—because the *Hipparchus* is Plato's boldest presentation of "eudemonism," or the characteristic Socratic reduction of the good to what is beneficial for oneself. Friedländer remarks (1958–70: vol. 2, p. 321 n. 16), "The questioning of the Platonic origin by Aelian . . . has no binding force, since neither the origin of the thesis nor any argument is given. In other places as well, Aelian rather prides himself upon such critical remarks."

[3] Indeed, some of the dialogues nowadays generally condemned or ignored—the *Theages, Alcibiades I,* and perhaps the *Cleitophon*—were judged by many ancient and medieval teachers or scholars to be *the* proper gateways to the Platonic corpus. See, e.g., Albinus 1892:149 (=1870:318); Diog. Laer. III 62; Alfarabi, pt. 2, beg.; Dunn (1976:59ff.).

was by no means, then, an uncritical acceptance of every so-called Platonic writing: the ancient scholarly community knew of dialogues, letters, and other pieces that circulated under the name of Plato but were excluded by scholars from the established canon of genuine works.[4]

Though there were earlier authoritative canonical arrangements of the dialogues (the most famous being that of Aristophanes of Byzantium, chief librarian at the library of Alexandria ca. 200 B.C.), the subsequently most influential version is that associated with Thrasyllus, the court astrologer of the emperor Tiberius and "apparently a very erudite scholar" (Chroust 1965:38).[5] Thrasyllus classified thirty-five dialogues in nine tetralogies (an arrangement modeled on the tragedians' supposed arrangements of their plays), completing the ninth tetralogy by treating all the epistles (of which he recognized thirteen as genuine) as one "work."[6] He placed certain spurious dialogues in an appendix. Because this Thrasyllan arrangement is reflected in most of the medieval manuscripts that are our sources for the works of Plato, the arrangement has become the basis for all modern complete editions of the Platonic corpus—even though few, if any, recent scholars have accepted either the Thrasyllan judgment as to the authenticity of all thirty-five dialogues and all thirteen letters or the tetralogical scheme. The latter was widely contested even in antiquity,[7] and the authenticity of some of the letters may also have

[4]Diogenes Laertius lists "the dialogues agreed to be spurious"; for a fuller list of "Platonic" works mentioned in ancient sources that seem to have been regarded as spurious by most ancient scholars, see Chroust (1965:38).

[5]For details as to what is known of Thrasyllus, see the references in Dunn (1976: n. 9).

[6]The question of the nature and the authenticity of each of the Platonic epistles would require a lengthy separate treatment, which would pay due regard to the fact that Thrasyllus (perhaps following the Alexandrians) joined the thirteen letters together as *one* work, one *dramatic* work, completing a dramatic tetralogy whose centerpiece is the *Laws*. Thrasyllus seems to have regarded the epistles as no more "historical" or genuinely "biographical" or "autobiographical" than Plato's Socratic dramas; one is tempted to say that he treats each of the thirteen letters much as he treats each of the twelve books of the *Laws* (Diog. Laer. III 57). Similarly, Aristophanes of Byzantium included the "epistles" (how many we do not know) as *one* work in one of his trilogies: he too treated the letters as a single dramatic whole, completing a larger dramatic whole whose centerpiece is the *Phaedo*. Consider here the remarks, from a rather different point of view, made by Müller (1975:17 n. 2).

[7]Diog. Laer. III 50–51, 61–62; Albinus 1892:149 (= 1870:318–19); Westerwink, ed., [Anonymous] *Prolegomena to Platonic Philosophy* 24–25. According to Diogenes Laertius (III 56), Thrasyllus claimed that Plato himself arranged the dialogues in tetralogies—but Thrasyllus' words as reported do *not* necessarily imply that he

been widely questioned in antiquity. But the authenticity of the thirty-five dialogues listed in the canon came into serious question only at the beginning of the nineteenth century, especially with the commentaries of Schleiermacher and his student Ast.

However intelligent the impulse may have been that spurred Schleiermacher's own animadversions, the critical tradition he originated rapidly drifted far from his reverential attitude toward Plato and the purportedly absolute unity of Plato's thought. To explain the course of this largely German tradition and the reason for its success would require lengthy consideration of a fascinating and poorly understood chapter in the history of modern thought. Suffice it to say that the doubts about much of the Platonic canon went hand in hand with similar suspicions about Homer, the Bible, and the classical historians; that these doubts came to be linked with a new and unprecedented concern with questions of historical and biographical development; and that this kind of approach waxed in the shadow of a belief in the historical progress of civilization in general and of philosophy in particular.[8] In other words, scholars came to be convinced that they had a new and superior understanding of what Plato could and could not have written at the same time that they succumbed to the delusion that they were in possession of a deeper understanding of the issues of philosophy than that held by Plato and the great medieval Platonists (e.g., Alfarabi). The modern atheteses were grounded for the most part on the supposed inconsistencies between what was claimed to be the teaching of the dialogue in question and what was supposedly "known" to be the doctrine and/or the "development" of Plato. Now, there are no doubt numerous extraordinary contradictions between Socrates' statements in such works as the *Republic* and his statements in several, or even all, of the lesser dialogues collected here, but there are at least as many,

thought his own tetralogies were the same as Plato's (Dunn 1976: n. 19). Other arrangements, some in trilogies—above all, that of Aristophanes of Byzantium—are reported by Diogenes. Whether any of these specific arrangements, including especially the tetralogies of Thrasyllus, go back to a very early date (perhaps even to the Academy of Plato's immediate successors) or whether they are of much later provenance remains a debated question. See Grote (1867:155, 169); Hoerber (1957); Philip (1970:296 n. 1); Müller (1975:23, 29 n. 1); Dunn (1976: n. 15); Solmsen (1981:106).

[8]Wilamowitz-Moellendorff opens the section of his *History of Classical Scholarship* that is devoted to the nineteenth century with the following remarkable declaration: "We have at last arrived at the threshold of the nineteenth century, in which the conquest of the ancient world by science was completed" (1982:105).

and as grave, contradictions within the *Republic* itself. These contradictions make each of the dialogues, and the Platonic corpus as a whole, truly educative. Precisely the fact that, in a dialogue such as the *Lesser Hippias,* Socrates' statements appear peculiar, not to say mad, when compared with what he seems to be presented as saying in the *Republic* makes the study of this strange little work valuable and enjoyable for people who love to have their minds prodded into wakefulness.

It is true that in the late nineteenth and early twentieth centuries the tide of doubt gradually receded somewhat. One by one, beginning with such works as the *Laws* and the *Apology of Socrates* (rejected by Ast) many "counterfeits"—at one time or another all but a quarter of the canon was vigorously rejected—were given back their legitimate birthright. It was stressed, for example, that the *Lesser Hippias* seems to be treated as perfectly genuine by Plato's friend and student Aristotle (*Metaphysics* 1025a6). Now, if Plato could create a Socratic conversation as delightfully odd as the *Lesser Hippias,* who is to say with confidence what Plato could and could not have written? More generally, what limits can be set to the artistry and playfulness of such a genius?[9]

In our view, when it comes to the less well known dialogues in the canon, contemporary readers, and even scholars, still remain too much under the spell of the doubts cast and the methods used by the great nineteenth-century critics. And yet in the midst of that same century George Grote (1867:132–69) defended the authenticity of the entire canonical listing with a strictly historical argument that seems to us to merit the most serious attention—even if it requires some major qualifications and supplements. Given the obscurity into which Grote's arguments have fallen, it is not inappropriate to rehearse his salient points. Grote begins by placing great weight on the implications of the fact that the school and library Plato himself founded was maintained in Athens for centuries:

> It provided not only safe and lasting custody, such as no writer had ever enjoyed before, for Plato's original manuscripts, but also a guarantee of some efficacy against any fraud or error which might seek to introduce other compositions into the list. . . . Speusippos and Xenocrates (also

[9]"Let us be frank to learn from the admission that without the explicit testimony of Aristotle, probably few critics would consider the *Hippias Minor* a genuine Platonic work" (Friedländer 1958–70; vol. 2, p. 146; cf. Calogero 1938:20).

Aristotle, Hestiaeus, the Opuntian Philipus, and the other Platonic pupils) must have had personal knowledge of all that Plato had written. . . . They had perfect means of distinguishing his real compositions from forgeries passed off in his name: and they had every motive to expose such forgeries (if any were attempted). . . . The original MSS. of Plato . . . were doubtless treasured up in the school as sacred memorials of the great founder, and served as originals from which copies of unquestionable fidelity might be made, whenever the Scholarch granted permission. . . . If we look back to the first commencement of the Alexandrine Museum and library, we shall be still farther convinced that the works of Plato, complete as well as genuine, must have been introduced into it before the days of Kallimachus . . . [The] favorable dispositions, on the part of the first Ptolemy, towards philosophy and the philosophers at Athens, appear to have been mainly instigated and guided by the Phalerean Demetrius: an Athenian citizen of good station, who enjoyed for ten years at Athens (while that city was subject to Kassander) full political ascendancy. . . . We learn that the ardour of Demetrius Phalereus was unremitting, and that his researches extended everywhere, to obtain for the new museum literary monuments from all countries within contemporary knowledge. . . . But Demetrius was a Greek, born about the time of Plato's death (347 B.C.), and identified with the political, rhetorical, dramatic, literary, and philosophical, activity of Athens, in which he had himself taken a prominent part. To collect the materials of Greek literature would be his first object. . . . Among all the books which would pass over to Alexandria as the earliest stock of the new library, I know nothing upon which we can reckon more certainly than upon the works of Plato. For they were acquisitions not only desirable, but also easily accessible. . . . Or if we even suppose that Demetrius, instead of obtaining copies of the Platonic MSS. from the school, purchased copies from private persons or booksellers . . . , he could, at any rate, assure himself of the authenticity of what he purchased, by information from the Scholarch. . . . If there were in the Museum any other works obtained from private vendors and professing to be Platonic, Kallimachus and Aristophanes had the means of distinguishing these from such as the Platonic school had furnished and could authenticate, and motive enough for keeping them apart from the certified Platonic catalogue. . . . When Thrasyllus set himself to edit and re-distribute the Platonic works, we may be sure . . . he accepted the collection of Platonic compositions sanctioned by Aristophanes and recognized as such in the Alexandrine library. . . . all the compositions recognized by Aristophanes (unfortunately Diogenes does not give a complete enumeration of those which he recognised) are to be found in the catalogue of Thrasyllus. And the evidentiary value of this fact is so much the greater, because the most questionable compositions (I mean, those which modern critics reject or even despise) are expressly included in the recognition of Aristophanes, and passed from him to Thrasyllus—*Leges, Epinomis, Minos, Epistolae*. . . . Exactly on those points on which the authority of Thrasyllus requires to be fortified against modern objectors, it receives all the support which coincidence with Aristophanes can impart. When we know that Thrasyllus adhered to Aristophanes on so many disputable points of the catalogue, we may infer pretty certainly that he adhered to him in the remainder. . . . it was perfectly natural that Thrasyllus should accept the recognition of the greatest library then existing: a library, the written records of which could be traced back to Demetrius Phalereus. He followed this external authority: he did not take each dialogue to pieces, to try whether it conformed to a certain internal standard—a "platonisches Gefühl". . . . the question between genuine and spurious Platonic dialogues was tried in the days of Thrasyllus, by external authority and not by internal feeling. . . . There was . . . unanimity, so far as the knowledge of Diogenes Laertius reached, as to genuine and spurious. . . . We may surely presume that this unanimity among the critics, both as to all that they accepted and all that they rejected, arose from common acquiescence in the authority of the Alexandrine library. [Pp. 132–69]

Grote's argument, as we have said, is today largely ignored or rejected. But on what basis? If we turn to perhaps the most important recent textual edition of one of the usually unaccepted canonical dialogues, we find that the editor dismisses Grote on the grounds that Grote's "hypothesis . . . was put to rest by Zeller" (Tarán 1975:5).[10] When we look back to the famous passage cited from Zeller (1888:52–54 = 1922:444–47), we find a half-paragraph argument that we suspect will strike many as tendentious, not to say lame. Zeller correctly notes that Grote's argument rests on a series of "uncertain

---

[10]The influence and the character of Zeller's presentation of Greek philosophy is conveyed by Wilamowitz-Moellendorff's discussion (1982:149–50). After summarizing the work of other major scholars in the nineteenth century who concerned themselves with Greek philosophy, Wilamowitz-Moellendorff remarks: "All this achievement pales into insignificance beside Eduard Zeller's great *History of Greek Philosophy*. It was Zeller who showed where the theological school of Tubingen had the advantage over the philologists by following the course of an intellectual movement through the persons of its leading figures: in other words, in addition to sorting out the different dogmatic systems to which it gave rise, studying its historical context. . . . His influence was incalculable and is still felt, even where scholarship has moved away from him" (ibid.).

propositions," propositions that may be challenged inasmuch as indubitable evidence is lacking. It *may* be that Plato's students, and/or the librarians and scholars at Alexandria, were not "scrupulous" guardians of his legacy. But why should we make this supposition rather than its opposite—especially given the existence of the canon? Zeller adduces only two answers, or grounds for impugning the scrupulousness of the pupils and scholars in question.[11] *First,* "the state of literary criticism in the post-Aristotelian period" makes it "unreasonable to credit the Alexandrians with having tested the authenticity of works bearing illustrious names, so carefully and accurately as Grote supposes" (see, in a similar vein, Thesleff 1967:13). But as regards *Plato scholars* at least, precisely the "state of literary criticism" is at issue or is that which Zeller is supposed to be establishing. What is the evidence for the state of Platonic criticism, and what are its implications? *Do* we know—have we sufficient evidence to question—the critical acumen and zeal or honesty of Plato's students and the Alexandrian Plato scholarship? Zeller's *second* argument or ground seems initially rather more substantial and avoids the circularity of the first; this second argument has certainly enjoyed truly amazing success and currency: "we are told," Zeller tells us, "that the high prices paid for writings in Alexandria and Pergamum gave great encouragement to forgery." For evidence, Zeller refers to only two original sources—Galen, commenting on Hippocrates, and Simplicius, in his commentary on Aristotle's *Categories.* But the fact is, both of these men are writing centuries after the events they speculate about. Moreover, Zeller himself here criticizes Galen for insisting, in the very passage quoted by Zeller, that there had been *no* forgery at all prior to the founding of the Alexandrian library. Which is it, one is tempted to ask Zeller—are we to rely on Galen's testimony, as regards the practice of Plato forgery centuries prior to him, or not? If not, then on *whom* or on what other evidence?

There is no question but that Galen's probable sources, the later Platonic commentators on Aristotle, repeatedly suggest forgery for

---

[11]Gomperz (1905:281 = 1925:221) asserts that "Plato's writings were not preserved in a library attached to his school." How Gomperz knows or thinks he knows this we have been unable to determine. Gomperz does more soberly add: "But there must have been a fairly large group of intimate disciples who were well able to distinguish what was genuine from what was spurious, and these men can have had no motive, worthy or unworthy, for remaining silent when occasion arose for a timely protest against fraud or error" (ibid.).

money as a major cause of the introduction of dubious or spurious works into the very shaky *Aristotelian* canon (Müller 1969:121; Moraux 1974:266–67). But now, even if these late commentators are right in their speculations about the works of *Aristotle,* the fate of Aristotle's Lyceum, and hence the loss or dispersal of his manuscripts, was determined by a very sad accident that may render all speculation about his canon quite irrelevant to the discussion of the history of *Plato's* works (see the elaborate contrast Grote draws between the two, 1867:137–40, and cf. Philip 1970:306). Besides, even assuming that forgery, even widespread forgery, was practiced on rich book collectors and lesser librarians in Antioch or Syracuse or God knows where, why should we suppose such fraud had any success with the scholarchs of the Academy or with the librarians and Platonic scholars at Alexandria? To this question the received opinion tends to reply that the centers of learning (e.g., Alexandria and Pergamum) themselves were probably the centers of commercial forgery operations because the scholars and librarians in these places were thirstiest for antiquities—any antiquities, even slightly plausible ones. But what evidence do we have to support such speculations apart from the surmises of commentators writing centuries later? In the total absence of evidence, how intrinsically plausible is the implicit characterization of the Alexandrian scholars (see, above all, Pfeiffer 1968: pt. 2, chaps. 1–6)? This whole doubtful line of argument has recently come under vigorous and entirely justified attack by Carl Werner Müller, who after a careful consideration of all testimony and arguments concludes: "Historically erroneous presuppositions and intrinsic implausibility, combined with a total lack of concrete examples for the theory in question, make it seem very difficult to understand how Galen, with his origins-hypothesis, has been able to find so many believers" (my trans.).[12]

To be sure, the confounding of Zeller's (or anyone else's) refutation of Grote does not constitute a full vindication of Grote's thesis. Although that thesis may be less certain, and the conclusion it points to less unambiguous, than appears in Grote's very attractive presentation, it remains, we submit, highly probable in the most important respect. At the very least, the canonical list of genuine dialogues quite

[12]Müller's acerbic conclusion deserves to be read in full: see 1975:14 n. 1. Cf. also Metzger (1980:10–11 and context): "That scholars in antiquity were able to detect forgeries, using in general the same kinds of tests as are employed by modern critics, is also well attested."

probably goes back to the very early days of Plato's Academy, and it is our impression that recent scholarship tends more and more to this conclusion. Pfeiffer (1968:65–66) regards it as "a fair guess that the first generations of [Plato's] pupils tried to collect, to arrange, and to copy the autographs of the master, and that this 'Academy Edition' became the basis of all the later ones" (cf. Reynolds and Wilson 1984:8). Philip (1970) goes further: "We must then imagine as the original source of our tradition papyrus manuscripts either in Plato's hand or executed under his eye. . . . we must have recourse to some form of the hypothesis that the Academy preserved an authoritative text of a corpus formed soon after Plato's death. Only some such hypothesis will account for the fact that the text of Plato has been so much better transmitted than that, for instance, of Aristotle or the historians" (p. 306). Or as Müller puts it:

> It is erroneous to suppose that in those days one had only to forge a short Socratic discourse, bring it on the market as by Plato, and right away people would snatch it up, above all the Alexandrian philologians—delighted to get a hitherto unknown work of the "divine man" for their library. When Aristophanes held up the *Minos* as a writing of Plato's he did so only because it was handed down to him as such and was *adequately* trusted as such. For it is wholly implausible, and contradicts the accustomed, methodical procedure of the Alexandrian Grammarians, that they themselves would have made such an attribution, when the work had not come to them by way of an unquestionable tradition. But such an authoritative tradition is unthinkable without the existence of a standard-setting edition of Plato's works. To its presence there is testimony especially in these pseudo-Platonic dialogues, which on account of their brevity were dependent from the outset on the support of a collected edition in order, in general, to survive. Now there is one and only one authority, which *prior* to that of the Alexandrians was in a position to have such a generally recognized Plato-Edition: the *ACADEMY.* It alone—besides Plato himself—could declare a writing "Platonic" and at the same time find recognition for its authority from critical readers." [1975:23–24; my trans.]

Summing up the recent literature, Solmsen declares (1981): "The tendency is to revert to the idea of a standard edition issued by the Academy, at a time not too distant from Plato's death" (p. 102).

But insofar as one reverts to this idea, it becomes harder and harder, at least on historical grounds, to avoid Grote's conclusion: it begins to seem perversely stubborn to continue to assert that more than one-fourth of the dialogues in the canon are counterfeit. If these dialogues are spurious, how did they enter the canon? The problem has been expressed almost plaintively by Philip (1970:307): "If a member or members of the Early Academy who had known Plato took a decision to conserve his writings either as holograph or as authoritative copy surely they would have had no trouble in knowing what should be included in the collection? Surely they would not have mistakenly included writings that were not Plato's but those of an imitator, as the dialogues of the fourth tetralogy certainly are [i.e., *Alcibiades I and II, Hipparchus, Lovers*]?"

The hope has been entertained that *within* the displeasing dialogues there might be found historical grounds for their rejection: linguistic usages or references to events, personages, and doctrines that certainly postdate anything Plato could have known. In the nineteenth and early twentieth centuries, considerable energy was devoted to trying to locate such signs of impurity (see especially the writings of Pavlu). But except in the case of some passages in the epistles and in dialogues *not* in the canon, every such attempt to find unambiguous evidence of anachronism failed to withstand critical scrutiny.[13] Gomperz expressed it well some years ago:

> There is only one kind of discrepancy which possesses absolute probative force—conflict with the ascertained facts of history, above all, references . . . such as may be shown by irrefragable proofs to have lain outside all possible knowledge of the alleged author of a given work. . . . The Platonic corpus, however, affords but few openings for the use of this critical weapon. . . . There is thus abundant need for caution; and additional warning is supplied . . . by the contradictions, bordering on the grotesque, which obtain between the subjective "feeling for what is Platonic" of this and that particular investigator. [1905:280 = 1925:221]

The historical evidence that we have now surveyed, we contend, leads to the conclusion that each of the dialogues that have come down to us as canonical deserves on historical grounds the presumption for which Woodruff has argued in the case of the *Greater Hippias*

---

[13]For a striking illustration of the undermining of purported discoveries of anachronisms in a canonical dialogue, see Friedländer's (1958–70: vol. 2, pp. 320–22), Calogero's (1938:22), and Souilhé's (1930:52–56) dissection of Wilamowitz-Moellendorff (1919: vol. 2, p. 415) and Pavlu (1910) on the *Hipparchus*. See also Thesleff (1967: p. 13 n. 5).

(1982): "The historical tradition creates a presumption in its favor" (p. 95).

Not that we have turned our backs on the intriguing line of approach recently opened up by Philip and, more extensively, by Müller. Given the conundrum that Philip describes so clearly—that is, facing strong evidence, on the one hand, that an authoritative canon was established at the Academy by students who were Plato's personal friends, and yet gripped, on the other hand, by the conviction that numerous dialogues in this canon cannot be Plato's own—these scholars advance the following suggestion: "If, as seems probable, Plato and his colleagues regarded the dialogues as written to enlist students for the study of philosophy, and to incite them to pursue those studies which prepared for philosophy, then, though they may have regarded Plato's works as performing these functions better than all others, they may have felt that the *First Alcibiades,* for instance, also performed it excellently and was worthy of a place in the collection" (Philip 1970:307). As Philip also remarks in this context, anyone taking the usual approach "may be misled by modern attitudes." The students of Plato were animated by zeal that was not so much philological as philosophic and didactic. Or in Müller's formulation, we may

> mistake the principal distinction between the Edition that a philosophic school would publish and a critical-philological edition. The two understand authenticity in somewhat different ways: while the latter aims to set forth the genuine text of the original work in its strict historical form, and bends its efforts to exclude alien interpretations and spurious writings, the former is not so opposed to interpolations and writings that are written, or seem, "in the spirit" of the author, and here the criteria are not so much formal as concerned with the nature of the contents. [Müller 1975:25–26; my trans.]

Müller further argues that the more philological approach may have set in (to the extent that it did set in, which is hard to determine) only with the later Academy and with the Alexandrian librarians, who may mistakenly have imposed *their* philological concerns on the compilers of the original "standard" edition.

We do differ from Müller in that we, like Philip, remain more impressed by the sort of doubt with which Philip (1970) rather uncomfortably concludes: "But surely the authors of non-authentic dialogues were known, even though they wrote essays in the manner of

Plato? Why were these essays not ascribed to their authors? Why were these, and these only (for we must assume the production of other such essays) preserved? These are questions that can be answered only by vague surmise" (pp. 307–308)—or (we would inject) by entertaining once again a presumption in favor of the authenticity of the entire canon.

But even supposing that a work included in the canon were by a student—Aristotle? Speusippus?—we would emphasize that its inclusion was in all likelihood a mark of very high esteem: the inclusion would indicate that intelligent and close pupils of Plato believed their teacher's thought and the dramatic integrity of his presentation of Socrates or the Socratic way of life to have been worthily continued. Accordingly, we would resist the tendency still evident in Müller to disparage the so-called "dubious" canonical dialogues. Moreover, we would hesitate to follow Müller's interpretative approach insofar as it seeks to downplay consideration of the relation between the disputed dialogues and the other, undisputed Platonic works.

The reader may wonder why there has been no discussion thus far of attempts to establish authenticity or inauthenticity on the basis of comparative stylistic and stylometric analysis of the disputed dialogues. The reason, in a word, is that such arguments turn out to be the slipperiest and shakiest of all. And this view, again, has become more and more the consensus of scholars. As Wilamowitz-Moellendorff put it: "Attempts to tie the great masters of Attic prose to hard and fast rules are doomed to failure. The microscopic examination of language, whose practitioners here often delighted in compiling statistical tables of average percentage frequencies, has sometimes achieved results. But equally often it has proved deceptive, because the mind cannot be mechanised. We must not despise little things— but neither must we forget that they are little" (1982:169).

Regarding Plato in particular, when we bear in mind that "it is no exaggeration to state that he makes use of a stylistic register far wider and far more subtle than any other ancient prosaist" and, what is more, that "he was constantly experimenting with new forms and constantly introducing different approaches and moods" (Thesleff 1967:7, 33), we should hardly expect to find any very clear or strict boundaries to "genuine Platonic style." Consequently, although Thesleff himself succumbs to the conventional negative judgment on the disputed canonical dialogues, he readily admits the subjectivity of this judgment. Concluding his study of Plato's styles, he remarks, "such

anomalies remind us of the elusiveness of stylistic criteria in determining the *inauthenticity* of particular passages or works. I have expressed
my personal opinion" (ibid., pp. 171–72). As for "stylometry," or
"that special branch of study which aims at solving problems of
chronology or authenticity by statistical accounts of the relative fre-
quency of linguistic or other peculiarities," Thesleff, like many other
careful students of style, remains largely skeptical and not only as
regards chronological conclusions: "Nor have questions of authenticity been settled with any more reliability by traditional stylometry,
than by other stylistic or non-stylistic methods. . . . The objections of
Natorp and Immisch to stylometry are still valid . . . except for Ritter,
who however is very cautious, first-rate Platonic scholars have been
inclined to reject a detailed stylometry" (ibid., pp. 8–9). On this point
Gomperz speaks with sober weight:

> Three of [Plato's] latest works (*Timaeus, Critias, Laws*) contain nearly
> 1500 words which are absent from his other works, and some, indeed,
> from the whole of the literature of his time. What, then, is proved if in a
> particular dialogue we detect a small number of words or phrases not
> met with elsewhere in Plato, or even if we find a few thoughts which
> have no close parallels in his other works? Indeed, we must be prepared
> to encounter serious contradictions, not only in thought, but in that
> which lies deeper and should therefore be less subject to change—in
> tone and sentiment. [1905:279 = 1925:220]

Nor on the other side must we let ourselves forget that "there is
always a chance that someone imitated Plato's art of writing to perfection" (Edelstein 1966:2). As for the numerous attempts to judge
particular disputed dialogues on the basis of their conformity or lack
of conformity to "true Platonic style," every example that we have
inspected exhibits the sorts of flaws Tarán (1975; cf. Woodruff
1982:94, 97) has exposed in such discussions concerning the *Epinomis:*

> Instead of an objective analysis of the grammatical and stylistic charac-
> teristics of the *Laws* and the *Epinomis* we find appeals to "the feeling of
> Plato's language" or dogmatic assertions that a certain expression,
> which is being compared with the "normal" one chosen from Plato, is
> un-Platonic. . . . the fact that a word or an expression in the *Epinomis* is
> not to be found in Plato could not by itself prove it to be un-Platonic,
> unless we possessed, as we certainly do not, evidence that Plato fol-
> lowed until the very end of his life narrow rules in his use of the Greek

language. But we find him attacked rather for his freedom of expression, his poetical turns, his coinage of new words, etc. . . . even among the obviously spurious dialogues included in the Platonic corpus there is probably not one that could be proved spurious on stylistic grounds alone. [Pp. 15, 16]

Essential to any judgment of authenticity, perhaps (in the final analysis) the only solid test available to us, is an interpretative study of the content—the drama, the arguments, the teaching—of each of these dialogues. But that enterprise will have difficulty ever getting under way if it is undertaken with a bias against the dialogue, or even with the intention of looking mainly for reasons to reject or accept the dialogue as genuine. In other words, we do *not* suggest, and we do not here present, new inquiries aimed principally at establishing authenticity or inauthenticity. It seems to us that the fruitlessness of that tack is visible in many or most of the studies executed in the nineteenth and early twentieth centuries, studies whose tenor has been properly censured by Müller, Friedländer, and others. Such investigations do not approach the dialogues in the spirit or with the questions and concerns that the author himself had or expected and sought in his audience. From the very start they therefore manifest little sympathy with, or at least are poorly attuned to, the *philosophic* project of the author. Besides, our preeminent concern, as human beings or as students of political philosophy striving to continue something like the Platonic tradition, ought to be not with philological questions of authenticity but with the truth about the human condition as that truth is illuminated in and by Platonic political philosophy—and in letting *this* concern guide us, we are attuned to the intention of the author.

We do not, then, claim to know with certainty what it seems to us only a god could know for sure—whether, and when, Plato in fact wrote each of the dialogues included here. Nor do we mean to pass silent judgment, by exclusion, on any of the other remarkable writings in the canon that we have not yet had time to study thoroughly. We limit ourselves to the contention that the dramatic and philosophic substance of the dialogues collected here is in every way worthy of Plato and consonant with his better known dialogues; and we hope to have given weight to this contention (among others) by our interpretative essays. Yet the essays are by no means intended as definitive pronouncements on the full meaning of any of these dialogues.

Our purpose will have been defeated if they substitute for the reader's own wrestling with the text or if they are allowed to preform his engagement with and reflection upon each dialogue. By placing each essay after its dialogue we mean to suggest that it be read only after the reader's immersion in the dialogue and formulation of some tentative hypotheses; then, for a reader so prepared, we hope our reflections will serve as stimulus to renewed reading and thinking.

The first six of the dialogues in the present volume have heretofore been readily available in English only in the Loeb Library series—in translations that are far from being literal. The four remaining dialogues are indeed included in the well-known Bollingen *Collected Dialogues*. But the *Laches,* and the two *Hippias* dialogues, are there presented in the old and loose Jowett renderings, and in the case of the *Ion,* though the translation (by Cooper) is surely superior to Jowett's, it still does not pretend to the standard of literalness to which we have aspired. The same must be said of more recent versions of these last four dialogues. Woodruff's translation of the *Hippias Major,* for example, does not scruple to introduce into the dialogue's oaths and other references to the divine a very unhistorical monotheistic or otherworldly tone. We do not assert that translations such as ours—as literal as possible within the limits of readable, though sometimes awkward, English—are the only permissible sort of translation, but we do insist that, for serious students and scholars who do not know Greek, such translations are indispensable. Through them, and only through them, can one begin to trace the variety, and the precise mutation, in the meaning of key terms in Plato's vocabulary. By the same token, only a literal translation compels the reader to confront the enormous difference between the Platonic, and our contemporary, sense of seemingly familiar and "obvious" notions (such as "soul," "city," "law," "virtue," "god," and "demonic"). Above all, literal translation throws the clearest light on the dramatic details—the oaths, the terms of address, the subtle changes in even brief responses to questions—that are sometimes as important in conveying Plato's meaning as the arguments themselves.

The texts upon which we have based our translations are those published in the Budé (Paris) and Oxford Classical Texts (Oxford) series. In his editorial review, the editor has found invaluable Carlini's extensive discussion of the manuscripts and the stemmata, and has made use of his fine apparatus for the *Alcibiades I, Hipparchus,* and *Lovers.* One major textual difficulty deserves special note: the status of the subtitles or alternative titles (see Hoerber 1957). With the exception of the *Hipparchus* and *Minos,* we incline to the generally accepted view that these titles were added by later scholars and have hence had them printed in brackets—but we are by no means certain.

Our brief footnotes supplement the translations by clarifying historical and literary allusions and explaining somewhat the complex meaning of certain important words. A number of such words occur in most or all of the dialogues, and rather than repeat the explanations in footnotes, we have appended a short glossary at the end of the volume. The reader is advised to peruse the glossary before reading the translations.

The editor thanks the John Simon Guggenheim Memorial Foundation and the Earhart Foundation for supporting him during a portion of the time he worked on this volume; John Podhoretz, for helping to get the project underway; David Bolotin and Wayne Ambler, for reviewing portions of the translations; Bernhard Kendler, of the Cornell University Press, for his sympathetic patience and assistance; and the anonymous reviewers for the Press, whose painstaking criticisms contributed much to improving the translations and the Editor's Introduction.

Bibliography

Listed here are works cited in the Introduction, as well as a few additional writings that in the editor's view are especially significant for the discussion of authenticity. For fuller bibliographical information, see Brisson, Cherniss, Friedländer, Geffcken, Shorey, and the bibliographies in Müller (1975) and Tarán.

Aelianus, C. 1866. *Varia Historia.* Ed. R. Hercher. 2 vols. Leipzig.
Albinus. 1870. *The Introduction of Albinus to the Dialogues of Plato.* In *The Works of Plato,* vol. 6. London. (A translation of the following item, by George Burges.)
———. 1892. *Isagogē.* In C. F. Hermann, *Platonis Secundum Thrasylli Tetralogias Dispositi,* vol. 6. Leipzig.
Alfarabi. 1969. *The Philosophy of Plato and Aristotle.* Trans. Muhsin Mahdi. Ithaca.
Alline, H. 1915. *Histoire du texte de Platon.* Paris.
Ast, F. 1816. *Platons Leben und Schriften.* Leipzig.
Azzolini, E. 1915. *Ricerche sull' Ipparco attribuito a Platone.* Modena.

Brisson, L. 1977. Plato: 1958–1975. *Lustrum* 20:5–304.

Burnet, J. 1900–1907. *Platonis Opera.* 5 vols. (Oxford Classical Texts.) Oxford.

Calogero, G. 1938. L'autenticità dell' 'IPPARCO' Platonica. *Annali della Scuola Normale Superiore di Pisa,* pp. 13–27.

Carlini, A. 1964. *Platone: Alcibiade, Alcibiade Secondo, Ipparco, Rivali.* Turin.

Cherniss, H. 1959 and 1960. Plato 1950–57. *Lustrum* 4:5–308 and 5:321–648.

Chroust, A. H. 1965. The Organization of the *Corpus Platonicum* in Antiquity. *Hermes* 93:34–46.

Clark, A. C. 1918. *The Descent of Manuscripts.* Oxford. (See chap. 12 for an authoritative introduction in English to the Platonic manuscripts.)

Diogenes Laertius. 1972. *Lives of the Eminent Philosophers.* 2 vols. Ed. and trans. R. D. Hicks. (Loeb Library.) Cambridge, Mass.

Dunn, M. 1976. Iamblichus, Thrasyllus, and the Reading Order of the Platonic Dialogues. In R. B. Harris, ed., *The Significance of Neo-Platonism,* pp. 59–80. Albany, N.Y., and Norfolk, Va.

Edelstein, L. 1966. *Plato's Seventh Letter.* Leiden.

Festugière, A.-J. 1969. L'ordre de lecture des dialogues de Platon aux Ve/VIe siècles. *Museum Helveticum* 26:281–96.

Friedländer, P. 1921–23. *Der grosse Alcibiades.* Bonn (in two parts). (Includes interpretation and defense of authenticity.)

———. 1958–70. *Plato.* 3 vols. Trans. Hans Meyerhoff. Princeton. (Defends and provides interpretive studies of *Hippias Major, Hipparchus, Theages, Alcibiades I*; also studies of *Laches, Ion,* and *Hippias Minor.* Footnotes afford a helpful guide to the literature. The English translation represents a revised and updated version of the German original.)

Geffcken, J. 1934. *Griechische Literaturgeschichte.* Vol. 2. Heidelberg.

Gomperz, T. 1925. *Griechische Denker.* Vol. 2. Berlin.

———. 1931. *Greek Thinkers.* Vol. 2. (A translation of the preceding by G. C. Berry.) London.

Grote, G. 1867. *Plato and the Other Companions of Socrates.* Vol. 1. London. (See especially chap. 4, "Platonic Canon, as Recognised by Thrasyllus," and chap. 5, "Platonic Canon, as Appreciated and Modified by Modern Critics," as well as discussions of particular dialogues.)

Guthrie, W. K. C. 1978. *A History of Greek Philosophy.* Vol. 5. Cambridge. (See chap. 6, "Doubtful and Spurious Dialogues," for an unusually well-balanced discussion of the question of authenticity.)

Hoerber, R. G. 1957. Thrasylus' Platonic Canon and the Double Titles. *Phronesis* 2:10–20.

Metzger, Bruce M. 1980. Literary Forgeries and Canonical Pseudepigrapha. In *New Testament Studies: Philological, Versional, and Patristic.* Leiden.

Moraux, P. 1974. La critique d'authenticité chez les commentateurs grecs d'Aristote. In E. Akurgal and U. B. Alkim, eds., *Mélanges Mansel,* pp. 265–88. Ankara, Turkey.

Müller, C. W. 1969. Die neuplatonischen Aristoteleskommentatoren über die Ursachen der Pseudepigraphie. *Rheinisches Museum für Philologie* 112:120–26.

———. 1975. *Die Kurzdialoge der Appendix Platonica.* Munich. See especially "Einleitung," pp. 9–44.

Oswiecimski, S. 1978. The Enigmatic Character of Some of Plato's Apocrypha. *Eos* 66:31–40.

———. 1979. The Ancient Testimonies in the Face of the Platonic Apocrypha. *Eos* 67:233–55.

Pavlu, J. 1910. *Die pseudoplatonischen Zwillingsdialoge "Minos" und "Hipparch."* Vienna.

———. 1913. *Die pseudoplatonischen Gespräche über Gerechtigkeit und Tugend.* Vienna.

Pfeiffer, R. 1968. *History of Classical Scholarship from the Beginnings to the End of the Hellenistic Age.* Oxford.

———. 1976. *History of Classical Scholarship from 1300 to 1850.* Oxford.

Philip, J. A. 1970. The Platonic Corpus. *Phoenix* 24:296–308.

Reynolds, L. D., and Wilson, N. G. 1984. *Scribes and Scholars: A Guide to the Transmission of Greek and Latin Literature.* 2d ed., revised and enlarged. Oxford. (See esp. chap. 1, "Antiquity," for a survey of what is known of the early history of textual transmission. Unfortunately, it repeats uncritically Galen's hypothesis about the deception of the great librarians by forgers [p. 7].)

Schleiermacher, F. 1817–28. *Platos Werke.* 6 vols. Berlin.

———. 1836. *Introductions to the Dialogues of Plato.* Trans. William Dobson. Cambridge.

Shorey, P. 1933. *What Plato Said.* Chicago.

Solmsen, F. 1981. The Academic and Alexandrian Editions of Plato's Works. *Illinois Classical Studies* 6:102–11.

Souilhé, J. 1930. *Platon: Oeuvres complètes.* Vol. 13, pt. 2. *Dialogues suspects.* (Budé Series.) Paris.

Taràn, L. 1975. *Academica: Plato, Philip of Opus, and the Pseudo-Platonic Epinomis.* Philadelphia.

Thesleff, H. 1967. *Studies in the Styles of Plato.* Helsinki.

Westerwink, L. G. 1962. *Anonymous Prolegomena to Platonic Philosophy.* Amsterdam.

Wilamowitz-Moellendorff, U. von. 1919. *Platon.* 2 vols. Berlin.

———. 1982. *History of Classical Scholarship.* Trans. Alan Harris. Ed. with an introduction by Hugh Lloyd-Jones. Baltimore.

Woodruff, P. 1982. *Hippias Major.* Indianapolis.

Zeller, E. 1888. *Plato and the Older Academy.* Trans. S. F. Alleyne and A. Goodwin. London. (A translation of the following item.)

———. 1922. *Die Philosophie der Griechen in ihrer geschichtlichen Entwicklung.* Pt. 2, vol. 1. Leipzig.

HIPPARCHUS;
or, The Lover of Gain

Translated by STEVEN FORDE

Socrates, A Comrade

225a SOCRATES: So what is the love of gain? Just what can it be, and who are the lovers of gain?

COMRADE: In my opinion, they are those who think it worthwhile to make a gain from worthless things.

SOC.: But do they, in your opinion, know these things are worthless, or do they not know? For if they don't know, you are saying the lovers of gain are fools.

Hipparchus was the son of the Athenian tyrant Peisistratus (see n. 8 below). According to popular Athenian tradition Hipparchus inherited the tyranny of Athens on his father's death (527 B.C.) and ruled until he was assassinated, when the tyranny passed to his brother Hippias. Socrates adopts the tradition in this dialogue (cf. 228b–229d): Hipparchus is a tyrant. According to Thucydides (VI 54–59), this Athenian tradition is erroneous, and Hippias inherited the tyranny directly from Peisistratus, so that Hipparchus was never more than a tyrant's brother. This version of the story is more widely accepted today. In any case, it appears that Hipparchus, as part of the ruling family, played a part in the encouragement of the arts at Athens, as had his father (cf. 228b–c; Aristotle *Constitution of Athens* XVIII 1; Herodotus V 55; VI 109, 123).

"Lover of gain" in Greek is one word, *philokerdēs*. The word appears throughout the dialogue and will always be translated "lover of gain." The construction of the word gives rise to all sorts of talk in the dialogue concerning love of other things, so it should be noted that "love" here is *philia*, the same word that applies to friendship. The other Greek word for love, *eros*, or "erotic passion," appears only once in this dialogue (at 229d); with that single exception, the word "love" in this translation always corresponds to *philia*.

b COM.: I say they're not fools but villains and evildoers who are overcome by gain. They know that the things from which they dare to
make gain are worth nothing, yet they still dare to be lovers of gain
through shamelessness.

SOC.: Then do you say that the lover of gain is of this sort, like a man
who is a farmer, who plants knowing his plant[1] is worth nothing and
raises it thinking it worthwhile to make a gain from that? Do you say
he is of that sort?

COM.: The lover of gain, Socrates, thinks he ought to make gain from
everything.

c SOC.: Don't answer me so aimlessly, as though you had suffered some
injustice from someone, but pay attention to me and answer as
though I asked you again from the beginning: don't you agree that
the lover of gain knows about the worth of this thing from which he
considers it worthwhile to make a gain?

COM.: I do, indeed.

SOC.: Now, who knows about the worth of plants, in what seasons
and soils it is worth planting them—if we too may throw in one of
those wise phrases with which people who are clever in the law-
courts beautify their speeches?[2]

d COM.: I suppose the farmer.

SOC.: And do you say that thinking it worthwhile to make a gain is
anything but thinking one ought to make a gain?

COM.: That's what I say.

226a SOC.: Then don't try to deceive me, an older man now, you being so
young, by answering as you did now with what you yourself don't
think, but speak truly. Is there any farmer, do you think, who knows
he plants a worthless plant and thinks to make a gain from it?

COM.: By Zeus, not I!

SOC.: And what about this: do you think that a horseman who knows
he is giving his horse worthless food doesn't know that he is harming
the horse?

COM.: I don't.

b SOC.: Then *he* doesn't think that he is making a gain from worthless
food.

COM.: No.

SOC.: What about this: do you think that a pilot who furnishes his ship

[1]The verb "to plant" (*phyteuein*) and the noun "plant" (*phyton*) have the same root
as the Greek word for "nature" (*physis*).
[2]Socrates' beautiful phrase is a sentence ending with the rhyming words *hora* and
chora—"season" and "soil"—in a pair.

with worthless sails and rudders doesn't know that he will suffer loss[3] and will run the risk of being destroyed himself and destroying the ship and everything he is carrying?

COM.: I don't.

SOC.: So *he* doesn't think that he is making a gain from worthless equipment.

c   COM.: No indeed.

SOC.: Furthermore, does a general who knows that his army has worthless arms think to make a gain from them or consider it worthwhile to make a gain from them?

COM.: Not at all.

SOC.: Or does an aulos player with worthless auloi,[4] or a citharist with a lyre, or an archer with a bow, or, in short, any one of the artisans at all, or any of the other men with intelligence, think to make a gain with tools or with any other equipment whatever that is worthless?

d   COM.: It doesn't appear so, at least.

SOC.: Then just who do you say are the lovers of gain? For I suppose that they are not the ones we have just gone through but[5] those who, knowing the worthless things, think they ought to make a gain from them. But in that case, as you say, you surprising fellow, there is not one lover of gain among human beings.

COM.: But I, Socrates, want to say that the lovers of gain are those who, out of greed, are always striving preternaturally for insignifi-

e   cant things of little or no worth in loving gain.

SOC.: Surely not knowing, best one, that they are worth nothing, for the argument just proved against us that that is impossible.

COM.: So it seems to me.

SOC.: And if they don't know it, clearly they are ignorant, thinking that worthless things are worth a great deal.

COM.: Apparently.

SOC.: Now, do not the lovers of gain love gain?

COM.: Yes.

SOC.: And do you say that gain is the opposite of loss?

---

[3] The Greek words for "to suffer loss" and "loss," which appear frequently in this dialogue, can also mean "to be punished" and "punishment," respectively.

[4] The aulos (plural *auloi*) was a musical instrument. See the Glossary.

[5] The word "but" does not appear in the manuscripts here, but something like it appears to be required for the sense. Another possible emendation would read "those who, knowing the worthless things, *do not* think they ought to make a gain from them."

227a COM.: I do.

SOC.: Is there anyone for whom it is good to suffer loss?

COM.: No one.

SOC.: Is it bad instead?

COM.: Yes.

SOC.: Human beings then are harmed by loss.

COM.: They are.

SOC.: Loss therefore is bad.

COM.: Yes.

SOC.: And gain is the opposite of loss.

COM.: The opposite.

SOC.: Then gain is good.

COM.: Yes.

b SOC.: So you call those who love the good, lovers of gain.

COM.: So it seems.

SOC.: At least you don't say the lovers of gain are madmen, comrade. But you yourself, do you love or not love whatever is good?

COM.: I do.

SOC.: Is there anything good that you don't love, or is it the bad instead?

COM.: By Zeus, not I!

SOC.: Perhaps you love all good things.

COM.: Yes.

c SOC.: Now ask me too if I don't as well; for I will agree with you that I too love the good things. But aside from you and me, don't all human beings seem to you to love the good things and to hate the bad?

COM.: So it appears to me.

SOC.: Didn't we agree too that gain is good?

COM.: Yes.

SOC.: Then everyone turns out in this way to be a lover of gain, but according to what we said earlier, no one is a lover of gain. Now, which of these arguments should one use to avoid error?

d COM.: I think, Socrates, that one would have to conceive the lover of gain correctly. It is correct to suppose that he is a lover of gain who is serious about those things and that he thinks it worthwhile to make a gain from them which the decent[6] wouldn't dare to gain from.

SOC.: But you see, sweetest one, that we have already agreed that to make a gain is to be benefited.

[6]The word *chrēstos,* "decent," can also mean "useful." I have translated "decent" throughout, but the ambiguity of the Greek should be borne in mind.

COM.: Well, what of it?

SOC.: Just this, that we agreed in addition that everyone wants the good things always.

COM.: Yes.

SOC.: Furthermore, the good want to have all gains, if these are good at least.

e COM.: Not, Socrates, gains from which they are going to suffer harm.

SOC.: Do you say that suffering harm is suffering loss or something else?

COM.: No, I say it is suffering loss.

SOC.: Is it by gain that human beings suffer loss or by loss?

COM.: By both: because they suffer loss both by loss and by evil gain.

SOC.: Well, does anything decent and good seem to you to be evil?

COM.: Not to me.

228a SOC.: And we agreed a little while ago that gain is the opposite of loss, which is bad?

COM.: I assent.

SOC.: And that being the opposite of bad it is good?

COM.: We agreed to that.

SOC.: So you see, you are trying to deceive me, purposely saying the opposite of what we agreed to before.

COM.: No, by Zeus, Socrates, you on the contrary are deceiving me, and I don't know how you are managing to turn everything upside down in the argument!

b SOC.: Hush![7] It wouldn't be right of me not to obey a good and wise man.

COM.: Who is that? What are you talking about?

SOC.: A fellow citizen of yours and mine, the son of Peisistratus[8] of Philaidae, Hipparchus, who was the oldest and wisest of Peisistratus'

---

[7]The word is *euphēmein,* which literally means "speak well" and was used especially in connection with sacred rites, during which an ill-spoken or improper word could taint the performance of the ritual and anger the god. In order to ensure that no improper word was spoken inadvertently during a ceremony, therefore, the practice was to maintain absolute silence, hence the word came to denote silence, especially the pious or awed silence in the presence of the god.

[8]Peisistratus first established tyranny at Athens, rising to the position of tyrant in 560 B.C. He was expelled from the city twice thereafter and returned twice, eventually passing the tyranny on to his sons. Hipparchus and Hippias were sons of Peisistratus by his wife, but he had at least two other children by another woman as well. According to Thucydides (VI 54, 55), Hippias, not Hipparchus, was Peisistratus' oldest son. The most likely construction of Socrates' reference to Philaidae is that it indicates the deme of Peisistratus' origin; according to the scholiast, Philaidae was a deme of the tribe of Aegeus.

children. His wisdom was displayed in many fine deeds; in particular, he first brought the Homeric epics to this land and compelled the rhapsodes at the Panathenaea[9] to recite them in relays, one after

c another, as they still do now. He also sent a fifty-oared ship for Anacreon of Teos,[10] to bring him to the city, and always had Simonides of Ceos[11] around him, persuading him by means of great pay and gifts. He did these things, wishing to educate the citizens, so that he would rule over people who were the best possible; being a gentleman, he thought that no one should be begrudged wisdom. Now, when the citizens from the city itself had been educated by

d him, and marveled at him for his wisdom, he, contriving to educate the people in the country as well, set up Hermae[12] for them along the road in the middle of the city and of each deme.[13] Then from his own wisdom, which he got both from learning and from his own discovery, he selected the things that he thought were wisest, put them himself into elegiac form, and inscribed them, his own poetry and

e examples of his wisdom, on the figures. This he did in the first place so that his citizens would not marvel at the wise Delphic inscriptions, "Know Thyself," "Nothing in Excess," and the like but would rather think the words of Hipparchus wise; but also so that in traveling back and forth they would read and get a taste of his wisdom and

[9]The Panathenaea was a great summer festival at Athens, which included horse races and musical contests and culminated in a great festive procession, on what was supposed to be the birthday of Athena, up to the acropolis. This procession is depicted on the famous frieze of the Parthenon.

[10]Anacreon was a lyric poet born at Teos, a Greek city in Asia Minor. He consorted first with the tyrant Polycrates of Samos and then with the Peisistratids at Athens. His poetry, even in his old age, sang mostly of love and wine.

[11]Simonides was a lyric poet born on Ceos, an island in the Aegean. He had a long and illustrious career at Athens during the rule of the Peisistratid tyrants and afterward, but later consorted with the tyrant Hiero of Syracuse. He was generally noted for his greed.

[12]The Hermae were figures representative of the god Hermes, generally consisting only of a square pillar with a phallus attached, and culminating in a head of the god. The worship of Hermes as the god of travelers was quite ancient, as was the practice of putting these figures on the streets and squares of towns. They sometimes bore inscriptions. Athens had an unusually large number of them on the streets and at the entrances to houses, and Attica, the territory of Athens, was somewhat unusual as well for having them on the country roads. There may be reason to link some of the Athenian Hermae to the Peisistratids (cf. Fustel de Coulanges, *The Ancient City*, IV 7.1).

[13]The Greek word *demos*—"deme"—refers either to a country district or to a town or village in the country. In Attica demes were legal or administrative districts outside "the city," Athens itself.

would come out of the countryside to complete their education. The
229a inscriptions are two in number: on the left side of each Hermes it is
inscribed that the Hermes stands in the middle of the city or of the
deme, while on the right it says:

This is a memorial of Hipparchus: Walk thinking just thoughts.

There are many other beautiful pieces of his poetry inscribed on other
Hermae. In particular there is one on the Steiria[14] road, on which it
says:

b   This is a memorial of Hipparchus: Don't deceive a friend.

Now, since I am your friend I would surely not dare to deceive you
and disobey such a one as this. After his death his brother Hippias
ruled as tyrant over the Athenians for three years, and you would
have heard from all the men of old that only for those three years was
there tyranny in Athens and that during the rest of the time the
Athenians lived almost as in the time when Cronos was king.[15]
c Indeed, it is said by the more cultivated human beings that his death
came about not in the way that the many think, on account of a
sister's being dishonored in the ritual basket carrying—since that is
silly—but because Harmodius was the favorite[16] of Aristogeiton[17]
and was educated by him; thus Aristogeiton prided himself on educating human beings and supposed himself to be a rival of Hip-
d parchus. Now, during the same time Harmodius himself happened to

[14]Steiria was a town on the southeast coast of Attica, in a deme of the tribe of
Pandion.
[15]The "reign of Cronos" in Greek mythology was an ancient period when Cronos,
the father of Zeus, ruled perfectly and dispelled all human ills (Hesiod *Works and Days*
109–26; Plato *Laws* 713b–714a, *Statesman* 269a–273e). On this analogy to the rule of
the Peisistratids, see Aristotle *Constitution of Athens* XVI 7. Thucydides says (VI 54)
that the rule of Peisistratus and his sons was generally mild and salutary and became
harsh only after the assassination of Hipparchus.
[16]The word *paidika* is derived from the word for "boy." One of its uses was, in the
terminology of pederasty, to denote the beloved, hence "darling" or "favorite."
[17]Aristogeiton was a man of the middle class, according to Thucydides (VI 54),
who was in love with the young and beautiful Harmodius. The two of them together
plotted against the tyranny and killed Hipparchus. Harmodius and Aristogeiton were
celebrated by the Athenian democracy of the fifth century as tyrannicides and cham-
pions of democracy. For the details of the story of Harmodius and Aristogeiton to
which Plato alludes here, see Thucydides' account.

be a lover of one of the beautiful and well-born youths of that period—they do say what his name was, but I don't remember it—and this youth for a while marveled at Harmodius and Aristogeiton for their wisdom, but later, after associating with Hipparchus, he despised them. They, being greatly pained by this dishonor, killed Hipparchus for that reason.

COM.: Well then, Socrates, it seems that either you don't consider me

e your friend, or if you do, you aren't obeying Hipparchus. For that you are not deceiving me in this argument—though I've no idea how—I will never be persuaded.

SOC.: But on the contrary, I am willing, as in a game of draughts, to let you change anything you want of what was said in the argument so that you won't think you are being deceived. Should I make this change for you, that the good things are not desired by all human beings?

COM.: No, no.

SOC.: Or that suffering loss, or loss, is not bad?

COM.: No, no.

SOC.: Or that gain and making gain are not opposite to loss and suffering loss?

230a COM.: Not that either.

SOC.: Or that making gain, as the opposite of bad, is not good?

COM.: It isn't always; change that for me.

SOC.: Then it is your opinion, it seems, that some gain is good, and some bad.

COM.: It is.

SOC.: Then I'll change that for you: Let some gain be good and some other bad. And neither of them is more gain than the other, neither the good nor the bad, is it?

COM.: Just what are you asking me?

SOC.: I'll explain. There is some food that is good and some that is bad?

b COM.: Yes.

SOC.: Well, is one of them more food than the other, or are they both similarly this same thing, food, and in this respect at least no different at all one from the other inasmuch as they are food but only inasmuch as one of them is good and the other bad?

COM.: Yes.

SOC.: And so for drink and everything else that exists, when some

things that are the same come to be good and others bad, the one does
c not differ from the other in that respect whereby they are the same?
Just as with human beings, I suppose, one is decent and another is
evil.

COM.: Yes.

SOC.: But neither of them, I think, is more or less a human being—
not the decent more than the evil nor the evil more than the decent.

COM.: What you say is true.

SOC.: Then are we not of this mind too about gain, that both the evil
and the decent sort are equally gain?

COM.: Necessarily.

SOC.: So then he who gets a decent gain doesn't make any more gain
d than he who gets an evil one; it appears rather that neither one is more
gain, as we agree.

COM.: Yes.

SOC.: For "more" or "less" is not attached to either one.

COM.: No, indeed.

SOC.: And how could anyone ever do or suffer anything either more
or less with something like that, to which neither of these things is
attached?

COM.: It is impossible.

SOC.: So now, since both are equally gain, and gainful, we have to
consider, on account of what you call both alike gain: what do you
e see in both of them that is the same? Just as if you were to ask me,
about the previous examples, on what account I call both good food
and bad food equally food, I would say to you that it is because both
are dry nourishment for the body—simply on account of that. You
would also agree, I suppose, that that is what food is, wouldn't you?

COM.: I would.

SOC.: And concerning drink the answer would be of the same man-
231a ner, that the wet nourishment of the body, whether decent or evil,
has this name, drink, and similarly for the others. Try therefore to
imitate me by answering in the same way. When you say that decent
gain and evil gain are both gain, what do you see to be the same in
both—the thing that is actually gain? If you are unable yourself to
answer again, consider what I say next: do you call a gain every
possession that one has obtained either by spending nothing or by
spending less and getting more?

b COM.: Yes, I think I would call that gain.

SOC.: Are you referring to some such things as this, where one is treated to a feast, spending nothing while being regaled, but then becomes sick?

COM.: By Zeus I am not!

SOC.: Becoming healthy instead from the feast, would he be getting a gain or a loss?

COM.: A gain.

SOC.: Then this at least is not gain, obtaining just any possession.

COM.: No, indeed.

SOC.: And it is not a gain whenever it is bad? Or will one not obtain a gain by obtaining just any good thing?

COM.: Apparently one will if it is good.

c SOC.: While if it is bad, will not one suffer a loss?

COM.: So it seems to me.

SOC.: Do you see then, how you are coming round to the same thing? Gain appears to be good, and loss bad.

COM.: Well, I don't know what to say.

SOC.: Not unjustly are you bewildered. But still, answer this also: if one obtains more than one has spent, do you claim that is a gain?

COM.: Not if it is bad, I say, but if one gets more gold or silver than one has spent.

d SOC.: Then let me ask you this: If one spends half a measure of gold and gets double in silver, has he got a gain or a loss?

COM.: A loss, surely, Socrates, for then his gold is only worth double instead of twelve times as much.

SOC.: Still, he has obtained more. Or isn't double more than half?

COM.: Not in worth, comparing silver and gold.

SOC.: So then it seems necessary to add the consideration of worth to gain. For now you are saying that silver, although more than gold, is not worth gold, while you say that gold, although less, is of equal worth.

e COM.: Absolutely; that's the way it is.

SOC.: Worth, then, is what is gainful, whether it is small or great, and the worthless what brings no gain.

COM.: Yes.

SOC.: Do you say that worth is worth anything except when it is possessed?

COM.: Yes, only when it is possessed.

SOC.: Furthermore, do you say that worth is the possession of what is disadvantageous or advantageous?

COM.: Surely what is advantageous.

SOC.: Now, isn't the advantageous good?

COM.: Yes.

232a SOC.: Well then, most courageous one, haven't we once again, for the third or fourth time, come to the agreement that the gainful is good?

COM.: So it seems.

SOC.: Do you remember from what point this discussion of ours began?

COM.: I think so.

SOC.: If you don't, I will remind you. You disagreed with me, arguing that the good do want to profit not from every gain but only from those gains that are good, not from the evil.

COM.: That's right.

b SOC.: And now doesn't the argument compel us to agree that all gains, small and large, are good?

COM.: For my part, Socrates, it has compelled rather than persuaded me.

SOC.: Well, perhaps later it will persuade you as well. Now, though, whether you are persuaded or however you are disposed, you do at least agree that all gains are good for us, both small and large?

COM.: Yes, I agree.

SOC.: Do you agree too that all decent human beings want all good things or not?

COM.: I agree.

c SOC.: And you yourself said that the evil for their part love gain, whether small or large.

COM.: Yes, I did.

SOC.: Then according to your argument, all human beings would be lovers of gain, both the decent and the evil.

COM.: Apparently.

SOC.: Then if someone reproaches another with being a lover of gain, it is not a correct reproach; for it so happens that the one making this reproach is himself of the same sort.

The Political Philosopher in Democratic Society: The Socratic View

ALLAN BLOOM

In an age in which not only the alternatives of action but also those of thought have become peculiarly impoverished, it behooves us to search for the lost, profound possibilities of human life. We are in need of a comprehensive reflection on the ends of politics, but we are confronted with a host of objections which make that enterprise seem impossible. A return to the origins of political philosophy—that is, a return to Socrates—is requisite if we are to clarify the nature of political philosophy and elaborate its intention and possibility. This attempt to recapture the original project of the political philosopher is a difficult one because we are searching without knowing quite what we are looking for, hence it is hard to know when we have found it. The best beginning is to focus our attention and efforts on those works which have least in common with our mode of treating problems and which were once taken seriously by serious men but are hard for us to take seriously. Writers like Isocrates and Xenophon have fallen into disfavor, but it is precisely from their rhetoric and restraint that we could learn of the taste of Thucydides and Plato and of the capital importance of the virtue of moderation in the political thought of the ancient authors. When we do not understand Isocrates and Xenophon, we do not understand Thucydides and Plato. We see in these latter concerns of our own, and they lose their liberating effect. Our horizon is protected from attack by a habit of not noticing what is not comprehended by it. As a result, what is unknown and important takes on the guise of the commonplace or trivial for us.

One of the best antidotes for this kind of myopia is the study of the smaller Platonic dialogues. They are short, which in one sense makes them easier; for it is almost impossible to devote the appropriate attention to every line, every word, of a book the length of the *Laws;* our eye skips over what ought to be perplexing; time does not permit the attention to the incredibly elaborate detail, nor are our intelligences ordinarily competent to the survey of such a large, complex whole. A dialogue which is a few pages long permits one to wonder over every detail, to ask innumerable questions of the text, to use on it every resource of intellect, passion, and imagination. In another sense, though, these small dialogues are much more difficult, for they are so strange. With the *Republic,* for example, a long tradition of philosophy tells us what the issues are; we know that the question is justice and the best regime. When we read the sections on the good and knowledge, we feel at home because we see them as parts of a great discussion which has been going on in Western thought for two and a half millennia, a discussion participated in by Locke, Kant, and Nietzsche, who use the same terms as does Plato. This sense of familiarity may be spurious; we may be reading the text as seen by the tradition rather than raising Plato's own questions, interpreting all of the foreign elements in the book in the light of questions posed to it by later thinkers. This is, of course, the danger; for if we cannot understand dialogues which do not contain the well-known themes, it means that we do not really know what Plato was about or what the dialogue form is and means. Still and all, we do feel at home in the big, famous dialogues. But when we come to a dialogue like the *Ion,* what are we to say about Socrates' meeting with a stupid reciter of the Homeric poems whom Socrates treats like an oracle, to whom he attributes divine inspiration, and who, at the end, in desperation at his incapacity to define himself in the face of Socrates' sophistic arguments, insists that he is Greece's greatest general? It all seems too mad. What is the philosophic significance of all this? Each of the smaller dialogues has this strange character. The scholarly reaction to such curious works has been to ignore them, to consider them spurious because Socrates would never have engaged in such discussions nor Plato recorded them, or to treat them as logical exercises, propaedeutic to real philosophy.

I would suggest that the big dialogues cannot be understood without understanding the little ones first, for the former are responses to problems elaborated in the latter, responses which become meaningful only against the background of those problems. Plato was more interested in posing the proper questions than in providing answers. Perhaps the most important question of all is what is philosophy, how is it possible, and why is it necessary? Philosophy emerges late in human history; it was still new in Socrates' time. It is not coeval with man as families, cities, and the useful arts seem to be. It could not be taken for granted. It also was suspected, ridiculed, and hated. It not only had to constitute itself; it had to defend itself. The little dialogues characterize Socrates', and hence philosophy's, confrontation with the opinions or conventions out of which philosophy emerged, the confrontation with the authoritative views of the pious, the poets, the statesmen, the people at large, etc. In other words, these dialogues sketch out the images on the wall of the cave, reveal their inadequacy, and point toward the road upward; they present the first, the commonsense horizon of man, the horizon which must be transcended but which must first be known in order to be transcended. Every explanation of the world presupposes a rich apprehension of the phenomena of the world; otherwise that explanation will be as impoverished as is the awareness which it seeks to clarify. Plato elaborates the commonsense horizon in the little di-

alogues. Each of the interlocutors represents an archetypical prejudice. Their arguments are always poor, but they are poor because something in their souls attaches them to falsehood. Thus, if we see the reasons for the poor arguments, we learn of the complexity of the soul as well as of the various views of what is most important to believe and know. These dialogues canvass the types of human soul and the most powerful prephilosophic opinions about the true and the good. They appear mad, because the common sense of this world is always somehow self–contradictory or askew; if pushed to its conclusion it leads to absurdity in thought and action, and it is precisely this character of common sense that necessitates philosophy and makes its emergence difficult. Philosophy, unlike the prejudices it seeks to replace, must be aware of its origins and its reason for being. The smaller dialogues are necessary to us because they unambiguously force us to learn Plato's mode of interpretation of the world and because they are almost indispensable aids to the enrichment of our consciousness so vital to any nonabstract pursuit of clarity about the most important questions.

Now, the *Hipparchus* is one of two dialogues Socrates carries on with an unnamed companion. The other is the *Minos*. Because the dialogue is acted out directly, we can learn nothing of the setting, the occasion for the meeting of the two men or any other detail which might reveal its intention. Both the *Hipparchus* and the *Minos* begin with the most profound Socratic question "What is . . . ?" the *Minos* investigating the nature of law and the *Hipparchus* that of profit, and both culminate in a provocative, extravagant, and unsubstantiated praise of a man usually thought to be an enemy of Athens, after whom the dialogue is named. A foreign oppressor is involved with respect to the law, a domestic tyrant with respect to profit. The similarities between the two dialogues make their differences interesting and revealing. Minos is the son of a God and has intercourse with him; Hipparchus is the son of a human being and no mention of the gods is made in the dialogue except for four oaths of the companion. Perhaps connected with the foregoing observations is the fact that Socrates is peculiarly brutal to his companion in the *Hipparchus*. This fact is certainly related to the further fact that Hipparchus, the man praised, was a tyrant.

The *Hipparchus,* like the *Minos,* has a double title; it is "Hipparchus or Lover of Profit" (I translate *philokerdes* as "profiteer," for that about matches the moral tone of the Greek). Perhaps the two are meant to be identical; if so, the praise of Hipparchus would be most revealing.

As already stated, the first words of the dialogue put the Socratic question, and it is put by Socrates himself. He is trying to learn from the companion, asking what kind of a thing profiteering is. It is a naive question, one that makes Socrates look like the unworldly inhabitant of the thinktank Aristophanes put him into, now venturing forth into the world to find out about the human things known to everyone else. We obviously enter a conversation that has already begun, and we do not know the reason Socrates puts his question to his companion, who is quite willing to instruct him, but we may suppose that the companion had said something denigrating about profiteers and Socrates wanted to know what was wrong with them.

"What is profiteering?" is indeed in the form of an authentic Socratic question, but it is really ill put, or a secondary question, for the answer to it depends on a prior answer to the question "What is profit?" The neglect of the more fundamental question results in the totally unsatisfactory character of the whole discussion, for the companion and the Socrates clearly mean different things, and the companion is unaware of even the possibility of such a difference. But this is not what we would today call a difficulty of communication, for it would clearly be beyond the capacity of the companion to grasp what Socrates holds to be profitable; if Socrates were to explain that to him, the companion would merely hear words. Although the discussion in that case might not arrive at its ultimate impasse, their agreement would be merely formal, for the companion would still continue prizing the things he had always prized. The difficulty in speech reveals a difficulty in the soul of the companion; the insufficiency of the conversation is a condition of a sufficient representation of that soul which necessarily holds self-contradictory opinions. The interesting thing about the conversation is its development of the views typically held by a man such as the companion and particularly the relation of those views to the life of Socrates.

The companion holds that money, or what it represents, is what is good. The word "profit" for him means what it means today to most men in commercial societies. They might be aware of a broader sense of the term, but that sense is not what they primarily mean when they use the term. The attachment to money is really identical to the attachment to life and comfort and, according to Socrates, is the motivation of the great majority of men. The companion, hence, belongs to, and represents, that lowest class of the *Republic* which Socrates calls the money-loving or profiteering class, even though the companion professes to berate profiteers. His exclusive concern for money is made explicit only at the end of the discussion, but it motivates his responses from the beginning. The discussion never moves beyond the companion's understanding of profit. It would have been easy to make it do so, for few men are willing in speech to admit that they care solely for safety and comfort; something forces them to recognize that there are nobler objects, but in deed most men care more for the useful than the noble. The *Hipparchus* investigates the moral taste of such men; Socrates facilitates this intention by not mentioning the companion's motive and only questioning its consequences, for in this way that motive operates unabashedly, unaffected by the shame exposure would cause.

225
a–b
Socrates asks a double question: what is profiteering and who are the profiteers? The companion chooses to tell who the profiteers are, proving that he is less interested in the nature of the thing than in

attacking a certain kind of man. He formulates it with rhetorical elegance: profiteers are those who think it is worth profiting from what is worthless. His meaning is immediately obvious—he means cheaters, those who sell useless things by deceit, the most common type of fraudulent business operators—but that meaning is not obvious to Socrates. He naively asks whether they know that the things are worthless, adding that they would be fools if they did not. Socrates, Candide-like, apparently does not know that there are men who would deceive others about the worth of things, and the companion is eager to inform him of the hard ways of the world, expecting to gain an ally in his war against the vicious. The companion in his assurance as to Socrates' meaning and his haste to make his condemnation of the profiteers fails to notice the ambiguity of Socrates' question. He takes it that Socrates wants to know if the profiteers make a profit by selling something the value of which they mistakenly overestimate; this would mean they could not be blamed; one must know one is committing a crime if one is to be considered responsible for it; since the companion wishes to blame the profiteers, he must insist on their full knowledge. But Socrates' question could, and should, be interpreted to mean that if something is simply worthless, one cannot profit from it, and only a fool would try to. There are two senses of worth here, worth for making profit and worth for the buyer. Socrates begins to play on their double sense, not to confuse the companion but because it represents a real, unresolved problem in the companion's own thought. The companion believes the profiteers actually do get something good, although he himself may be hurt by their doing so. He concentrates on the harm done to others, including himself, by profiteers, whereas Socrates seems indifferent to that and seems to concentrate on the efficacy of the profiteers' quest for profit. The companion, in reassuring Socrates that the profiteers certainly do know what they are doing, manifests a certain envy of the profiteers, calling them wicked and villains. Of course, he who makes a quick killing is no fool; he gets his own good at the expense of others. The companion believes, as do all those who speak in this way, that he knows what is profitable and that there is a conflict between private and public good, and he condemns the pursuit of private good in order to protect the public good. The profiteer is daring; he is shameless. Shame, fear of the opinion of others, prevents men from being profiteers; but shame or no shame, it remains that what the profiteer gets is truly profitable to him. The more advantageous the profiteer's dealings are, the more intense is the blame. Socrates, however, does not share the companion's ambivalence. Rather than looking naive, he might on closer examination appear shameless himself; he is not shocked at men's profiting from the worthless; he is merely curious as to whether it can be done. He attempts to indicate this to the companion by citing the example of a farmer. Would a farmer think it is worth profiting from planting a worthless plant? The companion, not responding to Socrates' hint, answers that a profiteer supposes he should profit from everything.

The example, to which the companion paid no attention, is actually quite revealing. The farmer and the profiteer both aim at increase; if a farmer's plants are worthless, they will not grow; if the profiteer sows worthless seeds of profit, they will not grow into profits. Judging from the point of view of the farmer and the profiteer, no worthless means can achieve their ends. The companion would readily admit this for the farmer, but he does not see the analogy between farmer and profiteer. The farmer's harvest is produced by nature and has a natural use value, whereas the profiteer harvests a crop of conventional money. It is precisely the disproportion between the natural or use value of things and what people will pay for them that the profiteer exploits and the companion complains about. But the companion is a lover of money and takes its pursuit to be natural. Thus he would really have to accept the comparison between a farmer's planting and a profiteer's investing and hence have to evaluate the worth of the means in relation to the achievement of the ends. Money, as Aristotle and Marx also saw, is ambiguous: it can represent the natural value of things, or it can be valuable in itself; in the former case it would be measured by the things, in the latter the things would be measured by it. Thus money can become an end in itself and can be desired in infinite amounts, divorced from any possible use, as opposed, say, to artichokes. The love of money, beginning from a natural desire for future power, gradually makes a man a prisoner of conventional value and alienates him from even the consideration of natural worth. The companion loves money and, at the same time, wants those who sell to him to be more concerned with natural worth or usefulness than money. The companion, in order to avoid contradiction, would have to distinguish between worth in money to the seller and worth in use to the buyer and elaborate the consequences of that distinction. But he is hopelessly confused about it, and this confusion is vitally linked to his whole view of men and things.

25b–
26a
Socrates responds brutally to the companion's assertion that the profiteer supposes he should profit from everything. He tells him to stop answering aimlessly like a man who has suffered some injustice at someone's hands. The sense of injustice suffered causes a man to make irrelevant answers, according to Socrates; he implies that indignation, at least in the companion's case, is only a form of selfish revenge and high principles only a form of self-protection. Indignation, outrage at injustice, only becloud serious consideration of important questions. Socrates, most uncharacteristically, banishes considerations of justice in favor of those of profit. At this point in the discussion he appears to deny the companion the possibility of saying that the profiteer is bad because he harms others, implying that the arguments against profiteering are merely made to protect one's own profit from cleverer seekers of profit. He treats the companion like an enemy, part of a conspiracy to deny him his own profit. He heightens this impression by making a contemptuous reference to the "wise phrases" clever men use in the courts of justice and mocking the rhetorical style of the companion's definition of profiteers. This moralism is a lot of high-flown talk designed to give a veneer of decency to a compact between men who do not believe in justice but wish to avoid suffering injustice, a compact made to inhibit a man from knowing what his true profit is. The courts are the instruments of this conspiracy. Socrates accuses the companion of wilfully trying to deceive him. As the companion feared deception in money matters, so Socrates fears it in speeches. It would seem that to avoid the deceptions of the profiteer there is a tendency to deceive potential profiteers about the nature of profit. What in another context might have been identified as considerations of justice Socrates here qualifies as the contrivances of hypocrisy. Socrates charges the companion with wanting Socrates to believe what the companion does not himself believe. Presumably for the sake of self-protection, he wants to convince Socrates of the badness of the profiteers; thus the companion could rely on him.

226
a–d
By thus browbeating the companion, Socrates turns the conversation away from the blame of profiteering and does not permit him to introduce considerations of justice or the effect of profiteering on

others. He takes the companion's assertion that the profiteers know that they are profiting from worthless things and converts it into the assertion that a profiteer is a knower, like all the artisans who know things. The farmer, the horse trainer, the pilot of a ship, and the general would never knowingly choose worthless means to gain their end; the ends of each of the arts mentioned is clear, and the worth of the means is determined by the end of the art. One would never, for example, judge of the worth of the manure used in farming by the discomfort it causes passersby. Similarly the profiteer's means would properly be judged in relation only to his end, which is profit, and not to the effects of those means on others. He would certainly not use worthless things for profit in this sense, for it would be both contrary to the nature of the knower and impossible. And thus it turns out that according to the companion's definition no one is a profiteer; he blames men who do not exist.

We are of course outraged by this terrible argument, but it really does the companion full justice in the deeper sense. He is selfish; he loves money overmuch, but at the same time he wishes to restrict the pursuit of money so that a community, the precondition of his making money, can exist. It is somewhat like Locke's solution to the political problem. In this perspective not the pursuit of profit but the means used are blamed. But that community has no dignity; it is no different from a band of robbers. Such a community's laws can hardly compel a man of superior power to abandon his pursuit of profit. The moral prohibitions become empty, mere attempts to dupe him. In the most radical way, Socrates' argument concludes that the ends justify the means. It is a dangerous conclusion. The only way for the companion to avoid its dangerous consequences is for him to reconsider the ends.

226d–
227c   This he now tries to do but in a fainthearted way, for neither his thought nor his tastes make him capable of discussing the hierarchy of goods—since he does not really believe there is one. He merely suggests that due to incontinence or insatiability men cling to things that are worth little or nothing. Thus he tries to find his way out of the maze by saying that profiteers are always worried about profit, meaning money, even when the gains are very small; uncontrolled passion causes them to be that way. This definition is an attack no longer on lack of shame but on lack of moderation. A man who controlled his passions would not want or need so much profit. The profiteer is motivated by a desire for gain which is not quite worth-

less but which is not worthwhile enough to justify his efforts. There is a praise of moderation implied in all of this, but there is no indication in the name of what; it is clear only that moderate men would not be likely to need to take advantage of other men, but what good moderation would be to its practitioners the companion in no way indicates. In order to salvage his condemnation of profiteers he now does speak of their ends and says that they are of very small weight; he is almost forced to say that profit is not important. Shame would cause a man to care about others and was a sufficient motivation for the comrade to encourage when he thought Socrates would share his concern; now he must argue that continence is good for the individual or that profit is not good. He can hardly believe this definition as he did the first, and Socrates easily overturns it. He rather illegitimately argues from their agreement about the means that the profiteers cannot know their ends are worthless. If they are ignorant, they cannot be blamed; they would need education. Men only pursue what they think to be good, so that, for the discussion, all that remains of the second definition is that profiteers have a passion for profit. Socrates establishes that profit is good, or even *the* good, by the negative road of getting the companion to admit that all loss is bad. The companion may have his doubts about profit for reasons of shame or fear, but loss he cannot accept. However, if profit is the opposite of loss, profit must be good. The companion and Socrates and all men love all good things and wish to possess them. Therefore all men are profiteers, and again profiteers cannot be blamed. The companion could only defend himself if he were to say that men should be judged on the basis of the adequacy of their understanding of the good, but he cannot, for he believes that the good is really known and its pursuit is shared by all men.

Socrates is gradually disarming the companion and breaking down all the barriers to selfish conduct to which the companion holds. He has tantamount to defended shameless daring in the use of the means to profit and immoderation in the pursuit of the end of profit.

227c–228b   The companion makes a last effort to defend his condemnation of profiteers. This he does by setting as a standard the conduct of decent men, or gentlemen, and applying it to the consideration of the ends and means of profit. He no longer insists that these ends or means are worthless; he has learned he cannot argue that. Instead he distinguishes between two kinds of men, the decent and the wicked, and asserts that the profiteer is among the wicked, for he is serious about things which no gentleman would be serious about and thinks it is worth profiting from things no gentleman would dare to profit from. If we can enter into the companion's world for a moment, we can see what he is trying to do. He knows that there are some admirable men, men faithful in their contracts, men whom one can trust. Such men are somehow superior; they are proof against the temptations ever present in human dealings. We blame profiteers because they do not behave as such men do, whether it is from shamelessness or extreme passion. The decent men, as it appears to the companion, are not motivated by profit; their conduct cannot be understood in terms of utility; decency and profit are irreducible, and if profit alone were pursued, there would be no decency left in the world. The companion thus both wishes profit and despises it in admiring those who are superior to it. Although he tries to maintain the notion of moral dignity, his view is in some sense low because he sees no profit in decency. He is forced to say that there are good goods and bad goods, and bad goods are those which are profitable but not such as are pursued by decent men. But decency is then without motivation; astonishingly, the companion's morality is like Kant's. Socrates, on the other hand, insists that all desire and action must be motivated by desire to possess the good; good and bad men are not distinguished from one another by the latters' caring for their own good while the former do not. On the companion's level, Socrates' teaching must appear corrupt, for as he understands it, that teaching encourages men to do whatever they want, or more specifically, to pursue money without restraint. Only by denying that increase of money is profit could that consequence be avoided, and this the companion will never do, at least in his heart of hearts. And Socrates thus has put his finger on the internal contradiction in the ordinary view of decency: it is not held to be profitable itself, hence it is either useful for some other goal or it is without ground and its practice folly. Profit has been conceded by the companion to be good, but he must also say it is bad, and so must anyone who is aware that there is a tension between profitable conduct and decent conduct. Socrates, in his pursuit of the good, must again accuse the companion of deceiving him because the companion tries to stop him from his pursuit by saying that the good is bad.

Now the companion has been told by Socrates that any way of profiting is good, that we should pursue profit insatiably and that good men do not differ from bad ones in this decisive respect; and thus he, with an oath, must counter by accusing Socrates of deceiving him. The arguments seem to have removed all restraints on what the companion must assume to be Socrates' desire to do him harm; and Socrates is destroying the horizon without which the companion cannot orient himself. The companion learns about a new kind of cheating, the use of worthless arguments which he cannot understand. He wishes to repress the profiteering of the man who seeks knowledge that might be damaging to him just as much as he wishes to repress the profiteering of the man who seeks monetary gains that might be damaging to him. Socrates, since he has apparently destroyed all grounds for the companion's trusting him, must hasten to reassure him.

228b– 229d   Socrates adopts a fantastic mode of reassuring the companion. He tries to show him that he is a disciple of a man who did not believe in deceiving others, or rather, friends. In doing so he must also show that his master is a man to be admired, and thus, in this backhanded and implausible way, Socrates introduces the hero of the dialogue, Hipparchus. Only this digression, which disrupts the surface movement of the discussion and is apparently irrelevant to it, permits us to see its true intention. Socrates' procedure is odd from any point of view, for in making Hipparchus his authority, he refers to a man who is popularly considered to have been a tyrant, the most extreme example of what the companion has been attacking, the ultimately successful profiteer who has gained possession of the city and everything in it. Rather than identify himself with what is respectable and thereby prove his own respectability, Socrates has the insolence to choose the greatest villain known to the Athenian democracy, praise him, and expect to be respected for it. He modestly introduces Hipparchus as "our fellow citizen." Socrates suggests that the profiteer will indeed be beyond the law, will take advantage of others, will not want to accept the rule of equality which is dear to the companion; but he further suggests that such a profiteer is a superior man and that, if the companion will only let himself be taken advantage of, he will profit from being ruled by him. Hipparchus is, above all, motivated by the love of wisdom; as money is profit for the companion, so is wisdom profit for Hipparchus, who was willing to spend money lavishly on procuring and displaying wisdom; he is a profiteer, a *philokerdes,* but in his case this is identical with being a lover of wisdom, a *philosophos.* This is a new kind of profiteering, unknown to the companion, an insatiable thirst, one which defies the laws of equality but the satisfaction of which does not depend on taking from others but rather provides plenty for others without loss to itself. This is what Socrates was referring to when he spoke of profit, and here we get a hint of his side of a discussion in which we have thus far seen only the companion's side. In this perspective, Socrates' conclusions, which seemed so sinister to the companion, are not only innocent but salutary. But the companion would condemn this form of profiteering just as he did the other. It does not obey the rules so essential to the companion's self-protection; his condemnation of the low form of profiteering includes a condemnation of the high form, and Socrates' apparent defense of the low form is really a defense of the high to a man who cannot even imagine its existence. This explains Socrates' anger with the companion; the companion, in all his apparent respectability, is the enemy of philosophy.

But in order to clarify all this, we must investigate the Hipparchus story and particularly Thucydides' account of it. In this way, we can see what Socrates is doing against the background of reality. The Athenians believed that Hipparchus was an unjust tyrant and that he was assassinated by Harmodius and Aristogeiton out of a noble love of freedom. They were thus in the deepest sense the founders of Athenian democracy and were sacrificed to as divine beings. The goodness and necessity of Athenian democracy were proved by the terribleness of the alternative to it; the attachment to the democratic regime was strengthened by this belief, and anyone diverging from the principles of the democracy could be accused of tyrannical ambitions. The fear of tyranny, grounded in alleged Athenian experience, was a valuable tool for demagogues. Thucydides, in the context of the Athenian condemnation of Alcibiades after the mutilation of the Hermae, takes the occasion to subject this essential part of the Athenian tradition to closer scrutiny. He shows that the rule of the Peisistratid family was excellent prior to the assassination of Hipparchus and that the bad behavior of the tyrants was a result of the tyrannicides' deed. The whole Athenian account belongs to the realm of political myth. All of the details are wrong. Hippias was the tyrant; the plot against Hippias failed and only his younger brother Hipparchus was killed. Harmodias and Aristogeiton were motivated not by love of freedom but by revenge in a tawdry, subpolitical erotic scandal. The two lovers had only the remotest connection with the establishment of democracy. They rather caused the tyranny to become tyrannical; it was the Spartans, foreigners, who deposed the

Peisistratids, and it is not at all clear that Harmodius' and Aristogeiton's deed had any part in producing this result. Thucydides in this
correction of the popular account implicitly asks the question
whether a tyranny is the worst possible alternative; he shows the
unreasoning element in the treatment of Alcibiades. He makes it
possible to think what is unthinkable and allows one to see out beyond the walls built in the mind by Athenian prejudice.

Socrates takes a different route to a goal not dissimilar to
Thucydides'. In discussion with an Athenian, he accepts the story
that Hipparchus was the ruler. He simply denies that the description
of Hipparchus is accurate. Hipparchus is the victim of a calumny of
the democrats, and if one were to understand the facts, one would
wish to be ruled by him again, for his was the golden age and the
Athenians lived as in the time of Cronos.

Socrates makes his own myth to counterpoise the Athenian one
and thus liberates from Athenian prejudice, finding within Athens
and its tradition a model for the regime and the man he understands
to be good.

The salient aspects of the description of Hipparchus are the following: he was a lover of wisdom and was motivated by the desire to be
admired for his wisdom. He therefore had to become an educator in
order to make his subjects good enough to admire his virtues. There
was a perfect proportion between his selfish interest and the common
good. In order to be admired for his own wisdom he had to become
an opponent of the prevailing wisdom, which was the Delphic
wisdom, expressed best in the two phrases "Know thyself" and
"Nothing too much." In response to these he set up Hermae
throughout Attica, engraved with such examples of his wisdom as
these: "Walk thinking just thoughts" and "Don't deceive a friend."

These two wise sayings do not appear to rival those of the Delphic
oracle, but reflection may at least help to give some indication of
what might be considered wise in them. A hint is provided by the
Charmides where the potential tyrant Critias in discussing moderation
interprets the two Delphic utterances as meaning the same thing; a
man who knows himself does nothing in excess; the Delphic teaching
is one of moderation. And in combating it Hipparchus carries forward the criticism of moderation which dominated the first part of
the dialogue. It was precisely the refutation of the arguments for
vulgar moderation that forced Socrates to try to find a substitute for it
that can guarantee decent human intercourse, and Hipparchus' say-

ings are supposed to be that substitute. Following Critias' lead, we
might suggest that Hipparchus' two sayings are also identical: justice
is not deceiving friends. To put it otherwise, a man should behave
decently toward others not because he has restrained his passions or
given up his satisfaction but because they are friends, because his
satisfaction comes from benefiting them. There are two opposed
notions of justice, the one conceiving of justice as unprofitable duty,
the other as the satisfaction of giving their deserts to those whom one
loves. The former, a more political view, concentrates on men's
opposition of interests and provides what is necessary for a community; the latter, more fitting to the private life, concentrates on what
men can have in common and the mutual satisfactions of worthy
men. Hipparchus' dictum in the principle by which Socrates guided
his life.

If one is not to deceive a friend, he must know the truth, and he
must find other men who are capable of learning it from him. The
real solution to the companion's impasse is not "Don't deceive a
friend" but philosophy, which that exhortation implies. It is the only
way of life which is both of profit to its practitioner and of benefit to
those with whom he associates. This is of course not a political
solution, for it implies a community composed only of the wise or
the potentially wise, which is impossible. But Socrates' description of
Hipparchus' politics contains a justification of his own life.

In order to support this praise of Hipparchus, Socrates must explain why he was assassinated and convert the conventional praise of
Harmodius and Aristogeiton into blame. He accepts without question that the motives were erotic, but this is in no sense blameworthy
in his eyes. Eros seems to constitute the core of life, and Hipparchus
founded a regime in which eros can enjoy its full rights. Education is
understood as an erotic activity or at least as closely bound up with it,
and Hipparchus' ruling is only education. The true story, according
to Socrates, is that Aristogeiton was a rival educator (perhaps of
Delphic persuasion) and had loved and educated Harmodius, who in
turn had loved a well-born boy. This boy began by admiring the
older men's wisdom but had come to despise them after meeting
Hipparchus. Because they were enraged at this dishonor, they slew
Hipparchus. In this account, Hipparchus was not the unrequited
lover who insulted the sister of Harmodius; Harmodius is the unrequited lover and Hipparchus an object of love. He was lovable be-

cause he was wise and was slain because his wisdom alienated the affections of the best of the young.

I submit that this tale of Hipparchus is nothing but a description of Socrates, and the intention of telling it is only to explain why Socrates was later put to death. Both Hipparchus and Socrates met death as a result of the envy of democrats who claimed that the youth were corrupted by their teachings. Socrates, like Hipparchus, was a lover of wisdom who benefited his friends by educating them and who competed with the Delphic oracle. He leads those who listen to him away from respect for the community and its leaders; he teaches them the immoderate pursuit of the good. Anytus, the major accuser of Socrates, was in later times said to have been a frustrated lover of Alcibiades, who himself said that he became a lover of Socrates. At all events, Anytus appears in Socrates' trial as the defender of the Athenian young against the Socratic seductiveness. I would suggest that as Socrates equals Hipparchus, Anytus equals Harmodius, and Alcibiades equals the nameless youth. Just as Harmodius turned to Aristogeiton, Anytus turns to his educator and lover, the Athenian *demos,* for aid in revenging himself on Socrates for stealing away Alcibiades. Just as Hipparchus and Aristogeiton were the real enemies there, Socrates and the *demos* are the real enemies here. Alcibiades despised the justice of the *demos,* and this was blamed, not totally without basis, on Socrates. Socrates silently exculpates himself by expressing reverence for the Hermae Alcibiades was accused of mutilating. But in spite of that, those Hermae were not meant to be protectors of the democracy, and Hipparchus is no friend to it. The little story of Hipparchus reiterates a well-known Socratic teaching: the wise should rule and should certainly never be ruled by the many.

Now, how does all of this relate to the companion and his argument? Very simply: the companion wants to impose the morality of the *demos* on Socrates and would ultimately be willing to destroy him if he does not accede. That morality consists in the restraint, according to the rules necessary to the existence of a community, of the pursuit of certain profitable things which are scarce and can be the sources of strife among men; it is the morality of private property. As revealed in the first section of the dialogue, Socrates cannot accept this morality, and his own teaching undermines it, at least in principle. One can say that the companion really holds that men are equal, in the sense that they all equally desire money and the things represented by it. The distinction among them is only in the way they pursue the satisfaction of that desire; the good men are those who play by the rules, the bad ones are those who do not. Men who pursue profit without restraint are enemies, and this is what Socrates does. It is a different kind of profit that the companion means, to be sure, but his net catches philosophers as well as bandits or embezzlers. Socrates' students would not be reliable citizens of a democracy, and Socrates himself does not hold that the lovers of wisdom should accept the way of life set down by the lovers of money. They want democracy; he is apparently a proponent of monarchy.

The first two parts of the dialogue present two kinds of lovers of profit, the lover of money and the lover of wisdom, and their necessary conflict. With the praise of Hipparchus, Socrates has revealed himself and manifested the source of the difficulty in the first part. The companion is really a praiser of Harmodius and Aristogeiton, for he can flourish in the regime of which they are the founders, just as Socrates would have flourished in the regime founded by Hipparchus. The first and second parts elaborate the conflict between the two men; the third is meant to be a resolution of sorts.

229d–230a   Not surprisingly, Socrates fails to persuade the companion of the validity of his earlier arguments by his invocation of Hipparchus. The companion says that either Socrates does not consider him to be a friend or he is not persuaded by Hipparchus. It would be hard for Socrates to disprove him on either count. Socrates' speeches seem to the companion to be like those of a profiteer; he deceives in argument, as do profiteers in business matters, but he is unable to find out quite where or how Socrates does it. He distrusts the cleverer, unconventional arguer. So Socrates inducts him into the art of dialectic to see whether he can learn and whether argument can persuade him. The companion is given the opportunity, as in chess, to change any of his earlier moves. Quite appropriately he returns to the attempt to distinguish between good and bad profit; he wishes to revoke his agreement that all profit is good. He appears to be thinking of something like the difference between money made in honest trade and that acquired in a bank robbery. He has steadily resisted the impetus of the argument tending to regard the one as just as legitimate as the other.

230a–231c   Socrates begins the examination of the companion's assertion by making explicit a general rule implied in that assertion: a thing is as much what it is whether it is good or bad; good does not relate to the being of a thing, it is rather something a thing undergoes, an accident of being. Bad food, drink, or men *are* as much as good food, drink, or men. This may be a questionable rule, but it certainly reflects the companion's view: the money in itself is still money—and desirable—no matter how acquired. He accepts it readily. The next step is to define profit. At last this most essential question is posed. Socrates suggests an answer. Profit is spending nothing or little and getting back more. This is, of course, also readily accepted by the companion. Then Socrates suggests an example: a man gets a free dinner and then gets sick from it. Is that a profit? By Zeus, no! (The companion's oaths always reinforce his powerful awareness of his own self-interest.) The companion is brought back from the world of money to that of nature; he sees that he must define profit not in terms of more or less money but in terms of its human effects. Health is naturally good and food must be judged in relation to it. Having begun from the premise that a thing does not exist more or less due to its goodness or badness, we now end with the companion's asserting that a thing does not exist if it is not good. The good, originally taken to be irrelevant to nature, comes back as the cause of being. There can be no such thing as bad profit.

In order to see the deeper sense of this curious result, we must apply it to one of the examples mentioned, apparently casually, by Socrates—man. It was admitted that a man is a man whether he is good or bad; now it would appear that if he is not good, he is not a man. Socrates defined food and drink in terms of their function, as nourishment of the body. If they do not perform that function, they are not food and drink but mere shadows. It would follow that a man who did not fulfill his function as a man is not a man.

Such a conclusion would have profound political consequences. What has the shape of a man but does not fulfill the function of a man would not be treated in the same way as one who does. Just as the companion does not want to admit a hierarchy of profits, he does not want to admit a hierarchy of men. This understanding of man is democratic: all men are equal and have equal rights in the political community, the only distinction among them being made on the basis of their obeying the rules of that community. But Socrates, in the same way he has forced the companion to deny the equality of profits, or that much of what appears to be profit is profit, silently forces him to deny the equality of men, or that many who appear to be men are men. Food was judged in relation to health of the body;

men would be judged in relation to health of the soul. Socrates' understanding is profoundly aristocratic or even monarchic. The companion may have thought he was protecting the principle of equality in all of its forms in accepting the general rule; further probing resulted in his being forced to abandon the principles on which he bases his life.

231c–
232b
At this reversal of his position the companion confesses himself at a loss, in an *aporia,* or, as I would like to translate, without means. No amount of money or power can help him out here. Socrates tells him that it is not unjustly that he is without means, applying a new standard of justice, and reiterates the earlier definition of profit, spending less and getting more. The companion testily replies that he does not mean that getting more of something bad is profitable, but it is profitable if one gets more gold or silver. Socrates asks if it is a profit to spend a certain weight in gold and get twice that weight in silver. The companion eagerly replies that it would be a great loss. It is clear that it is not more or less that determines profit but worth. Gold is worth more than silver. One must know worth first of all; one wants more of what is worth something. The companion throughout has thought that determination of worth is a simple matter; everybody knows the worth of things measured in money. But how is it determined that gold is worth more than silver? That is merely a convention which has no relation to the human benefits connected with each, and it is the human benefits Socrates has been talking about. The companion is hopelessly conventional.

Money is what is worthwhile, according to the companion; the only way of distinguishing among men, then, is in their way of pursuing it, their means. For Socrates there are various levels of worthwhile things, and the primary way of distinguishing among men is in what they pursue as worthwhile, their ends. The political consequence of this is that, for the companion, the purpose of law would be to regulate the means of pursuing profit in such a way as to ensure the possibility of the existence of civil society, which, in its turn, is necessary for the pursuit of profit. Law would inevitably be the will of the community of lovers of money expressing their self-interest. For Socrates the primary standard for a law would be that which conduces to the benefit of the members of the community of true human beings. One can see why the companion and Socrates are at war.

The companion, because he is torn between his belief that everything can be measured and bought with money and his awareness that there are natural goods like health, does again have to agree that profit is benefit and consequently that the profitable is always good, thus contradicting himself. He does not really see that it is the value of money that is called into question; he believes that it is the basis of morality that has been placed in doubt by Socrates. That would indeed be the result of Socrates' teaching for a man who believed money to be profit, since men should pursue the good and profit is good. It is hence a dangerous teaching.

₂₃₂
_{b–c} The companion must now accept that good men want all possible profit, whether great or small. He can no longer blame the profiteers. But he must if he is to protect his vital interests. He can see no unbridled pursuit of profit which would not be dangerous. Socrates tells him that the argument has compelled them to accept that the good men are profiteers. The companion responds that he is compelled but not persuaded. That does not seem to disturb Socrates; for if a man's passions prevent him from responding to the persuasion of reason, if his limitations, intellectual and moral, make it impossible for him to care for truth rather than gain, he should not be allowed to rule those who are capable of reason. He must be compelled, at least to the extent he impinges on the life of the others. Socrates is introducing a new tyranny, based on the force of argument. This accounts for his praise of Hipparchus and his tyrannical tone with the companion. If he cannot rule the companion, the companion will rule him. He tells the companion that his blame of profiteering is only hypocrisy inasmuch as he himself is a profiteer. His blame is his way of protecting his own profit at Socrates' expense. To compromise with him would be to compromise the higher with the lower, true profit with sham profit. Although this can in no sense result in a practical political proposal, the analysis of the companion and his thought indicates that he should not be treated with the concern or respect due a human being. The *Republic* is an attempt to find a regime in which philosophers are not ruled by such men, and the observations made by Socrates in this dialogue have a profound effect on the way he lives his life in democratic Athens, which is not the *Republic*. Maimonides sums up the teaching of the Hipparchus when speaking of the way in which a philosopher should live among his fellows: "He should . . . regard all people according to their various states with respect to which they are indubitably either like domestic animals or like beasts of prey. If the perfect man who lives in solitude thinks of

them at all, he does so only with a view to saving himself from the harm that may be caused by those among them who are harmful if he happens to associate with them, or to obtaining an advantage that may be obtained from them if he is forced to it by some of his needs." This is the resolution, provided in the third part, of the antagonism presented in the first two parts of this very radical statement of the ancient view of the relation between the wise man and civil society.

MINOS;

or, On Law

Translated by THOMAS L. PANGLE

Socrates, A Comrade

313a SOCRATES: What is law, for us?[1]

COMRADE: And what sort of laws are you asking about?

SOC.: What? Is there some way in which law differs from law in regard to this very thing, in regard to its being law? For just consider what I now happen to be asking you. I am asking this just as if I had asked, "what is gold?"—if you thus asked me what sort of gold I was speaking of, I think you would not be asking a correct question. For
b presumably gold doesn't differ from gold, or stone from stone, at least in regard to being stone and in regard to being gold. And thus neither does law, presumably, differ at all from law, but they are all the same thing. For each of them is law to the same degree—not one more so and another less. This is the very thing I am asking: what is law as a whole? So if you have the answer at hand, speak.

COM.: What else would law be, Socrates, except the things that are lawfully accepted?[2]

Minos was the legendary founder of Crete and the bitter enemy of Athens. As the dialogue indicates, the accounts surrounding him are of two sorts. According to one tradition, he was tyrannical, harsh, and imperialistic; according to another, he was the greatest of lawgivers, inspired directly by Zeus, his father. See *Laws* 624–25, 706; Plutarch *Theseus* xv–xvi; Strabo *Geography* X iv 8, 19; Diodorus Siculus IV 60 and V 78.

[1]This sentence is ambiguous; it could also mean, "What is the law among us?" In the Greek, the first words in the dialogue are "The law."

[2]The word I have translated "lawfully accepted" is a participle formed from the verb *nomizō*, which has the same root as *nomos* ("law"). Like *nomos, nomizō* has a wide

53

soc.: And so is speech in your opinion the things that are spoken, or sight the things that are seen, or hearing the things that are heard? Or

c does speech seem something different from the things that are spoken, and sight something different from the things that are seen, and hearing something different from the things that are heard, and law, indeed, something different from the things that are lawfully accepted? Is this the way it seems to you, or how else?

com.: Now it does appear to me different.

soc.: So then law is not the things that are lawfully accepted.

com.: It doesn't seem to me to be.

soc.: So what then would law be? Let's investigate it in the following way. If someone had asked us, in regard to the things said just now,

314a "Since it is by sight that you declare that the things that are seen are seen, by the sight's being what are they seen?"—we would have replied to him that it is by its being this perception that shows matters[3] through the eyes. And if, again, he had asked us, "What then? Since it is by hearing that the things that are heard are heard, by the hearing's being what does this take place?"—we would have replied to him that it is by its being this perception that makes voices manifest to us through the ears. In the same way, then, if he should ask us, "Since it is by law that the things lawfully accepted are

b lawfully accepted, by the law's being what are they lawfully accepted? Is it by its being some perception, or some showing, as the things that are learned are learned by the science that shows them, or some discovery as the things that are discovered are discovered—for instance, the things pertaining to health and sickness by the medical art, and, on the other hand, the things the gods think (as the diviners claim) by the divining art? Since for us art is presumably a discovery of things; isn't it?"

com.: Certainly.

soc.: So which of these would we especially take law to be?

c com.: In my opinion at least, these official opinions and decrees

---

range of possible meanings, including "practice or use customarily," "be legal or customary," "enact as legal or as legal custom," and "acknowledge, accept, or believe"—often "in the lawful or customary way." In order to highlight the connections with law and with belief or opinion that are paramount in this dialogue, I have usually translated *nomizō* as "lawfully accept"; where it was not possible to do so, I have placed an asterisk after the word or words that translate *nomizō*. The reader should bear in mind that the word may have a more active connotation than the English "accept" might suggest.

[3]Two lesser manuscripts read: "shows *colors to us*."

passed by votes; for what else would one declare law to be? So as a result it's likely that what you've asked about, this whole, law, is the official opinion of the city.

SOC.: What you're saying, it is likely, is that law is political opinion.

COM.: I do say so.

SOC.: And perhaps what you say is nobly put. But probably we will know better by proceeding as follows. You say some are wise?

COM.: I do say so.

SOC.: Aren't the wise wise through wisdom?

COM.: Yes.

SOC.: What then? The just are just through justice?

COM.: Certainly.

SOC.: And aren't the lawful lawful through law?

COM.: Yes.

d SOC.: And the lawless lawless through lawlessness?

COM.: Yes.

SOC.: And the lawful are just?

COM.: Yes.

SOC.: And the lawless unjust?

COM.: Unjust.

SOC.: Aren't justice and law most noble?

COM.: That is so.

SOC.: And injustice and lawlessness most shameful?

COM.: Yes.

SOC.: And the one saves cities and everything else, while the other destroys and overturns?

COM.: Yes.

SOC.: So then one ought to think about law as being something noble and seek it as good.

COM.: How could one not?

SOC.: Didn't we declare law to be the official opinion of the city?

e COM.: We did so declare.

SOC.: So what then? Are not some official opinions worthy but others wicked?

COM.: That is the case.

SOC.: And now law, at any rate, was not wicked.

COM.: No, indeed.

SOC.: So then it is not correct to answer thus, without qualification, that law is the official opinion of the city.

COM.: Not in my opinion, at least.

SOC.: So then it wouldn't fit harmoniously for the wicked official opinion to be law.

COM.: Certainly not.

SOC.: And yet even to me law comes to sight as being *some* opinion; but since it is not the wicked opinion, then hasn't this now become manifest, that it is the worthy—if law is indeed opinion?

COM.: Yes.

SOC.: But what is worthy opinion? Is it not true opinion?

315a   COM.: Yes.

SOC.: Isn't the true, the discovery of what is?

COM.: It is indeed.

SOC.: Law, then, wishes⁴ to be the discovery of what is.

COM.: How is it then, Socrates, if law is discovery of what is, that we don't at all times use the same laws in the same matters—if the things that are have indeed been discovered by us?

b   SOC.: The law wishes, nonetheless, to be the discovery of what is, but the humans who, in our opinion, do not at all times use the same laws are not at all times capable of discovering what the law wishes—what is. For come, let's see if from this point onward it becomes manifest to us whether we at all times use the same laws, or different ones at different times, and whether all use the same or different peoples use different ones.

COM.: But this at least, Socrates, is not difficult to know—that the same people do not at all times use the same laws and that different peoples use different ones. Because, for example, among us it is not the law to sacrifice humans, but it is instead impious, while the

c   Carthaginians do perform the sacrifice as something that is pious and legal for them, and some of them even do these things with their own sons, for the sake of Kronos⁵—as perhaps you too have heard.⁶ And

---

⁴"Wishes to be" is a literal rendering of a phrase (*bouletai einai*) that usually has the colloquial meaning of "tends to be"; this helps explain the companion's response. But as Socrates makes clear in his next utterance, he means to bring to the surface the literal meaning (Aristotle sometimes does the same—see, e.g., *Politics* 1259b6 and context).

⁵Kronos was the father of Zeus and came to power by leading a revolt of his brothers and sisters ("the Titans") against his father, Ouranos. It was prophesied that he in his turn would be overthrown by a son of his own, and to forestall the prophecy he ate his own children, but his wife, Rhea, hid the baby Zeus from him, and Zeus lived to fulfill the prophecy (see Hesiod *Theogony* 131–38, 207–10, 453–506, 629–735). Diodorus Siculus (XX 14) tells how the Carthaginians sacrificed their noblest sons in honor, and in imitation, of Kronos.

⁶One of the major manuscripts reads, "as perhaps you have *not* heard."

it's not just barbarian human beings who use laws different from ours, but these people in Lycaea[7] and the descendants of Athamas[8]—what sort of sacrifices do they perform, even though they're Greeks! As to ourselves, presumably you too know, from having heard yourself, what sort of laws we used to use in regard to the dead, slaughtering the sacred victims before the carrying out of the corpse and sending for the women who collect the bones in urns; and again, the

d people who lived still earlier used to bury the dead where they were, in the house. But we do none of these things. Someone could tell of ten thousand such things; for there's plenty of room for a demonstration that neither we among ourselves nor mankind at large at all times lawfully accept the same things.

SOC.: It's no wonder, best of men, if what you say is correct, and this has escaped my notice. But so long as you tell how things seem to you by speaking in your own manner, with lengthy speech, and I in

e turn do so, we will never get together on anything, I believe. If, on the other hand, the investigation is set forth as a common one, perhaps we would come to agree. So if you wish, investigate in common with me by asking me something; or if you wish, do the answering.

COM.: But I'm willing, Socrates, to answer whatever you wish.

SOC.: Come then, which do you believe—that the just things are unjust and the unjust things just, or that the just things are just while the unjust things are unjust?

COM.: For me it is that the just things are just and the unjust things unjust.

316a SOC.: And isn't it believed in this way by everyone, as it is here?

COM.: Yes.

SOC.: And isn't it so among the Persians?

[Lacuna][9]

[7]Lycaea was a town in Arcadia, near a mountain that was one of the places supposed to be Zeus's birthplace. It was the site of an important sanctuary and cult founded by Lycaon. In founding the cult, Lycaon sacrificed a boy to Zeus. This offering angered Zeus, but despite the punishments he sent, the inhabitants continued the practice, and it was said that every nine years a boy was sacrificed and his flesh eaten (cf. *Republic* 565d; Pausanias VIII ii 1–2 and VI viii 2; Apollodorus III vii 1).

[8]Herodotus (VII 197) tells of human sacrifices offered by Greeks who lived in the area of the town of Alus in Achaea, in connection with a cult of the hero Athamas; Athamas was supposed to have founded Alus and, through a complicated intrigue, was deceived into attempting a human sacrifice. One of Sophocles' lost tragedies was about him (cf. Pausanias I xliv 11 and IX xxxiv 4–5; Apollodorus I vii 3 and III iv 3).

[9]The manuscripts lack any reply from the comrade: some brief reply has probably been lost, though one cannot rule out the possibility that the companion simply remained silent.

SOC.: But at all times, surely?

COM.: At all times.

SOC.: Is it believed here that the things that weigh more are heavier, and the things that weigh less lighter, or the opposite?

COM.: No—but that[10] the things that weigh more are heavier and the things that weigh less lighter.

SOC.: And isn't it so in Carthage and in Lycaea?

COM.: Yes.

b SOC.: The noble things, as is likely, are everywhere lawfully accepted as noble and the shameful things as shameful but not the shameful things as noble or the noble things as shameful.

COM.: That is so.

SOC.: And it is the case, to speak universally, that the things that are are lawfully accepted as being, not the things that are not—both by us and by all the others.

COM.: That is my opinion, at least.

SOC.: So then he who errs about what is, errs about the legal.

COM.: Thus, Socrates, as you say, the same things come to sight as

c legal, both for us at all times and for the others. But when I reflect that we never stop changing the laws, this way and that, I can't be persuaded.

SOC.: Perhaps because you do not reflect that these things, being moved as draughts pieces, remain the same. But join me in observing the things in the following way: now, have you ever encountered a writing about the healing of the sick?

COM.: I indeed have.

SOC.: You know, then, to what art this writing belongs?

COM.: I do know: medicine.

SOC.: Don't you call "doctors" the men who have knowledge about these things?

COM.: So I declare.

d SOC.: Is it the case that the same things are accepted*, about the same matters, by those who have knowledge, or different things by different ones?

COM.: The same things, it seems to me at least.

SOC.: Is it the case that the same things are accepted* only by the Greeks among Greeks or also by the barbarians among themselves and among the Greeks as well—in regard to matters they may know?

---

[10]One of the two best manuscripts has "No—but it is believed* here that (etc.)."

COM.: Surely there is a great necessity that those who know—Greeks and barbarians as well—agree with themselves in accepting* the same things.

SOC.: You're answering nobly. And isn't this the case at all times?

COM.: Yes, at all times.

e SOC.: And don't doctors write, about healing, things that they accept* as being so?

COM.: Yes.

SOC.: Then medical, and medical laws, is what these writings of the doctors are.

COM.: Medical they indeed are.

SOC.: So then, too, agricultural writings are agricultural laws?[11]

COM.: Yes.

SOC.: Whose, then, are the writings and legal customs concerning the working of gardens?

COM.: Gardeners'.

SOC.: So then for us these are gardening laws.

COM.: Yes.

SOC.: Belonging to those who have knowledge of how to rule gardens?

COM.: Who else?

SOC.: And it is the gardeners who have knowledge.

COM.: Yes.

SOC.: And whose are the writings and legal customs concerning the preparation of cuisine?

COM.: Cooks'.

SOC.: So then these are cooking laws?

COM.: Cooking.

317a SOC.: Belonging, as is likely, to those who have knowledge of how to rule the preparation of cuisine?

COM.: Yes.

SOC.: And the cooks, as they claim, have the knowledge?

COM.: For they do have the knowledge.

SOC.: Well, and whose, indeed, are the writings and legal customs concerning the organizing of a city? Don't they then belong to those who have knowledge of how to rule a city?

COM.: In my opinion, at least.

---

[11]Two lesser manuscripts have "geometrical" (*geometrika*) instead of "agricultural" (*georgika*).

SOC.: Are they who have the knowledge any others except the statesmen and the kings?

COM.: These are indeed the ones.

SOC.: So then these things which human beings call laws are political writings—the writings of kings and good men.

b COM.: What you say is true.

SOC.: Well those, certainly, who have knowledge will not write different things at different times about the same things?

COM.: No.

SOC.: Nor will they ever, concerning the same matters, change one set of legal customs for another.

COM.: No indeed.

SOC.: So if we see certain persons doing this anywhere, will we declare the ones doing this to be those who have knowledge or those who lack knowledge?

COM.: Those who lack knowledge.

SOC.: And won't we declare that which is correct to be the legal custom for each—either medical or cooking or gardening?

c COM.: Yes.

SOC.: But that which is not correct, this we will no longer declare to be the legal custom?

COM.: No longer.

SOC.: So then it becomes lawless.

COM.: Necessarily.

SOC.: And then in the writings about the just and unjust things, and in general about ordering a city and about how a city ought to be organized, what is correct is kingly law, while what is not correct—what seems to be law to those who don't know—is not. For it is lawless.

COM.: Yes.

d SOC.: So then we were correct in agreeing that law is the discovery of what is.

COM.: So it appears.

SOC.: But further, let's look into the following aspect of it: who has knowledge of distributing[12] seeds on the earth?

---

[12]The word for "distributing" (*dianeimai*) has the same root as the word for law (*nomos*). The original meaning of this root seems to have been the idea of appointing pasture to herds, and the Greek word for "law" seems to have retained an echo of this original notion of fair or reasonable distribution. The word for "distributing" also means "pasturing," and the word for "herdsman" or "pasturer" is the same as the word for "distributor" (see Emmanuel Laroche, *Histoire de la racine NEM en Grec ancien* [Paris, 1949]).

COM.: The farmer.

SOC.: And this man distributes the suitable seeds to each part of the earth?

COM.: Yes.

SOC.: The farmer, therefore, is a good distributor of these things, and the laws and distributions of this man, to these things, are correct?

COM.: Yes.

SOC.: And who is a good distributor of notes to songs, and distributes the suitable ones, and whose are the correct laws?

e COM.: Those of the aulist and the citharist.

SOC.: The most knowledgeable about law, then, in these matters, is the one who is most knowledgeable about the aulos.

COM.: Yes.

SOC.: And who is best at distributing food to the bodies of humans? Isn't it he who distributes what is suitable?

COM.: Yes.

SOC.: So then the distributions of this man, and the laws, are the best, and whoever is most knowledgeable about the law concerning these things is also the best distributor.

COM.: Certainly.

SOC.: Who is this?

318a COM.: The trainer.

SOC.: This man is the most capable of pasturing the human herd of the body?[13]

COM.: Yes.

SOC.: And who is the most capable of pasturing a herd of sheep? What is his name?

COM.: Shepherd.

SOC.: So then the laws of the shepherd are the best for the sheep.

COM.: Yes.

SOC.: And those of the cowherd for the cattle.

COM.: Yes.

SOC.: And whose laws are best for the souls of humans? Aren't they those of the king? Declare it!

COM.: I do declare it.

b SOC.: Now you're speaking in a noble fashion. Would you then be

---

[13]W. R. M. Lamb, the translator of the Loeb edition, points to this line as perhaps the strongest stylistic evidence that Plato could not have written the *Minos*. E. B. England, on the contrary, uses this line as a basis for introducing an emendation into the *Laws*: see his authoritative philological commentary, *The Laws of Plato* (Manchester, 1921) at 808d3.

able to say who among the ancients became a good lawgiver as regards the laws of the art of aulos playing? Perhaps you don't have it in mind, and want me to remind you?

COM.: By all means.

SOC.: Well, then, is Marsyas spoken of, and his boyfriend Olympos, the Phrygian?[14]

COM.: What you say is true.

SOC.: Their aulos tunes are indeed most divine, and alone move and reveal those who are in need of the gods. And now they alone still

c   remain, because they are divine.

COM.: These things are so.

SOC.: And who of the ancient kings is said to have become a good lawgiver, whose legal customs even now remain, as being divine?

COM.: I don't have it in mind.

SOC.: Don't you know who among the Greeks use the most ancient laws?

COM.: So then you're speaking of the Lacedaemonians and the lawgiver Lycurgus?

SOC.: But these, at any rate, are not perhaps three hundred years old,

d   or a little more. But where do the best of these legal customs come from? Do you know?

COM.: They claim, at any rate, from Crete.

SOC.: Then don't these latter people use the most ancient laws among the Greeks?

COM.: Yes.

SOC.: Do you know, then, who were the good kings of these people?—Minos and Rhadamanthus, the sons of Zeus and Europa:[15] these are their laws.

COM.: They claim that Rhadamanthus, at least, was a just man, Socrates, but that Minos was someone savage, harsh, and unjust.

SOC.: Best of men, you're telling an Attic myth, from tragedy!

e   COM.: What? Aren't these things said about Minos?

[14]Marsyas was a satyr who was supposed to have invented the first music for the aulos. He challenged Apollo to a musical duel, claiming his new music was superior to Apollo's; he lost and was flayed alive for his impudence. Olympos, his lover, invented a number of songs and melodies. Both are mentioned prominently in the *Laws* (677d; cf. *Symposium* 215b, c, e; *Republic* 399e; *Euthydemus* 285d; *Ion* 533b). Phrygia was a country in Asia Minor, and the Phrygians were not Greeks.

[15]Europa was the daughter of Phoenix; Zeus fell in love with her and carried her off to Crete, where she bore him the three sons, Minos, Rhadamanthus, and Sarpedon. See *Iliad* XIV 321.

SOC.: Not, at any rate, by Homer and Hesiod, and yet they, indeed, are more trustworthy than all the tragic poets taken together, from whom you have heard the things you're saying.

COM.: But what, then, do these say about Minos?

SOC.: I shall certainly tell you, so that you will not also be impious, as the many are. For there is nothing more impious than this, nothing more to be guarded against, than to err in speech and deed regarding the gods and, second, regarding divine human beings. Nay, it's nec-319a essary to exert very great foresight every time you go to blame or praise a man, so that you won't speak incorrectly. This is why it's necessary to learn how to distinguish worthy from wicked men. For the god is indignant[16] when someone blames a man who resembles him or praises a man who is the opposite of him: and the former is the good man. For you shouldn't suppose that, while stones are sacred, and pieces of wood, and birds, and snakes, human beings are not. Rather, of all these things,[17] the most sacred is the good human being, while the most polluted is the wicked.

Now then, as regards Minos, this is why I'm going to explain how b Homer and Hesiod eulogized him: in order to prevent you, a human being sprung from a human being, from erring in speech regarding a hero who was a son of Zeus. For Homer, in saying about Crete that many human beings are in it, "and ninety cities," declares:

And among them is the great city of Knossos, where Minos
In the ninth season reigned as king, the confidant of great Zeus.[18]

c Now this is a Homeric eulogy regarding Minos, spoken with bre-vity, the likes of which Homer has not composed for a single one of the heroes. For that Zeus is a sophist and that the art itself is entirely noble he makes clear in many other places and especially here. For he says that in the ninth year Minos got together with Zeus to talk, and visited him to get educated—as though Zeus were a sophist. Now, that this prize, of being educated by Zeus, is not distributed by

---

[16]The word for indignation, *nemesis*, has the same root as *nomos* (see n. 12 above).
[17]One of the two best manuscripts has "of all things."
[18]*Odyssey* XIX 172–79. The speaker is the hero Odysseus, who is telling a long and convincing lie to his wife in which he claims to be the grandson of Minos. Socrates omits several lines between the beginning and the ending of the section he quotes and fails to complete Homer's sentence. The translation "in the ninth season" renders a phrase whose meaning is somewhat obscure.

d   Homer to any other hero except Minos—this is amazing praise. And
in the raising of the dead spirits in the *Odyssey*,[19] he has portrayed
Minos, not Rhadamanthus, holding the golden scepter and judging;
he hasn't portrayed Rhadamanthus judging these, and he has nowhere portrayed him getting together with Zeus. It's because of these
things that I assert that Minos was eulogized more than all others by
Homer. For to be the child of Zeus, the only one to have been
educated by Zeus, is praise that cannot be surpassed, and this is what
is signified by the verse

   In the ninth season reigned as king, the confidant of great Zeus

e   —that Minos was a disciple of Zeus. For "confiding" is talking, and a
"confidant" is a disciple in talking, so Minos visited the cave of Zeus
at intervals of nine years, on the one hand to learn things, and on the
other hand, to show things—the things he had learned from Zeus in
the previous nine-year period. There are some who take "confidant"
to mean drinking companion and playfellow of Zeus, but one may
use the following evidence to show that those who take it thus are
320a saying nothing: of the many human beings both Greek and barbarian,
none refrain from drinking parties and from this play that takes place
where there is wine except the Cretans, and second the Lacedaemonians who learned from the Cretans. And in Crete this is one among
the laws which Minos established—not to drink together with one
another to the point of drunkenness. Yet it is manifest that the things
he lawfully accepted as being noble were the things he established as
b   legal customs for his citizens as well. For surely Minos did not, like a
paltry human, believe* some things but create others contrary to the
things he believed*. Rather, this intercourse was, as I say, one that
took place through talking, with a view to education in virtue,
whence he established for his citizens these laws, by means of which
Crete—as well as Lacedaemon—is happy for all time, ever since it
began to use them, for they are divine.

c   Rhadamanthus was indeed also a good man, for he had been educated by Minos. To be sure, he had been educated not in the whole of
the kingly art but in the art of ministering to a king—enough to
preside in the judicial courts. It was for this reason that he was said to

[19]*Odyssey* XI 568–72. Odysseus is the speaker, describing what he saw in his trip to
the underworld.

be a good judge. For Minos used him as a guardian of the laws for the town and Talus[20] for the rest of Crete. For Talus made a circuit three times a year through the villages and guarded the laws in them by having the laws written down on bronze tablets—as a result of which he was called "brazen."

d   Hesiod too has said things akin to these about Minos. For when mentioning his name he declares:

Who came to be the most royal of mortal kings,
and held sway over the most neighboring humans,
possessing the scepter of Zeus; and by it he reigned over cities.[21]

And when he speaks of the scepter of Zeus, he means nothing other than the education which came from Zeus, by which he governed Crete.

COM.: On account of what, then, Socrates, has this report ever gotten
e   spread about concerning Minos, that he was an uneducated and harsh fellow?

SOC.: On account of something that will make both you, best of men, if you are sensibly moderate, and every other man who cares for good repute, guard against ever incurring the hatred of any poetical man. For the poets wield great power over opinion, whichever sort they create among human beings, either by eulogizing or by pronouncing evil.[22] This, indeed, was where Minos erred: in warring against this city here, in which there exists much other wisdom and all sorts of poets, of tragedy especially, along with the rest of poetry.
321a Now tragedy is an ancient thing here; it did not, as they suppose, originate with Thespis or with Phrynichos, but if you're willing to reflect, you will discover that it's a very ancient discovery of this city here.[23] And the poetry that is the most pleasing to the populace and the most soul-alluring is tragedy—which, indeed, is the kind of verse

[20]According to the other mythic traditions that have come down to us, Talus was a bronze man given to Minos by Zeus to help guard Crete from enemies. See Apollonius of Rhodes IV 1639ff. and Apollodorus I ix 26.

[21]These verses are nowhere to be found in our texts of Hesiod; the meter of the first line is imperfect.

[22]One of the two best manuscripts has "accusing" instead of "pronouncing evil."

[23]Thespis was the traditional founder of Attic tragedy, supposedly the first poet who introduced an actor in dialogue with the reciting chorus. Phrynichos was another early contributor to the emergence of the actor; he lived in the late sixth and early fifth centuries, and only the titles of some of his plays survive.

we stretch Minos on the rack of, in retribution for his having compelled us to pay those tributes.[24] So this was where Minos erred—incurring our hatred, from whence, indeed, comes what you asked

b about, his having gotten a worse reputation. For the greatest evidence of his having been good and lawful—as we said earlier, a good pasturer—is this: his laws are unchanged, since they belong to one who discovered well the truth of what is, in regard to organizing a city.

COM.: You seem to me, Socrates, to have found[25] a likely account.

SOC.: Then if I'm saying what's true, don't the Cretan citizens of Minos and Rhadamanthus seem to you to use the most ancient laws?

COM.: They do appear to.

c SOC.: So then these were the best lawgivers among the ancients, and pasturers and shepherds of men—just as Homer declared the good general to be "shepherd of peoples."[26]

COM.: By all means.

SOC.: Come then, in the name of Zeus, the god of friendship! If someone should ask us: "In the case of the good lawgiver and pasturer for the body, what are these things he distributes to the body in making it better?"—we would say, replying in a noble and brief fashion, that they are food and toils, by the former of which he makes the body itself grow and by the latter of which he exercises and makes it firm.

COM.: Correctly put, indeed.

d SOC.: If, then, after this he should ask us: "And whatever, indeed, are those things which the good lawgiver and pasturer distributes to the soul in making it better?"—by answering what, would we not be ashamed of ourselves and of our years?

COM.: This I can no longer say.

SOC.: But surely it is shameful for the soul of either of us to be manifestly ignorant of those things in it in which good and base inhere, while having investigated the things that pertain to the body and the rest!

---

[24]Minos compelled the Athenians to send seven maidens and seven youths to Crete every year, to be eaten by the Minotaur.

[25]In Greek, the word for "found" can also mean "invent." I have here adopted the reading agreed upon by six secondary manuscripts; the two best manuscripts read "uttered" (*eirēkenai*) rather than "found" (*heurēkenai*).

[26]A frequent epithet for kings and princes in Homer.

On the *Minos*

Leo Strauss

The *Minos* has come down to us as a Platonic work immediately
preceding the *Laws*. The *Laws* begins where the *Minos* ends: the
Minos ends with a praise of the laws of the Cretan king Minos, the
son and pupil of Zeus, and the *Laws* begins with an examination of
those laws. The *Minos* thus appears to be the introduction to the
Laws. The *Laws* more than any other Platonic dialogue needs an
introduction, for it is the only Platonic dialogue in which Socrates is
not mentioned or which is set far away from Athens, in Crete. The
Minos thus also appears to be entirely preliminary. Yet it is the only
work included in the body of Platonic writings which has no other
theme than the question "What is law?" and the answer to it. It could
appear strange, and it ought to appear strange, that this grave question which is perhaps the gravest of all questions is, within the body
of the Platonic writings, the sole theme only of a preliminary work.
But we must remember that in Xenophon's Socratic writings Socrates never raises the question, "What is law?"; according to
Xenophon, it was Socrates' ambiguous companion Alcibiades who
raised that Socratic question in a conversation with Pericles while
Socrates was absent. The strangeness is enhanced by the fact that
Plato's Socrates raises his question concerning law, not as is his wont,
after proper preparation, but abruptly; he seems to jump at an un-
suspecting companion with his bald question. He thus brings it about

"On the *Minos*" originally appeared in Leo Strauss, *Liberalism Ancient and Modern*
(New York: Basic Books, 1968), pp. 65–75, copyright © 1968 by Leo Strauss, and is
reprinted by permission of Basic Books, Inc., Publishers.

that nothing accidental or particular—like the question of Socrates' own law-abidingness in the *Crito*—distracts our attention from the universal question in all its gravity. We are not even distracted by the name of the companion; that companion remains nameless and faceless; we perceive only what he says. Since no one else appears to be present at the conversation, the work could not carry as its title, as most Platonic dialogues do, the name of a participant in a Socratic conversation or of a listener to it: the name which is mentioned in the title is the name of a man of the remote past who is only spoken about in the conversation.

While the question with which Socrates opens the conversation is abrupt, it cannot be said to be unambiguous. It is not clear whether he asks the companion, "What in our opinion is law?" or "What is the law to which we (we Athenians [?]) are subject?" The first question might be called universal or theoretical, and the second question might be called practical or particular. The practical question is again ambiguous; it may refer to a whole legal order or to any particular law. While being distinct, the theoretical and the practical questions are inseparable from each other. One cannot know to which law one is subject without having some knowledge, however vague and dim, of law as such; one cannot know what law as such is without possessing at least a directive toward the law to which one is subject. For the time being Socrates makes his initial question unambiguous by limiting the conversation to the theoretical question. But the practical question is only driven underground: the dialogue ends with the suggestion that the law deserving the highest respect is the law, not of Athens, but of Crete.

Socrates illustrates the question "What is law?" first by the question "What is gold?" and then by the question "What is stone?" Gold is most valuable, and a stone may be entirely worthless. "Gold" is never used in the plural, whereas "stone" is; one cannot say "a gold" as one can say "a stone": there are wholes each part of which is a whole or complete, and there are wholes no part of which is complete. We are thus induced to wonder whether law, properly understood, is more like gold or more like stone. But regardless of whether any particular law or even any particular code can be said to be a whole, Socrates' question is concerned with a whole—the whole comprising all laws. Just as gold does not differ from gold in respect of being gold and stone does not differ from stone in respect of being stone, law does not differ from law in respect of being law. Does this mean that a bad law is as much law as a good law?

The companion's first answer to Socrates' comprehensive question is to the effect that the law is the whole consisting of whatever is "held" or whatever is established by law. Socrates convinces him by suitable parallels that just as in other cases what we may call the acts of the human soul are not the same as the things in which these acts issue, law as an act of the soul is not the same as that in which that act issues. Law is then so far from being something inanimate (like gold or stone) that it is an act of the soul: is it manifestation or science or is it finding (invention) or art? In his answer (the second and central answer to Socrates' comprehensive question) the companion does not meet the issue. He says that law is the decision of the city. He means by this that the law is not an act of the soul, but something in which certain acts of the soul issue. Yet it is now clear to him that law is the outcome of some act of the soul, whereas his first answer would have been compatible with the view that law is custom of which no one knows whence it came or, as one might say, which is not "made" but has "grown." Socrates rephrases the second answer in such a way as to make it an answer to the particular question which he had addressed to the companion: the act of the soul which is law has the character, neither of science nor of art, but of opinion; it is the city's opining about the affairs of the city.

A simple consideration suffices to show that this answer is insufficient. We assume that there is a connection between law and justice. Perhaps a man may be law-abiding without being just, but surely a lawless man is unjust. In a way law and justice seem to be interchangeable; hence law will be something high. But a city's opinions may be low. We are then confronted with a contradiction between two most audible opinions which are so audible because they are opinions of the city: the opinion that the law is the opinion of the city and the opinion that the law is something high. Socrates, without any hesitation and without giving any reason, chooses the second opinion and therewith tacitly rejects the opinion that the law is the opinion of the city. Since the opinions of the city are self-contradicting, even the best of citizens cannot simply bow to them. Law is indeed an opinion, according to Socrates; but he does not yet say whose opinion it is; for the time being he only says that it is a high opinion, hence a true opinion, and hence the finding out of what is. "Finding out," and hence law, appears to be between "finding" or art on the one hand and "manifestation" or science on the other.

Only one more step is needed in order to bring us to the third and final definition of law, the only definition proposed by Socrates: the law wishes to be the finding out of what is. The last step is a step back. Socrates qualifies the apparent result according to which the law is the finding out of what is. He does not give a reason for his qualification, but the compelling reason comes to sight immediately afterward: if the law were the finding out (the having found out) of what is, and what is (what is without any admixture of nonbeing) is always the same, law would be simply unchangeable, and hence all or most of the things which we call laws and which differ from time to time and from place to place would not be laws at all. But if law only wishes, or tends, to be the finding out of what is, if no law is necessarily the finding out of what is, there can be an infinite variety of laws which all receive their legitimation from their end: The Truth. The companion fails to grasp the qualification; he believes that Socrates has left it at suggesting that law is the finding out of what is. Given the fact, he argues, that we constantly find out the same things as things which are (sun, moon, stars, men, dogs, and so on), all men should always use the same laws, and they manifestly do not. Socrates replies to the effect that the variety in question is due to the defects of human beings and does not affect the law itself. The implied distinction between the infallible law and the fallible human beings suggests to us that law is indeed an act of the soul, but perhaps not necessarily of the human soul. Besides, Socrates regards it as an open question whether human beings do use different laws at different places and in different times. He thus compels the companion to prove the fact that laws vary. But when he has completed that proof, Socrates seems to reject it as an irrelevant "long speech." In brief, Socrates tries to be silent about the variety of laws—about a fact which had induced him to say that the law wishes to be—that is, is not necessarily—the finding out of what is.

The companion proves the variety of laws by the examples of laws concerning sacrifices and burials; the examples concern sacred things. They confirm to some extent Socrates' definition of law; they show that at any rate the most awe-inspiring laws are based on more or less successful attempts to find out what is in the highest sense, namely, the gods and the soul and hence what the gods demand from men and what death means. The examples show the great difference between present Athenian practice and the practice of the earliest past, of the age of Kronos, as it were. They seem to show that in the beginning men were savage, whereas in present-day Athens they are gentle; hence present-day Athenian laws will be superior to the oldest laws,

Greek or barbarian. This finding obviously presupposes that laws differ temporally and locally. Perhaps Socrates treats the changeability of law in so gingerly a manner because it is the premise of the finding mentioned—of a finding with which he is not satisfied.

Socrates attempts now to bring about a meeting of minds with the companion by means of short speeches, or short questions and answers. The companion prefers to answer Socrates' questions rather than to question Socrates. He grants to Socrates that people everywhere and always hold that the just things are just, the noble things are noble, the unjust things are unjust, and the base things are base—just as all people, regardless of whether they hold it lawful or impious to bring human sacrifices, hold that the things that weigh more are heavier and the things that weigh less are lighter. The final result of this reasoning confirms the unqualified definition of law according to which law does not merely wish but is the finding out of what is. The companion, who through his own fault is compelled to give short and rather quick answers and cannot, as we can, read and reread Socrates' questions, is unable to lay bare the sophism to which Socrates draws our attention while committing it: the universal agreement regarding the opposition of the just or noble things to the unjust or base things does not establish universal agreement as to the content of "the just and the noble." Nevertheless, the companion remains entirely unconvinced, for Socrates' result manifestly contradicts what the companion himself observes with his own eyes in Athens every day, namely, that "we" (that is, we Athenians) unceasingly change the laws.

What one may call Socrates' second proof of his definition of law is not a mere repetition of the first. In the second proof Socrates tacitly contrasts "the just things" and "the heavier things"; he thus draws our attention to two questions: (1) Can justice be a matter of degree as is weight? (2) Is disagreement regarding weight as widespread and as profound as disagreement regarding justice? Besides, the first proof was still related to the opinion that law is the opinion of the city; that opinion plays no role in the second proof. We are thus being prepared for the suggestion that law is the mental act, not of the city (that is, of the assembly of the citizens) or of the citizen, but of men of a different description.

Reading on, we observe that what we have called Socrates' second proof of his definition of law is in fact the first section of his tripartite defense of his definition of law; that tripartite defense forms the second or central part of the dialogue. At the beginning of the central section of the central part, Socrates abruptly turns to the writings of men who possess an art. We can discern the reason for the apparent change of the subject. Socrates had raised the question whether law is a science or an art. He assumes now that law is an art. He seems to justify this assumption as follows. Laws are prescriptive writings; but the arts, being a kind of perfect, final, fixed knowledge which is the same for all, necessarily find their appropriate expression in prescriptive writings; hence laws belong to the same genus as the arts. This reasoning suffers from an obvious flaw: it is not necessary for either arts or laws to present themselves in writings. For instance, the farmers, that is, the experts in farming, do not necessarily compile or even read writings on farming.

If laws belong to the same genus as the arts and are therefore prescriptive writings composed by experts of a certain kind, namely, the kings (or statesmen), there is no reason why laws should be the work of the city or of Greeks: neither citizens nor Greeks are, as such, experts in the kingly art. The prescriptions ordinarily called "laws" may differ from place to place; but regarding things of which men possess knowledge, all knowers agree, as Socrates asserts, regardless of where they live or whether they are Greek or barbarians. When the companion emphatically assents to this assertion, Socrates praises him for the first time. Furthermore, the prescriptions ordinarily called "laws" may differ from time to time; but where there is knowledge, there is no change of thought; or vice versa, where there is change of thought, there is no knowledge; the frequent change of "laws" for which Athens was so notorious is then a clear proof that the Athenian legislature is ignorant, and hence its findings or decisions do not deserve to be called laws or to be respected as laws; in fact those "laws" must be particularly bad. The companion does not object to this tacit result; in other words, he has now become convinced of the truth of Socrates' definition of law or, more precisely, of the fact that law is an art. It looks as if Socrates has succeeded in appealing from his pro-Athenian prejudice to his antidemocratic prejudice. We on our part realize that the answer to the theoretical question "What is law?" has supplied at least a negative answer to the practical question "What is the law to which we are subject?" In spite of the agreement reached, there remains at least one difference between Socrates and the companion—a difference which comes to light in the very center of the dialogue: the companion is more certain than Socrates that cookery is an art; Socrates' uncertainty regarding the status of cookery is matched in the *Minos* only by his uncertainty regarding the status of soothsaying, that is, of the art by which men claim to know what goes on in the minds of the gods. The companion is also more certain, at least to begin with, that knowers agree always and everywhere than that experts agree always and everywhere; perhaps he knew in advance that good legislation requires knowledge of the subject matter to be regulated by law, but was doubtful that that knowledge must be expert knowledge: knowledge of the pertinent facts as distinguished from their causes may be sufficient for good legislation.

In the last section of the central part Socrates proves that law is an art by assuming that art consists in distributing properly the parts of some whole to the parts of another whole—of a herd, as it were. In some cases the distributor assigns to each member of the herd the same quantity of the whole to be distributed as to every other member. In other arts, however, the distributor must consider the fact that the "herd" consists of qualitatively different parts or that different things are good for different parts or different individuals. What human beings call laws would then be the distributing, say, of punishments and rewards to the members of the city or in the best case the distributing of the proper food and toil to the souls of human beings by the king. The king assigns to each the work best for him, that is, most conducive to his becoming a good man: he does not treat the human beings whom he rules as parts of a herd. But if to be a good man is the same as to be a good citizen, a good member of the city, one can also say that the king assigns each man to the place or the work for which he is best fitted. In this section writings are no longer mentioned: assigning to each soul what is good for it cannot be done well except orally, by the king on the spot. It would be more simple to say that such assigning cannot be done well by any law. Socrates prefers to say that it is best done by the best laws, the laws of the king. He thus implies that laws ought to be infinitely variable. Whereas according to the preceding argument, law as art entails that law must be always and everywhere the same and hence that at least almost all so-called laws do not deserve to be called laws, according to the present argument, law as art entails that law must be as variable as the individuals and their individual situations and hence that no so-called law deserves to be called law. On the other hand, by now speaking of the best laws Socrates restores the common view according to which certain decisions of ignoramuses or of assemblies of ignoramuses may also be regarded and respected as law. Yet the best laws prove to be unwritten laws of a certain kind—not indeed the unwritten laws of unknown origin which say the same things always and everywhere, but certain acts of a wise soul.

Socrates had opened the central part of the dialogue with the suggestion that there is universal agreement regarding the just and the noble things. This suggestion taken by itself could be thought to refer to the unwritten laws which are always and everywhere acknowledged to be laws and which for this reason cannot be the work of human legislators (Xenophon *Memorabilia* IV.4.19). But the *Minos* is silent about the unwritten laws thus understood. One may say that in this dialogue Socrates turns from unwritten laws of unknown origin first to written laws and then to unwritten laws of known origin, viz. the distributing by the king of the proper food and toil to each man's soul.

The third and last part of the *Minos* deals with the laws of Minos. The transition is not explained and is therefore abrupt. We are supposed to have learned what law is and what makes a law good; we must then seek the best laws. What we have learned may have made us doubtful whether the best laws can be of human origin. The lesson conveyed through the last part of the dialogue may provisionally be said to be that the best laws are the laws of Minos because Minos received them from the highest god, his father Zeus. What must surprise us is that the laws of Zeus do not consist in assigning to each man's soul the food and toil best fitted for him, and besides that Zeus did not communicate his laws to all men: he communicated them only to a single privileged man, to Minos, whom he appointed also as the highest judge of the dead (*Gorgias* 523e–524a). Perhaps Zeus did not wish to rule directly so that man, within certain limits left to himself, would be compelled or enabled to choose as long as he lives. Furthermore, if Zeus had communicated his law to men directly, men would necessarily be able to know the thoughts of Zeus, that is, soothsaying would necessarily be a genuine art; but there is no need for soothsaying if there is an intermediary between Zeus and men, an intermediary like Minos who, as participating in divinity, does not need a human art to be aware of the thoughts of his father and as participating in humanity can communicate his father's thoughts to men just as human legislators communicate their laws to men.

Socrates leads up to the laws of Zeus by speaking first not simply of the best laws but of laws (prescriptive and distributive acts) both good and ancient regarding flute playing. As we could have learned from the companion's long speech, the good is in no wise the same as the ancient: certain ancient laws commanded human sacrifices to the then highest god. But an ancient law which is now still in force approximates the unchangeability which appeared to be a mark of goodness. Law must be not only good or wise but also stable: could the best laws be laws which are both wise and stable? The example of flute playing—of an art which reminds most forcibly of speech and yet which cannot be practiced while one speaks—draws our attention to the quality of the divine as distinguished from the ancient and the good. The flute songs invented by certain ancient barbarians are most divine because they alone move and bring to light those who are in need of the gods; yet the divine character of those flute songs explains why they still retain their force. Not everything ancient is divine, but perhaps everything divine necessarily lasts for a very long time. Could the stability of the best laws be due to the unspeakable or mysterious power of the divine which rules chance and may rule it in favor of the good? We are thus prepared for Socrates' suggestion that the oldest Greek laws—the laws which Minos gave to his fellow Cretans, rather than, for instance, the Egyptian laws or the Lacedaemonian laws which were popularly traced to Apollo, the victor over Marsyas and his art of flute playing—combine the qualities of oldness, goodness, and divinity.

The companion, who has been brought to admit that law is an art and hence that the Athenian laws are either not laws at all or in the best case only bad laws, refuses to bow to the Cretan laws. He does not deny that Minos was an ancient king of divine origin, but he denies that he was a good king. Socrates tells him that he is under the spell of an Athenian myth; he sets out to liberate him from the spell of the Athenian myth as he has liberated him from the spell of the Athenian laws. In a speech whose length surpasses by far the length of the companion's long speech, Socrates appeals from the Athenian tragic poets who had originated the myth, according to which Minos was bad, to Homer and Hesiod, the most ancient poets, and thus proves that Minos and hence his laws are good. From Homer, Socrates has learned that Minos was the only one of the children of Zeus educated by Zeus in his art, the noble art of sophistry, which may be identical with the legislative art and certainly is identical with the kingly art; the education took place in a cave, if in the cave of Zeus. Law is so far from being the opinion of the city that it is, or is based upon, an art, the highest art, the art of the highest god. In order to judge of Socrates' contention, one would have to consider in their contexts the few Homeric verses to which he appeals; one would have to see whether they express the view of Homer or of a Homeric character; in the latter case one would have to consider whether that character can be presumed to possess both the knowledge and the truthfulness required in a matter of such importance. As Socrates indicates, the decisive Homeric passage could be thought to mean that Minos associated with his father Zeus, not in speeches devoted to education in virtue, but in drinking and playing. He disposes of the suggestion that Minos associated with Zeus in drinking to the point of drunkenness by a consideration which, it must be admitted, is not free from begging the question. He does not dispose of the suggestion that Zeus and Minos associated for other purposes which have nothing in common with education to virtue. It is not advisable to speculate on the alternatives which are not mentioned. It suffices to say that, as Socrates makes clear at the very end, the whole conversation is based on ignorance of the function of the good legislator: the whole praise of Minos' laws must be reconsidered, as it is in the *Laws*.

The audible proof of Minos' goodness is balanced by an inaudible doubt of that goodness. The difference between proof and doubt corresponds to the difference between two Socratic exhortations. The proof is preceded by an exhortation to piety, for Socrates challenges the Athenian myth regarding Minos in the name of piety: it is impious for a human being to speak ill of Minos, that is, a hero who was the son of Zeus; the god may resent this more than if one speaks ill of him. The proof is followed by an account of how the myth of Minos' badness arose: Minos waged a just war against Athens, defeated Athens, and compelled the Athenians to pay "that famous ransom": to send fourteen young Athenians at regular intervals to Crete as a kind of human sacrifice; hence Minos became hateful to "us," the Athenians, and we take our revenge on him through the tragic poets who present him as bad; this revenge is effective because tragedy is in its way as pleasing to the people and as apt to lead the soul as flute playing itself. While stating these things, Socrates addresses his second exhortation to the companion—the exhortation to be on his guard, not against acts of impiety, but against incurring the hatred of any patriotic poet. As is shown by the example of Minos, one cannot comply in all cases with both exhortations, although each exhortation demands compliance in all cases. While complying with his first exhortation Socrates was compelled to praise most highly the most ancient enemy of Athens to whom he will owe, if indirectly, the postponement of his execution decreed by the city of Athens (cf. *Phaedo* 58a–c).

The end of the dialogue renders doubtful its chief result. This ending is not entirely unexpected, for the suggestion that Minos' laws are the best laws implies the view that law can be the finding out of what is and hence can be unchangeable, whereas Socrates' definition of law implies the view that law can never be more than the attempt to find out what is and hence is necessarily changeable. According to the first view, men can be experts—can possess full knowledge— regarding the matter with which law is concerned; according to the second view, men are ignorant regarding that matter. One can re- solve this difficulty by suggesting that while men cannot be experts regarding that matter, they necessarily are knowers of it. The funda- mental difficulty can also be stated as follows: law is always and everywhere the same and therefore one; law must be as variable as the needs of individuals and therefore infinitely many. If one accepts the second view, one reaches this conclusion: whereas in the case of man, justice, dog, the one (man as such, justice as such, dog as such) is of higher dignity than the many (the individual men, just things, dogs); in the case of law the one (the universal rule) is of lower dignity than the many (the assignment of the proper food and toil to each man's soul) and in fact spurious.

We could touch only on some of the things which the reader of the *Minos* must consider much more carefully than we have been able to do here. For instance, we did not speak of the circumstances in which Socrates and the companion address each other by name or in other ways. The companion addresses Socrates eight times by name and never in any other way. Socrates never addresses the companion by name (which does not necessarily mean that he does not know his name), but addresses him three times by an expression which we may render "you excellent one." In conversations between two men one uses the name of the other especially in two cases: when the other says something apparently absurd and one tries to call him back to his senses, and when one is pushed to the wall by the other and begs for mercy. Socrates addresses the companion twice as "you excellent one" immediately after the companion has addressed him as "O Socrates"; the first time the companion was dissatisfied with Socrates' praise of Minos, and the second time the companion failed to understand how the good Minos could have acquired the reputation of being bad. As for the character of the companion, we suspect that he was no longer quite young, that he was concerned with civic fame, that he was what one might call free from prejudices, and that he believed that one can be just while being savage and unaccommodating.

The *Minos* raises more questions than it answers. In order to see how the thoughts suggested by the *Minos* are best continued, one must turn to the other dialogues. It is of little use to look up parallels in the other dialogues to this or that passage of the *Minos,* for the meaning of the parallels depends on their contexts, that is, on the whole dialogues within which they occur. One must then study the other dialogues. With every other dialogue a new land comes to sight; the experience resembles that of one's becoming aware of an unexpected turn of the road at what seemed to be the end of the road. The dialogue most akin to the *Minos* is the *Hipparchus.* The *Minos* and the *Hipparchus* are the only dialogues between Socrates and a single nameless companion. They are the only dialogues whose titles consist of the name of someone who is not present at the conversation but was dead a long time before the conversation; their titles resemble the titles of tragedies. They are the only dialogues which open with Socrates' raising a "what is" question. While the *Minos* begins with the question "What is law?", the *Hipparchus* begins with the question "What is the quality of gain-loving? Who are the gain-loving ones?" If the beginning of the *Minos* corresponded strictly to the beginning of the Hipparchus, it would read: "What is the quality of lawful? Who are the law-abiding ones?" If not law itself, surely law-abidingness is generally praised, while love of gain is generally blamed: the *Minos* need not vindicate law-abidingness and law, while the *Hipparchus* is devoted to vindicating love of gain. While the *Minos* may be said to end in the praise of the Cretan legislator Minos, the *Hipparchus* may be said to culminate in the praise of the Athenian tyrant Hipparchus. The vindication of the love of gain is the vindication of tyranny, if the tyrant is the most outstanding lover of gain (cf. Aristotle *Politics* 1311a 4–11). Tyranny is the opposite of law or rule of law; the *Minos* and the *Hipparchus* together deal with the two fundamental alternatives. The connection which we indicated between "love of gain" and "Hipparchus" is not made explicit in the *Hipparchus*. Hipparchus is mentioned there because a saying of Hipparchus throws light on the conversational situation. Socrates charges the companion with trying to deceive him, and the companion charges Socrates with in fact deceiving him. (No such charge is made in the *Minos*.) Thereupon Socrates quotes, after proper preparation, the saying of Hipparchus "Do not deceive a friend." The saying does not disapprove of deceiving people who are not friends. From the context it would appear that not deceiving friends is a part of justice or, in other words, that justice consists in helping one's friends and hurting one's enemies. Love of gain is generally despised because it seems inseparable from deception. However this may be, Socrates praises the Athenian tyrant Hipparchus as a good and wise man, the great educator of the Athenians in wisdom, whose reign resembled the age of Zeus's father Kronos. If we put the *Minos* and the *Hipparchus* together, we become haunted by the suggestion that an Athenian tyrant rather than the Athenian law (and even than the Cretan law) was good and wise. Accordingly, just as in the *Minos* Socrates explicitly rejects the Athenian myth regarding Minos, in the *Hipparchus* he takes issue with what "the many" in Athens say about Hipparchus: Harmodios and Aristogeiton, who were magnified as liberators by the people of Athens, murdered˙ Hipparchus for no other reason than because they were envious of his wisdom and his effect on the young; the nonlegal murder of Hipparchus foreshadows the legal murder of Socrates.

The *Hipparchus* questions the view that love of gain is simply bad, just as the *Minos* may be said to question the view that law is simply good: a law may be bad just as gain may be good. These facts recommend the view that both law and gain by themselves are neutral just as man may be said to be neutral: a high-class man is not more nor less a man than a low-class man (*Hipparchus* 230c). But just as the *Minos* leads up to the view that a bad law is not a law, the *Hipparchus* leads up to the view that bad gain is not a gain. With what right do we then say of a low-class human being that he is nevertheless a human being?

LOVERS

[or, On Philosophy]

Translated by JAMES LEAKE

Socrates

132a SOCRATES: I entered the place of Dionysius[1] the schoolteacher, and there I saw those of the young who are reputed to be most remarkable for their looks[2] and the good repute of their fathers. I also saw their lovers. Two of the boys happened to be disputing then, but about what, I did not plainly overhear. They appeared, however, to

b be disputing either about Anaxagoras[3] or about Oinopides.[4] At any rate, they appeared to be describing circles and were imitating certain ecliptics with their hands and had taken it very seriously. And I—for I was sitting next to the lover of one of the two—nudged him with my elbow and asked him what the two boys were so serious about. And I said, "Presumably it is something great and noble on which the two have bestowed such great seriousness."

He said, "What do you mean 'great and noble'! They are babbling about the heavenly things, and they are talking nonsense, philosophizing."

The title *Lovers* (*Erastai*) appears in all the major manuscripts BDTW. Some editors follow a marginal correction of B that reads *Rivals* (*Anterastai*), perhaps because that is how the dialogue is titled in Diogenes Laertius' list of genuine Platonic dialogues.

[1]Plato as a boy had a teacher named Dionysius (Dio. Laert. III 5). Could Plato have veiled himself behind one of the anonymous boy disputants?

[2]*Tēn idean* ("looks," "appearance"). This is the same word used for the "forms" or "ideas" in Plato's account of how we know and how things are ordered. Cf. *Rep.* 479a, 486d, 507b.

[3]The philosophy of nature of Anaxagoras was of the utmost interest to the young Socrates (cf. *Phaedo* 97b6–98b6).

[4]Oinopides was a philosopher accomplished in astronomy and geometry.

c   And I, marveling at his answer, said, "Young man, does it seem to you to be shameful to philosophize? Or why do you speak so harshly?"

And the other youth, for he happened to be sitting near him and was his rival in love, upon hearing my question and his answer said, "You're not acting as becomes you, Socrates, even to ask this fellow if he considers philosophy to be shameful. Or do you not know that this one has passed his whole life putting others in a headlock, stuffing himself, and sleeping? So what did you suppose he would answer except that philosophy is shameful?"

d   Now, of the two lovers, this one had spent his time on music; the other, whom he was abusing, had spent his on athletics. And it seemed to me that I ought to dismiss the other one, whom I had been questioning, since he didn't even claim to be experienced in speeches, but rather in deeds; and it seemed that I ought instead to question thoroughly the one who claimed to be wiser, so that I might also, if I could, receive some benefit from him. Accordingly I said: "I asked the question of you in common. But if you suppose you could answer more nobly than this one, I ask you the same question I asked him, whether it seems to you to be noble or not to philosophize?"

33a   Now, just as we were saying these things, the two boys, who had overheard us, became silent, and they themselves ceased from their dispute and became our listeners. I don't know what the lovers felt, but as for myself, I was stricken wild. For I'm always stricken wild by the young and beautiful. Anyway it seemed to me that the other as well was no less in agony than I. Nevertheless he did answer me in a manner that showed his great love of honor.

b   "Now, Socrates," he said, "if ever I should consider it shameful to philosophize, I would not even hold myself to be a human being, nor would I anyone else so disposed." Here he pointed to his rival in love and spoke in a loud voice so his favorite might hear him plainly.

And I said, "So then it does seem to you noble to philosophize?"

"Most certainly," he said.

"What then?" I said. "Does it seem to you to be possible to know with regard to anything whether it is noble or shameful, if one doesn't know to begin with what it is?"

"No," he said.

c   "Do you know then," I said, "what it is to philosophize?"

"Very well," he said.

"What is it, then?" I said.

"What else than [what it is] according to the saying of Solon? For

Solon said somewhere, 'I grow old, always learning[5] many things,' and thus it seems to me that the one who is going to philosophize ought always to be learning at least some one thing, both when he is younger and when he is older, so that he may learn as much as possible in his life."

And at first he seemed to me to be saying something, but subsequently, when I had reflected somewhat, I asked him whether he held philosophy to be much learning.

d   And he said, "Certainly."

"And do you," I said next, "consider philosphy to be merely noble, or also good?"

"Also good," he said, "very much so."

"Do you see this sort of thing as peculiar to philosophy, or does it also seem to you to be the case in the other things? For instance, do you consider love of athletics to be not merely noble but also good? Or don't you?"

To this, very ironically, he spoke in a double fashion. "Let it be said by me to this fellow that it is neither; to you, however, Socrates I grant that it is both noble and good. For I hold that to be correct."

e

So then I asked, "Well then, in the case of athletics do you hold that much exercising is love of athletics?"

And he said, "Certainly, just as I hold that much learning in the case of philosophizing is philosophy."[6]

And I said, "Do you think, then, that those who love athletics desire anything other than that which will cause them to be in good bodily condition?"

"It's that," he said.

"And does much exercise," I said, "cause the body to be in good condition?"

134a   "Yes—for how," he said, "could anyone be in good bodily condition from little exercise?"

---

[5]The speaker replaces Solon's word, *didaskomenos* ("learning" or "being taught"), with *manthanein* ("to learn") in his interpretation. The primary sense of the word Solon had used is "being taught" (as a father has his son brought up to be a good citizen), whereas the speaker's word has a primary sense of learning for oneself. Solon's word embraces learning how to live, while the speaker's word often implies more intellectual learning. See Liddell and Scott, *A Greek-English Lexicon,* 9th ed. (Oxford, 1940), s.v. *didaskomenos* and *manthanein.*

[6]*Philosophia* ("philosophy") in Greek is literally "love of wisdom." Thus the youth's argument is more apparent in Greek than it appears in the translation: much exercising is love of athletics as much learning is love of wisdom.

Here it seemed to me that the lover of athletics should be aroused, so that he might help me through his experience of athletics. So then I asked him, "Why are you being silent, excellent one, while he is saying these things? Does it seem to you, too, that men are in good condition, with regard to their bodies, from much exercise, or is it from the measured amount?"

"As for me, Socrates," he said, "I supposed, that even a pig[7]—as the saying goes—would have known that a measured amount of
b exercises causes bodies to be in good condition. So how would a man who is sleepless and unfed, whose neck is unchafed and who is thin from anxious thoughts not know this?"[8]

And the two boys were pleased when he said this and burst into laughter, while the other one blushed.

And I said, "Well, then, do you now concede that neither many nor few exercises cause human beings to be in good condition with regard to their bodies, but the measured amount? Or will you fight it out with the two of us concerning the argument?"

c   And he said, "I would very gladly contend against this one, and I know well that I would be capable of supporting the thesis which I have put forward even if I had put forward one still weaker than this, for he is nothing. But against you, I haven't the slightest desire to seek victory contrary to my own opinion. And I agree that not much athletics but the measured amount produces good condition in human beings."

"And what about food? Is it the measured amount or much?" I said.

He agreed it was the same in the case of food.

d   Then I compelled him to agree that also in all other things having to do with the body the measured amount, not much nor little, is most beneficial. And he agreed with me that it was the measured amount.

"What then," I said, "about the things having to do with the soul? Is it the measured amount of things or those without measure which, when administered, are beneficial?"

[7]Here, with Burnet, I follow Hermann's emendation of manuscripts B and T, which gave a reading that strained grammar. The emendation seems more plausible in that a similar formulation is found at *Laches* 196d9.

[8]His rival appears to the lover of athletics much as the young Socrates appeared to the horseman Pheidippides in Aristophanes' *Clouds* 100–104; cf. *Birds* 1553–64. The "unchafed neck" indicates lack of wrestling practice.

"The measured," he said.

"And are the things that can be learned one of the things administered to a soul?"

He agreed.

"Then of these things, too, the measured amount, not the large amount, is beneficial."

He assented.

e   "Whom, then, would we justly ask what sort of exercises and foods are measured with regard to the body?"

The three of us agreed that it was a doctor or a trainer.

"And whom would we ask about the sowing of seed, how much is the measured amount?"

And about this, we agreed that it was the farmer.

"Whom would we justly ask about the planting and sowing in the soul of the things to be learned, how much and what sort is the measured amount?"

135a   Thereupon we were all completely at a loss. And I playfully asked them, "Are you willing, since we are at a loss, for us to ask these boys here? Or are we perhaps ashamed, as Homer says[9] the suitors were, who didn't deign that there be another who would string the bow?"

Then, since they seemed to me to be disheartened about the argument, I tried to pursue the investigation in another way, and I said, "What sort of things that can be learned do we guess to be especially those which the one philosophizing[10] must learn, since he is not to learn all or even many of them?"

b   Here the wiser one responded by saying, "These would be the noblest of things that can be learned, and the fitting ones, from which one might have the greatest reputation for philosophy. And one would have the greatest reputation if he were reputed to be experienced in all the arts; or if not, in as many as possible and especially the noteworthy ones, through having learned as much of them as is fitting for the free to learn, as much as belongs to the understanding rather than to manual work."

"Well," I said, "do you mean this in the same way as in the case of
c   carpentry? For there you could buy[11] a carpenter for five or six minae; but you couldn't buy a first-rate architect even for ten thou-

----

[9]*Odyssey* XXI 285–86.

[10]The major manuscripts are divided here. I follow B and D, which give *philosophounta* ("the one philosophizing"). T and W read *philosophon* ("the philosopher").

[11]As a slave.

sand drachmae. Indeed, there would be few of them even among all the Greeks. Is it something like this that you mean?"

And when he heard me he granted that he too meant this sort of thing.

Then I asked him if it weren't impossible for the same one to learn even two individual arts this way, much less many great ones. And he said, "Don't take me to be saying, Socrates, that the one philoso-
d phizing must know precisely each of the arts, just as he who possesses the art himself, but rather he must know them as is fitting for a free and educated man who is able to follow what is said by the craftsman in a way that distinguishes him from those present and who can himself contribute his judgment, so as to be reputed most refined and wisest among those who are present at any time when things are said and done concerning the arts."

And I, for I was still uncertain about his argument, as to what he
e intended, said, "Do I have in mind what sort of man you mean by the philosopher? For you seem to me to mean those who are like the pentathletes[12] in relation to the runners and the wrestlers, in competition. For they too are inferior to those others in their particular events, and are second to them, but are first among the other athletes and victorious over them. You, mean perhaps, that to philosophize likewise brings about some such thing in those who practice this
136a pursuit, that they are inferior to the first-raters in understanding of the arts, but by having the second place, they are superior to the others, and thus the one who has philosophized becomes a sort of second-best man in everything. You seem to me to be pointing to someone of this sort."

"You appear to me, Socrates," he said, "to have a noble conception of what has to do with the philosopher, in likening him to the pentathlete. For he is simply[13] the sort of person who is not enslaved to any matter and who hasn't labored at anything to the point of
b precision (so as to be deficient in all the other things, as the craftsmen are, because of his concern for this one) but has touched upon everything to a measured degree.

After this reply I was eager to know with certainty[14] what he

---

[12]The pentathlete competed in an exercise consisting of wrestling, jumping, running, throwing the discus, and boxing. To win he had to do well in all five events.
[13]*Atechnōs* (literally, "artlessly").
[14]For an explanation of this translation of *saphōs*, see n. 5 of the essay that follows this dialogue.

meant, and so I inquired of him whether he conceived of those who are good as being useful or useless.

"Surely useful, Socrates," he said.

"Then if the good are useful, are the wicked useless?"

He agreed.

"What else? Do you regard the philosophers as being useful men or not?"

c   He agreed that they are useful, and furthermore he said he regarded them as being most useful.

"Come now, let us judge, if what you say is true, where these second-best men are also useful to us. For it is plain that the philosopher is inferior to each of those who possess the arts."

He agreed.

"Come now," I said, "if either you yourself or one of your friends, whom[15] you regard with great seriousness, happened to be sick, would you, in your wish to acquire health, bring that second-best man, the philosopher, into your household, or would you get the doctor?"

d   "For my part, both," he said.

"Don't say 'both,'" I said, "but tell me which one you would rather have, and first."

"No one," he said, "would dispute about this, that he wouldn't rather have the doctor, and him first."

"What else? In a storm-tossed ship, to which one would you rather entrust him[16] and your property, to the pilot or to the philosopher?"

"I would prefer the pilot."

"Then is it like this in everything else as well: as long as there is some craftsman, the philosopher is not useful?"

"It appears so," he said.

e   "And therefore, do we now see that the philosopher is somebody useless for us? For there are surely craftsmen at our disposal. But we have agreed that the good are useful and the evil are useless."

He was compelled to agree.

---

[15]The best manuscripts are divided as to whether this word is singular or plural. Burnet takes it as plural.

[16]I follow the reading of manuscripts T and W, "him," which I take to refer to one of the friends "you regard with great seriousness." Manuscripts B and D here read "yourself." The reading I have adopted preserves the ambiguity present elsewhere in this section as to whether the "usefulness" of the philosopher is in the first instance to others or to himself.

"Then what comes next? Shall I ask you, or is it too rude to ask?"

"Ask what you want."

"Well," I said, "what I seek is nothing else than to summarize what we've agreed upon. And the matter stands somewhat like this. We agreed that philosophy is noble and that we ourselves are philosophers; that philosophers are good, the good are useful and the wicked useless; again, we agreed that philosophers are useless as long as there are craftsmen but that there are always craftsmen. Haven't these things been agreed upon?"

"Certainly," he said.

"It looks as if we were agreeing, then, according to your argument at least, that, if to philosophize consists in their being knowledgeable about the arts in the way you say, they are wicked and useless as long as there are arts among humans. But I suspect, my friend, that this isn't so, and that to philosophize isn't to have become serious about the arts nor to live as a busybody, stooping down and learning many things, but rather something else, since I supposed that this was in fact a matter of reproach and that those who have become serious about the arts were called illiberal.[17] But we shall know with more certainty whether what I say is true if you answer this: who are those who know how to punish horses correctly? Is it those who make them best[18] or others?"

"Those who make them better."

"What else? Don't those know how to make dogs better who also know how to punish them correctly?"

"Yes."

"Then the same art makes them best and punishes them correctly."

"It appears so to me," he said.

"What else? Is the art which makes them better and punishes them correctly the same as that which also knows[19] the ones who are good and the ones who are evil, or is it some other?"

"The same," he said.

"Will you be willing, then, in the case of human beings as well, to agree that the art that makes humans best is the one that both pun-

137a

b

c

d

[17]*Banausous*, properly speaking, refers to those artisans who devote themselves to one art and earn their living by manual labor.

[18]The manuscripts vary throughout this section, at times speaking of an art that makes animals and men "better," at times saying it makes them "best." The apparatus criticus prepared with the greatest care is that of Carlini.

[19]*Gignōskein* (to "know," "distinguish," or "judge").

ishes correctly and knows thoroughly[20] the ones who are good and evil?"

"Certainly," he said.

"Then if there is some art which is applicable to one it also is applicable to many, and if there is one that is applicable to many it also is applicable to one?"[21]

"Yes."

"And so too with horses and all the others?"

"Yes, I say."

"What, then, is the science that correctly punishes the unrestrained and lawbreakers in the cities? Isn't it the judicial?"

"Yes."

"Do you also call any science justice other than this one?"

"None but this one."

e   "Then don't they know those who are good and evil by the same [science] as that by which they punish correctly?"

"By the same."

"And he who knows one will also know many?"

"Yes."

"And he who is ignorant of many is also ignorant of one?"

"Yes, I say."

"If, then, one were a horse and were ignorant of the good and wicked horses, would one also be ignorant of oneself, of what sort one is?"

"Yes, I say."

"And if one were an ox and were ignorant of the wicked and good ones, would one also be ignorant of himself, of what sort one is?"

"Yes," he said.

"And so too if one were a dog?"

He agreed.

138a   "What then? When one who is a human being is ignorant of the good and evil human beings, isn't he ignorant of himself, as to whether he is good or evil, since he is himself also a human being?"

He conceded this.

"And is to be ignorant of oneself to be moderate or not to be moderate?"

---

[20]*Diagignōskein* (to "distinguish," "discern," or "judge thoroughly").

[21]I follow here the readings of manuscripts B and D. Burnet reads with T and W: "Then that art which applies to one also applies to many, and that which applies to many also applies to one."

"Not to be moderate."

"Then to know oneself is to be moderate?"

"Yes, I say," he said.

"It looks, then, as if this is what the writing[22] in Delphi exhorts: to practice moderation and justice."

"So it seems."

"And by this same [science] do we also know how to punish correctly?"

"Yes."

b   "Then isn't it justice by which we know how to punish correctly and moderation by which we know how to know thoroughly both oneself and others?"

"It looks like it," he said.

"Then both justice and moderation are the same thing?"

"It appears so."

"And indeed, it is thus that the cities are well managed: whenever those who do injustice pay the penalty."

"What you say is true," he said.

"And so this is also the political art."

He concurred.

"And what about when one man correctly manages a city? Isn't his name tyrant and king?"

"Yes, I say."

"Then he manages it by the kingly and tyrannic art?"

"Just so."

"And these are the same arts as the former ones?"

"They appear to be."

c   "What about when one man manages a household correctly by himself? What name is he given? Is it not household manager and master?"[23]

"Yes."

"Then would this one too manage the household well by justice or by some other art?"

"By justice."

---

[22]"Know thyself."

[23]Here and in what follows, the words translated "master" and "masterful" (*despotēs, despotikos*) refer primarily to the ownership of slaves in a household but may mean more generally "despot" and "despotic"; the words translated "household," "household manager," and "economic" all refer to the household (*oikos*) and its supervision.

"It looks as if they are the same thing, then, a king, a tyrant, a political man, a household manager, a master, a moderate man, a just one. And it is one art that is kingly, tyrannic, political, masterful, pertaining to household management, justice, moderation."

"It appears to be that way," he said.

d   "Then if it is shameful for the philosopher, when a doctor says something about the sick, neither to be able to follow what is said nor to contribute anything concerning what is said or done, and likewise whenever any other of the craftsmen is involved, is it not shameful, when a judge or a king or any other of those we've just now gone through is involved, for him neither to be able to follow nor to contribute concerning these things?"

"How is it not shameful, Socrates, to having nothing to contribute especially with regard to such great matters?"

e   "So then," I said, "which shall we say: that he should be a pentathlete and second best about these things too and that the philosopher, taking second place in all of this, is indeed good for nothing as long as one of them is available? Or that, first, he ought not to entrust his own household to another nor have second place in this but rather sit in judgment and punish correctly himself if his household is going to be well managed?"

He conceded this to me.

139a   "Next, presumably, if his friends entrust matters for arbitration to him, or if the city commands him to decide or judge some judicial matter, is it shameful, comrade, to come to light as second or third in these affairs, rather than to lead?"

"It seems so to me."

"Therefore, you best one, to philosophize is far from being much learning[24] and preoccupation with the arts."

On my saying these things, the wise one, who was ashamed at what he had said earlier, was silent, but the ignorant one said that it was so, and the others praised what had been said.

---

[24]Polymathia ("much learning") is attested by manuscript B. Two important manuscripts, T and W, have philomath[e]ia ("love of learning").

On the Original Meaning
of Political Philosophy: An
Interpretation of Plato's *Lovers*

CHRISTOPHER BRUELL

The question posed by my title is a historical question, and therefore my hope is to uncover Plato's view. But the answer to a historical question may be of more than historical interest. The place of political philosophy within the discipline of political science has for some time been a matter of uncertainty or dispute. Political philosophy as we know it is concerned with "values," claiming to be able to provide rational guidance as to what is good and just in politics. Since Max Weber, however (see his essay "Science as a Vocation"), many political scientists have held that reason, or science, cannot, by itself, supply such guidance and that, insofar as political philosophy seeks to supply guidance as to what is good and just, it is not as rational or scientific as it claims. Others within the profession, students of political philosophy especially, refuse to accept this conclusion. Moved by awareness of the need for "normative" political guidance as well as by respect for science as the only unquestioned authority of our age, they insist that science must and can supply this guidance in the form of a political philosophy that is at once normative and scientific. But they have been unable to establish to general satisfaction either that such a political philosophy already exists (whether in the work of contemporary students or past masters) or that it is possible for it to be developed in the future. As a result, the study of political philosophy within our discipline remains something of an embarrassment as well as an anomaly: it reminds us of the shortcomings of a value-free political science without, apparently, being able to show how they might be remedied.

The premise of the study that follows is that the uncertainty as to the place and worth of political philosophy must be understood in the light of a crucial change in its character that emerged in the course of its history. If we are to understand this change and its significance, we must first see what political philosophy was prior to it or originally; we must return to the origin of political philosophy in the thought of Socrates. I argue that this origin is most clearly and directly presented in the *Lovers,* a dialogue that has been generally neglected or despised—so much so that doubts have been raised as to whether it is a genuinely Platonic work. Since these doubts appear to be based on a judgment as to the merits of the dialogue rather than on any hard external evidence (see, for example, the Introduction of Schleiermacher), a secondary aim of the study is to help lay them to rest.

The *Lovers* is one of only four dialogues narrated from beginning to end by Socrates, the others being the *Republic, Charmides,* and *Lysis.* This fact may tell us something as to the place of these dialogues within the Platonic corpus. When he was obliged to defend himself publicly against charges of impiety and corrupting the young, Socrates gave the Athenians an account of his way of life as a whole. However memorable that account is, its adequacy—that is, its truthfulness and completeness (*Apology of Socrates* 17b8)—may have been adversely affected by the circumstances in which Socrates was forced to present it: his audience was of questionable friendliness and openness, and he was allowed to speak for only a legally prescribed period of time (*Ap. Soc.* 37a6–b2). At any rate, Socrates himself suggested that his account had struck some of his hearers— perhaps not the least discerning—as ironical (*Ap. Soc.* 38a1). The dialogues just mentioned, on the other hand, present occasions on which Socrates, without apparent compulsion, provides accounts of his life, or of significant episodes in it, to companions who are familiar with philosophy and friendly to it—to judge at least from hints supplied in two of the cases.[1] Thus the defects of circumstance that may have inhibited Socrates in his public defense are not present there or are not present in the same degree.[2]

[1]The person or persons to whom the *Lovers* is narrated are familiar not only with Anaxagoras but also with Oinopides. The one to whom the *Charmides* is narrated is more familiar with Socrates' companion Chairephon than with Critias.

[2]The *Phaedo* could not have been narrated by Socrates, but its audience (both that to which the dialogue is narrated and that present at the original conversation) would qualify it for inclusion in this group; moreover, the *Phaedo* culminates in Socrates' narration, to the companions present, of most significant experiences of his youth (96a1–100a8). In the *Theaetetus,* one of those reported as present at the original

In the *Lovers,* Socrates recounts to one or more people a conversation in which he successfully defended philosophizing against the assertion of a young athlete that it is frivolous or ridiculous, if not also shameful. Socrates had entered a grammar school full of those among the young considered to be most decent in appearance (and to come from noted fathers) and the lovers of these boys. Two of the boys were disputing—about what Socrates was not very able to hear. But as he tells whomever he is narrating the encounter to, he conjectured that it was about Anaxagoras or Oinopides, for the boys appeared to draw circles and to imitate certain slopes with their hands. The athlete was a lover of one of the two boys. By asking him what the boys had become so serious about—"surely some great and noble thing"—Socrates innocently or deliberately provoked the attack on philosophizing. In putting his question to the athlete, Socrates had, not so innocently, withheld from him the fact that he had already formed a conjecture as to what the dispute was about, as to the identity of that which he called "great and noble."

Socrates' defense of philosophizing took the form of a refutation of the athlete's rival in love, a culture vulture who regards himself as a philosopher. This "philosopher" asserted, in response to the athlete's attack, that philosophizing is noble, but he proved unable to back up his assertion. The encounter of Socrates with the two lovers took place in the presence of the two boys, who broke off their philosophical-astronomical dispute in order to listen to it; the boys as well as the others accepted the results of the argument directed by Socrates.

Most of Socrates' account is taken up by his narration of this argument. In the course of describing how the discussion began and how it came to take the form that it did, Socrates appears to allude to his famous turn in philosophy (from concentration on things or deeds to concentration on speeches: cf. *Phaedo* 99d4–100a7 with *Lovers* 132d4–5), and he calls attention to his notoriously erotic nature (133a; cf., e.g., *Protagoras* 309a). These facts, together with the inconclusive character of pre-Socratic natural philosophy (reflected, perhaps, in

conversation in the *Phaedo* reads, to a companion also reported as present there, a record of a conversation that he claims was narrated to him by Socrates. In the *Republic,* as in the narrative portions of the *Protagoras* and *Euthydemus,* Socrates recounts an experience that he has just had, and may have wished to fix in his memory by reliving it. The episodes recounted in the *Charmides, Lysis,* and *Lovers,* on the other hand, occurred at some unspecified time in the past. Cf. *Charmides* 153a1 with *Republic* 327a1, *Protagoras* 309d3–310a8, and *Euthydemus* 271a1, 272d4–e7.

the boys' dispute), appear to form the background against which the argument of the *Lovers,* which is more narrowly the topic of this essay, must ultimately be understood. The argument itself went as follows.

The Argument

I. Socrates asked the "philosopher" whether it was his opinion that it is possible to know with regard to anything at all whether it is noble or shameful if one doesn't know to begin with what it is. When the "philosopher" said it was not, Socrates asked him whether he knew what philosophizing is. "Certainly." "What is it then?" According to Socrates' interpretation of the "philosopher's" response, which the "philosopher" accepts, philosophy is *polymathia* (the knowledge which consists in having learned, and thus knowing, many things).

In recounting this last exchange, Socrates as narrator indicates that he had some doubt as to the adequacy of such a view of philosophy. This alerts us to a shift that had just taken place or was about to take place in the course of the argument. Socrates' next questions, which appear designed, as we might have expected, to examine the nobility of philosophy as polymathia, were in fact designed to test the adequacy of this view of philosophy: to test it by seeing whether philosophy as polymathia would be noble. (What permitted or required this shift was the fact that the "philosopher," despite his agreement that one must know what a thing is before one can know whether or not it is noble, had greater confidence in the nobility of philosophy than in any particular view as to what it is. If he came to believe, then, that philosophy, according to his view, would not be noble, he would more readily modify or abandon his view than agree that philosophy itself is truly not noble.) More precisely, the view in question was to be tested by examining the goodness of philosophy as polymathia. But the question of goodness is linked to that of nobility in the following way. The noble things appear to us to be also good. If the nobility of something is believed to imply its goodness, we can ultimately accept as noble (or high or serious) only what can be established as good. The meaning to be given here to "goodness" will be clarified as the argument proceeds.

Socrates began by asking whether the "philosopher" held that philosophy is only noble or also good. "Also good, certainly." Did the "philosopher" see this in philosophy alone, or was he of the opinion that it is the case in other things too? For example, did he hold that love of athletics (*philogymnastia*) is not only noble but also good? When the "philosopher" agreed that he did, Socrates asked him whether he held, in athletics, that love of athletics is the performance of many exercises (*polyponia*). The "philosopher" was quite ready to see the situation in athletics as parallel to the one he had claimed to see in philosophizing. Socrates thereupon asked him whether the lovers of athletics desire anything other than what will make their bodily condition a good one. He replied that this is what they desire. "Do the many exercises then make one's bodily condition good?" How could this come about from few exercises? the "philosopher" responded.

At this point, Socrates appealed to the experience of the athlete (or, as he is called here, the lover of athletics) to establish the fact that human beings achieve good bodily condition not through many exercises, nor indeed through few, but through a "measured" amount. (Socrates' appeal is perhaps not as superfluous as it might appear to be. "Measured" [*metrios*] is indeed so flexible a term as to be applicable to any quantity that is beneficial, but for that very reason it might be applicable to a very large or even to the largest possible number of exercises as long as that number is beneficial. That is, a "measured" amount might not be different from many. That it is different—or indeed the same—could not perhaps be established without the assistance of the relevant experience.) The "philosopher" yielded the point to Socrates and the athlete. He agreed also that the case with food was the same, and beyond that he was forced by Socrates to agree that, with all other things having to do with the body, "measured" rather than great or small amounts are most beneficial. What then about the things having to do with the soul? Is it the measured things, or those without measure, that, when administered, are beneficial? Whether because a question phrased in this way admits of only one answer, or because he accepted the suggestion that Socrates' procedure conveys—that what holds true for the body holds true for the soul—the "philosopher" answered, "The measured things." He then agreed that one of the things administered to a soul is *mathēmata* (things learned or to be learned). It followed that, of these, too, a "measured" amount, and not many, is beneficial.

Philosophy, then—if, being noble, it must be good, indeed good for a soul—must be learning, or having learned and thus knowing, a "measured" amount of things. But what things? Without waiting for the amended view of philosophy to be stated or expressly agreed to, Socrates went on to ask a series of questions designed to uncover the expert to be consulted concerning mathēmata, as to the amounts and kinds that are "measured." "Whom would we justly ask which exercises and foods—with regard to the body—are measured?" The three interlocutors agreed that this was a doctor or trainer. "Whom concerning the sowing of seed—how much is a measured amount?" Here again they agreed (on the farmer). "Whom would we justly ask, concerning the planting and sowing of mathēmata in a soul, how many and which are measured?" Here, according to Socrates' account, the interlocutors were all at a loss. Apparently, they didn't know of any such expert or expertise. It seems to be clear, then, if this was the case, that they didn't know what mathēmata are good for a soul or that any are good for a soul.

Nevertheless, Socrates was able to keep the conversation going by asking the others more directly which "we guess" to be the mathēmata the one philosophizing must learn, since these are neither all nor many. The "philosopher" replied to this question without characterizing his reply as a guess. In asking it, Socrates was asking which mathēmata they guessed to be "measured," beneficial to a soul. That is, a distinction was implicitly made here, or rather was confirmed, between a philosopher and the expert they had been seeking. A philosopher is taken to be something other, at any rate something more than the possessor of an expertise. He is closer to the lovers of athletics spoken of earlier than to a doctor or trainer. While a lover of athletics was indeed consulted regarding exercises, such lovers were said to desire only what will make their bodily condition a good one. What forms these lovers, we can say, is a desire to benefit from, rather than to exercise or even to possess, the expertise regarding exercises. Similarly, a philosopher, it was now implied, must learn the mathēmata that are "measured," must acquire the learning that benefits a soul.

The "philosopher's" reply, however, spoke of the mathēmata that would be noblest and fitting and referred to reputation (what they make one seem to be) rather than benefit to a soul (what they make one to be truly) as their goal and fruit. He didn't appear to think of benefit. But this would be simply true only if he now separated the noble things from the good things, only if he had dropped his insistence that the noble things be also good, good for us.

According to his reply, the mathēmata from which one would have most reputation for philosophy would be noblest and fitting, and one would have most reputation if one were reputed to be experienced in all of the arts,[3] or in as many as possible and especially in the noteworthy ones, through having learned the portions of those arts that are fitting for the free to learn—the portions that belong to the understanding rather than to manual work. Socrates forced the "philosopher" to reformulate his suggestion by raising a difficulty that would apply especially to the great or noteworthy arts that he had in mind: is it not impossible for the same person to learn in the indicated way two such arts, let alone many?[4] What he requires of the one philosophizing, the "philosopher" now said, is not precise knowledge of each of the arts, like the one who possesses the art, but rather what is to be expected of a free and educated man: superior ability to follow things said by a craftsman and to express a judgment himself, so as to be reputed most refined and most wise of those who happen to be present whenever there are words or deeds concerning the arts.

This answer still left open the possibility that the "philosopher" required of one who is philosophizing knowledge of a different and higher kind than that belonging to the arts: for example, knowledge deriving from reflection on the ends of the arts and their importance to us. (See Socrates' remark at 135d8 that he was still uncertain as to the "philosopher's" meaning.) Socrates' next inquiry, however, and the response it elicited made it clear that the "philosopher" did not have any such knowledge in mind. Philosophizing proved in his view to make those who engage or, rather, who have engaged in it something like pentathletes of the arts—inferior, concerning the arts, to those who excel in the relevant understanding but, as second-raters,

---

[3] *Technai*, which, in the Greek usage, include such diverse "arts" as medicine, farming, piloting, shoemaking, and poetry.

[4] Charles H. Fairbanks, in his valuable work on the *Lovers* ("Reason, Technique, and Morality in Plato's *Lovers*," a paper presented at the Annual Meeting of the American Policital Science Association, San Francisco, August 28–31, 1975), has explained Socrates' stratagem here. Socrates took as his example a most difficult art, architecture, which is exercised almost entirely with the understanding. According to the "philosopher's" first formulation, the one who is philosophizing would be required to have learned all of this art together with many others. See Fairbanks, "Reason, Technique," pp. 23–25.

superior to the others. But what Socrates saw as mediocrity or deficiency our "philosopher" saw as strength. It is the very failure of the philosopher to be a slave to any one matter or to have labored at anything to the point of precision that has made it possible for him, as opposed to the craftsmen, to have—to a "measured" degree—laid hold of all.

Our "philosopher's" view of the mathēmata required of a philosopher was thus clarified. They had recommended themselves to him, as we saw, for what he took to be their nobility. It remained to be seen whether he still required of noble mathēmata, as of noble things in general, that they also be good—indeed good for the souls of those who have learned them. (See Socrates' mention at 136b3–4 of his "being eager," after this last answer, to know "with certainty"[5] what the "philosopher" would say.) Socrates ascertained that the "philosopher" took it that those who are good are useful (useful to others: 136c4, c7–e2) and that those who are wicked are useless. Socrates then asked him whether he held that philosophic men are useful or not. In asking this question, Socrates was asking about the goodness of philosophers. For if the good in every case are useful, the useful may be good, while the useless are surely not. Our "philosopher" agreed that philosophers are useful and added that he held them to be most useful. We infer from this response that he still expected the noble mathēmata to benefit the philosopher, that he expected them indeed to benefit him in such a way as to make him good—and hence useful. But to infer is not yet to know "with certainty."

If our "philosopher" still required noble mathēmata to benefit the philosopher (and to benefit him in the manner or to the extent now indicated), Socrates should be able to impugn in his eyes the nobility of the mathēmata under discussion by showing that they do not make one who has learned them useful, as they would unfailingly do, according to our "philosopher," if they made him good. Socrates showed this by stressing the inferiority of the philosopher, as dabbler or second-rater in the arts, to the possessor of each of the arts. This inferiority is most striking where dependence on art is greatest, where one's life or the life of a friend or relative for whom one cares in a serious way is at stake. In such cases, our "philosopher" himself would choose to rely on a doctor or pilot, for example, rather than on

---

[5]On this translation of *saphos,* see Burnet's edition of the *Phaedo* (Oxford, 1959), notes at 57b1, 61d8, and 85c3. Cf. *Gorgias* 453b5–c1, 454b8–c5, and 489d1–3.

a philosopher. It thus became clear that a philosopher is not useful whenever a craftsman—possessor of an art— is available. But given the general availability of craftsmen, this conclusion seems to mean, as our "philosopher" was forced to agree, that the philosopher is useless simply. And since the good have been agreed to be useful, what follows?

Having indicated the direction that an examination of our "philosopher" should take, Socrates broke off to summarize the argument to this point in a manner authorized by the anticipated but not supplied completion of the examination: "We agreed that philosophy is noble and that we ourselves are philosophers; that philosophers are good, the good are useful and the wicked useless; again, we agreed that philosophers are useless so long as there are craftsmen, but that there are always craftsmen. Have not these things been agreed upon?" The "summary," admittedly rough (*pōs* at 137a1), included points that had not been stated previously: that "we" are philosophers, that philosophers are good. By granting that he had agreed to these points, the "philosopher" now showed that, as far as he was concerned, these previously unstated points had always been understood. In suggesting that the goodness of philosophers had been taken to follow from the nobility of philosophy, and their usefulness from their goodness, the summary brings to light what the examination was expected to help confirm.

Socrates then stated the argument's conclusion as follows: "We were agreeing then, as it looks, according to your argument at least, that if philosophizing consists in their being knowledgeable about the arts in the way you say, they are wicked and useless so long as there are arts among human beings." Anticipating, however, the "philosopher's" reaction to such a conclusion concerning philosophizing or the mathēmata that constitute it, Socrates offered at once another interpretation of the outcome of the argument: philosophers may not be wicked and useless, because philosophizing may not consist in having become serious about the arts, in poking about, becoming involved in many matters (being a busybody), any more than it consists in having learned many things—but may rather consist in something else. From the latter part of the argument (the agreement that the good are useful and the emphasis on the usefulness of the arts), we might wonder whether philosophizing does not consist in having become serious enough about some one art to learn it well, whether it does not consist in being or becoming useful through the acquisition of such expertise. This possibility seems to be ruled out by an apparently casual remark that Socrates added here, without objection on the part of the "philosopher." He thought, he said, that seriousness about the arts was a matter of reproach and that those who have become serious about the arts are called "banausic." Indeed the reproach in question, if applied to dabblers in many arts, was no doubt applied still more strongly to the craftsmen or experts proper. It thus reminds us of the "philosopher's" earlier rejection of the precise knowledge belonging to craftsmen as inappropriate to a philosopher. In other words, despite the recognition that has been given in the meantime to the fact that the mathēmata with which craftsmen are concerned confer usefulness, these are still not held to be noble mathēmata. (If the implication is that they are not held to confer the benefit expected of noble mathēmata—that is, to make us good— then we have an indication that the usefulness of craftsmen, at any rate, is not held to be human goodness, whatever may be the case with any other sort of usefulness.)

The argument still remained, then, in the impasse it had reached when it became clear that Socrates' interlocutors, if not also Socrates himself, did not know what mathēmata are good for a soul, or whether any are good for a soul. The reason is in part the fact that a single set of assumptions has governed the argument throughout. The "argument" in fact has been nothing as much as the gradual, just-completed uncovering of these assumptions. What is noble is held to be also good—that is, is held to benefit us. Good human beings—that is, those who have been benefited in a fundamental way—are taken to be also useful (to others). But it is not clear that all useful human beings are held to be good: perhaps only those useful in a certain way are held to be (also) good; perhaps human goodness is held to be something more than usefulness. Philosophy is held to be noble and therefore also good—that is, it is believed to benefit us. And since it consists in mathēmata, which affect the soul, it is believed to benefit our souls, indeed to make us good. From the perspective determined by these assumptions or expectations, what philosophy or philosophizing is will be unknown as long as mathēmata that so profoundly benefit a soul are unknown.

II. In suggesting that philosophizing may consist in something other than what has already been proposed, Socrates now implied that *he* knew, or had an opinion about, what philosophizing is. He had withheld this suggestion, which had the effect of shifting the initiative in the argument entirely to him, not only until the "philosopher" had been chastised for presuming to know what philosophizing is, but also until the assumptions or expectations of the "philosopher" regarding philosophy had been brought to light. Socrates thus did his best to ensure that his own "proposal" would be greeted and later examined with these expectations in mind.

The elaboration of Socrates' proposal took place in two stages. First he called attention to the links among three kinds of knowledge for dealing with (punishing, improving, judging) animals of concern to human beings (horses, dogs, human beings)—identifying them, for each kind of animal, as a single art. The art or science applying to human beings he further identified with justice and moderation as well as with the science or art by which a city or household is managed correctly. Then Socrates suggested that, in part to avoid what is shameful, the philosopher must master this art. His argument went as follows.

Those—only those—who know how to improve beings of a certain kind ("make them better" or "best") know how to punish those beings (horses, dogs, or human beings) correctly. (The implication is that punishment is a necessary means to improvement and that improvement is the only correct end or purpose of punishment, that punishment for any other end is incorrect, not to say tyrannical or despotic. If punishment were not necessary to improvement, one might have knowledge of improvement without knowledge of correct punishment; if there were correct ends of punishment other than improvement, one might have knowledge of improvement without the whole knowledge of correct punishment.) And this twofold art of improvement and correct punishment and no other is that which judges (*gignōskein*) of the beings it is set over, which are good and which evil, or distinguishes (*diagignōskein*) the ones from the others—whether it is a question of one such being or many. (Such judging is more clearly necessary to an improving-punishing art than to any other.)

The science that correctly punishes the unrestrained and unlawful in the cities is the judicial science, also called justice. And the science by which they punish correctly is the one by which they judge which are the good human beings and which the evil, whether it is a question of one or of many. If, then, as is the case, judging (gignōskein) which are the good and evil human beings is necessary to human beings who are not to be ignorant of themselves, of whether they are good or evil; and if, as is also asserted to be the case, to know (gignōskein) oneself is to be moderate, since to be ignorant of oneself is to be immoderate, the writing in Delphi ("Know thyself") is apparently an exhortation to practice moderation and justice. Justice, the science by which we know how to punish correctly, is the same as moderation, the science by which we know how to judge (diagignōskein) both oneself and others. (Knowing whether one is good or evil, in other words, which requires the ability to judge others too in this respect, is not merely necessary to self-knowledge but is its core. Cf. *Charmides* 167a1–7.)

Moreover, cities are well managed whenever those doing injustice pay the penalty: the science we are considering is then a political one, too. And when one man manages a city correctly, he does so by the kingly and tyrannic art: these arts, too, then, are the same as those others. And the arts by which one man manages a household correctly are apparently the economic (household) and despotic (master) arts; since by justice and no other art he, too, manages the household well, we can conclude that this one art is at once kingly, tyrannic, political, despotic, economic, and justice and moderation.

Our "philosopher" had implied earlier that it would be shameful for the philosopher to be able neither to follow when a doctor says something concerning the sick nor to make a contribution of his own concerning the words or deeds of a doctor or any other of the craftsmen. Is it not shameful, then, for him to be able neither to follow nor to contribute when the speaker (or doer) in question is a judge or king or one of the others just mentioned? Must the philosopher here be a pentathlete and second-rater, useless as long as one of those is available? Or rather is it for him, first, not to turn his own household over to another but, sitting in judgment himself, to punish correctly, if his household is to be well managed? Next, if his friends turn over to him matters for arbitration, or the city orders him to decide or give judgment on something, is it shameful to come to light as a second or third-rater in these matters rather than to lead?

When our "philosopher" had conceded these points, Socrates drew the conclusion that philosophizing is far from being polymathia or preoccupation with the arts. This statement reduced our "philosopher," who was ashamed at what he had said earlier, to silence, while the athlete declared it was so, and the others (that is, the boys) praised what had been said.

Discussion

The search for the mathēmata that constitute philosophy was thus brought to an apparently successful end. Socrates had pointed in a direction in which, he suggested, lie mathēmata that the philosopher must master, and his words had met with approval—especially on the part of the boys, for there is no reason to suppose that "what had been said" refers to Socrates' concluding statement alone. But several clouds darken this picture, among them the concluding statement itself. Why did Socrates choose to leave his listeners and interlocutors with a merely negative statement? Moreover, what basis do we have for supposing that the mathēmata to which he had pointed, even if they truly exist, are noble in the sense indicated in the first (or destructive) part of the argument, that they fill the great bill of expectations regarding philosophy that was uncovered there with such care? Surely the fact that the mastery of such mathēmata would make the philosopher useful can by now be dismissed in advance as conclusive evidence of their being noble. Nor is the fact that they are not open to the other objections advanced against our "philosopher's" suggestions positive evidence of their adequacy. Indeed, lacking as we do any explicit Socratic assertion to this effect, what basis do we have for supposing that Socrates himself, the philosopher of ignorance (*Ap. Soc.* 21d4), regarded them as noble in the indicated sense?

It will be argued on the other side, I suspect, that, as I have admitted and even stressed, the most important audience of Socrates on the spot, those who have shown by deed their potential for philosophy, that is, the boys (consider 135a1–5), must have understood him to be recommending these mathēmata as noble. To admit the possibility of what I have tentatively suggested is, then, to admit the possibility that Socrates left the boys with what he regarded as a false impression. This objection can be regarded as conclusive only as long as one regards it as certain that Socrates had no reason for leaving the boys, even temporarily, with a false impression. For purposes of indicating what such a reason might be, I will assume that what I have tentatively suggested is true: that Socrates did not regard the political mathēmata as noble, that indeed, as he once in the dialogue went so far as to indicate, he didn't know of any mathēmata that are noble in the required sense.

It must be recalled that, at the outset of the dialogue, the boys were seriously engaged in an astronomical-philosophical dispute. Socrates conjectured, at any rate, that their quarrel concerned Anaxagoras or Oinopides—that is, he linked their concerns to those of pre-Socratic, nonpolitical philosophy (see also 132b9). Socrates seemed to have conjectured as well, on the basis of their manifest seriousness or earnestness, that they regarded the object of their concern as noble. It is not very significant for our purposes that our "philosopher" acknowledged openly his opinion that philosophizing is noble; it is much more significant that Socrates' questioning of the "philosopher" on this point silenced the boys and drew their attention to the Socratic discussion. Their attitude toward philosophizing may not have been very different from that of the young Socrates himself, in whose opinion the wisdom called "inquiry into nature"—to know the causes of each thing—was a "splendid" thing (Phaedo 96a5–10, cf. Lysis 215e1–216a2). That is, the seriousness of the boys is due to the fact that they regard the object of their concern, the wisdom or learning they strive for, as serious or high or noble. But the question "What is noble?" was not, as far as we can tell, a part of their inquiries.

In these circumstances, Socrates' examination of our "philosopher" must have begun to awaken in the boys this question, or the question of what is implied in our holding something to be noble. Moreover, it must have aroused in them some doubt as to the adequacy of their own activity in terms of the standard being brought to light: is astronomy, or philosophy as they have been pursuing it, good for the soul? They were thus prepared to greet Socrates' proposal toward the end with the enthusiasm with which they apparently did greet it. If their praise is sincere, they are about to turn from astronomy or natural philosophy to political philosophy. Socrates will have brought about in them the very change in philosophic orientation that he apparently underwent himself. But this statement is not quite correct. The enterprise that must have been embraced by Socrates in full awareness of its character and possible limits will be embarked on by the boys as the result of a false impression as to its worth for which Socrates is in some sense responsible.

We are back to our original dilemma. The boys will have changed the object of their studies but not their expectations from them. But this very fact may now begin to suggest a solution. For what the boys expected earlier—without being aware of it—from their natural studies, may, to repeat, not differ greatly from what was always expected from philosophizing as long as philosophizing was regarded as a way of life. The choice to philosophize, to give one's life to philosophizing, is after all a human choice, made for human reasons, on the basis of some human concerns—among which the concern to know is not likely to have played the sole, perhaps not even the leading, part. The thought that philosophy or wisdom or the knowledge of the causes of all things is noble or high or serious may always have had great weight in this choice. (Consider, regarding the objects of philosophy, *Laws* 889e6 and a4–5; cf. Aristotle, *N. Ethics* 1141a 18–22 and 34–b3). But if this is the case, the unique significance of political philosophy is immediately apparent. What is, at the outset at least, the unexamined assumption prompting philosophizing of every sort becomes a necessary object of critical examination in philosophizing of only one sort, political philosophy. This, at least, is the suggestion of Plato's *Lovers,* where the nobility of anything is first shown to imply its goodness—that it makes us good—and where political science is then equated with knowledge of what makes us good. By putting the boys on the path to political philosophy, Socrates was putting them, then, on the path to self-knowledge.[6] (Among other things, the attempt to acquire knowledge of what makes us good will require us to consider whether the punishing done "in the cities" accomplishes this goal. The goodness of horses and dogs is clear because we understand by that goodness their usefulness to us. Clear too, then, is the role of punishment in making them "good," that is, in molding them in accordance with our needs or desires. But we saw that, by the goodness of human beings, we may mean more than our usefulness to one another. We must wonder, then, whether the standards imposed by the punishing done "in the cities" are ultimately different from usefulness or whether the art of improvement is there, as is proper, setting the standards of good and evil for the punishing art to follow or vice versa.)[7]

[6]That Socrates should make a proposal with one thing in mind while giving part of his audience the impression that he has something else in mind, is wholly consistent with the definition of irony suggested by his remark at 133d8: saying two things at the same time with a view to the differences among one's addressees. Cf. Fairbanks, "Reason, Technique," p. 11. In other words, Socratic irony is not totally absent from the *Lovers*.

[7]Once "the cities" have been mentioned by Socrates, he ceases to refer by name to the improving art. Note also the improper conversion—the wicked are useless, there-

If Socrates put the boys on the path to self-knowledge, he must have regarded self-knowledge as good. He was, then, not as unaware of mathēmata that are good for a soul, not as innocent of expertise in that respect, as he occasionally suggested and I supposed. Only two "virtues" are mentioned in the *Lovers* by name: justice and moderation. Since justice, the art of punishing correctly, has to do principally with the improvement of others and is, at any rate, only what *brings* a soul into good condition, I surmise that moderation, that is, self-knowledge, is this good condition itself. Moreover, if human goodness is or presupposes self-knowledge, we can understand why punishment is necessary to improvement: becoming aware of what one thought one knew but did not know cannot be so free from pain as to make it unreasonable to speak of it as punishment.

But in what sense is self-knowledge the good condition of a soul? Does it render one perfect and free from needs or rather good *for* something? (This question is justified by the fact that self-knowledge was said here to be moderation, i.e., a virtue, only on the basis of a false conversion.) In the exchange on experts, it was clear that a doctor or trainer is to be consulted, as to exercise and foods, for the sake of the body and its good condition. But it was unclear whether the farmer is to be consulted, as to the sowing of seed, for the sake of the crop or for the sake of the land and its good condition, or for both (cf. Xenophon, *Oeconomicus* 17.1–11). What, then, about the planting of mathēmata or seeds of mathēmata in a soul—in particular the political mathēmata whose seeds Socrates planted in the boys toward the end? In what sense will they, or the self-knowledge to which they may lead, make the boys better?

It is unlikely that a single dialogue, especially one as short as the *Lovers,* will supply a definitive answer to such a question. Each dialogue presents only a part of Plato's view and must eventually be put together with all the others, beginning with those most closely associated with it in one way or another. If we are to confine ourselves here then to what can be established on the basis of the *Lovers* alone, we must rest satisfied with certain indications of what the answer

---

fore the useless are wicked—at 136b7–8 and e3 and 137a10–b1, which may have the function of calling our attention to a kindred and more important improper conversion. This difficulty may also lie behind the association of the political art with tyranny and despotism. Note the coordination of justice and despotism at 138c7–10 (the items that advance a place in the second list).

might be. While mentions of "philosophizing," "philosophy," and "philosopher(s)" abound in the dialogue, as we would expect, given its theme, Socrates and our "philosopher" use these terms in somewhat different ways. Socrates speaks first of "philosophizing" (132c2), the "philosopher" of "philosophy" (132c7). The "philosopher" speaks of what must be learned by "the one who is going to philosophize" (133c7–8) and again of what must be known, though not with precision, by "the one who is philosophizing" (135c8–d7 and also 135b5; cf. 136a6–b2, the three uses of the perfect tense). Socrates, when not absolutely prevented by the need to present the "philosopher's" view, speaks of what "the one who is philosophizing" must learn (135a8–9) or of what philosophizing does for those who are engaging in it (135e6–7; cf. 136a3 and 137a9–b6). Socrates appears to understand by "philosophy" (or "philosophizing") a process of learning, while our "philosopher" takes it to be possession of a body of knowledge. (Consider also Socrates' initial approval and subsequent rejection of the "philosopher's" first definition, at 133c4–11.) Once we have observed this difference in usage, we are likely to be surprised by Socrates' apparent insistence toward the end of the dialogue that the political mathēmata must be mastered by the philosopher. But the difficulty disappears once we remember that the political mathēmata are never identified as philosophy. If we are cautious and do not go beyond what Socrates suggests, we can only take them, or rather "political philosophy," to be a needed preliminary to philosophizing. This is the most important meaning of the purely negative ending of the dialogue. Every explicit definition of philosophizing suggested is rejected. The only definition that has not been rejected, that remains, is the one supplied by the boys at the beginning by their deed.[8] We can expect, then, that there will be a vindication, within the Platonic *corpus,* of astronomy and its kindred sciences. This expectation is borne out by the *Laws* (especially 966d6–968a1 and 888a7–d2). Socrates' advice in the *Lovers* to two unnamed boys to turn from astronomy to political science is answered there by a demonstration of the importance of astronomy given to two old citizens by an unnamed Athenian.

The foregoing suggestions admittedly leave many questions unan-

---

[8]Cf. Fairbanks, "Reason, Technique," p. 9. On the investigation of political or human affairs as a necessary preliminary to the investigation of heavenly or divine things, cf. Xenophon, *Memorabilia* I 1.11–12. This is a part of the passage in which Xenophon presents Socrates' critique of his philosophic predecessors.

swered. For example, in what context, at what stage of reflections, does the return to "astronomy" first take place? Is political philosophy only preliminary to philosophizing proper, or is this its primary or most important, rather than its sole, function? But to repeat, these questions may not be answerable within the limits of a consideration of the *Lovers*. Even the question posed by the title considered in the light of Socrates' description of the opening scene of the dialogue— was Socrates himself one of the "lovers," or what is the connection between philosophizing and love?—may be posed but not answered by the dialogue. And this question in turn may be linked to that of the *way* in which political philosophy or self-knowledge is a necessary preliminary to philosophizing, the question of its bearing on the capacity to philosophize.

There is a parallel in the *Charmides* (155b9–156d3) to the scene at the beginning of the *Lovers* (133a), and the *Charmides* seems to be more intensely and narrowly concerned with its importance and meaning. In addition, with regard to all these questions, we should never forget the suggestion conveyed by Socrates' question to the athlete regarding exercise: to answer some questions we must first acquire the relevant experience.

Conclusion

As we can see with the help of the *Lovers,* political philosophy emerged in a situation that was in many significant respects, though not in all, the opposite of ours. Philosophy or science, far from being the only universally respected authority, was suspect in the eyes of many citizens of ordinary decency (represented in the *Lovers* by the athlete), who would not think of looking to it for guidance as to what is good and just even if they felt the need for such guidance. What evidence or authority the political and moral values of the time had did not stem from their being put forward or confirmed by any allegedly scientific or rational teaching. Science had not yet had a widespread impact on ordinary moral-political life; rather, the values respected by ordinary citizens were likely and even bound to exercise on scientists—on those citizens who undertook to engage in philosophy or science—an influence that had not yet learned to disguise itself in professions of scientific objectivity or neutrality. In that situation, it was somewhat more obvious than it is now that, if philosophy or science is to have clarity about itself, its first task is to come to grips with its own motivations.

According to the *Lovers,* Socrates turned to political philosophy to meet this challenge. That is, the only "value" that political philosophy originally intended to put on a rational basis, or to prove, was the value of philosophy or science as a way of life. Only in this respect was it originally concerned to establish a rational set of values. It is true that, as the *Lovers* also shows, political philosophy seemed from the beginning, inevitably, to promise more—to promise to provide general guidance for political life. Nor could it count on never being asked, or never needing, to deliver on the broader promise it apparently held forth. But it is not perfectly clear that Socrates considered political philosophy, as he originated it, to be capable of providing such guidance: it is at least conceivable that the studies to which he directed the boys in the *Lovers,* which he himself must have undertaken previously, achieve their primary goal without ever equipping one to accomplish this additional task. (Cf. *Laches* 186b8–c5.) More precisely, it is not clear that Socrates regarded the truths discovered by political philosophy as *directly* relevant to the guidance of political life. And indeed, the first philosopher in the Socratic tradition who seriously attempted the broader task found it necessary to borrow certain fundamental assumptions from decent political life that, for the purpose at hand, were simply accepted as the starting points of discussion (Aristotle, *Ethics* 1095a30–b8 and 1098a33–b4). Only with their help—in respectfully clarifying, modifying, and applying these, the very assumptions whose questioning and challenging had been necessary to its primary task—was Socratic political philosophy able to fulfill its secondary but politically most important task, which, accepted by all subsequent political philosophy, eventually came to be regarded as the primary task. In the process, there took place the crucial change in the way the task was approached to which I referred at the beginning of this chapter. It came to be believed that scientific truth (e.g., the truth uncovered by investigation of the state of nature) is directly relevant, without such mediation as Aristotle had relied on, to the guidance of political life. As a result, the claim to scientific validity was raised much more loudly or boldly on behalf of certain modern doctrines than it had been by Aristotle. (Cf., e.g., the conclusion of the second part of Hobbes' *Leviathan* with *Ethics*

1094b11–27 and 1098a26–b8.) And this claim in turn was forcefully rejected by Weber, who thus helped to bring about or call attention to our present predicament.

If the foregoing analysis is correct, it may be possible, by reflecting again on the reasons for Aristotle's procedure and for his caution, to see more clearly both the basis of the difficulty that concerned Max Weber and the solution to it. But to do so, it will be necessary first to come to grips, as I have tried to begin to do, with political philosophy as Aristotle himself first knew it, as it was bequeathed to him by Socrates and Plato, with the original meaning of political philosophy.

CLEITOPHON
[or, Exhortation]

Translated by CLIFFORD ORWIN

Socrates, Cleitophon

406 SOCRATES: Cleitophon, the son of Aristonymos, as someone was just telling us, was conversing with Lysias and criticized spending time with Socrates, while he could not praise too highly the company of Thrasymachos.[1]

CLEITOPHON: Whoever that someone was, Socrates, did not recount accurately for you the arguments that I made about you to Lysias. For while there were some things for which I for my part did not praise you, there were also some for which in fact I did. But since it is plain that you are holding this against me, for all that you pretend that you couldn't care less, I would very gladly go over these same arguments with you myself—now that we happen to be alone—so that you will be less inclined to think that I have a low opinion of you. For as things stand now, perhaps you have been misinformed, and that is why you appear to be more harshly disposed toward me than you ought to be. So then, if you give me permission to speak frankly, I would very gladly accept it, as I wish to explain.

407a SOC.: Why, it would be shameful indeed, when you are so eager to

"Exhortation" translates the Greek *protreptikos,* an adjective from a verb meaning "to urge onward or impel"; of speeches, "exhortatory" or "admonitory"; in medical usage, "stimulative." The adjective occurs twice elsewhere in Plato (*Euthydemus,* 278c and 282d); the verb, several times.

[1]Cleitophon (active 411–405 B.C.) was an Athenian statesman; Lysias (ca. 459–ca. 380), the great Attic orator; Thrasymachos (ca. 460–ca. 400), from Chalcedon on the Hellespont, a leading sophist, or itinerant teacher of rhetoric. Cleitophon's historic and Platonic significance is discussed in my essay.

benefit me, not to submit to it. For clearly, once I have learned my bad and good points, I will practice and pursue the one and shun the other with all my might.

CLEIT.: Then listen. When I was together with you, Socrates, I was often amazed at what I heard. You seemed to surpass all other human beings, so very finely did you speak, whenever, taking human beings

b to task like a god on the tragic stage,[2] you declaimed as follows, "Whither are you borne, O human beings? Know you not that you do nothing of what you ought, you to whom all that matters is laying up riches for yourselves? While that your sons, to whom you will bequeath them, will know how to use them justly, that you neglect. Nor do you find them teachers of justice—if indeed it is to be acquired through study—or, if through exercise or training, people to train them and exercise them sufficiently. Nor have you even first provided for yourselves in this regard. But when you see that you

c yourselves and your children have learned sufficiently letters and music and gymnastic—which indeed you regard as a complete education in virtue—and that you are as a result not a whit less vicious where riches are concerned, how is it that you neither disdain the present manner of education nor search for people who will put a halt to this unmusicality? Yet surely it is because of this dissonance and heedlessness, and not because of a want of measure in keeping step with the lyre, that brother strives with brother and city with city,

d clashing without measure and discordantly, and in the heat of war do and suffer the utmost. Now you claim that it is not from want of education or from ignorance but voluntarily that the unjust are unjust. But then to the contrary you dare to declare that injustice is disgraceful and hateful to the gods. How then could anybody voluntarily choose an evil of this kind? Somebody, you reply, who is no match for pleasures. But then surely he is so involuntarily, is he not, if to prevail is voluntarily done? So in every way the argument proves that injustice is done involuntarily and that we must pay greater

e attention to it than we now do, every man privately and at the same time all the cities publicly."

---

[2]Literally, "just like a god on a tragic contrivance" (or "machine"), the contrivance in question being that by means of which gods made soaring entrances and exits on the Greek stage and addressed the other characters from on high. Often the god would harangue the mortal characters while rescuing them from an otherwise impossible predicament; as early as the time of Aristotle, expressions akin to the present one had become proverbial and have come down to us through the Latin deus ex machina.

These things, then, Socrates, when I hear you so often pronounce them, I admire greatly, and I praise them wondrously. And so too when you utter the sequel to this, that those who exercise their bodies while neglecting their souls are doing something else of this sort— (they are neglecting that which rules while concerning themselves with that which is ruled). And again, when you declare that whatever someone does not know to make use of, better that he relinquish the use of it. If, then, someone does not know how to make use of his eyes or his ears or his body as a whole, better for him neither to hear nor to see nor to put his body to any other use whatever than to make use of it in any which way. And so too with regard to art. Whoever 08a does not know how to make use of his own lyre clearly will not know how to make use of his neighbor's, and whoever does not know how to make use of that of others will not know how to make use of his own—or of any other instrument or possession.

This speech of yours ends finely, too—that, for anyone who does not know how to make use of a soul, it's better for him to keep his soul at rest and not to live and act on his own. If, however, there should be some compulsion to live, better for such a one to pass his b life as a slave than as a free man and to hand over the rudder of his thought, as of a ship, to another, who has learned the art of piloting human beings—which, Socrates, is the name that you often give to statesmanship, saying that this very same art is that of judging and justice.

These speeches, then, and others like them, very many and very finely spoken, to the effect that virtue is teachable and that one should bestow one's cares upon oneself before all else—these I have hardly c ever contradicted, nor do I suppose that I shall ever do so hereafter. I believe that they are stirring[3] and helpful in the highest degree and truly such as to wake us, as it were, from our slumber. And so I set my mind on attending to what would come next. At first, Socrates, it was not you whom I questioned further but your contemporaries and those who shared your aspirations, or comrades or whatever name one should give their relation to you. Of these the first I questioned further were those of whom you have a particularly high opinion: d inquiring as to what argument came next, I put the matter to them rather after your own fashion. "Best of men," said I, "how ever do we take Socrates' exhortation of us to virtue? As if there were nothing

---

[3]Literally, "hortatory in the highest degree" (*protreptikōtatous*).

more, it not being possible to see the business through and grasp it completely, and is our task throughout life but this, to exhort those who have yet to be exhorted, who will then do the same to others in

e   their turn? Or ought we, once we have agreed that this is just what a human being should do, go on to ask Socrates and one another, 'then what?' How do we say that we ought to begin to go about the study of justice? Just as if someone were exhorting us to bestow our cares upon the body, seeing that just like children we had no notion that there was any such thing as gymnastic and medicine, and therefore reproached us, saying that it is disgraceful to bestow the whole of one's care on wheat and barley and vines and however many things we toil to acquire for the sake of the body, without seeking to discover some art or contrivance for the body itself, in order that it might be as good as possible—even though such a thing exists. Say

409a that we questioned further the person who was thus exhorting us. 'What are these arts you speak of?' He would probably say that they were gymnastic and medicine. So, then, in the matter at hand, what do we assert to be the art having to do with the virtue of the soul? Let it be stated." The one of them who was reputed to be the most formidable in these matters answered me, saying that this art was just that one (said he) "of which you hear Socrates speaking, none other than justice." To which I said: "Don't just tell me its name, but look

b   at it this way. It is said, presumably, that there is an art of medicine: and of this the aims are twofold: the continuous production of physicians in addition to the existing ones; and health. Of these the latter is an art no longer but rather a result of the art which both teaches and is taught, which result is just what we call health. And there is to carpentry, by the same token, a house and carpentry; the one the result, the other the teaching. Of justice, then, let it likewise be granted that it produces just men, exactly as the other arts do their various practitioners. As for that other thing, however, the result that the just man is capable of producing, what do we say that it is? Tell

c   me." The same one as before replied, as I suppose, that it was the advantageous; someone else, the needful; yet another, the beneficial; still another, the profitable. Upon which I replied as follows: "But there too these very same terms apply to each of the arts; to act correctly, to do the profitable things, the beneficial things, and so on. As to what all of these things refer to, however, each art states that concern which is peculiar to itself. Take carpentry: it will declare what it is well to do, what it is fine to do, what it is needful to do, in

order that implements made of wood come into being—which are not themselves art. So let the business of justice be stated in just this
d same way." Finally, Socrates, one of your comrades did answer me, one indeed who was reputed to speak in a most accomplished manner. He answered that the result peculiar to justice, and to no one of the other arts, was to produce friendship in the cities. Upon further questioning, he proceeded to maintain that friendship was a good and never an evil. When asked, however, about the friendships of children and beasts, to which we do refer by that name, he refused to admit that they were friendships. For this followed from his admission that relations of this sort were harmful more often than they
e were good. To avoid the implications of this statement he declared that such relations were not friendships at all and that those who so name them name them falsely. That which was really and truly friendship was most clearly oneness of mind. Asked whether by oneness of mind he meant oneness of opinion or rather knowledge, he dismissed oneness of opinion. For there were of necessity among human beings many and harmful instances of oneness of opinion, while he had agreed that friendship was wholly a good and a result of justice. Therefore he maintained that oneness of mind was the same and was knowledge and not opinion.

410a   Now, when we were at this point in the argument and at a loss, the bystanders were able to jump on the man and declare that the argument had gone in a circle to the very point where it had been at first. "Medicine too," they said, "is a kind of oneness of mind, as are all the arts, and they are able to say what it is that they have to do with. But as for the 'justice' or 'oneness of mind' you speak of, what it aims for has gotten clean away, and whatever its result might be is anything but clear."

    Finally, Socrates, I questioned you yourself about these things, and
b you told me that it belonged to justice to harm enemies and to do good to friends. Later, however, it appeared that the just man never harms anyone, for in all matters he acts for the benefit for all. After pressing you in this way not just once or twice but sticking it out for a long time, I gave up. For I had come to believe that when it came to exhorting to concern with virtue, of all human beings you did it most finely, but that one of two things must be so. Either you are capable of this much only but nothing more—as might happen also with respect to any other art, as in the case of a man who although not a
c pilot might apply himself to a praise of that art, as worth a great deal

to human beings—and so too with respect to the other arts. Now, someone could perhaps bring the same charge against you as regards justice, that you are none the more a knower of justice just because you eulogize it finely. Not, of course, that this is my position. Still one of two things must be so: either you don't know or you are unwilling to share the knowledge with me. And that is why I will continue to go about, yes, to Thrasymachos and whomever else I am able, for I am at a loss. If, however, you are even now willing to

d desist at last in my case from these speeches of exhortation, just as if, having exhorted me with respect to gymnastic that the body ought not to be neglected, you were to deliver the sequel to the speech of exhortation, declaring of what sort my body is by nature and of what sort of treatment it therefore has need—let just that be done in the present case. Take it that Cleitophon agrees that it is ridiculous to concern oneself with other things while neglecting the soul, for the

e sake of which we toil at the other things. And suppose now also that I have recited in this way all the other things that follow these—things that as a matter of fact I just went through.

I speak now as one who is entreating you not, by any means, to do otherwise; so that I shall not, just as I do now, praise you to Lysias and the rest in some ways but in others blame you somewhat. For I shall maintain, Socrates, that to a human being who has not been exhorted, you are worth everything but that to one who has been exhorted, you are almost even a stumbling block in the way of his arriving at the goal of virtue and becoming a happy man.

On the
Cleitophon

CLIFFORD ORWIN

The *Cleitophon* is by far the shortest of the dialogues ascribed to Plato. It is also the only one that features an unanswered blame of Socrates. These facts encouraged many critics of the last century to try to pronounce it spurious. None of the ancient grammarians, however, is known to have regarded it as suspect, and there are no compelling philological reasons for assigning it to anyone but Plato. Today its authenticity is generally conceded, although some scholars do view it as unfinished.[1]

The Hellenistic critic Thrasyllos, who arranged the dialogues in their present tetralogies, grouped the *Cleitophon* with the *Republic, Timaeus,* and *Critias.* By placing the *Cleitophon* before the *Republic,* he affirmed the many and clear connections between the two. As will appear below, the thematic affinities are very great; the dramatic ones are perhaps more striking still. The *Cleitophon* is the only other dialogue in which all the characters named—Cleitophon, Socrates, Lysias, and Thrasymachos—figure in the *Republic* as well as the only one named after a character in the *Republic*. Of the speakers in the

"On the *Cleitophon*" originally appeared as "The Case against Socrates: Plato's *Cleitophon*," copyright © 1982 by the *Canadian Journal of Political Science*, in *CJPS* 15:4 (December 1982):741–53. It is reprinted here by permission of the author and the journal.

[1]Despite a recent upsurge, critical commentary on the *Cleitophon* is sparse. The best review of it is provided by David L. Roochnik at the beginning of his "The Riddle of the *Cleitophon*," *Ancient Philosophy* 4:2 (1984):132–45. Roochnik's article and that of Jan Blits, "Socratic Teaching and Justice: Plato's *Cleitophon*," *Interpretation* 13:3 (1985):321–34, are responses to the earlier version of this chapter and should be consulted by the serious reader.

Republic, moreover, Cleitophon is the only one who neither addresses Socrates nor is addressed by him, merely sparring with Socrates' companion Polemarchos (340a–b). He is the only one who leaves the discussion as he had entered it, at odds with Socrates.[2] The *Cleitophon* depicts the "missing" confrontation between Cleitophon and Socrates, implied by the *Republic* but absent from it. To interpret the former is thus necessarily to explore its relation to the latter.

Cleitophon's foray into the conversation of the *Republic* is provoked by the return to it of Polemarchos, whose name means "War Leader" and with whom Socrates has just concluded an alliance to do battle on behalf of justice (335e). Thus far Socrates has done all the fighting, but when Polemarchos breaks in to applaud the discomfiture of Thrasymachos, Cleitophon rallies to the latter's defense.

Thrasymachos has gotten in trouble by asserting both that justice is the advantage of the stronger—by which he means the rulers—and that it is obedience to the laws that the rulers make (338e). When reminded that the rulers are fallible and sometimes make laws to their disadvantage, he is made to see that he has contradicted himself. If justice is obedience to law, it is not necessarily the advantage of the stronger—and vice versa (339b–e). As he falls silent to try to regroup, Polemarchos glories in his defeat, and Cleitophon rushes into the breach.

Cleitophon's opening sally underlies the dramatic context: a mock trial of Socrates in which Thrasymachos plays the accuser (compare with 337d). It is also a sneer at Polemarchos: it is not for him, an alien, to testify in an Athenian proceeding. In turn, this assault provokes a defensive reply. Cleitophon speaks not merely for the city (as Thrasymachos at first plays at doing) but for Athens in particular. As a citizen he better represents the city than the professional foreigner from far-off Chalcedon.

In fact, however, Polemarchos proves an excellent witness, correctly restating the argument. It is Cleitophon himself who proves unable or unwilling to do so. As Polemarchos asserts and Socrates appears to agree (340b–c), the position that Cleitophon defends is not quite that of Thrasymachos.

According to Cleitophon, if Thrasymachos has implied that it is ever just to do what is disadvantageous for the stronger, he has done so because he has "set down that to do what the rulers bid is just"

<hr/>

[2]Cf. *Republic* 450a–b with 498c–d.

(340a).[3] Cleitophon takes for granted that here is the premise from which the rest of Thrasymachos follows; when Polemarchos reminds him that justice was also the advantage of the stronger, he interprets this as merely another way of stating that the just is the legal: "But . . . he said that the advantage of the stronger is what the stronger believes to be his advantage. This is what must be done by the weaker, and this is what he set down as the just."[4]

In fact Thrasymachos has said no such thing and denies emphatically that he meant it (340c). Preferring to clutch instead at the other horn of his dilemma, he develops the notion of the genuine advantage of the stronger, in the strongest and strictest sense (340d and following). He thereby replaces the legal with the artful, as the standard for the law and everything else. His commitments and requirements as practitioner of art prevail, and we hear no more from him of the just as the merely legal.

Cleitophon is thus the only speaker in the *Republic* who not only begins with but holds fast to the notion that justice is doing what the rulers say. He asserts what Socrates gets Thrasymachos to deny, that the will of the rulers is beyond appeal. He maintains what is everywhere the position of the rulers themselves and so of the cities whose official spokesmen the rulers are. Once Socrates has induced Thrasymachos to abandon this position, he has separated him from Cleitophon, the rhetorician from the spokesman for the city. Cleitophon will not again come to the defense of Thrasymachos. In never wavering from his interested attachment to legal justice, he is the sole character in the *Republic* who stands first and last for the city as it is. That is another way of formulating his obvious enmity toward Socrates, the questioner par excellence of the authority of the laws of the city.

Cleitophon's attachment to legal justice is an interested one because he himself is a ruler or rather, inasmuch as Athens is a democracy, a "leader" or ambitious servant of the rulers. Socrates' brushes with him are those surprisingly rare occurrences in Plato, encounters with a practicing statesman.[5]

Cleitophon was in fact a public man of some, if not the first,

[3]Citations of the *Republic* are from the translation of Allan Bloom (New York, 1968).
[4]*Republic,* 340a–b. One might render the first sentence as: "By the advantage of the stronger he meant what the stronger believes to be his advantage."
[5]Cf. *Apology of Socrates,* 21c–e.

importance. Active from 411 to 405 (the epoch of the dramatic date of the *Republic*), he was known for his advocacy of the "ancestral laws" (or "regime"), presumed a compromise between democracy and oligarchy. As a close associate of Theramenes, he may have shared the twists and turns of the latter's dazzling career "acting as a good citizen under all regimes." Aristophanes pairs the two as adepts of the sophists. A third leader of their faction was Anytos, later the accuser of Socrates.[6]

The career of Cleitophon thus confirms the plausibility of the role that Plato assigns him: a sometime companion of Thrasymachos whose attachment to the city and its laws comes between them. It also establishes his credentials as a representative of the city in its quarrel with Socrates; here again we note that he figures in the *Republic* as a hostile witness in a mock trial of Socrates that foreshadows the real one. This fact is worth keeping in mind as we approach the *Cleitophon*.

If the cast of the *Cleitophon,* and its theme of justice, clearly link it with the *Republic,* its dramatic structure no less clearly recalls that of the *Apology*. In the *Cleitophon,* however, the accused is Cleitophon; in this dialogue so full of blame of Socrates, it is not he who is on the defensive (406a).[7] Far from looking incomplete, the dialogue resembles an Athenian trial brought to completion: the accused receives the last word.[8] The "one-sidedness" of the *Cleitophon,* then, like that of the *Apology* itself, would reflect this context of accusation and reply.

Indeed, if we may take Cleitophon as the champion of the authority of the city, we might regard this dialogue as a kind of counter-*Apology*. A leading citizen responds, before the fact, to the strain in Socrates' self-defense that is most an accusation of the city: his insistence that it undervalues virtue and himself, the arch exhorter to virtue (*Apology* 29d–30c). For Cleitophon's objection to Socrates is not that his exhortations are unnecessary, but rather that they are insufficient. While invaluable to the unexhorted, Socrates is useless and even harmful to those who are no longer so (410c).

[6]The ancient sources are (on Cleitophon) Aristophanes *Frogs* 967; Aristotle *Athenian Constitution* 29 and 34; (on Theramenes) Thucydides 8.68, 89–94; Aristophanes *Frogs* 967–70; Xenophon *Hellenica* 1.7, 2.3, and 2.24–56; Aristotle *Athenian Constitution* 28 32–34, 36–37. On these see also Roochnik, "Riddle," and Blits, "Socratic Teaching."
[7]Hereafter all textual references are to the *Cleitophon* unless otherwise noted.
[8]Heinrich Brunnecke, "Kleitophon wider Sokrates," *Archiv fürGeschichte der Philosophie* 26 (1913):452–57.

In the *Apology* Socrates sometimes seems to confuse exhorting the citizens to virtue with success in educating them to it. On this confusion, in fact, rests his claim to have proved himself their greatest benefactor.[9] In distinguishing as firmly as Cleitophon does between Socrates' skill at exhortation and his incapacity to proceed beyond it, we discern a possible reply of the city to Socrates' gravest charge against it. Not its unwillingness to learn virtue, but Socrates' inability to teach it, explains his failure to persuade it of the greatness of his benefactions. That the city gets the last word here compels us at least to consider whether the city might not deserve it.

As mentioned, Cleitophon does not wholly deprecate Socratic exhortations: they are fine as far as they go. The example of one that he recounts verbatim is of considerable interest, for there is no other anywhere in Plato. Only here does Socrates step forth to address all human beings, collectively and indiscriminately (407b); only here are we witness to the first stage of Socratic confrontation—the only one that most Athenians would have known firsthand.

The exhortation as Cleitophon relates it is to greater concern with justice. Justice at first appears, in accordance with common opinion of it, as one discrete aspect of the proper conduct of everyday life— here, of the proper employment of wealth (407b–c). Its goodness emerges indirectly, from the badness of the results of injustice; ultimately, it seems, from the badness of suffering injustice (407c–d). Injustice is disharmony, but the emphasis is less on the proper attunement of the individual or his soul so that its parts form a harmonious whole than on the discord that injustice sows among citizens and cities. The positive or intrinsic goodness of justice for the individual remains something shadowy.

Perhaps for this reason, Socrates anticipates the objection that injustice is undertaken not for want of a proper education but willingly, that is, with both eyes open and not necessarily in ignorance of what is good for oneself. The intrinsic badness of doing injustice is not altogether obvious (cf. *Republic* 357a–6e). Socrates answers this objection by appealing to the opinion that injustice is "disgraceful" and "hateful to the gods"—sanctions necessary only where something is otherwise (that is, intrinsically) attractive (cf. *Republic* 362d–67e). Because of these sanctions, injustice appears to be too great an evil to be chosen willingly, or as Socrates means, knowingly. To choose it,

[9]Cf. *Apology,* 29d–30c with 36d–e.

then, is, as previously asserted, a symptom of want of education. This would be persuasive, however, only if the present contemptible education (407c) did not inculcate an awareness that injustice is disgraceful and hateful to the gods. Yet to just this awareness Socrates now appeals. Therefore, either it is not universal, or though universal, it does not suffice to persuade all men that justice is not to be undertaken willingly. In either case some further persuasion is required concerning the badness and hence involuntariness of injustice.

To the further objection that some do choose the evil of injustice willingly, namely those whose pleasures get the better of them, Socrates denies that such men are willingly bested: men will victory, not defeat. Suppose, however, that men will victory because it is pleasant, while defeat is painful. If, then, as Socrates suggests, pleasure impels to injustice, it would follow that injustice is what men do willingly and justice only under the painful constraint of fear of suffering injustice or punishment. (Such is in fact the assertion of ancient conventionalism.) These are only some of the problems with the claim that vice is ignorance and virtue knowledge. Cleitophon himself will raise others.

The question that proves to trouble Cleitophon is the relation of justice to the other arts. That justice is in fact an art is a version of the claim that virtue is knowledge. Socrates implies it in this first exhortation by casting concern for justice as a search for competent teachers or trainers, also likening it to music, both in the individual and in the city.

At 47e, the manner of Cleitophon's relation changes. He no longer quotes Socrates verbatim. He is now recounting, he says, the sequel to what has preceded. It is unclear whether we are to take this sequel as intended for the same general audience and as uttered in the same oracular manner. It makes a very different argument for justice, superfluous to anyone who has already been convinced but a plausible response to others who remain to be satisfied that justice is a good for the man who practices it. Unlike the prior exhortation, moreover, this one depends upon a remarkable transformation of the usual meaning of justice.

This transformation will appear from the following considerations. Earlier justice figured as a particular aspect of the proper use of things (407b–c). Now it appears instead as knowing how to use something. So too the object of use has undergone considerable elevation: from using property justly we move to justice as the art of making use of the human soul. Justice now seems the same as wisdom, and hence more clearly of intrinsic benefit to the just. Many men are willingly rogues, but few are willingly fools. Socrates resolves the problem of whether a wise man would be just by redefining justice as wisdom.

What lends this resolution some plausibility is the understanding of art to which justice is assimilated. Socrates presents art as knowledge of how to use any one of a given class of objects. The "art" of employing one's soul is therefore that of employing others, souls being no less interchangeable than lyres for the person who knows how to make use of one. Thus the art that we would most wish to know in order to live happily ourselves appears the same as the political and judicial arts and as justice.

We may question whether all of the inferences that Socrates draws from his scheme are correct. That the lyre player can play any one lyre well does not mean that he can play many of them at once; similarly, that I know how to use my own eyes and body does not mean that I know how to use those of others—not even if I would know how to use any body or eyes that were my own. Only I can use my eyes. Yet the statesman or judge or just man is like the lyre player playing many lyres at once or the man using many bodies not his own. And can we even speak of using our souls? If the soul is used, what is it in us that uses it? But if the soul is the unused user, then does the "art" of the soul, the summit of art in Socrates' scheme, conform at all to the model of art with which he presents us? Art is here knowledge of how to use, and the soul is not an object of use. It rather seems the seat or subject of such knowledge.

(A possible resolution to these questions about the soul would involve understanding it as composite, one part of which is "user" and the other or others are "used." Similarly we might understand the soul as the seat of knowledge about, among other things, itself. Any such understanding would imply the dependence of justice upon the soul's self-knowledge, that is, upon the wisdom at which philosophy aims.)

Last, if justice is the art of living well, what incentive has the knower of this art to practice it for the benefit of others? The merely formal identification of the art of living well with justice blurs the possibility that this art might teach indifference to others or even exploitation of them. It obscures, in other words, the possible tension between doing what is good for oneself and doing what is good for others. It thus raises the question whether there is any activity free of

124   Clifford Orwin

this tension; the known arts do not seem to qualify (cf. *Republic* 333e–34b).

408b–
410a   So far, however, so good, as far as Cleitophon is concerned. His difficulties arise in grasping this most important of arts. He airs them initially not to Socrates himself but to those who consort with him—as Cleitophon evidently does not. He may be leery of Socrates or of acquiring a reputation for consorting with him, or he may hope to impress Socrates' companions while diminishing their esteem for Socrates. His choice enables us to compare the response of the "Socratics" to his objections with the later one voiced by Socrates himself.

Cleitophon poses the question of how Socrates' harangues are to be taken. Is there nothing beyond exhortation—of oneself by Socrates and of others by oneself—or can we go about studying the art that Socrates eulogizes? If the latter, the first step is to locate that art. This becomes and will remain the problem of the dialogue within the dialogue.

Cleitophon wants justice explained on the analogy of gymnastic and medicine. The question that he raises on this basis ("What is the art concerned with the virtue of the soul?"), however, suggests that he is not entirely clear as to the place of justice in the analogy. Is it like gymnastic and medicine, the arts concerned with the body, or is it rather like health, the result at which these arts aim? Socrates has spoken of justice as an art, but we are used to regarding it as a virtue. Virtue, the well-being of the soul, is analogous to health, not to gymnastic and medicine. Yet as an art, justice would resemble these latter. Even in Socrates' presentation, it so much resembles virtue that in order to grasp that it is rather an art we must bear firmly in mind that the soul is an object for it rather than its subject or that of which it is an attribute. This perplexity, clearly grasped or dimly sensed, may account for the hesitancy of Cleitophon. Instead of asking what art procures justice or what justice procures, he simply asks what art procures virtue.

Having received the answer that this art is justice, the very one of which he has heard Socrates speak, Cleitophon demands to know the product or result (*ergon*) of this art. This question may seem superfluous; have we not just learned that this result is virtue? Perhaps, however, it is not so clear just what virtue is. Most people, after all, would say that justice is a virtue.

Each art, as Cleitophon explains, is guided by two concerns: self-perpetuation through renewing the ranks of its practitioners and the achievement of its particular result. Medicine produces physicians and health; justice, just men and what? "The fitting," "the needful," "the helpful," "the profitable," reply the companions. But the fitting, and so on, with regard to what? Each art can name that particular result in respect to which its particular procedures are fitting. So what is that result in the case of justice? Specifically Cleitophon distinguishes between the end of each art that is the art itself—by which he means its continued practice, which it assures by training new artisans—and the end that is "no longer" (*ouketi*) the art. The ends of carpentry, for instance, are carpentry itself and things made from wood; the ends of justice, justice itself and some result apart from justice, to which the practice of justice is a means. The difficulty lies in specifying that result.

To this one of the companions replies that the work specific to justice is the production of friendship in cities (409d). This answer seems to jibe very well with the first stage of Socrates' protreptic (cf. 407c–d). True friendship this Socratic defines as being of one mind— or sharing the same knowledge, for when pressed he distinguishes friendship from merely being of one opinion (409d–e). The auditors then cry that the argument has run about in a circle. Every art consists of "oneness of mind" or agreement on the basis of shared knowledge but always, once again, with respect to the specific province or product of the art. Carpenters share knowledge and are thus of the same mind concerning the production of wooden objects, not concerning politics or poetry. The attempt to define the product of justice has failed to specify this product and so to distinguish the place of justice among the arts.

10   Foiled at learning from the Socratics (or successful in embarrassing
–e   them), Cleitophon had turned to Socrates himself. At first Socrates had told him that justice was helping friends and harming enemies (cf. *Republic* 332b–336a). So to understand justice is in effect to equate it with friendship, where friendship is conceived politically as loyalty to one's comrades in a common quest for scarce goods. Clearly this definition could not have dispelled Cleitophon's perplexity. For it necessarily raises, rather than settling, the problem that has been troubling him, the relationship between justice and the arts. What goods in particular does justice confer, and how are these related to the ones conferred by the arch providers of particular goods, the arts? (Cf. *Republic* 332c–334b.)

So too with the other point that Cleitophon reports, that it had turned out that the just man would in fact harm no one (410a–b). The reasons supporting this remark are left unstated, and the formulation of the outcome differs from that of the parallel argument in the *Republic* (335b–e). Again, however, that the just man allegedly "acts in all things to the benefit of all" can hardly have satisfied Cleitophon. It leaves as urgent (and so open) as ever the questions of what benefits justice confers, that is, of its distinctive task or product.

Nor do either of the assertions that Cleitophon ascribes to Socrates address the question of how justice is itself beneficial, that is, an aspect of the good of whoever practices it. There is the suggestion that the just man acts in all things to the benefit of *all,* which, taken strictly, must include his own. This suggestion, however, remains undeveloped and therefore mysterious.

It seems, then, that Cleitophon's sessions with Socrates (whom, he stresses, he has queried repeatedly) have made no progress toward resolving his problem, while pointing unmistakably to it. Is justice an art or is it a good: if an art, what good does it produce; if a good, what good and produced by what art?

We noted above that the attempt to define the result of justice had failed to specify that result and so to distinguish the place of justice among the arts. Perhaps just this failure, however, marks some progress in understanding justice. That an answer intended to specify its product (e.g., health) should be interpreted by the bystander as describing the art itself (e.g., medicine) or even art as such—surely this could happen in the case neither of medicine nor of any other "art" but justice. It may reflect less our regrettable ignorance of the product of justice than the failure of justice to conform to the model of art and product.

Cleitophon, it will be recalled, had posited that one end of justice (as of every art) was the continuous production of new practitioners ("the art itself"). He had asked the companions to identify the other, the specific result beyond itself (that which "is no longer the art") that justice (like every art) must strive to produce. In at least one respect this formulation of the dual end of art is misleading. The "art itself" cannot claim a status equal to that of the specific result as an end of the art concerned, for the production of practitioners, like their practice, is merely a means to producing the result. Cleitophon should have distinguished not between the two aims of the practice of art but between the practice (which yielded crates) and the teaching of it (which yielded carpenters). The two are equally means to one end, the crates.

At first glance this correction of Cleitophon offers no comfort to the companions. For it means that, as long as we are ignorant of the specific result of justice, we cannot even grant it its apparently non-controversial end of the production of more just men. We cannot train artisans to fashion we know not what. In the absence of an agreed-upon result, justice collapses entirely: there can be no knowledge without something to know about. In the case of art, that something is the specific result. Without it justice cannot plausibly claim to qualify as shared knowledge ("oneness of mind")—if by knowledge we mean anything conforming to the model of art.

Perhaps, then, we should reconsider the notion that an art is what justice is. It first came to light as *either* the art that procured the virtue of the soul *or* that virtue itself. Cleitophon's first question to the companions had hedged the issue. Asked point blank what the art was that procured the virtue, they had responded as if justice were the former rather than the latter. This answer, however, has led nowhere. The result of justice collapses into justice itself, defying the necessary distinction between art and result. Justice is agreement about producing agreement or knowledge about producing knowledge. However absurd this conclusion when considered on the model of the arts, it makes a certain sense as an account of justice.

Thus far two different "results" have been ascribed to the "art" of justice: the virtue of the soul (409a) and friendship in the cities (409d). These are, however, in a sense synonymous: where there is virtue in the citizens, there will be friendship in the cities (cf. with 407c–d). Both of these "results," moreover, are such that their production might be thought synonymous with that of just men. In which case justice, unlike the arts, aims at a result identical with, and so exhausted by, the perpetuation of justice itself through the training of more practitioners. Justice, then, is an art the practice of which is reducible to its teaching. As such it would inhabit a middle ground between teaching and the arts or, if one prefers, between teaching and the other arts. For teaching, which Cleitophon's formulation has failed to disentangle from all the other arts to which it is ancillary, is a case of an art other than justice that aims merely at the production of agreement. It yields no result beyond agreement on the basis of knowledge, any further one being not that of teaching but rather that of the art taught. Rather like the "wage-earning art" of the *Republic*

(345b–347a), teaching accompanies the other arts while remaining distinct from them. Unlike the money-making art, it serves them rather than being served by them.

As for justice, it must stand somewhere in between teaching and the other arts. Like teaching it produces "oneness of mind" and nothing more; like the rest and unlike teaching, its province is some kind of knowledge distinct from that of transmitting knowledge. Lacking the practical orientation of the other arts, it lacks the merely ancillary character of teaching. Or is it ancillary to what came to be called theoretical knowledge?

Inasmuch as justice is the result of the exhorting that comprises its practice, it might well seem a *virtue* the practice of which is reducible to its teaching. This ambiguity of justice as virtue and art may explain why the companions answer at 409d that the result of the "art" of justice is friendship in the cities, forgetting that at 409a they have accepted the inference that it is the virtue of the soul. If justice is the art that produces virtue (in oneself or in others), then we need to look no further than virtue to find that produce which is "no longer [the] art that produces virtue (in oneself or in others), then we need to look no further than virtue to find that product which is "no longer [the] art [itself]." If justice is a virtue, however, then we might be tempted is. The difficulty of here distinguishing knowledge from virtue hints at their identity, in a context suggesting some of the problems that this identification poses.

Last, we may doubt that the practice of the "art" of justice is wholly reducible to its teaching. If it were, we would be at a loss to explain why it is good to be just. Teaching, after all, benefits not the teacher but the person taught. For this very reason, however, we could not conceive of the benefit of justice to the person taught if its only effect were to make him a teacher. If justice indeed departs from the model of the arts in producing no identifiable result beyond prac-titioners of justice, we have still to grasp how it might benefit these.

A clue to resolving this question is the prominence in the *Cleitophon* of the art of gymnastic. Cleitophon first offers gymnastic to Socrates, along with medicine, as the model to which their exposition of justice should conform (408e), and gymnastic alone will frame his final chal-lenge to Socrates (410a). Yet gymnastic signifies the road not taken in the dialogue, for Cleitophon proceeds to develop his demand on the companions along the lines of medicine alone (409a–b), and the final challenge to Socrates will go unanswered. This matters, for the model of an art afforded by gymnastic differs from that offered by medicine, and does so in just the respects of concern to us.

The differences are two. Unlike medicine, but apparently like justice, gymnastic is without tangible result apart from the "art itself," that is, the practitioners that it produces, thereby perpetuating itself. Whatever it produces in addition to these is produced within them, namely their health. Second and accordingly, while medicine is only incidentally of benefit to its practitioners—physicians are only incidentally sick, and otherwise their art benefits others, from whom they require compensation—gymnastic is so essentially. Justice as producer of shared knowledge, but without discernible practical result, and justice as analogous to gymnastic, that rare art the practice of which procures the good of the practitioner, a good moreover that parallels the virtue of the soul—these hints should help us fare better than the companions in facing the problems posed by Cleitophon.

As Socrates' *Apology* in response to the city's accusation of him necessarily expresses his accusation of it, so Cleitophon has replied in kind to what he takes to be Socrates' indictment of him. It is because his defense is accusatory that the dialogue seems incomplete without Socrates' response. Formally, however, as we have suggested, the work may be accounted complete. Again, the defendant gets the last word; as in the *Apology*, the final verdict is the reader's.

As for Socrates, he has never suggested an intention of replying to Cleitophon. His concern is neither to teach nor to refute him but to learn whatever may be learned from him (406e–407a). Nor is his silence surprising when we consider that the only alternative superior to it would be to provide an account of justice satisfactory to Cleitophon. At this task Socrates has already failed repeatedly (410b). Obviously Cleitophon does not expect him to succeed at it now, and neither should we or Socrates. No: Socrates has known from the outset, or has learned from Cleitophon's recitation, that his chances of satisfying him are nil.

Is Cleitophon innocent of the charge of blaming Socrates, not because he has not blamed him, but because Socrates is blameworthy? Cleitophon is of some help in refining the problem: either Socrates cannot say what justice is, or he will not say it to Cleitophon (410c). Or (a third possibility) is Socrates willing to say what justice is but unable to say it to Cleitophon?

It is striking that in this dialogue Socrates has arrived at the same point as in his conversation with Polemarchos in the *Republic* and has gone no farther. There further progress depends on raising the question of the relation of justice to the comprehensive human good (357a–367e); only through addressing this concern of his interlocutors is Socrates able even to begin considering what justice is (cf. 354b–c). This question Cleitophon never raises: the priority of the knowledge of the good to that of justice is suggested only by the "most accomplished" companion (409d–e) and implicitly by Socrates himself. Otherwise the very word for good (*agathos*) is absent from the *Cleitophon*. This is an index of the low ceiling of the dialogue, one of the few that never mentions philosophy. For the problem of justice, incredibly, proves an aspect of that of philosophy, the quest for knowledge transcending the realm of practice and the arts (*Republic* 474b–480a). Justice in this sense can come to light only through raising the question of the good and thereby doubting the goodness of justice. Can it be that Cleitophon is inferior as an interlocutor to Glaucon and Adeimantos precisely because he takes the goodness of justice too much for granted?

Be this as it may, from the perspective of Cleitophon and the city, Socrates must prove a disappointment. As the *Republic* confirms, Socrates can say what justice is, but only in the sense of achieving a comprehensive articulation of the problem of the relation of one's own good to the demands of the city. He can offer only problematic and paradoxical definitions of justice, and none that would gratify in the least any actual city.

The health of the soul, and the end of justice conceived as art or "treatment" (410d), is virtue. In the *Apology* Socrates states the main thing of which the city cannot be persuaded: that human happiness consists in a life spent *discussing* virtue and other things.[10] The city feels with Cleitophon that happiness depends on *arriving* at the summit of virtue (410e), with speech serving the ancillary purpose of pointing out the way. The Socratic formulation, however, implies that there can be no end to discussing virtue—and therefore no begin-

---

[10]"And if, on the other hand, I say that it even so happens that *the greatest good for a human being is this, to talk every day about virtue* and the other things about which you hear me conversing and examining myself and others, and that the unexamined life is not worth living for a human being—still less would I persuade you by saying these things. And yet they are so, just as I say, men, although to persuade of them is not easy" (*Apology*, 38a, italics added; author's translation). The greatest good for a human being is to *talk* about virtue every day, not, evidently, to practice it as opposed to just talking about it. By "the examined life" Socrates means a life spent in examining.

ning to practicing it. Practically speaking, the search replaces the object sought. Philosophy is not, as Socrates' protreptic seems to suggest, a means to specifying the virtuous life: it takes the place of that life.

In other words, justice never keeps its promise to the ordinary justice-loving man. It had offered relief for the city from the quarrels and other evils ascribed to injustice (407c–d). Justice is allegedly concord or agreement in the city, yet the nature of the agreement has remained elusive. While exhorting to the scrutiny of those common opinions that support such agreement as does unite citizens, philosophy proves unable to replace them. It fosters not harmony but a new kind of discord—between itself and the city.

That justice should prove to be an aspect of the discussion of justice may vindicate the justice of Socrates. It would suggest, however, a surprising answer to the question that Cleitophon first put to the companions (408d–e). Yes, justice may be studied—and yes, it does resemble a perpetual chain letter of exhorting. Given that Cleitophon, like the city, craves above all a clear *answer* to the problem of justice, we should not be surprised to find him impressed with the specious clarity of Thrasymachos. The seeming futility of the quest for justice rooted in nature has prepared him for the conclusion that it is merely convention.

THEAGES
[or, On Wisdom]

Translated by THOMAS L. PANGLE

Demodocus, Socrates, Theages

121a   DEMODOCUS:[1] Socrates, I have been needing to talk to you in private about some matters, if you have leisure, and even if you don't and your business is not very important, make some time for my sake.

SOCRATES: Why, I happen to be at leisure in any case and indeed for your sake very much so: if you wish to speak about something, you may.

DEM.: Then would you like to go over here out of the way, into the portico of Zeus the Liberator?[2]

SOC.: If you like.

b   DEM.: Come, let's go.

Socrates, all the things that grow very likely follow the same course—both the things that grow from the earth and the animals, man as well as the others. And as regards the plants, it is very easy for us who farm the earth to make all the preparations that precede the planting and to do the planting itself, but when what has been planted

c   takes on life, then a great, difficult, and vexatious tending begins. And it seems likely that the same holds concerning human beings

---

[1]This Demodocus may be the general mentioned by Thucydides (IV 75). He and Theages are mentioned in the *Apology of Socrates* (33e), where Theages is said to be deceased. Theages is mentioned prominently in the *Republic* (496b–c). The *Demodocus* is a dialogue listed among the noncanonical "Platonic works" (see the Editor's Introduction).

[2]This was built in worship of Zeus as the patron of Greek liberty, especially from the Persians.

(from my own business I draw inferences about the rest). For as regards this son of mine here, the planting, or the child begetting—whichever one ought to call it—was the easiest of all things, but the upbringing has been vexatious and has made me anxious, with constant fear concerning him. There are many other things that might be mentioned, but the desire that is now present in him is for me a great source of fear—for it's not ignoble, but it is risky—since here he is

d   before us, Socrates, desiring, as he declares, "to become wise." In my opinion, certain of those who are of his own age and deme,[3] having gone down into the city, get him worked up by recounting certain discussions; these he envies, and he has for a long while been giving me trouble, demanding that I look after him and pay money to one of the sophists,[4] whichever one will make him wise. For me the money

122a is not such a concern, but I do consider that he's entering into no small danger where he's heading. Now, for a while I held him back with placating talk, but since I can't any longer, I consider it best to give in to him, lest perchance he be corrupted by frequenting someone when I'm not there. So now I've come for this very purpose: to place this boy with one of those who are reputed to be "sophists." You have therefore showed up at a fine moment for us—you whom I would especially like to take counsel with when I am actually going to do something about such matters. So if you have some counsel to

b   give about what you've heard from me, you may, and ought, to give it.

soc.: Well, Demodocus, it is said, certainly, that counsel is a sacred thing. If indeed it is ever sacred, it would be in this case, concerning the matter on which you are taking counsel. For a human being could not take counsel about anything more divine than about education, both for himself and for those who belong to him. First, though, let's you and I come to an agreement as to whatever this may be about

c   which we are taking counsel. Otherwise, if I should take it to be one thing, and you another, then after we've been together for a while we will perceive ourselves as laughable—I the one giving counsel and you the one being counseled—because nothing of what we're considering is the same.

dem.: Why, what you say seems to me correct, Socrates, and that's the procedure that ought to be followed.

---

[3]One of the traditional rural districts of Athens.
[4]The word comes from the word for wisdom (*sophia*).

soc.: I am indeed saying what's correct, though not entirely. I change it slightly. For it occurs to me that this youth may desire not this

d thing that we suppose him to desire but something else, and then again we would be even more absurd—taking counsel about something else. What seems most correct to me, therefore, is to begin with this youth himself, thoroughly inquiring into just what it is he desires.

DEM.: Most likely it's best to proceed in the way you say.

soc.: Tell me, then, what is the noble name of the youth? How shall we address him?

DEM.: His name is Theages, Socrates.

soc.: Noble indeed, Demodocus, is the name you've bestowed on

e your son—and benefitting what is sacred.[5] Tell us, Theages, do you affirm that you desire to become wise, and are you asking your father here to search out the company of some man such as will make you wise?

THEAGES: Yes.

soc.: Which do you call "Wise": the ones who know, concerning the matter (whatever it may be) about which they are knowers, or the ones who don't?

THE.: The ones who are knowers, I say.

soc.: What then? Didn't your father teach and educate you in the things in which the other sons of gentlemanly fathers here are educated—such as letters, cithara playing, wrestling, and the other kinds of contest?

THE.: Yes, he has.

123a soc.: Do you still suppose, then, that you are lacking in some knowledge which it is fitting that your father look to on your behalf?

THE.: I do.

soc.: What is this? Tell us, so that we may gratify you.

THE.: *He* knows, Socrates; because I've often told him. But he says these things to you on purpose, as if he didn't know what I desire. With other talk of this kind he battles against me and isn't willing to place me with anyone!

b soc.: But the things you said to him before were said, as it were, without witnesses; now, however, make me your witness, and in my

---

[5]The name Theages (from *theos* and *age*) would seem to mean either "revering god" or "envying god."

presence declare what this wisdom is that you desire. Come now, if you were desiring the wisdom by which human beings pilot ships, and I happened to ask you: "Theages, what wisdom do you lack, that you blame your father because he isn't willing to place you with those by whom you could become wise?" What would you answer me? What would it be? Wouldn't it be the piloting art?

THE.: Yes.

c   SOC.: And if you were desiring to be wise in the wisdom by which they pilot chariots, and in that case blamed your father, and again I asked what this wisdom was, what would you answer that it was? Wouldn't it be the charioteer's art?

THE.: Yes.

SOC.: And that which you now happen to be desiring: is it something nameless, or does it have a name?

THE.: I for one suppose it does have.

SOC.: Then do you know of it but not the name or also the name?

THE.: Also the name.

SOC.: So what is it? Speak!

d   THE.: What else, Socrates, would anyone declare its name to be other than wisdom?

SOC.: Isn't the charioteer's art also wisdom? Or does it seem to you to be ignorance?

THE.: Not to me.

SOC.: But wisdom?

THE.: Yes.

SOC.: Which we use for what? Isn't it that by which we have knowledge of how to rule a team of horses?

THE.: Yes.

SOC.: Isn't the piloting art wisdom?

THE.: It seems so to me.

SOC.: Isn't this that by which we have knowledge of how to rule ships?

THE.: That is indeed what it is.

e   SOC.: And what is the wisdom which you desire? That by which we have knowledge of how to rule what?

THE.: Human beings, it seems to me.

SOC.: The sick?

THE.: No indeed!

SOC.: Because that is the medical art, isn't it?

THE.: Yes.

SOC.: Then is it that by which we have knowledge of how to rule the singers in choruses?

THE.: No.

SOC.: Because that is the musical art?

THE.: Of course.

SOC.: Then is it that by which we have knowledge of how to rule those who are exercising?

THE.: No.

SOC.: Because that is the gymnastic art?

THE.: Yes.

SOC.: Then of those who are doing what? Make a spirited endeavor to say, along the lines of what I've said to you in what's preceded.

124a THE.: Those in the city, it seems to me.

SOC.: Aren't the sick also in the city?

THE.: Yes, but I'm speaking not only of them but also of the rest in the city.

SOC.: Now, then, do I understand which art you're speaking of? For you seem to me to be speaking not of that by which we have knowledge of how to rule reapers and harvesters and planters and sowers and threshers, because that's the farming art, by which we rule these, isn't it?

THE.: Yes.

b SOC.: Nor, I suppose at least, that by which we have knowledge of how to rule sawyers and borers and planers and turners, all taken together—you're not speaking of that, because isn't that the art of carpentry?

THE.: Yes.

SOC.: But perhaps that by which we have knowledge of how to rule all these, as well as the farmers, and the carpenters, and all the public craftsmen, and the private noncraftsmen, both women and men— this perhaps is the wisdom of which you're speaking.

THE.: This Socrates, is what for a long time I've wanted to say.

c SOC.: Can you say, then, whether Aegisthus, who killed Agamemnon in Argos,[6] ruled over these of whom you speak—over the public

---

[6]For the legend of Aegisthus' murder of the legitimate king Agamemnon and usurpation of the throne, see the *Electra* plays of Euripides and Sophocles and Aeschylus' *Oresteia*.

craftsmen and the private noncraftsmen, both men and women, all together, or was it over certain others?

THE.: No, it was over these.

SOC.: What then? Didn't Peleus[7] the son of Aeacus rule over these same, in Phthia?

THE.: Yes.

SOC.: Have you already heard of how Periander[8] the son of Cypselus ruled in Corinth?

THE.: I have.

SOC.: Didn't he rule over these same people in his city?

d   THE.: Yes.

SOC.: What then? Don't you consider that Archelaus[9] the son of Perdiccas, who recently ruled in Macedonia, ruled over the same?

THE.: I do.

SOC.: And over whom do you suppose Hippias,[10] the son of Peisistratus, ruled when he ruled in this city? Wasn't it over these?

THE.: How could it be otherwise?

SOC.: Then would you tell me what appellation Bacis and Sibyl, and our countryman Amphilytus, have?

THE.: What else, Socrates, except soothsayers?

e   SOC.: What you say is correct. But try to answer in the same way as regards the following: what appellation do Hippias and Periander have on account of their identical rule?

THE.: I suppose, tyrants; what else?

SOC.: Then does he who desires to rule over all the human beings in the city desire the same rule as these—the tyrannical and to be a tyrant?

THE.: So it appears.

SOC.: Isn't this what you affirm you desire?

THE.: That's likely, at least, from the things I've said.

SOC.: Scoundrel! Out of a desire to tyrannize over us, you have been
25a   blaming your father all this while because he wouldn't send you to

---

[7]After committing fratricide, Peleus (later the father of Achilles) fled from Aegina to Phthia, where he married the king's daughter and was given a third of the kingdom.

[8]An effective but stern tyrant often counted as one of the seven sages.

[9]A bastard who usurped the throne through a series of crimes but who then ruled quite effectively: cf. *Gorgias* 470d.

[10]See the *Hipparchus* and the first note there.

some school for tyrants? And you, Demodocus, aren't you ashamed that, while knowing for a long time what this youth desires, and having a place where you could send him to make him a public craftsmen in the wisdom which he desires, you begrudge it to him and are unwilling to send him? But now—do you see?—since he has accused you in my presence, shall we in common, I and you, deliberate about whom we should send him to and by means of whose company he might become a wise tyrant?

b   DEM.: Yes, by Zeus, Socrates! Let's deliberate indeed, since to me it certainly seems that this matter requires no ordinary deliberation!

SOC.: Take it easy, good fellow. Let's first make our thorough inquiry of him in an adequate way.

DEM.: Go ahead and make the inquiry.

SOC.: What, then, if we invoke Euripides, Theages? For Euripides declares somewhere:[11]

> Tyrants are wise through keeping company with the wise.

Now suppose someone were to ask Euripides: "Euripides, through
c keeping company with the wise in *what,* do you declare that tyrants are wise?" Just as, if he said:

> Farmers are wise through keeping company with the wise,

and we asked, "the wise in *what?*"—what would be his answer to us? would it be anything other than "in the things of the art of farming?"

THE.: No, this would be it.

SOC.: What then? If he said:

> Cooks are wise through keeping company with the wise,

and we asked, "the wise in *what?*"—what would be his answer to us? Wouldn't it be, "in what belongs to cooks?"

THE.: Yes.

SOC.: And what, if:

----

[11]Here and in the *Republic* (568a), Socrates attributes this line to Euripides, following Aristophanes in the *Thesmophoriazusae* (21). But the scholiast on the latter passage, and several other ancient references, indicate that in fact the line comes from Sophocles' lost play, *Ajax of Locrus.*

Wrestlers are wise through keeping company with the wise,

were what he said, and we asked, "the wise in *what?*"—wouldn't he declare, in what belongs to wrestling?"

d THE.: Yes.

SOC.: But since he said:

Tyrants are wise through keeping company with the wise,

and we are asking, "the wise in *what,* are you speaking of Euripides?"—what would he say? What sort of things would he say these are?

THE.: But by Zeus, I don't know!

SOC.: Well, do you want me to tell you?

THE.: If you want to.

SOC.: These are the things Anacreon declared that Callicritē[12] knew. Or don't you know the song?

THE.: I do.

SOC.: What then? Do you too desire company of such a sort with
e some man who happens to have the same art as Callicritē the daughter of Cyanē and who "knows the things of the tyrannic art" as the poet declares she did—so that you too may become tyrant over us and the city?

THE.: For a long time, Socrates, you have been mocking and joking with me!

SOC.: What? Didn't you assert that you desire this wisdom, by which you might rule over all the citizens? If you did thus, would you be anything other than tyrant?

THE.: For my part I would pray, I suppose, to become tyrant—
126a preferably over all human beings and, if not, over as many as possible, and so would you, I suppose, and all other human beings—or, moreover, probably rather to become a god. But this is not what I said I desire.

SOC.: But whatever is it that you do desire? Didn't you assert that you desire to rule over the citizens?

12 The ode is lost. Callicritē and her mother, Cyanē, helped rule part of Lipara in the Aeolus Islands off Sicily (cf. Diodorus Siculus V 7). Anacreon was a famous poet who consorted with several different tyrants (see *Hipparchus,* n. 10).

THE.: Not by violence, or as the tyrants do, but over those who are willing, in the manner of the other men in the city who are in good repute.

SOC.: Do you mean, then, in the manner of Themistocles, and Pericles, and Cimon[13] and whoever has become wonderously adept in the things that pertain to the art of politics?

THE.: By Zeus, these are the ones I mean!

b SOC.: What then? If you happened to desire to become wise in the things that pertain to the art of horsemanship, to which persons would you suppose you would have to go to become a wonderously adept horseman? Would it be any others except those versed in the art of horsemanship?

THE.: By Zeus, no, I say!

SOC.: But, again, it would be those who are wonderously adept in these things, who own horses, and who use them all the time—both their own and many belongings to others?

THE.: Obviously.

SOC.: Then, if you wanted to become wise in the things that pertain to the art of javelin throwing, wouldn't you suppose that you would be wise by going to those versed in the art of javelin throwing—those to

c whom javelins belong and who use javelins all the time, both many belonging to others and their own?

THE.: So it seems to me at least.

SOC.: So tell me: since, indeed, you wish to become wise in the things that pertain to the art of politics, do you suppose that you will be wise by arriving at any other men except those versed in the art of politics—these very men who are wondrously adept in the things that pertain to the art of politics and who all the time use their own city and many others, carrying on business with both Greek and barbarian cities? Or is it your opinion that you will be wise, in these matters which these men practice, by having intercourse with certain others rather than with these men themselves?

d THE.: Well, I have heard, Socrates, the arguments they assert you present, to the effect that the sons of these men versed in the political art are in no way better than the sons of shoemakers,[14] and it is my opinion that what you say is very true, from the things I am able to

[13]Famous Athenian statesmen who all contributed to the growth of the Athenian empire: cf. *Gorgias* 503c, 515d–19a.

[14]Cf. *Meno* 93cff., *Protagoras* 319eff., *Alcibiades* 118d–e.

perceive. So I would be mindless if I were to suppose that one of these men would hand over his wisdom to *me* but benefit his own son not at all—if he were able to bestow any benefit, regarding these matters, on any human being.

soc.: How then, best of men, would you comport yourself, supposing you had a son and he were to give you trouble along such lines, e declaring that he desired to become a good painter and blaming you the father because you were unwilling to spend the money on him for these things—and yet holding in disesteem the public craftsmen of this very thing, the painters, and not wishing to study with them? Or treating in the same fashion the aulists while wishing to become an aulist? Or the citharists? Would you have an idea what to do with him and where else to send him, since he was unwilling to study with these?

the.: By Zeus, not I!

27a soc.: Now, then, when you yourself are doing these same things to your father, are you amazed, and do you blame him, if he is at a loss as to what to do and where to send you? For we will place you with whomever you might wish of the gentlemen—Athenian at least—versed in the things that pertain to the political art, who will keep company with you gratis. On the one hand, you won't spend any money and, on the other, you will get a much better reputation among the mass of human beings than if you kept company with someone else.

the.: Look here, Socrates: aren't you one of the gentlemen? Because if *you* would be willing to keep company with me, that will suffice and I will seek no one else.

b soc.: What's this you're saying, Theages?

dem.: Oh, Socrates, what he says isn't bad, and at the same time it would gratify me; for there's nothing I would consider a greater godsend than if this boy were satisfied with your company and you were willing to keep company with this boy. Indeed, I am even ashamed to say how intensely I wish it! But I beseech both of you—you to be willing to keep company with this boy and you not to seek c to have intercourse with anyone else except Socrates. And you will relieve me of many fearful thoughts. For now I am very fearful on his account, lest he fall in with someone else such as will corrupt this youth.

the.: Fear no more now, father, on my account, if indeed you are able to persuade this man to accept my company!

DEM.: You speak very nobly. Socrates, the discourse that comes next at this point would be addressed to you. For I am ready to put at your disposal (not to be long-winded) both myself and whatever I have

d that is most my own—for whatever you might need, in brief—if you welcome this Theages here and do him good in whatever way you can.

SOC.: Demodocus, that you are so earnest does not make me wonder, if you really supposed that I especially would benefit this boy of yours (for I don't know what someone of intelligence might be more earnest about than that his son be the best possible), but where you came by this opinion that I especially, rather than yourself, would be able to benefit your son with a view to his becoming a good citizen and where this youth came by the supposition that I rather than you

e might benefit him—this very much makes me wonder. For in the first place, you are older than I, and then, you have now ruled in many great offices for the Athenians and are held in high esteem by the Anagyrasian demesmen and no less by the rest of the city, while neither of you sees in me any of these things. Moreover, if Theages here looks down on the company of men versed in the art of politics and seeks certain others who proclaim themselves capable of educating young persons, there are here Prodicus of Ceos, and Gorgias of

128a Leontini, and Polus of Agrigentum,[15] and many others, who are so wise that they go into the cities and persuade the most well born and richest among the young—who may keep company with any of the citizens they wish, for nothing—to leave the company of those others and to keep company with themselves and to lay down in addition a great deal of money as a fee while feeling gratitude. It would be reasonable for your son and you yourself to choose some of these, but

b to choose me is not reasonable. For I know none of these blessed and noble subjects of knowledge—I wish I did. Rather I always say, surely, that I happen to know so to speak nothing, except a certain small subject of knowledge: what pertains to erotic love. As regards this subject of knowledge, to be sure, I rank myself as wonderously clever beyond anyone, whether human beings of the past or of the present.

THE.: Do you see, father? Socrates is still not at all, in my opinion,

c willing to spend some time with me! Since for my part, I am ready if he were willing—but he says these things to us in jest. Because I

[15]For Prodicus, see esp. *Protagoras;* for Gorgias and Polus, see *Gorgias.*

know boys of my age and a little older who before they kept company with him were of no account but since they started to frequent this man in a very brief time became manifestly superior to all those to whom they were previously inferior.

soc.: Do you know, then, what sort of thing this is, child of Demodocus?

the.: I do, by Zeus: that if you wish, I too shall become like those.

d   soc.: No, good fellow, but it has escaped your notice what sort of thing this is. I shall explain to you. For there is something demonic which, by divine dispensation, has followed upon me beginning from childhood. This is a voice which, when it comes, always signals me to turn away from what I am going to do but never urges on, and if one of my friends consults with me, and the voice comes, it's the same—it turns away, and will not allow, the action. And to these things I will furnish you witnesses.

e   Now you know this Charmides[16] who has become so beautiful, the son of Glaucon: he once happened to impart to me that he was going to train to race for the Nemean games, and immediately when he began to say that he was going to train, the voice came; I opposed him and said, "As you were speaking the voice came to me, that of the demonic thing: just don't train."—"Probably," he said, "it signals to you that I shall not win; but even if I am not going to win, if I exercise during this time, I shall be benefited." So saying, he trained;

129a   now it's worth hearing from him the things that befell him on account of this training.

And if you wish, ask the brother of Timarchus,[17] Cleitomachus, what Timarchus said to him on his way to his death, contrary to the demonic thing,[18] together with Euathlos, the racer, who harbored Timarchus as a fugitive; for he told us that his brother told him these things.

the.: What?

soc.: "Cleitomachus," he said, "I am now going to my death because I wasn't willing to heed Socrates." Now why, then, did Tim-

b   archus ever say this? I'll explain. When Timarchus got up from the

[16]See *Charmides*.

[17]These men, and their story, are otherwise unknown (though on the name Heroskamandrus see Paul Friedländer, *Plato*, 3 vols. [Princeton, 1958–70], 2:153).

[18]The text may be corrupt here: "the demonic thing" may be a mistaken insertion, in which case the word translated "contrary to" (*euthu*) would mean "straight" (to his death).

banquet together with Philemon, the son of Philemonides, to kill Nicias, the son of Heroskamandrus, the two of them alone knew the plot, but Timarchus as he got up said to me, "What do you say, Socrates? You people go on drinking, but I need to get up and go somewhere; I'll be back a little later, if I'm lucky." And the voice came to me, and I said to him, "No, don't," I said, "get up; for the

c   accustomed demonic sign has come to me." And he held back. And after some time passed he again had the impulse to go and said, "I am going, Socrates." Again the voice came. Again therefore I compelled him to hold back. The third time, wishing to escape my notice, he got up without saying anything more to me and did escape my notice, by watching until I had my attention elsewhere. Thus he went off and executed the deed on account of which he was on his way to his death. Which is why he said to his brother what I am now telling you—that he was going to his death on account of not heeding me.

d   Moreover, concerning the numbers who were in Sicily,[19] you will hear from many the things I said about the destruction of the expedition.

And as regards things that are past, it is possible to hear from those who know; but it is also possible to make trial now of the sign, to see if it does say anything. For when the beautiful Sannion went out on campaign the sign came to me, and he is now on an expedition with Thrasyllus against Ephesus and Ionia.[20] I therefore suppose he will either die or undergo something similar to this, at any rate, and I am in great fear for the sake of the rest of the army.

e   I have told you all these things because this power of this demonic thing is also all-powerful when it comes to the intercourse of those who spend time with me. For it opposes many, and it is impossible for these to be benefited by spending time with me, so that I can't spend time with them. There are many, again, whose intercourse it doesn't prevent, but who are in no way benefited by the intercourse. But those whose intercourse the power of the demonic thing contributes to are the ones you have noticed: because they immediately make

130a rapid progress. And again, of those who progress, some retain the benefit in a firm and lasting way, but many, for as long a time as they spend with me, make amazing progress, but when they go away

---

[19]The great disaster described in Books VI and VII of Thucydides.

[20]This expedition occurred in 409 B.C. (thus furnishing a very precise date for the setting of the dialogue) and led to an Athenian defeat at Ephesus (Xenophon *Hellenica* I ii 6–10; Plutarch *Alcibiades* 29).

from me, are once again no different from anyone. It is this that Aristides, the son of Lysimachus, the son of Aristides, once experienced.[21] For by spending time with me he made enormous progress in a short time; then there was a certain military expedition and he sailed away. He returned to find Thucydides, the son of Melesius, the
b son of Thucydides, spending time with me. Now Thucydides, the day before, had quarreled with me. So when Aristides saw me, after having given a greeting and discussed other matters, he said: "But I hear that Thucydides, Socrates, bears himself in a solemn manner toward you and complains, as if he were somebody."—"That indeed," I said, "is the way things stand."—"What? Doesn't he know'" he said, "what sort of a slave he was, before he was in your company?"—"It seems not," I said, "by the gods!"—"But I too,"
c he said, "am laughable, Socrates."—"Why exactly?" I said.—"Because," he said, "before I sailed away I was able to converse with any person whatsoever and appear inferior to none in arguments, so that I sought out the intercourse of the most refined; but now, on the contrary, I flee anyone whom I perceive to be educated, so ashamed am I of my vulgarity."—"Well," I said, "did this power leave you all
d at once, or little by little?"—"Little by little," he said.—"And when it came to you," I said, "did it come when you learned something from me, or in some other way?"—"I'll tell you," he said, "Socrates, something that is—by the gods!—incredible but true. For I never learned anything from you, as you yourself know; but I made progress when I was together with you even if I was only in the same house and not in the same room: more when in the same room and, it seemed to me, much more when I was in the same room and looked
e at you when you were talking as opposed to when I looked elsewhere—and I progressed especially much, and most, when I sat beside you, holding and touching you. But now," he said, "all that condition has melted away." Therefore, Theages, such is our intercourse: if it should be dear to the god, you will make very great and rapid progress, but if not, not so. Consider then, whether it would not be safer for you to be educated by one of those who are themselves in charge of the benefit by which they benefit human beings rather than, with me, to act according to what turns out by chance.
131a THE.: To me, Socrates, it seems that we should do thus: make trial of this demonic thing by keeping company with one another, and if it

[21]For the personages in this story, see *Laches,* and *Theaetetus* 151a.

permits us, this will be best. But if not, then at that time we shall immediately deliberate on what we ought to do—whether we shall keep company with someone else, or whether we will try to placate the divine thing that comes to you, with prayers, and sacrifices, and in whatever other way the diviners prescribe.

DEM.: Don't oppose the lad any longer in these matters, Socrates; for what Theages says is well spoken.

SOC.: But if it seems that that's the way it has to be done, then that's the way we'll do.

On the *Theages*

THOMAS L. PANGLE

As the subtitle suggests and as is confirmed by even a cursory reading, the theme of the *Theages* is wisdom.[1] This dialogue thus stands with the four other dialogues that treat thematically the cardinal virtues (*Republic, Charmides, Laches,* and *Euthyphro*). It would be surprising if Plato did not regard wisdom as the crown of the virtues; yet contrary to what one then expects, the discussion portrayed in the

"On the *Theages*" originally appeared in a slightly different version as "Socrates on the Problem of Political Science Education" in *Political Theory* 13:1 (February 1985):112–37, copyright © 1985 by Sage Publications, Inc. It is reprinted by permission of Sage Publications, Inc.

[1] The authenticity of the *Theages,* as a work of Plato, was never questioned—as far as we know—in antiquity (cf. Joseph Souilhé, *Platon: Dialogues suspects* [Paris, 1930], p. 137). Moreover, as John Rist has remarked, "later writers too were equally convinced of its authenticity" ("Plotinus and the *Daimonion* of Socrates," *Phoenix* 17 [1963]:20–21: Rist himself rejects the dialogue as inauthentic, however). I believe it is fair to say that the strictly philological doubts have never been the strongest or even the principal grounds for the excision of this dialogue: as Souilhé says, "Le style est bien attique et imite assez heureusement celui de Platon" (*Platon,* p. 141). Besides, these strictly philological suspicions, such as they are, seem to have been answered by Paul Friedländer (*Plato,* 3 vols. [Princeton, 1958–70], 2:326–29; see also the appendix of Seth Benardete's unpublished master's thesis, "The Daimonion of Socrates: A Study of Plato's Theages," University of Chicago, 1953). For the most part, the dialogue's genuineness has been questioned on the basis of claims that its substance cannot be understood in a way that makes it cohere with the rest of Plato's works. See especially, as the fountainhead of these objections, *Friedrich Schleiermacher's Introductions to the Dialogues of Plato,* trans. William Dobson (Cambridge, 1836), pp. 321–25. The interpretation that follows is meant to respond to these doubts by demonstrating how the *Theages,* properly read, not only fits together with, but throws indispensable new light on, the portrait of the Socratic way of life provided by the other Platonic dialogues (above all the *Gorgias, Theaetetus, Symposium, Republic, Laches,* and *Laws*).

Theages seems considerably less weighty than the conversations depicted in the other dialogues just mentioned. If we do not seek to elude this disappointment induced initially by the *Theages,* if instead we confront it squarely, we are spurred to begin to think why Plato might have decided to give wisdom such short shrift.

Let us begin from the observation that wisdom is the only cardinal virtue whose name is regularly used as a term of blame. We do not speak pejoratively of the courageous, the moderate, or the just except perhaps in jest, but we do speak with blame of "wise guys" (as did the ancient Greeks, in their use of the term *sophos*). Part at least of what underlies this usage is our awareness of a difficulty peculiar to the excellence of wisdom. Knowledge and intelligence, which lie at the heart of wisdom, can all too easily tempt men to try to escape from the constraints of conventional fair play. Indeed, some degree of emancipation from ordinary restraints seems intrinsic to wisdom, since wisdom reasonably claims the role of guide and leader in life. To suppose that one is wise, or to seek to become wise, is to move toward a condition of independence from, if not superiority over, others who are less wise. The traditional response that seeks to limit this tendency is an insistence on the radical limitations of human knowledge. True wisdom, the wisdom of the Seven Sages, for example, is then knowledge of our limits as human beings. It is knowledge of our dependence on divine guidance or assistance (Diogenes Laertius I 28–29, 82–83). The Bible (to look in another quarter) praises wisdom above all other virtues—but draws a sharp distinction between full, divine wisdom and the wisdom available to man, the "beginning" of which is "fear of the Lord" (Proverbs 9:10). Plato's Socrates shows considerable agreement with this kind of thinking when he says that the "god" teaches through him that "human wisdom is worth little or nothing" (*Apology of Socrates* 23a).

Yet Socrates makes this pious pronouncement when on trial for his life on the charge of impiety and corrupting the young. Near the beginning of his defense speech he stresses that the official charges and accusers are less terrible than a much older set of accusers who have for a long time been "slandering" him. These slanders are to the effect that "there is a certain Socrates, a wise man [wise guy], a thinker about the things aloft, who investigates all the things under the earth and makes the weaker argument stronger"; those who hear this "consider that those who investigate these matters do not believe in gods" (*Apol. Soc.* 18b–c). More generally, Socrates goes on to show, these slanders associate Socrates not only with natural scientists like Anaxagoras—who claims that the sun and moon, worshiped by Greeks and other peoples as gods, are mere stone and earth—but also with those remarkable teachers, such as Gorgias, Prodicus, and Hippias, who are known as the "wise ones" or "sophists" (19c–e, 26d). The sophists claimed to teach for money the skills that assured political success. These men were widely suspected of taking over the insights into nature that had been provided by natural philosophers and of using such insights to liberate their students from the conventional beliefs that restrained the use of tricky rhetoric and of other unscrupulous tactics in politics.

Socrates indicates that among the "first accusers" who directed slanders against him one stands out by virtue of his fame and influence: the comic poet Aristophanes (18d, 19c). If we turn to the *Clouds,* we gain a more vivid and detailed impression of just what "wisdom" Socrates claims to have been tarred with. Only then do we begin to comprehend fully the extraordinary touchiness of the issue of "wisdom"—and thus the delicate context within which the *Theages* was written.[2] The foreground hilarity of the *Clouds* and its comic caricature lead into a deep, complex, and serious critique of the Socratic way of life. I can offer only a reminder here of some of the chief elements of that critique that are most relevant to an understanding of the *Theages* and its major theme.

In Aristophanes' eyes, the scientific or philosophic enterprise is necessarily corrosive of the attachments that are the bulwark of a healthy republic. Socrates' questions and discoveries debunk religious faith and with it the sacredness of both familial and civic bonds. Moreover, Socrates brings into the open the lack of pleasure or reward, and hence the irrationality, of manliness—of the spirited willingness to dedicate, or even sacrifice, oneself to public service for the sake of nobility or duty. Yet Aristophanes does not accuse Socrates of being an ordinary sophist (of the type, say, of a Prodicus, who is also mentioned in the play, and contrasted with Socrates); he portrays Socrates as an unerotic, impoverished ascetic and contrasts him sharply with the erotic, feisty, and hedonistic "Unjust Discourse," who is the representative in the play of vulgar sophistry. Aristophanes insists, however, that Socrates cannot help but supply to such sophistry some of its most powerful ammunition: the Unjust

[2]Cf. John Burnet, *Greek Philosophy: Thales to Plato* (London, 1964), 87–88.

Discourse is associated with, even used by, Socrates. Nor can Socrates keep his poisonous thoughts hidden. Sooner or later, half-corrupted citizens like the farmer Strepsiades seek out Socrates for the sake of the power they sense might be theirs if they or their sons could learn to exploit what the philosopher knows. According to Aristophanes, no safe coexistence is possible between the wisdom of philosophy or science and even the minimum virtue required by a republican society—a society on which the philosopher-scientist, in his humanity, depends. But then, the philosopher-scientist is not truly wise, for he lacks human wisdom or prudence. Only the poet, the comic poet, can be wise or can wisely pursue wisdom. Only the comic poet can question and inquire in such a way as to deepen our understanding without undermining society.

In a sense, the whole of the Platonic corpus can be said to represent a reply to this Aristophanean diagnosis of what Nietzsche was later to call "the Problem of Socrates." But in the *Theages* we find perhaps the most pointed response to the *Clouds* that Plato ever wrote (cf. Benardete, pp. 1–3). This statement does not by any means imply that the work answers all of Aristophanes' criticisms; nevertheless, when read in the light of Plato's other dialogues, the *Theages* makes an essential contribution to our understanding of the Platonic conception of philosophy's role as a source of political education in a republic. The dialogue does so by showing Socrates' relationship to three rival sources of political education: the pious and manly upbringing of a traditional democracy; the new models provided for the youth by an expansionist and more individualistic democracy; and the education or goals supplied by the sophists.

The Opening and the Setting

121a1–
b1 The dialogue opens with Demodocus telling Socrates he needs to speak with him in private if Socrates has leisure—or even if Socrates lacks leisure, and his present business is not too pressing. Demodocus apparently does not know Socrates very well: he is not aware that Socrates is always, so to speak, "at leisure" or has no "business" that would be recognizable as such to Demodocus (cf. Benardete, p. 4). We learn presently that Demodocus is a well-to-do farmer who rarely comes into the city but who nonetheless has taken an active role both

in local affairs and in the city's democratic government (127e). In a dialogue that highlights the significance of the meaning of names (122d–e, 123c), Demodocus' name as well as his situation link him to the *demos* and to the rural *demes* that are the backbone of the traditional, conservative democratic faction celebrated by Aristophanes. At Demodocus' instigation, the conversation takes place in the portico that is one of the most visible memorials to the political freedom Zeus helped these pious old democrats—the Marathon fighters—win from Persian and every other form of tyranny. The *Theages,* we may say, is one of the very few dialogues in which Socrates is portrayed conversing with a statesman or active, mature citizen; and in this case it is with a democratic *politikos* of the old school (cf. Benardete, p. 5).

Demodocus' Problem

21b1– The old democrat's outlook is determined by the fact that his life is
22b1 rooted in the soil and concerned with tending the things that grow (*phuta*) from the earth. He is, as we would say, close to nature (*phusis*). As a result he is oblivious to nature, and, partly as a consequence, the term "nature" is conspicuously absent from this dialogue. For to conceive of *phusis* is to distinguish man from the other beings, while Demodocus' experience has produced in him the conviction that there is no fundamental distinction between the "way" of the human being and the "way" of all the other "things that grow." The goal or fulfillment of human growth is no more problematic than the term or fruition of the crops (contrast *Laws* 765e–766a). This viewpoint has left Demodocus quite unprepared for the difficulties involved in tending his son's growth—a tending that he finds not only "vexatious," like the tending of the crops, but also the source of "the anxiety of constant fear."

The father's most pressing fear is occasioned by his son's "desire to become wise." Demodocus knows that this desire is somehow respectable and reveals something lacking on the farm: though the desire is "risky," it is "not ignoble." Precisely what, then, about the desire, is so frightening? Demodocus does not say specifically and is probably unable to do so, but he believes that in his son's case the desire springs from an "envy" brought into being by the creeping influence of certain "discourses" that are carried out to the country folk by youths who have frequented the city and sophists there, around whom Demodocus scents "corruption." Demodocus considers that he can no longer resist the new urban impulse. A point has been reached in the development of democracy in Athens at which the sons can no longer, like all the other things that grow, be kept on the farm.

The trouble Demodocus finds himself in, with and because of his son (and indirectly because of the dynamic of Athenian democratic society), and his turning to Socrates as a guide to the "sophists," cannot help but remind of the more extreme or ridiculous plight of another rural father who turned to Socrates: Strepsiades. Through his choice of characters and situation, Plato presents in the *Theages* his most direct dramatic reply to the *Clouds*. Plato here seems to portray a situation that comes as close as "realistically" possible (in his eyes) to Aristophanes' extravagant situation and then seems, in effect, to invite the reader to compare the two dramas in order to see just how wrong Aristophanes was about both the circumstances in which Socrates was likely to come into contact with rural fathers and the way he handled such contacts.

According to Plato's drama, the rural father whom Socrates is likely to encounter is not one driven to economic desperation by the development of Athenian society. The Platonic counterpart to Strepsiades does not urge his son to learn from a sophist how to evade the law: he is not himself corrupt, and he does not regard the sophists in anywhere near such a dark light. Moreover, Demodocus, unlike Strepsiades, knows Socrates by name and knows that he is not a sophist. As Plato would have it, Socrates appears to the old farmer-statesman as a trustworthy intermediary between the citizen-farmers and the not altogether reputable, but by no means simply corrupt, sophists.

The Examination of Theages

122b2–   The Platonic Socrates' response to the paterfamilias is a model of
126c9   prudence and seems at first to be a model of piety as well. To prevent their intercourse from being "perceived as laughable"—as fit for comedy à la Aristophanes—Socrates suggests that before proceeding a step they make sure the two of them agree as to the goal of their

deliberation (cf. *Clouds* 221ff.). When Demodocus heartily concurs, Socrates makes a "slight change" in his proposal: to somewhat less eager paternal assent, Socrates brings it about that the youth's own understanding of his "desire" will predominate over the understanding or wishes of the father in determining the goal of deliberation (cf. *Clouds* 1105–13). The Platonic Socrates, it would seem, caters more to the young than does the Aristophanean. But he manages to do so while evincing respect for the old or the fathers.

What then does "Theages" (the "god revering"—or is it the "god-envying"?) understand by "being wise?" Socrates begins to try to find out by asking the youth to make a choice seemingly so obvious that we wonder at first why the question is even asked (122e). On reflection we see that the way Socrates poses the alternatives has the effect of steering the conversation away from the possibility that the wise are the ones who also know that, and what, they do *not* know (cf. *Charmides* 167aff.). In proceeding thus Socrates follows, and lays the foundation for testing, Theages' own outlook. For Theages desires, not to become a "lover of wisdom," but rather to "become wise": to acquire the virtue or excellence of wisdom (cf. St. Augustine *City of God* VIII 2).

Yet since Theages has been educated by his father in the things the sons of gentlemen learn, what scientific knowledge (*epistēmē*) is he lacking, in order to be wise? In response to this question, Theages gives bold, not to say insolent, expression to the antagonism he feels toward his father and the restrictiveness of what is now seen to be "gentlemanly education." (With a view to what will soon follow, we note that Theages here reveals himself to be neither shy nor passionless; it would seem that neither of these characteristics can explain the remarkable dullness of his answers to Socrates' subsequent questions.) Socrates, taking the side of the younger generation, declares that he will serve as the son's witness against the father. In the questions that follow (123b–124b), he tries to lead Theages to articulate what the science is on account of whose absence he blames his father and traditional gentlemanly education. Socrates' very first analogies disclose that he has already divined that Theages wants to know political science—how to "pilot" (*kuberneō*) or "rule." But Socrates apparently wants to find out the extent to which this longing has crystallized in Theages' mind and how well he has thought about or can be stimulated to think about what he wants. The results are very unencouraging; the chief practical, or dramatically significant, lesson this section provides is the demonstration of the severe limitations of Theages' intellectual capacities.[3]

On the way to discovering Theages' capacities and character, Socrates offers a number of examples or analogies that (if we do not fail the test, like Theages) usher us into the Socratic view of the alternative ways political wisdom may be understood—or must be understood if it is to be justified in its claim to embody scientific knowledge (*epistēmē*). Socrates begins by introducing a pair of arts. He first speaks as if the leading member of the pair were the piloting of ships; driving chariots comes second and is at first described as another form of "piloting" (123c2). Now, if we try to follow Socrates' implicit suggestion and think of the political art on the model of piloting a ship, we realize that we are regarding it as an art whose principal task is locating the goal that society seeks and steering the city to that goal over a route that is discernible only to the pilot. Certainly if we follow the Platonic Socrates' use of this analogy in other contexts, we see that the job of imposing discipline on the "ship's company" (the city's inhabitants) is conceived as a subordinate art that is not necessarily practiced by the same man who exercises the higher, pilot's art (*Republic* 488a–89c; *Laws* 961e, 963a and context). But presentation of the pair of analogies with piloting in the lead rings no bells with Theages. It does not help him bring into focus the wisdom he desires (123d1). So Socrates reverses the pair: he brings "ruling" a team of horses to the fore and speaks of piloting as if it were just another form of "ruling." If we bear in mind the fact that in Plato's time chariots were used mainly in racing competition, we recognize that conceiving of the political art on the model of charioteering means conceiving of it as an art in which locating the goal and steering for it is not all that difficult. Everyone knows the track and sees it as well as the finish line clearly; the challenge, the art, lies in disciplining one's team and driving it to victory against competing teams, whether native or foreign (see *Laws* 906e). We observe that both of Socrates' analogies point to the rule of one man, untrammeled by the "rule of law" in his relations with the ruled. The pilot image, however, besides being less coercive and competitive, suggests a greater consciousness of the

---

[3]The *Theages* thus clarifies the meaning of Socrates' ambiguous reference to Theages in the *Republic* (496b–c): Theages is not adduced as an example of someone with a philosophic nature, but rather his illness is an example of one way in which men with philosophic natures might be saved from politics.

weakness of the guiding art and hence a more lively awareness of the need for assistance from other, subordinate arts as well as from the gods (cf. *Laws* 709c).

Only when he stresses the charioteer and his "ruling" does Socrates strike a spark in Theages: prompted by Socrates, Theages says it "seems" to him that he wants to *rule* "human beings" (123e1). The paradigm of ruling horses in a race seems, for the time being at least, to have taken precedence over that of piloting ships at sea.

Socrates does not demur but insists that the condition of the ruled be made more precise. He offers three suggestions, each of which is rejected by Theages; each rejection appears to be confirmed by Socrates. The second, or central, rejected candidate is "music," or the rule "over those singing in the choruses." In both the *Laws* and the *Republic* it is argued that music or the choral art is the art by which the city gives to healthy souls the exercise that perfects them and that music or the choral art is therefore the summit of the political art. Yet at the same time, in both these dialogues a doubt is raised as to whether the knowledge of the soul that the art of music claims to possess—and must possess, if it is to be completed—is available, to statesmen or even to Socratic philosophers (see esp. *Republic* 402b–d and context with *Laws* 963a–end). Here in the present dialogue, the rejection of music, or the relegation of its sphere of "rule" to the subpolitical, would seem to confirm, if not to suggest an explanation for, the defeat of the piloting paradigm. Theages has no serious interest in a political art that culminates in the "music" needed for the soul's health and perhaps sees very little connection between "music" and politics. Given Socrates' limited success in outlining such a "music" in other dialogues, perhaps Theages' standoffish attitude here has greater justification than he could ever realize.

At any rate, "music" is certainly not the first of Socrates' three suggestions as to the "rule" Theages seeks to learn how to wield. The first candidate is the rule over those who are sick. Why is this Socrates' first suggestion? How are we to understand the movement of his thought here? Our wonder is sharpened when, after Theages has made the vague but not wholly unilluminating suggestion of "those in the city" as the subjects of the rule he seeks, Socrates returns to the rejected art of ruling the sick (124a2). Socrates insists on making Theages see that the rule over the city *is,* in part at least, a rule over the sick. But Theages does not want to focus on the sick. Socrates' dogged emphasis on the sick is not sufficiently explained as an allusion to the fact that Theages is himself probably very sickly even at this time and therefore foolish in thinking of a political career (*Republic* 496c). The three arts suggested are those concerned, respectively, with the care of sick bodies (medicine), with the exercise of healthy souls (music), and with the exercise of healthy bodies (gymnastic): missing, plainly, is the art that knows the care of sick souls. According to the *Gorgias* (464b–c, 517cff.), *Republic* (405aff.), and *Laws* (719eff., 857c–e), this is the art of punitive or corrective justice, which in each of the three mentioned dialogues is said to be analogous to the art of medicine. This apparently low but ever-necessary and somehow noble aspect of politics could give some moral substance to the charioteer paradigm and to its implications. As the *Gorgias* shows, the art of corrective justice embraces not only the dealing with crime but also the restraining of an entire people's appetites, hopes, and fears. An example of a statesman who possessed justice so understood is Aristides, in contrast to his imperialist rival Themistocles, and the latter's successors Pericles and Cimon (*Gorgias* 515c–519a, 526a–b). The perfection of such rule requires a ruler who dominates the city as if he were a member of a superhuman species, on the analogy of a man ruling domestic animals (516a–b; cf. *Laws* 713c–e). But just as the medical art would remain incomplete if it only diminished sickness but had no clear conception of the body's healthy exercise or perfection, so politics, if it is to be wisdom, would seem to have to transcend the care of sick souls. This longing is very dimly reflected in Theages' insistence that the desired art rule over more than just sick men.

The most obvious or crude answer to longings of this kind—that is, longings for some purpose in political life beyond law and order—is one suggested by the charioteer image: the city may be disciplined for the sake of winning glorious victories over other cities. But Socrates ceases to permit the charioteering image to predominate; he introduces a new pair of much less coercive analogues, by which he leads up to a third paradigm for political science: the architectonic art.[4] Viewed in this light, the art of ruling is apparently understood to deal mainly, though not exclusively, with those who are not sick; taking over human beings whose souls have already been disciplined,

---

[4] In describing the farming art, Socrates makes no reference to the tending of animals; he keeps his architectonic examples or analogies as far as he can from the charioteer analogy and its implications.

or "cured of illness," by some sort of "driver's" or "herdsman's" art, the ruler transforms many or most into "public craftsmen" (*demiourgoi*) and orchestrates their various expertises into an ordered whole that satisfies the needs of all—"private" persons as well as "public craftsmen." Theages is perfectly satisfied with this suggestion. Yet the obvious unanswered question is: what is the overall good or product with a view to which the orchestration is executed? If political life were to be guided by true political science, would it aim solely at the securing of economic goods (like food and buildings, the objects of the arts mentioned here as analogies)? Or would it have some higher purpose? Can the need for a "piloting art," or a musical gymnastic of the soul, be circumvented? Moreover, if politics, conceived as an architectonic art, does have "higher" goals, which of the two arts mentioned here might politics resemble more: is it like farming, whose "architectonic" thought is aimed at cultivating some organic growth (recall Demodocus' earlier implicit suggestion about the nature of education), or is it more like carpentry, a constructive art (as Aristotle was later to suggest—*Politics* 1332a26–b11; *Ethics* 1152b1–3)—and if so, with a view to what are its constructions made? To the extent that these perplexing questions cannot be answered, it becomes difficult to see what prevents the return to the second and central, charioteering, paradigm (i.e., to something like a Machivaellian conception of political science).

Socrates has now layed out three alternative but not at all mutually exclusive paradigms of what a science of politics might claim to know or of what sorts of questions it might claim to answer. By using images that provoke and require imaginative interpretive thought, he has also allowed his audience to think through for themselves the major difficulties involved in each suggested version of the project of developing a science of politics. At the same time, he has discovered that his primary addressee, Theages, is not a suitable student with whom to pursue such inquiries. He therefore decides to try to shock or shame Theages into abandoning his quest for teachers of political science and to lead the boy back to a more traditional or at least civic perspective on the "art of politics." (Theages' reaction to this attempt of course sheds additional light on his character and especially his moral character.) Abruptly and without preparation, Socrates shifts to an investigation into how those who possessed political science would rule if and when they put their knowledge into action. He thereby opens up the darker implications of the quest for political science, as he has adumbrated it. The practitioners of such a science would be tyrants. Socrates establishes this point through an argument that is very much ad hominem. But at the heart of his tongue-in-cheek assertion there lies a serious point, which was foreshadowed by the fact that in describing political science as the architectonic art Socrates spoke as if political science regarded the inhabitants of the city as either "public craftsmen" or as "private persons, women and men." If the architectonic art were to come into operation, it would leave no room for the public life of "citizens" or "gentlemen." All important tasks would be directed by expert specialists, governed by the expert of experts—the practitioner of political science. A farmer like Demodocus in particular would exercise the farming art—and no more. The rough and tumble of a free democracy such as the Athenian, where the unwise and the wise or semiwise gather periodically to thrash out their affairs in the absence of any architectonic experts, would disappear. Or if it were needed as a kind of exercise of the soul, it would take place within limits prescribed by the art that takes care of souls (psychology), put into practice by the ruling expert, the practitioner of political science (consider here the meaning of "citizenship" in relation to the terms "public craftsman" and "private person" in the *Republic:* 370c, 389b–c, 423d, 428c–d). After all, if there really did exist an architectonic political science, a scientific knowledge about the ends and organization of society, who could reasonably or legitimately oppose its authority? At the center of Socrates' list of historical tyrants is Periander, one of the traditional Seven Wise Men: Socrates thus unobtrusively reminds us that even the most respectable tradition associates the rule of the wise, if and when it exists, with absolute, that is, tyrannical, authority.

Still, the first and last tyrants named—the most exposed and striking parts of the list—have shocking records indeed, and mention of them is calculated to put tyranny in the worst possible light. Moreover, just before Socrates leads Theages to pronounce the word "tyrants," and thereby to make tyranny the explicit theme, he reminds forcibly of the presence of the oracles by which the gods seem to provide decisive guidance to man. Does not absolute political authority, when it is based on a claim to possess scientific knowledge of human affairs, presume to surpass the limits set upon human knowledge and power by the eternal gods? Yet none of this seems to faze Theages, who rather blithely agrees that "it is likely, at least, from the things I have said," that he desires to be a tyrant.

So Socrates suddenly starts reviling the "rogue" Theages for his desire to tyrannize over "us" (i.e., "us free Athenians"). Socrates talks like a manly and pious citizen, outraged by what he has discovered in Theages. He speaks so out of character, and with such exaggerated severity, that he almost sounds like someone acting a role in an Aristophanean comedy. Besides, his reviling is rendered paradoxical or absurd when in the next breath he turns to blaming Demodocus for failing to gratify his son's desire, and then insists that the two older men must now deliberate about whom to send the boy to in order that he may become a "wise tyrant." Socrates' attitude toward the youthful desire for tyrannic authority based on wisdom is ambiguous in the extreme. He treats the desire as if he knew (from personal experience of it?) that it is a demonic force that cannot be resisted, that must be gratified no matter how shocking it seems. Again we see that, even while he tries to alter or discourage Theages, Socrates continues to draw out, for us to see, the full implications of the desire Theages claims to have—but that in fact is present only as a flicker in his soul. Through his passionate and contradictory speech at this point Socrates highlights the fundamental antagonism present in a very pale version in the tension between Demodocus and his son: the antagonism between attachment to the pious and patriotic roots of republicanism and the desire to acquire the wisdom or science of politics. Plato leaves us to guess what side Socrates would have taken in this quarrel if Theages were of a more promising nature; "fortunately" for his wish to rebut Aristophanes, the particular case with which Plato has chosen to deal in his dialogue on wisdom is one in which Socrates is not for too long tempted to take sides with a son against a father.

However puzzled Demodocus may be by Socrates' contradictory outburst, his own excited response (which includes the dialogue's first oath, an oath by Zeus—in whose portico they are standing) shows that what has been uncovered in his son's heart has measurably intensified his anxieties about sending Theages to some teacher of "wisdom." Demodocus' need or dependence on Socrates has accordingly increased almost to the point of desperation. Yet by heightening the father's alarm Socrates has progressed only a short way toward his goal of discouraging father and son from seeking teachers of political science. Socrates therefore moves to a third stage in his examination of Theages, finally approaching a version, at least, of the question he was originally called upon to deliberate over: in whose company can the boy become wise? In this section, which is in a way the most important, at least from a practical point of view (as well as being the most dangerous for Socrates' reputation), Socrates appeals for the first time to higher authority. He invokes the poets and first of all Euripides—the "wise man" who is second only to Socrates as a target of Aristophanes' moral censure (see *Clouds* 1370ff. and *Thesmophoriazusae* as a whole). The bow to poetic authority is nevertheless not as deep as initially appears. Socrates ignores the original context of the line he quotes (that context—if it ever really existed: see the scholiast on line 21 of *Thesmophoriazusae*—is lost to us, and hence our understanding of this section is somewhat hampered). He treats Euripides as a kind of oracle whose gnomic utterance requires a dialectical interpretation, and the interpretation he develops here is rather different from the one suggested for the same line in the *Republic* (568a–b).

In trying to lead Theages through the interpretation, Socrates once again proceeds by way of analogies. The central analogy this time is cooking, which Socrates carefully refrains from treating as an art. Is he trying to lead his audience to wonder whether tyranny or political science, at least as it is *actually* carried on by its *known* practitioners and teachers (e.g., the sophists and their students or models), is only a pseudoart, a knack of gratifying certain people (*Gorgias* 462ff.)?

But the main focus here is on the question of the people with whom one should keep company in order to become wise in tyranny. Whatever "Euripides" may have intended, Socrates interprets him as meaning that tryants become wise *in their business as tyrants* by frequenting other, already wise, knowers of the tyrannic things. Or at any rate, that is the manifest implication of the way Socrates deploys his analogies. Yet Theages fails to follow out the analogies in the obvious way and complete the thought. Instead, he curses by Zeus. He has become highly impatient with Socrates' questions or with his own inability to answer them. (His curse *is* a kind of inadvert answer; for is not Zeus the very model of the tyrannic rule of the wise?) But is his inability to answer this time due solely to his slow wit, or does he glimpse something impossible or unacceptable in saying that "to become a wise tyrant one must keep company with someone who is wise in the tyrannic things"? If we look again at the analogies, we see that they suggest that the one seeking to become wise in an art must *subordinate* himself to the person who already possesses the wisdom. Theages himself has direct experience of this in the third case (cf. 122e11), and above all in the first of the cases mentioned, since he has surely been learning the farming art from his father, whose instructing was combined with complete authority over Theages. Analogously, it would seem that to learn the tyrannic things Theages would have to leave his father's mild supervision and go subjugate himself to some tyrant. Moreover, the poetic tradition suggests that not only the student but also the knower of political science is, qua knower, indistinguishable from a smart woman (125d–e). Manliness has only a coincidental overlap with political science. Theages is sure that Socrates is now mocking him, but he also now recalls—if only vaguely—that there is an incompatibility between the authority and knowledge he longs for and the manly independence he has been brought up to respect. After Socrates introduces (for the first time in the discussion of political science) the notion of rule over *citizens,* Theages therefore insists that it is republican authority, rule on the basis of the consent of free and independent fellow citizens, that he has desired all along.

To be sure, Theages admits that he (like everyone, in his view) would *pray* to become the tyrannical ruler over as many people as possible or, taking this thought a step further, to become god. If he could become a tyrant through prayer, that is, through divine assistance, Theages would circumvent the necessity of having to subordinate himself to a tyrannic human teacher. But would he know how to maintain his rule without political science? And would his rule be manly and independent? It seems that only by becoming a god, a being who transfigures human science and manliness, could he be certain that he could resolve the tension between tyranny, based on science, and manly independence. The concentration of oaths by Zeus in this immediate section (125d7, 126a10, b3) reminds us that Theages discloses his remarkable prayer for tyranny while standing in a place consecrated to Zeus, the patron god of political liberty. The boy is either fatuous or very cavalier in his attitude toward Zeus or both. Nevertheless, we must not be hasty in dismissing his emulation or envy of god as altogether unreasonable. Given the manifest bungling and bad luck that dogs every version of man's rule over man, is it any wonder that men long to share in god's art of rule? Put more generally: can any political tradition, whether grounded in piety or in reason, remain unqualifiedly attached to republicanism, manly independence, or democratic authority? Are not the roots of the desire for authoritarian rule already present in man's longings for either divine or scientific guidance (cf. *Laws* 713aff.)?

But whatever may be revealed by Theages' prayer, Theages draws a sharp distinction between what he prays for and what he desires. He *desires* only what is possible without divine intervention and without sacrificing manly independence. That means (he now realizes) that he desires to become, not a wise tyrant, but someone who resembles the "reputable he-men" (*ellogimoi andres*) of the great democratic (i.e., imperialist) political history of Athens.

Socates has not exactly purified Theages' soul, but he has succeeded in rekindling in the youth's heart the distinction between tyranny and civic glory. Since Theages' models are now Themistocles, Pericles, and Cimon, has Socrates thereby shifted the boy's aim away from the pseudo–political science that is correlative with cooking? Or has he merely shifted it to another, democratically more respectable version of "political cooking" (cf. *Gorgias* 518c–519a)? Socrates tries to make Theages discover for himself—once again by way of suggestive analogies—just what kind of instruction he is seeking when he seeks to learn the sort of thing Athenian statesmen know. This time, Socrates carefully avoids any reference to scientific knowledge. Instead he speaks of those who are "wise" in a new sense: he speaks of men who are "marvelously adept" (*deinos*) at managing things they own and use, or practice with, as their own (e.g., horses and weapons). He thus seems to suggest that the "wisdom" of the great actual statesmen, far from being a matter of science, is a kind of knowledge rooted in practiced familiarity with, and attachment to, their own peoples or countries. Yet at the same time he points to a dark implication or tendency of this nonscientific, democratic, and patriotic or noble approach to political "wisdom." He speaks as though the same men who enjoy using, and learn to use well, their own horses and weapons are also accustomed to using horses and weapons "belonging to others." What he is getting at becomes clearer when he goes on to characterize the statesmen Theages is seeking to imitate as men who "made use" not only of their own city (Athens) but of "many other" cities, Greek as well as barbarian. The patriotic statesman's "marvelous cleverness," grounded as it is in a powerful and discerning love of his own people and its wants or demands, all too easily grows into the imperialism that was the hallmark of the democratic movement inspired and led by

Themistocles, Cimon, and Pericles. In trying to reconcile young
Theages to his city's republican tradition, Socrates has no illusions
about that tradition's justice or its adherence to its originally rural and
gentlemanly or preimperialist roots. Nevertheless, unlike Aristophanes or his "Just Discourse," Socrates makes no effort to arouse nostalgia for either the preimperialistic Athens (represented above all
perhaps by Aristides, the opponent of Themistocles) or its closest
recent equivalent, the anti-Periclean policy (represented especially by
Thucydides the son of Melesias; see n. 6). Compared with the poet,
the philosopher seems less hopeful about, or less able to contribute
to, a revival of even nostalgia for this conservative spirit.

Socrates' Problem

126d1–   Socrates now seems to have led Theages back from a quest for
128c8 teachers of political science to a desire for associating with—well, if
not with traditional gentlemen like his father, then at least with contemporary (imperialist) democratic politicians. But suddenly an unexpected and unwelcome Socratic fly settles on the ointment. Theages reveals that the sophisticated discourses of which he has heard
and by which he has been excited include certain Socratic discourses
that cast grave doubt on the ability of statesmen to teach anything
about the political art to anyone, including their own sons. Socrates,
it transpires, is an indirect source of Theages' rebellion against his
father's tutelage. Theages assumes that the Socratic discourses he has
heard are meant, not to draw into question the existence of political
science, but only to reveal the didactic incapacity of statesmen. But as
Socrates hints by the analogies he uses in his response (painting and
instrumental music), he may just as well have meant to draw attention to the rarity of natural talent among young aspirants to political
science (cf. *Meno* 94a–b; *Protagoras* 320a; and especially *Alcibiades I*
118d–e). By now we know Theages well enough not to be surprised
when he fails to notice the unflattering insinuation. However this
may be, certainly Socrates cannot deny that the discourses quoted are
his, nor does he offer a word in refutation of them. Instead, he tries to
recover the upper hand by pleading with Theages to sympathize with
a father's point of view. Is this one of the very few places in the
Platonic dialogues where Socrates is caught somewhat flat-footed, or
is at least momentarily taken aback, by an unexpected development?

Such a moment would not be inappropriate in a dialogue meant as an antistrophe to the *Clouds*. As a last ploy Socrates adds two further incentives: if Theages frequents native Athenian gentlemen, instead of foreign sophists, they will charge no fee, and (considerably more telling with the youth) he will not risk tarnishing his reputation among the many.

"What then, Socrates? Aren't you, also, one of the gentlemen?" It is hard to determine just how long Theages has entertained the thought of seeking to make Socrates his mentor, but Socrates surely appears to be a plausible compromise between the desires of the son and the now-heightened fears of the father. Demodocus promptly and passionately seconds the proposal. But Socrates with equal vigor opposes it. Socrates did not seek this conversation, and from it he has learned enough about Theages to know that he has no wish to assume responsibility for the boy in any way. These are not, of course, the thoughts to which the urbane Socrates gives voice. He begins by identifying his perspective with that of a good father: he asserts he knows of nothing an intelligent person could be more seriously concerned with than the betterment of his own son. Precisely on this account, he claims to be amazed at the opinion that he could work more benefit than the boy's father, with a view to the boy's becoming a good citizen. (Socrates does not deny, then, that he could benefit the boy in many ways and even with a view to his becoming a good citizen.) And if the boy looks down on time spent with political men, it is reasonable for him and his father to choose, instead of Socrates, one of the "wise men" like Prodicus, Gorgias, or Polus (the last being the praiser of tyranny and in particular of Archelaeus: cf. 124d with *Gorgias* 471a–c). We note that Socrates locates himself slightly nearer to the sophists than to the political men or the good citizens. Socrates would obviously prefer to have the boy remain under the tutelage of his father or some other citizen; but in order to avoid having to spend time with Theages, he is finally ready to introduce the boy to any of the sophists he wishes. This attitude should not shock us; the Platonic Socrates frequently led young men to become students of the sophists (*Theaetetus* 151b; cf. *Laches* 180b–c, 200c–d; and the opening and closing of *Euthydemus*). The sophists may be boasters, insofar as they claim to possess science or wisdom in political matters, but that does not mean they teach nothing of importance pertaining to politics and even virtue (cf. *Meno* 91a–92a). As for their putative undermining of pious democratic traditions, Socrates elsewhere defends them against that charge (*Republic* 492aff.): at the worst, they merely cater to the forces of egalitarianism, egoism, and majoritarianism already poisoning democratic politics. In some cases they may refine and temper those impulses. Perhaps Theages will prove to be such a case, especially if Socrates advises him in his choice of a sophist. At any rate, Socrates has done all he can do or wishes to do to save Theages' soul. Socrates is not an "intellectual," and he does not revere "intellectualism," but neither is he an "anti-intellectual." He differs from both the intellectuals and their enemies, from both the sophists and the traditionalists, in that he is aware, and openly declares, that he does not know the "blessed and noble subjects of knowledge" they claim—each in their different ways—to know. He cannot teach either "good citizenship" (gentlemanliness) or political science (tyranny) because he does not have knowledge of either—though he wishes that he did. As he "always" (cf. *Symposium* 177d) says, he knows scientifically (*epistamenōs*) only a certain small subject (*mathēmaton*), namely, what pertains to erotic love.

To begin to understand this cryptic but obviously important utterance, we need to keep squarely before us the teaching of the *Symposium* to the effect that erotic love is love for that which one needs or lacks. Then we are in a position to appreciate what can be learned by juxtaposing this description, in the *Theages,* of Socrates' limited knowledge or wisdom with Socrates' kindred characterization of his wisdom in the *Apology*. In the *Apology* Socrates says that he learned that "human wisdom," which he has come to realize he possesses, consists in knowing that one does not know what is "good and noble" (*Apol. Soc.* 21d). When we put these two different characterizations of Socratic wisdom together with the teaching of the *Symposium,* we are led to the following reflection. As rational but needy beings, aware, especially, of our mortality and finitude, we humans are prone by nature to become possessed by a consuming passion for completion, or at any rate compensation, achieved through attachment to a good that is noble or beautiful and therefore apparently lasting. Some humans—those whom Diotima calls "erotic"—experience this passion to a much greater degree than others. Once a man of this kind, a man like the Socrates whom Diotima describes, has come to know that he does not have knowledge of a complementary goodness or nobility such as he seeks, once such a man has experienced self-consciously what his ignorance means while refusing to ignore, or compromise with, or hide from the consequences, his original passion necessarily alters. He becomes possessed by a desire to make progress in reducing his ignorance, in remedying his inability to find solutions to his needs and perplexities. Now, if this new or altered thirst were a merely personal experience—if what Socrates at some point became aware of had been only his own ignorance of the truly noble and good or of true gentlemanliness—then there would be no sound reason why the requisite answers should not be secured through closer contact with the regular community authorities. Nothing would prevent Socrates or anyone else from quenching their thirst by consulting and studying with the priests, the poetic and traditional texts, the statesmen, the old city fathers, and (above all) the laws, in order to learn the proper way to behave and the proper beliefs in which to have faith. But as the whole *Apology* makes clear, Socrates' knowledge of ignorance, and consequent thirst, was rooted in a ceaseless public and private examination and refutation (*elenchus*) of the political, technical, and poetic or religious authorities. The conversation in the *Theages* helps us to understand better what might have been the substance of those refutations. For here Socrates lays out what knowledge would be required of anyone who made good his claim truly to *know* the political things, to *know* the common good or justice in the full sense. We thus catch a glimpse of the enormous disproportion that Socrates must have discovered between what the acknowledged authorities actually know and what they ought to know—or would have to know in order to substantiate their claim to be moral and political authorities (cf. Socrates' investigation into law in the *Minos*). By revealing this disproportion, and kindred difficulties, Socrates may be said to justify his life as a philosopher. He thus vindicates his refusal to be guided simply by the established moral authorities; he explains his turn away from ordinary civic duties to a life devoted to an independent (though still socially responsible) quest for true gentlemanliness on the basis of *knowledge* of whatever can be known about the just, the good, and the noble. Of course, the Socratic sort of quest might peter out, or might even prove destructive, if it turned out that no progress were possible. But as has been at least indicated by what has preceded in this dialogue, such is not the case—at least for a man with the natural strength of a Socrates.

It thus transpires that Socratic knowledge of ignorance, rooted at least partly in knowledge of what would constitute a genuine political science, implies a sovereign, rational, or objective "value judgment" about life and the ways of life open to human beings. Socrates knows what is the "best life," or, even more cautiously stated, what is the greatest good, and most defensible life, available to human beings: "It so happens that this is the greatest good for man, each day to make discourses about virtue and the other things about which you have heard me conversing, and examining myself and others; and the unexamined life is not worth living for a human being" (*Apol. Soc.* 38a). Such knowledge does not have the character of an abstract observation made from the outside about the existence of some being named "man" but is rather the expression, from the "inside," of a specific kind of experience. This experience, this eros, as outlined here, Plato presents Socrates as having possessed to a degree unequaled by any other human known to him.

To Theages, however, Socrates' extraordinary, if obscure, declaration of his erotic science is a totally incomprehensible sort of "jesting." It explains and justifies nothing; it does not even provoke questions or thought. It simply conveys Socrates' stubborn and unreasonable refusal to help Theages become a shrewd thinker and clever talker like other boys he knows have been transformed by Socrates' company. Because this is the "bottom line" for Theages: no matter how idiosyncratic Socrates and his knowledge may be, Theages knows from personal observation that Socrates is a very great teacher. Socratic *eros* necessarily includes a procreative love or need for certain other human beings.

The Demonic Power

128d1– Because of the success of his past didactic deeds, and because that
end success is widely known among the young, Socrates' speech attempting to avoid tutorial responsibility has failed. He cannot elude that responsibility, in the present circumstances, by showing that his paltry erotic knowledge, or awareness of ignorance, sets him apart from the other gentlemen and the other sophists—and indeed from *all* other human beings past and present (see *Republic* 496c). At this juncture it would seem that Socrates is confined to one of two disagreeable options: either he must take on responsibility for a headstrong and very unpromising student, or else he must admit—by speech or by silence—his unfavorable opinion of the boy. Whichever

he chooses, he is likely to wind up antagonizing a proud father who is very influential in Athens. But Socrates' rhetorical quiver is not yet empty. Taking a dramatic new tack, he elaborates a different explanation of what sets him apart from all other men, an explanation that takes fully into account his remarkable powers as an educator but absolves him of all responsibility for the effects of his influence. According to the speech with which Plato has his Socrates draw to a close the dialogue on wisdom, the philosopher's success as a teacher was entirely the work of "the god" (129e, 130e6), of whom Socrates was merely the pious vehicle or obedient instrument. In other words, Plato shows that, in the pedagogical sphere of the Socratic philosopher's life, wisdom becomes indistinguishable from piety. Equally important, Plato here shows that Socrates was capable of convincing some of his most unpromising students that their wisdom, such as it was, depended entirely on the favor of the gods. The Platonic Socrates was surely not guilty of irresponsibly teaching young people disbelief in the gods.

Socrates' account of his "divine dispensation" is rich with wonders. It is true that "it should be observed that nothing in this account of his reliance on a spiritual sign fails to agree with what we find recorded of him elsewhere,"[5] but it is also true that Socrates' manner of expression is that of a raconteur whose stories are so tinged with the uncanny as to be downright spooky. To understand why he talks as he does we must bear in mind that the present company is rural and comes from an environment rife with what we might call "superstitious gossip." Theages' response to Socrates speaks volumes. With peasantlike shrewdness, he in effect says, "Let's give it a try, and either we'll meet with the divine thing's approval or, if not, Dad and I will start bargaining with it, following the advice of the Diviners." Whereas the talk of erotic knowledge was unintelligible to him, the talk of the uncanny "divine thing" makes perfect sense to Theages and is convincing: Socrates' closing speech "talks the language" of his interlocuters and therefore succeeds in having the intended effects.

Socrates begins by speaking very briefly about how the demonic thing intervenes in his own affairs: since childhood, there has been a "voice" that, when it comes, always "signals" him to turn away from some action but never urges him on toward anything. He then

[5]W. R. M. Lamb, "Introduction to the *Theages*," in *Plato: Charmides, Alcibiades I & II, Hipparchus, Lovers, Theages, Minos, Epinomis* (Cambridge, Mass., 1955), p. 343.

adds that when a friend consults with him, the voice may in this case too "turn away *and not allow* the action" (128d7). Socrates speaks more emphatically of the voice's preventative power when he refers to the way in which it manifests itself as regards the intentions of his friends: in these cases, of course, the friends learn of the prohibition only through Socrates' speech. Socrates next offers "witnesses of these things." For obvious reasons, he fails to provide witnesses to the voice's interdictions of his own actions. Yet he also refrains from providing any examples of such occasions; since Socrates speaks in this dialogue with a view to Demodocus and Theages, he wishes to speak here almost exclusively of how the voice guides others— through the intermediary, to repeat, of speeches uttered by the lips or voice of Socrates. The examples Socrates recounts seem to imply that the voice comes only in response to something apprehended by Socrates' mind (*nous:* 129c; see Benardete, pp. 23–25), that it manifests itself on behalf more of individuals than of multitudes, and that it tends to help beautiful young men like Sannion and Charmides (the latter's being the only case mentioned in which the voice intervened on a less than life-and-death matter). When the voice comes, it requires some interpretation, but the story of Charmides suggests that it is wise to intrepret the proscription broadly rather than narrowly. We are forced to guess the terrible grief that must have been the outcome of Charmides' attempt to give a narrow interpretation, but the other cases described, cases in which the voice was simply disobeyed, resulted in death for the disobedient. Socrates thus leaves his hearers with the impression that, if at some point the accustomed sign should oppose Theages' intention to study with Socrates, or if it should veto Theages' desire to study with any particular sophist, the consequences of his refusal to obey would be grave indeed.

The dire tales of those who sought to evade the demonic injunctions are only a portion of Socrates' story, however. The prohibiting voice proves to be only a small part of the demonic force, which is "all-powerful" as regards the intercourse of those who spend time with Socrates (129e). The voice itself is purely inhibitory, but it is only one side, one expression, of a power that is at least as much stimulative, fertile, and procreative as it is forbidding and denying. The way in which this demonic power operates causes those who spend time with Socrates to fall into four categories. Socrates dwells on only one of the categories and illustrates it with the story of Aristides, the son of Lysimachus—a youth who recalls the peak of old, conservative Athenian political tradition by his name and lineage (but—alas!—*only* by his name and lineage). Aristides was one of those who, as Socrates puts it, "immediately made swift progress." Or as the nobly named Aristides himself said in retrospect, he "never learned a thing" from Socrates, although while he was with Socrates—especially when he looked into his eyes and touched him—it "seemed" to Aristides as if he were making enormous progress. So long as he absented himself only for a short time and remained at no great distance from Socrates, he felt able to converse with anyone and "appeared" inferior to none in the gift of gab. But the "power" gradually "flowed out and away" until, when he stayed away from Socrates for an extended period, it left him entirely (cf. *Theaetetus* 150e–151a). Having told this story Socrates apostrophizes the nobly named Theages as follows: "Of such a kind, therefore, is our being together, oh Theages; if it is dear to the god, you will progress very much and rapidly. If not, you won't." Theages is *at most* another Aristides, son of Lysimachus, and perhaps not even that.[6]

The *Theages* teaches us that the Platonic Socrates' talk of his demonic or divine power is an alternative way of talking about his eros, in some of its manifestations.[7] To grasp Plato's or Socrates' understanding of this demonic power adequately, we would have to compare carefully all the Platonic accounts of eros and the demonic. But on the basis of what the *Theages* contributes to our understanding of this central element in the personality of Socrates as portrayed by Plato, this much seems reasonably certain: in Socrates the thirst engendered by the knowledge of ignorance took on unprecedented strength because it came into being in a man whose nature, whose "instincts" (to use a modern expression) were well suited to a re-

---

[6]Socrates' story associates Aristides with his friend Thucydides, the son of Melesias, who bears the name—and only the name—of the great statesman. Thucydides sounds even less intelligent than Aristides, by whom he is scorned for lacking sufficient self-knowledge. Are we meant to wonder whether Theages might not be closer to Thucydides than to Aristides in talent? The *Theages,* it may be observed, provides a sequel to the *Laches* that explains the outcome of the proposal tentatively accepted by Socrates at the end of that dialogue; after reading the *Theages* we understand better the implications of Socrates' reference to the favor of "the god" at the very end of the *Laches.* For a fuller discussion of the intricate relation between the *Laches* and the *Theages,* see Benardete, pp. 5–7 and 26.

[7]Cf. Leo Strauss, *Studies in Platonic Political Philosophy* (Chicago, 1984), 46–47; Friedländer, vol. 1, chap. 2 ("Demon and Eros"), as well as pp. 129–30, and vol. 2, pp. 151–52; W. K. C. Guthrie, *Socrates* (Cambridge, 1984), 78–85; Benardete, pp. 32ff. and esp. 38; Gerhard Krueger, "Der Dialog Theages" (diss. Griefswald, 1935), 20–21.

markable degree. In speaking of eros as demonic or divine, Socrates describes in "religious" language something that was, in fact, intelligible as an extraordinary concentration and eruption of natural forces.[8] Like every kind of dominating love, the love of knowledge as Socrates experienced it was a positive force accompanied by or inextricably associated with very strong negative or repulsing forces. Just as, for example, the most passionate and shrewdest lover of gain (cf. the *Hipparchus*) is the man most sensitive to bad deals and has an instinctive aversion to those circumstances in which his love may be wasted or thwarted, so Socrates had an uncanny "nose" for souls and a sixth sense that alerted him to otherwise undetectable threats to the pursuit that he loved with every fiber of his being. For those who could share or appreciate Socrates' passion, even to a small extent, to be in Socrates' presence was to experience something that is not improperly described in terms of the uncanny; to a degree that is unusual even in the case of great teachers, his presence was truly inspiring. But the inspiration, the sense of exaltation and sudden, awesome insight, was all too often a kind of beautiful illusion that melted away in his absence. Socrates' power of love therefore led frequently to acute disappointments, not only for those who sought him out and were repulsed, but also for many of those he initially welcomed (for whatever reason). These negative effects of Socratic eros—Socrates' refusal or inability to satisfy the hopes of various individuals—were most likely to arouse dislike and hatred. Hence Socrates most often and most emphatically spoke of the negative side of his eroticism as coming from some higher power, for which he could not be held responsible (cf. Xenophon *Symposium* viii 5, and Guthrie, p. 83).[9]

---

[8]Note that the two dialogues (*Theages* and *Apology of Socrates*) in which the demonic thing figures most prominently are dialogues in which Socrates refrains almost completely from mentioning nature. The sole reference to nature—*Apol. Soc.* 22c—supports the suggestion that Socrates' talk of a demonic influence in his own life replaces, or is an alternative pious way of speaking about, a natural gift or inspiration he experienced.

[9]It is a mistake, however, to suppose that the *Theages* is the sole Platonic dialogue in which Socrates suggests that the demonic voice is part of a power that urges him forward in a positive way. We must not forget that a no or negative often implies a yes, as is most evident from the story of the Delphic Oracle: according to Socrates, when the oracle replied no to Chaerephon's question ("Is there anyone wiser than Socrates?"), it meant, in effect, to lay down the program or goal of Socrates' entire life. Similarly, the demonic sign is often described as prohibiting Socrates from doing one thing in order to guide or impel him toward another: *Apol. Soc.* 40b–c, *Alcibiades I* 105e–106a, *Euthydemus* 272e, *Phaedrus* 242b–c (on this last passage, see Rist, p. 15).

Conclusion

In the *Theages* wisdom is treated in a partial or incomplete way.
The most obvious sign of the limitation Plato imposes on himself is
the dialogue's silence about philosophy—not to speak of its silence
about nature and about the soul. The discussion is strictly governed
by a primarily defensive purpose: the "wisdom" of Socratic philosophy is considered in the light of the demand made upon it that it make
a contribution to society and to civic education—that it help to provide education in a science of politics. Such knowledge above all—
the knowledge of how to guide society rather than the knowledge of
"nature"—men mostly seek and praise, or fear and blame, when they
speak of wisdom (see *Clouds* 95–118, 129–30, 238–41, 655–59, 895–
98, 1024–27).

Through the *Theages,* Plato shows, in the first place, that Socrates
is clear about the various but related spheres of knowledge that are
lacking, and hence that are sought, when human beings seek the
wisdom that is political science. On the basis of that clarity, Socrates
knows that such wisdom or science is unavailable to man. What
Socrates calls his expertise in erotics is in fact his knowledge of the
neediness of humans; such knowledge or awareness frees him from
the unjustified hopes that underlie the great claims made by the expo-
nents of various versions of political science or wisdom. Socrates also
knows, however, that our neediness is not an unmitigated affliction;
for one thing, political science does not sit easily with self-govern-
ment. But this means that republicanism is haunted by a moral difficulty: as rule of the non-expert, republicanism would seem to depend
on ignorance of the true common good; and without such knowledge, there would seem to be no firm barrier preventing the drift
from proud republican freedom to glorious, but despotic, imperialism. Still, agreeing with Greek tradition, Socrates values highly, if
much more provisionally, the virtues that are fostered by, and in turn
help foster, political self-rule. The absence of a completed political
science apparently does not prevent Socrates from garnering from his
confrontation with tradition a partial knowledge of man's needs and
thereby a standard for evaluating politics. In other dialogues, especially the *Republic* and *Gorgias,* Socrates proves by deed that a
dialectical critique of tradition enables us to make marked progress in
our comprehension of the divisions and perforce of the whole, of the
sought-for political science; in the *Laws* Plato even shows that this

unfinished Socratic inquiry, or "human wisdom," can provide decisive, if not definitive, concrete guidance to practicing statesmen. Generally speaking, the Socratic political philosopher tries to show how the traditional virtues can be made more consistent, intelligible, and self-conscious. In part, that is, he tries to show how the life that moves within the horizon formed by traditional excellence can be opened up to greater wonder or questioning without being fatally undermined in the process. For Socrates does doubt strongly whether tradition possesses as well founded an understanding of man's needs as it claims. He is therefore not surprised by, and indeed has considerable sympathy with, the quest—associated with the sophists—for scientific knowledge of man's situation. Nor is he surprised, or altogether dismayed, at the transformation of conservative republicanism into a more dynamic and expansionist society animated by all sorts of uncertain, restless longings—or types of eros.

Having been prompted by the *Theages* to take greater cognizance of this complex situation in which Socrates prosecutes his researchers, we are made more aware of how difficult and pressing is the question: how does Socrates understand and manage the effects on the young of his philosophic activity—especially the effects on those of the young who, though drawn to him, are unsuited to participate with him in his inquiry? The bulk of the *Theages,* and especially its drama, are devoted to this question. By means of the depiction of Socrates in action trying to manage an unusually delicate father-and-son relationship, Plato both responds to Aristophanes' critique and allows us to think through for ourselves Socrates' way of dealing with a range of similar cases. Most memorable and revealing of all, we are given to understand the manner and the meaning of Socrates' clothing his passionate relations with his students in the mysterious garb of the "demonic." We learn that Socrates introduced a new and strange demonic thing into Greek piety not in order to undermine that piety but to shore it up, even while liberalizing it (and thereby protecting himself and his friends). For though Socrates continued to favor a traditional upbringing for most young people, he was very skeptical about the capacity of the tradition to maintain its decisive influence over education. Socrates formed and promulgated no educational policy for society at large; his interventions and guidance took place strictly on a case-by-case basis. But in some of those cases he was apparently willing to facilitate the transfer of young men's allegiance away from the old republican ways and to the radical

Periclean or imperialist democracy—and beyond that, even to the politically neutral or independent educational activities of the sophists. He did so with the hope of moderating—in the manner we have seen illustrated in this dialogue—the attachment to the new order.

In one respect, and that the most important, we may say that the situation presented in the *Theages* is the same as our situation, or at any rate we have thus far been offered, it seems to me, no argument that compels us to suppose otherwise. A Socratic, or "erotic," theorizing about politics remains as possible today as it was when Plato wrote. Yet it should go without saying that we cannot directly apply, in our time, what we learn from the *Theages* about the educational effects of such theorizing. Both our original tradition and our present-day political system differ in major ways from those of ancient Athens, and for many reasons it would be a grave injustice to identify today's political scientists and journalists with men such as Protagoras or Prodicus. Still, these very differences between our situation and that of Socrates, however great they may be, are in large part the result of later philosophers' attempts (through political speech and action) to overcome the problems revealed by Plato. It follows that lucid insight into the Platonic analysis of the problematic political position of those who try to teach and study political science provides the indispensable foundation for any adequate effort to analyze our different, yet derivative, difficulties.

ALCIBIADES I
[or, On the Nature of Man]

Translated by CARNES LORD

Socrates, Alcibiades

103a SOCRATES: Son of Kleinias,[1] I suppose you wonder why it is that I, who was the first to become a lover of yours, alone persist in it now that the others have left off and yet have not so much as spoken to you during the many years the others came clamoring to converse with you. Of this the cause has been no human thing but a certain b demonic opposition; you will learn later of its power. Now, as it no longer opposes me, I have approached you in this way; and I am hopeful it will not oppose me in the future. Through observing you during that time, I pretty thoroughly understand how you behaved toward these lovers: though they were many and thought greatly of themselves, there is not one who was not exceeded by you in such thinking and put to flight. As for the reason that made you think 104a excessively of yourself, I would like to explain it. You assert you are not in need of anyone among human beings for anything, since what belongs to you—beginning with the body and ending in the soul—is so great that you need nothing. For you suppose first of all that you are very handsome and very tall[2] (and indeed it is plain for all to see that in this you do not speak falsely) and next that you belong to a family that is very distinguished in your own city, the greatest of

[1]Alcibiades, depicted here as an adolescent, later became one of the leaders of Athens and perhaps the most extraordinary political genius of classical Greece. His exploits fill the pages of Thucydides' and Xenophon's histories.
[2]*Megistos:* imposing or "great" in a physical sense—generally considered an attribute of the gods.

b   Greek cities, and that you have there through your father many and excellent men as friends and relatives who could serve you in case of need and others through your mother neither worse nor fewer than these. Greater than all the things I have spoken of, however, is, as you suppose, the power that is available to you in Pericles, son of Xanthippus, whom your father left as guardian to you and your brother—a man who is able to act as he wishes not only in this city but in all of Greece and among many and great barbarian peoples. I

c   shall add that you belong among the wealthy, though it seems to me you think greatly of yourself least of all on this account. It is by boasting about all of these things, then, that you have overcome your lovers, and they through being more needy have been overcome, and this has not escaped you. I know well, then, that you are wondering what I have in mind when I do not abandon my love and what I can hope for by standing my ground when the others have fled.

d   ALCIBIADES: Perhaps Socrates, you don't know that you have barely anticipated me. For I had intended to approach you first and ask these same things—just what it is you want and what hope you look to in making such a nuisance of yourself, always taking such trouble to be present wherever I happen to be. I really do wonder what you are about, and it would please me very much to learn of it.

SOC.: It is likely that you will listen to me eagerly, then, if, as you assert, you desire to know what I have in mind; and I will speak on the assumption that you are going to listen and remain.

ALC.: Certainly. Speak on.

e   SOC.: See that you are sure. For it would be nothing to wonder at if I were as slow to leave off as I have been to begin.

ALC.: Speak, my good man; I shall listen.

SOC.: Then speak it is. And though it is difficult for a lover to come to grips with a man who never succumbs to lovers, I must be bold all the same and tell you my mind. For if, Alcibiades, I saw you content with the things I just mentioned and supposing you ought to spend your life in the midst of them, I would long ago have abandoned my

105a love, or so at least I persuade myself. But I will now accuse you to your face of having other things in mind—by which you will understand what constant attention I have paid to you. For it seems to me that if one of the gods were to say to you—"Alcibiades, would you wish rather to live, having what you now have, or to die at once if it were not permitted you to acquire more?"—you would choose, it seems to me, to die. But as to what hope it is you now live on, I shall

tell you. You believe that if you come shortly before the people of
b Athens—and you believe this will occur within a very few days—
upon coming forward you will prove to the Athenians that you are
deserving of being honored more than Pericles or anyone else who
has ever existed and, having proved this, that you will have very
great power in the city; and if you are very great here, that you will
be so as well among the other Greeks, and not only among the
Greeks but also among the barbarians who share the mainland with
us. And if this same god were again to say to you that you must hold
c sway here in Europe but will not be permitted to cross into Asia or to
interest yourself in affairs there, it seems to me you would again be
unwilling to live on these terms alone, without being able to fill with
your name and your power all mankind, so to speak. And I suppose
you believe that, apart from Cyrus and Xerxes,[3] no one deserving of
mention has ever existed. That this is the hope you have, then, I
know very well—I am not guessing. Perhaps, then, since you know I
speak the truth, you will say: "What has this to do, then, Socrates,
d with the account you said you would give of why you don't abandon
me?" I will tell you, dear son of Kleinias and Deinomache. It is not
possible for all these things you have in mind to be brought to a
completion without me.[4] So great is the power I suppose myself to
have regarding your affairs and you, and I suppose this is why the
god did not allow me to converse with you for so long, and I waited
for him to permit it. For just as you have hopes of proving before the
e city that you are invaluable to it, and having proved this, of immediately having the power to do anything, so I too hope to have the
greatest power with you after having proved that I am invaluable to
you, and that no guardian or relative or anyone else is capable of
bestowing the power you desire apart from me, though with the help
of the god. When you were younger and not yet teeming with so
much hope, the god, it seems to me, would not permit our convers-
06a ing, in order that I not converse to no point. Now he has granted it,
for now you may listen to me.
ALC.: You now appear much stranger still to me, Socrates, since you
have begun to speak, than when you followed in silence; yet you
were something to see even then. As to whether I have these things in

[3]Cyrus was the founder of the Persian Empire; the Persian king Xerxes led the
invasion of Greece that culminated in the battles of Plataea and Salamis (480–79 B.C.).
On the Persian kings generally, see *Laws* 694a–698a.
[4]Socrates' language seems consciously heroic: cf. *Iliad* XIX 107, XX 369.

mind or not, you have, as it seems, decided the question, and if I deny it I will be no closer to persuading you. All right; if I've really had these things in mind, how is it, then, that I will obtain them through you but could not have them without you? Can you say?

b   soc.: Are you asking whether I have some long speech to deliver, of the sort you are accustomed to hear? Such is not my way. But I would be able, I suppose, to prove to you that matters stand this way, provided you are willing to do me only one small service.

ALC.: Unless the service you speak of is something difficult, I am willing.

soc.: Does answering questions seem difficult?

ALC.: No, not difficult.

soc.: Then answer.

ALC.: Ask.

soc.: Shall I assume in my questioning that you have in mind these
c   things I assert you have in mind?

ALC.: Be it so, if you like, so that I can know what you are going to say.

soc.: Well, then. You have in mind, I assert, to come before the Athenians before much time has passed to advise them. If, then, I took hold of you as you were about to go up to the platform and asked—"Alcibiades, what is it that the Athenians have in mind to deliberate about that has caused you to get up to advise them? Are these matters that you have greater knowledge of than they?"—what would you answer?

d   ALC.: I would surely answer that these are matters I know better than they.

soc.: On those matters you happen to know about, therefore, you are a good adviser.

ALC.: How could it be otherwise?

soc.: Do you know only the things you have learned from others or discovered yourself?

ALC.: What else is there?

soc.: Is it possible, then, that you could ever have learned or discovered anything if you had not been willing to learn it or to investigate it yourself?

ALC.: It is not.

soc.: What then? Would you have been willing to investigate or learn what you supposed you had knowledge of?

ALC.: By no means.

e SOC.: What you happen to have knowledge of now, therefore, at one time you did not believe you knew?

ALC.: Necessarily.

SOC.: Now, what you have learned, at any rate, I also know, or nearly so—but tell me if anything has escaped me. You learned, at least according to my memory of it, letters, cithara playing, and wrestling, for you were not willing to learn to play the aulos. These are the things you have knowledge of unless you have learned something in a place where you escaped my notice; which I don't suppose, at least, since you never left home to go there, either by night or during the day.

ALC.: I have never gone to any others than these.

107a SOC.: Is it when the Athenians deliberate about letters and how to write correctly, then, that you will get up to advise them?

ALC.: Not I, by Zeus!

SOC.: But when they deliberate about strokes of the lyre?

ALC.: Not at all!

SOC.: Nor, indeed, are they accustomed to deliberate in the assembly about wrestling holds.

ALC.: Indeed not!

SOC.: When they deliberate about what, then? Not, presumably, about house building, at least.

ALC.: By no means!

SOC.: For in these matters, at least, a house builder will advise better than you.

b ALC.: Yes.

SOC.: Nor when they deliberate about divination?

ALC.: No.

SOC.: For, again, in these matters a diviner will do it better than you.

ALC.: Yes.

SOC.: Whether he is short or tall, fair or ugly, well born or not well born.

ALC.: How could it be otherwise?

SOC.: For advising on any matter belongs, I suppose, to the man who knows, not to the wealthy man.

ALC.: How could it be otherwise?

SOC.: But whether the man counseling the Athenians is poor or

c wealthy will make no difference to them when they deliberate about the health of those in the city, but they will seek an adviser who is a doctor.

ALC.: That is likely, at any rate.

SOC.: Then what will they be considering when you get up to advise them—if you are to be right in doing so?

ALC.: Their own affairs, Socrates.

SOC.: Those concerning shipbuilding, you mean—what sort of ships they ought to build?

ALC.: Not I, Socrates.

SOC.: For I suppose you do not have a knowledge of shipbuilding. Is this the cause or something else?

ALC.: No, this.

d SOC.: But what do you mean? When they are deliberating on what sort of affairs of their own?

ALC.: When they are deliberating on war, Socrates, or on peace, or some other of the city's affairs.

SOC.: You mean, therefore, when they deliberate concerning whom they ought to make peace with, and whom war, and in what manner?

ALC.: Yes.

SOC.: Ought it not to be with those with whom it is better to do so?

ALC.: Yes.

e SOC.: And at whatever time is better?

ALC.: Certainly.

SOC.: And for as much time as is better?

ALC.: Yes.

SOC.: Now, if the Athenians were to deliberate with whom they ought to wrestle and with whom they ought to spar and in what manner, would you or a trainer advise them better?

ALC.: A trainer, surely.

SOC.: Can you tell me, then, what the trainer would look to in advising them with whom they should or should not wrestle, and when, and in what manner? I'm referring to some such thing as the following: should they wrestle with those with whom it is better to do so or not?

ALC.: Yes.

108a SOC.: And as much as is better?

ALC.: As much.

SOC.: And also at whatever time is better?

ALC.: Certainly.

SOC.: Now, one who sings must sometimes accompany the song with cithara playing and dancing?

ALC.: He must.

soc.: And at whatever time is better?

alc.: Yes.

soc.: And as much as is better?

alc.: I agree.

b soc.: Now, what of this? Since you used the term "better" in the case both of cithara playing to accompany a song and of wrestling, what do you call "better" in cithara playing—in the way I call it in wrestling "gymnastical"?[5] What do you call it in that case?

alc.: I cannot bring it to mind.

soc.: Well, try to imitate me. For presumably what I answered is, what is correct in every instance, and what is correct is surely what comes about according to art—or is it not?

alc.: Yes.

soc.: Was the art not gymnastic?

alc.: What else?

c soc.: I said that the better in wrestling is gymnastical.

alc.: You did.

soc.: Didn't I speak in a fine way?

alc.: It seems so to me at least.

soc.: Come, then, and tell me yourself—for presumably it would suit you as well to converse in a fine way[6]—what the art is, first of all, to which correct cithara playing, singing and dancing belong. What is it called as a whole? You still cannot say?

alc.: No, indeed.

soc.: Then try it this way. Who are the goddesses to whom the art belongs?

alc.: Do you mean the Muses, Socrates?

d soc.: I do. Now, consider: what name deriving from them does the art have?

alc.: It seems to me you are speaking of music.

soc.: That is what I'm speaking of. Now, what is it that comes about correctly in accordance with this? Just as in the other case, in gymnastic, I told you what is correct in accordance with the art, so too here, then—what do you say? How does it come about?

alc.: Musically, it seems to me.

soc.: You speak well. Come, then, with respect to what is better in

---

[5]*Gymnastikon;* the word in Greek of athletic skill.

[6]There is a verbal play on the idiom *kalōs legein* ("to speak in a fine or beautiful way") and Alcibiades' good looks (cf. 104a, 113b).

e waging war or keeping peace, what term do you use for better in this
sense? Just as you said what the better is in each of the other cases—
that it is the more musical or in the other case the more gymnastical—try to say what the better is here.

ALC.: Nothing occurs to me.

SOC.: But what a shameful thing! If it was about food you were
speaking and advising—that this is better than that and at this time
and so much of it—and someone then asked you, "What do you
mean by better, Alcibiades?" you could say in this case that it is the
healthier, even though you do not claim to be a doctor. Yet concern-
109a ing something that you claim to be knowledgeable about and will get
up to give advice on as one who knows, aren't you ashamed to have
nothing to say, as it appears you do not, when you are asked about
this? Or does it not appear shameful?

ALC.: Very much so.

SOC.: Consider, then, and be eager to tell me; the better in keeping
peace and waging war with whom one should—to what does this
refer?

ALC.: I am considering but cannot bring it to mind.

SOC.: Don't you know that when we make war we begin to wage war
after accusing each other of some affront and what term we use when
we begin?

b ALC.: I do—we say we have been deceived, or done violence to, or
deprived of something.

SOC.: Stop there. How are we affronted in each of these cases? Try to
tell me what difference there is between one way and another.

ALC.: By "way," Socrates, do you mean justly or unjustly?

SOC.: This very thing.

ALC.: Certainly they are wholly and entirely different.

SOC.: Now, what of this? Whom will you advise the Athenians to
wage war against, those behaving unjustly or those practicing the just
things?

c ALC.: What you are asking is a terrible thing; for even if someone had
it in his mind that war ought to be waged against those practicing the
just things, he would not admit to it, at least.

SOC.: For this is not lawful, it would appear.

ALC.: No indeed, nor does it seem to be anything noble.

SOC.: Is it with a view to this kind of justice, therefore, that you too
will make your speeches?[7]

----

    [7]This sentence reads ungrammatically in all but one minor manuscript (Paris,
1811), on which this translation is based.

ALC.: Necessarily.

SOC.: Then that "better" in relation to waging or not waging war against those we ought or ought not and when we ought or ought not, which I was just asking about—does it happen to be anything other than the more just? Or not?

ALC.: It appears so, at any rate.

d SOC.: Yet how is this, dear Alcibiades? Has it escaped you that you have no knowledge of this, or did it escape me that you were learning and going to a teacher who taught you to recognize the more just and the more unjust? And who is this? Tell me as well, so that you can introduce me and I too can become his pupil.

ALC.: You are mocking, Socrates.

SOC.: By the Guardian of Friendship,[8] mine and yours, whom I would least of all forswear, I am not! But if you can, tell me who he is.

e ALC.: What if I cannot? Do you not suppose I could know something otherwise about the just and unjust things?

SOC.: Yes, if, that is, you discovered it.

ALC.: But do you not believe I could discover it?

SOC.: Certainly, if you investigated.

ALC.: Then you not suppose I could investigate?

SOC.: I do, if, that is, you supposed you did not know.

ALC.: Then was there not a time when I was in that state?

110a SOC.: What you say is fine. Can you tell me, then, at what time you supposed you did not know the just and unjust things? Come, was it last year that you were investigating and did not suppose you knew? Or did you suppose you did? Answer with the truth, so that our conversations may not be to no point.

ALC.: I supposed I knew.

SOC.: And two, three, and four years ago—was it not the same?

ALC.: I agree.

SOC.: But before that you were a child, were you not?

ALC.: Yes.

SOC.: I well know, however, that at that time you supposed you knew.

ALC.: How do you know this so well?

b SOC.: When you were a child I often heard you, when you were throwing dice or playing at some other kind of play at your teachers' or elsewhere, instead of being at a loss about the just and the unjust

---

[8]One of Zeus's epithets and roles.

things, speak rather in a very loud and confident way about one or another of the children being wicked and unjust and behaving unjustly. Or am I not speaking the truth?

ALC.: But what was I going to do, Socrates, when someone behaved unjustly toward me?

SOC.: What should you do, you mean, if you happened at that time to be ignorant of whether you were being unjustly treated or not?

c   ALC.: By Zeus, I was not ignorant but knew clearly that I was being treated unjustly!

SOC.: You supposed, therefore, that you had knowledge of the just and unjust things even as a child, as it appears.

ALC.: I did and I did have the knowledge.

SOC.: At what time did you discover it? For surely it was not at the time you supposed you knew.

ALC.: No indeed.

SOC.: Then when do you believe you were ignorant? Consider, for you won't find that time.

ALC.: By Zeus, Socrates! I cannot say.

d   SOC.: Therefore you do not know these things by discovering them.

ALC.: It appears I don't.

SOC.: And yet you just asserted you do not know them by learning either. But if you neither discovered nor learned them, how and from where do you know them?

ALC.: Perhaps I did not answer you correctly in asserting I know by discovering them myself.

SOC.: Then how is it?

ALC.: I suppose I learned them too, in the same way as everybody else.

SOC.: We come back to the same argument. From whom? Tell me, too.

e   ALC.: From the many.

SOC.: These are hardly weighty teachers you are taking refuge with when you refer it to the many.

ALC.: Why? Are they not fit enough to teach?

SOC.: Not even what makes for skills at draughts and what does not, yet I suppose these things are slight, compared with the just things. What about it? Do you not suppose it is this way?

ALC.: Yes.

SOC.: If they are unable to teach slighter things, can they teach weightier ones?

ALC.: I would suppose they can; at any rate, they are able to teach other things that are weightier than draughts.

SOC.: What are these?

11a ALC.: I, at least, learned Greek from them, for example. I couldn't say who my teacher was: I would refer you rather to the very ones you assert are not weighty teachers.

SOC.: But, well-born fellow, the many are good teachers of this, and they may be justly praised for the teaching.

ALC.: Why?

SOC.: Because as far as these things are concerned they have what good teachers ought to have.

ALC.: What do you mean by this?

SOC.: Do you not know that those who are going to teach anything b ought first to know it themselves? Or is it not so?

ALC.: How could it be otherwise?

SOC.: And that those who know ought to agree with one another and not differ?

ALC.: Yes.

SOC.: If they differ about certain things, will you assert they know these things?

ALC.: No indeed.

SOC.: Then how could they be teachers of these things?

ALC.: In no way.

c SOC.: Now, what of this? Do the many seem to you to differ about what sort of thing a piece of stone or wood is? And if you ask someone, do they not agree they are the same thing, and do they not go toward the same things when they want to get a piece of stone or wood? And the same holds for all such things. For by having a knowledge of Greek I take it something like this is what you mean. Or not?

ALC.: Yes.

SOC.: Is it not the case, then, as we said, that in these things they agree with one another and with themselves taken as individuals and—taking them as a public—that cities do not dispute with one another over these things, some saying they are one thing and others something else?

ALC.: They do not.

SOC.: It is likely, therefore, that of these things at least they would be good teachers.

d ALC.: Yes.

SOC.: If we want to make someone know these things, then, we would be correct in sending them to be taught by this many?

ALC.: Certainly.

SOC.: What then? If we had wanted to know not only what human beings or horses are but also which of them are skilled at running and which not? Are the many still fit to teach this?

ALC.: No indeed.

e SOC.: And the sufficient evidence, for you, that they neither know nor are good teachers of these things, is that they don't agree among themselves about them?

ALC.: For me that is the case.

SOC.: What then? If we had wanted to know not only what human beings are but which are healthy or sick, would the many be adequate teachers for us?

ALC.: No indeed.

SOC.: And it would have been evidence for you that they are bad teachers of these things if you had seen them differing?

ALC.: For me that is the case.

SOC.: Then what of this? Do the many now seem to you to agree with
112a themselves or with one another concerning just and unjust men and affairs?

ALC.: Least of all, by Zeus, Socrates!

SOC.: But they disagree most of all about these things?

ALC.: Very much so.

SOC.: I suppose, at any rate, that you have never seen nor heard of human beings differing so vehemently about the healthy things and the not healthy as to fight on account of these things and kill one another.

ALC.: No indeed.

b SOC.: But as far as just and unjust things are concerned, I know that, even if you have not seen this, you have heard about it at any rate from many, and especially from Homer. For you have heard the *Odyssey* and the *Iliad*.

ALC.: Of course, Socrates.

SOC.: Aren't these poems about a difference of just and unjust?[9]

ALC.: Yes.

SOC.: At any rate, it was on account of this difference that there came

---

[9]Socrates plays on the word *diaphora*, which means "quarrel" as well as "difference."

to be battles and deaths between the Achaians and the Trojans and between the suitors of Penelope and Odysseus.

c ALC.: What you say is true.

SOC.: And for the Athenians, Lacedaemonians, and Boeotians who died at Tanagra, I suppose, and those who died later at Coronea, and among them your own father Kleinias, the difference that led to the deaths and the battles was about no other thing than the just and unjust.[10] Is it not so?

ALC.: What you say is true.

SOC.: Shall we assert, then, that these men have knowledge of the
d things they differ so vehemently about as to inflict on each other the last degree of harm in their disputes?

ALC.: It doesn't appear so, at least.

SOC.: Is it to such teachers that you refer, then, when you yourself agree they do not know?

ALC.: It seems so.

SOC.: How, then, is it likely that you should know the just and unjust things, when you are in such uncertainty and have plainly never learned them from anyone nor discovered them yourself?

ALC.: From what you say, it is not likely.

e SOC.: Do you see that this was not spoken in a fine way, Alcibiades?

ALC.: What?

SOC.: When you assert I said these things.

ALC.: Why? Do you not say I have no knowledge about the just and unjust things?

SOC.: No indeed.

ALC.: But I do?

SOC.: Yes.

ALC.: How so?

SOC.: You will know in the following way. If I ask you whether one or two is greater, you will say two?

ALC.: I will.

SOC.: By how much?

ALC.: By one.

SOC.: Then which of us is the one saying that two is greater than one?

ALC.: I am.

[10]The battles of Tanagra and Coronea—both of them Athenian defeats—took place in 456 B.C. and 447 B.C., respectively (cf. Thucydides I 107–108, 113, *Menexenus* 242a–b).

SOC.: And I was asking and you answering?

ALC.: Yes.

113a SOC.: Then am I, the questioner, or you, the answerer, the one who is plainly saying these things?

ALC.: I am.

SOC.: What if I ask you what letters there are in "Socrates," and you tell me—who is the one saying it?

ALC.: I am.

SOC.: Come then, say in a single speech: when there is question and answer, who is the one saying something, the questioner or the answerer?

ALC.: The answerer, Socrates, it seems to me at least.

b SOC.: Haven't I just now been the questioner throughout?

ALC.: Yes.

SOC.: And you the answerer?

ALC.: Very much so.

SOC.: Now, then, which of us has said the things that were spoken?

ALC.: From what has been agreed, Socrates, it appears to be I.

SOC.: And what was spoken was that Alcibiades the fair, the son of Kleinias, does not have knowledge concerning just and unjust things but supposes he does, and is about to go to the assembly to advise the Athenians on things he knows nothing about? Was this not it?

c ALC.: It appears so.

SOC.: The result, therefore, is as Euripides has it: you have, I'm afraid, heard "from yourself these things, not from me,"[11] nor am I the one saying them but you, and it is pointless for you to hold me responsible. Nevertheless, you have spoken well. For it is a mad thing you intend to undertake, excellent fellow—to teach what you do not know, having taken no trouble to learn it.

d ALC.: I would suppose, Socrates, that the Athenians and the other Greeks rarely deliberate as to which things are more just or more unjust; for they believe such things are evident, and so they let these matters go and consider which things will be advantageous to those practicing them. For just and advantageous things are not, I suppose, the same, but many have profited from committing great injustices, and I suppose there are others who performed just acts that were not to their advantage.

SOC.: Now, what of this? If just and advantageous things are as

---

[11] *Hippolytus* 352.

e different as they can possibly be, do you not still suppose that you know these things that are advantageous for human beings and why they are so?

ALC.: What prevents me, Socrates? Unless you are going to ask me again whom I learned it from or how I myself discovered it.

SOC.: What a thing this is you are doing! If you say something that is not correct, and this can be proved on the basis of the earlier argument, you suppose you ought to hear something new, and different proofs, as if the earlier ones were like worn-out old clothes that you

14a will no longer put on, but someone will bring you clean and fresh evidence. But I will let pass your little counterattacks in the argument, and ask you nevertheless where you learned your knowledge of the advantageous things and who your teacher is, and all those earlier things I shall ask in a single question. But it is evident that you will come to the same point and will be unable to prove that you know the advantageous things either by discovering them or by learning them. But since you are given to luxury and would not find it pleasant to taste the same argument again, I shall let pass this question of whether you know or do not know what is advantageous

b to the Athenians. As for the question of whether just and advantageous things are the same or different, why did you not prove something there? If you wish, question me as I did you, or present your own argument yourself.

ALC.: I don't know whether I would be able to present it to you, Socrates.

SOC.: Good fellow, imagine that I am the assembly and people; for even there you will have to persuade each man by himself, will you not?

ALC.: Yes.

SOC.: Does it not belong to the same man to persuade each indi-

c vidually and many together about the things he knows, just as the teacher of letters persuades, presumably, both one and many about letters?

ALC.: Yes.

SOC.: And the same man, therefore, will persuade both one and many about number?

ALC.: Yes.

SOC.: And this will be the man who knows, the one who is skilled at number?

ALC.: Certainly.

soc.: Then the things you can persuade many of, can you not also persuade one of?

alc.: It is likely, at any rate.

soc.: And these are clearly the things you know.

alc.: Yes.

d soc.: Is there any other difference, then, between an orator in front of the people and one in some such intercourse as this than that the one persuades men in a crowd, regarding the same things, and the other one by one?

alc.: I'm afraid not.

soc.: Come then, since it appears to belong to the same man to persuade many and one, practice on me, and try to show me that the just is sometimes not advantageous.

alc.: You are insolent, Socrates!

soc.: Now, at any rate, I shall be insolent enough to persuade you of the opposite of what you are not willing to persuade me of.

alc.: Speak, then.

soc.: Just answer my questions.

e alc.: No, you do the speaking yourself.

soc.: What? Do you not want to be persuaded as much as possible?

alc.: By all means!

soc.: Would you not be persuaded as much as possible if you yourself say "the matter stands thus"?

alc.: It seems so to me at least.

soc.: Answer, then. And if you yourself do not hear from yourself that the just things are advantageous, do not believe another saying it.

alc.: I won't, but answer it is. I don't suppose there is any harm in it.

115a soc.: You are skilled at divining. Now tell me: you assert that of the just things some are advantageous and some not?

alc.: Yes.

soc.: What of this? Are some of them noble and some not?

alc.: What do you mean by this question?

soc.: Has anyone ever seemed to you to do things that are shameful yet just?

alc.: That has never seemed the case to me, at least.

soc.: But all the just things are also noble?

alc.: Yes.

soc.: Again, what of the noble things? Are all of them good, or are some good and others not?

ALC.: I at least would suppose, Socrates, that some noble things are bad.

SOC.: And some shameful things good?

ALC.: Yes.

b SOC.: Do you mean some such things as this, then—that many who have gone to the aid of a comrade or relative in war have been wounded or killed, while others did not give such aid when they should have and got away safely?

ALC.: By all means.

SOC.: Then such aid you call noble with respect to its being an attempt to rescue those who should be rescued, and this is courage? Or not?

ALC.: Yes.

SOC.: But bad, in respect to the deaths and wounds? Or what?

ALC.: Yes.

c SOC.: Then isn't the courage one thing, the death another?

ALC.: Certainly.

SOC.: Coming to the aid of friends is not, therefore, noble and bad in the same respect, at least?

ALC.: It appears not to be.

SOC.: Consider, however, whether something is not in fact good insofar as it is noble, as in the other case. For you agreed that aid is noble with respect to courage; now consider this very thing— whether courage is good or bad. Consider it in this way. Which would you choose to have for yourself, good things or bad?

ALC.: Good things.

d SOC.: And above all the greatest?

[Lacuna][12]

SOC.: And you would choose least of all to be deprived of these?

ALC.: How could it be otherwise?

SOC.: Then what do you say about courage? For what price would you choose to be deprived of it?

ALC.: I wouldn't choose to live if I were a coward.

SOC.: Cowardice seems to you, therefore, the ultimate among bad things?

ALC.: It does to me, at least.

SOC.: On an equality with death, as it seems.

---

[12]A brief response has probably been dropped from the manuscripts, though one cannot rule out the possibility that Plato has Alcibiades remain silent here.

ALC.: That is what I assert.

SOC.: And life and courage are most opposed to death and cowardice?

ALC.: Yes.

e SOC.: And the first you would want for yourself above all, and the others least of all?

ALC.: Yes.

SOC.: Is this because you believe the former to be best, the latter worst?

ALC.: Certainly.

SOC.: You believe courage to be among the best things, therefore, and death among the worst.

ALC.: I at least do.

SOC.: Coming to the aid of friends in war, therefore, insofar as it is noble, an action of courage that accords with goods, you call noble?

ALC.: It appears I do, at least.

SOC.: But bad, at any rate, as an action of death that accords with bad?

ALC.: Yes.

SOC.: Each of these actions, then, we may justly speak of in the following way. If you call one bad insofar as it produces something
116a bad, you must call the other good insofar as it produces something good.

ALC.: It seems so to me, at least.

SOC.: And therefore noble insofar as it is good and shameful insofar as it is bad?

ALC.: Yes.

SOC.: In saying, then, that aiding friends in war is noble but bad, you are speaking no differently than if you called it good but bad.

ALC.: What you say seems to me true, Socrates.

SOC.: None of the noble things, therefore, to the extent it is noble, is bad, and none of the shameful things is good to the extent it is shameful.

b ALC.: It appears not to be.

SOC.: Consider it, however, in the following way as well. Whoever acts nobly, does he not also act well?[13]

ALC.: Yes.

SOC.: And are not those who act well happy?

[13]The expression *eu prattein* means not only "to act well" but "to do well," i.e., to prosper.

ALC.: How could they not be?

SOC.: Are they not happy through the acquisition of good things?

ALC.: Above all.

SOC.: And they acquire these things through acting well and nobly?

ALC.: Yes.

SOC.: To act well, therefore, is something good?

ALC.: How could it not be?

SOC.: Is acting well not something noble?

ALC.: Yes.

c SOC.: Again, therefore, it appeared to us that noble and good are the same thing.

ALC.: It appears so.

SOC.: Whatever we may find to be noble, therefore, we shall find to be good as well, at least on this argument.

ALC.: Necessarily.

SOC.: What of this? Are good things advantageous or not?

ALC.: They are advantageous.

SOC.: Do you remember, then, what we agreed about the just things?

ALC.: That, I suppose, those who practice the just things necessarily practice noble things.

SOC.: And those who practice the noble things necessarily practice good things?

ALC.: Yes.

d SOC.: And that the good things are advantageous?

ALC.: Yes.

SOC.: The just things, therefore, Alcibiades, are advantageous.

ALC.: So it seems.

SOC.: Now, then, are you not the one who is saying these things, and I am the one questioning?

ALC.: I appear to be, as it seems.

SOC.: If, then, someone gets up to advise either the Athenians or the Peparethians[14] and, supposing he knows the just and unjust things, asserts that the just things are sometimes bad, would you do anything

e else than laugh at him, since you too happen to say that just and advantageous things are the same?

ALC.: But by the gods, Socrates! I myself don't know what I am

[14]Peparethus, a small island off the coast of Thessaly, appears to be cited for the insignificance of its political life.

saying, and I seem like someone in an altogether strange condition; for at one time things seem a certain way as you question me but at another time another.

SOC.: Then you are ignorant, my friend, of what this experience is?

ALC.: Very much so.

SOC.: Do you suppose, then, that if someone asked you whether you had two eyes or three, or two hands or four, or some other thing of this sort, you would answer a certain way at one time and a different way at another, or would always answer the same thing?

117a ALC.: I am already afraid for myself, but I would suppose the same.

SOC.: Is it not because you know? This is the cause?

ALC.: I at least suppose so.

SOC.: As for the things where you involuntarily answer in opposite ways, it is clear that you do not know about them.

ALC.: It is likely, at any rate.

SOC.: Is it not concerning things just and unjust, noble and shameful, bad and good and advantageous and not, that you assert you wander about in your answers? Is it not clear, then, that it is because you do not know about these things that you wander in this way?

b ALC.: It is, to me at least.

SOC.: Well, then, isn't this the way it is? Whenever someone does not know something, he necessarily wanders about in his soul concerning this?

ALC.: How could it be otherwise?

SOC.: What of this? Do you know a way in which you can ascend to heaven?

ALC.: By Zeus, not I, at least!

SOC.: Does your opinion concerning these things wander about?

ALC.: No indeed.

SOC.: Do you know the cause, or shall I tell you?

ALC.: Tell me.

SOC.: It is, friend, because you do not suppose you have knowledge of this while not in fact having it.

c ALC.: What do you mean by this?

SOC.: Look at it in common with me. What you do not have knowledge of but know that you do not know—do you wander about concerning things of this sort? You know that you do not know, surely, about preparing relishes?[15]

---

[15]The word for "relish" (*opson*) signifies whatever was eaten with bread and has a connotation of luxury; cf. *Republic* 372cff.

ALC.: Certainly.

SOC.: Then do you yourself make guesses as to how you should prepare these things and wander about, or do you entrust it to someone who has knowledge?

ALC.: The latter.

d SOC.: What if you were to sail in a ship—would you make guesses as to whether the rudder ought to be moved in or out and wander about as one not knowing, or would you entrust it to the pilot and remain quiet?

ALC.: To the pilot.

SOC.: You do not wander about, therefore, concerning the things you do not know, as long as you know that you do not know?

ALC.: It appears I do not.

SOC.: Do you understand, then, that going wrong in one's actions[16] comes about through this sort of ignorance—the ignorance of one who supposes he knows when he does not?

ALC.: What do you mean by this?

SOC.: Do we undertake to act when we suppose we know what action to take?

ALC.: Yes.

e SOC.: And when men—or some of them, at least—suppose they don't know, they hand the matter over to others?

ALC.: How could it be otherwise?

SOC.: Of those who don't know, then, such men live without going wrong, by entrusting these things to others?

ALC.: Yes.

SOC.: Then who are the ones who go wrong? For they are not, presumably, those who know.

ALC.: No indeed.

SOC.: Since they are neither those who know nor those of the non-
118a knowers who know they do not know, are any others left besides those who don't know but suppose they do?

ALC.: No, just these.

SOC.: This very ignorance, then, is a cause of evils and a reprehensible form of stupidity?[17]

ALC.: Yes.

---

[16]A more precise rendering might be: "culpable errors [hamartēmata] in action." Hamartanein and derivatives will regularly be translated "to go wrong" or "going wrong."

[17]The word rendered "stupidity" (amathia—literally "lack of learning") carries a strong connotation of moral obtuseness or boorishness.

SOC.: And it is most damaging and disgraceful when it concerns the greatest things?

ALC.: Certainly.

SOC.: Now then, can you tell me of any greater things than the just, noble, good, and advantageous things?

ALC.: No indeed.

SOC.: Is it not concerning these things that you assert you wander about?

ALC.: Yes.

SOC.: If you wander about, therefore, is it not clear from what has
b gone before that you are not only ignorant of the greatest things but suppose you know them when you do not?

ALC.: I'm afraid so.

SOC.: Alas, then, Alcibiades, what a condition you have come to be in! I hesitate to use the term, but as we two are alone, I shall say it all the same: it is stupidity, excellent fellow, in its most extreme form, that you are living in the midst of, as the argument accuses you as well as you yourself. This is why you are rushing toward the political things before you have been educated. But you are not the only one in this condition—the many among those who practice the things of
c this city are also, except for a few at any rate, perhaps including your guardian Pericles.

ALC.: And in fact, Socrates, it is said that he became wise not spontaneously but through keeping company with many wise men, including Pythokleides and Anaxagoras, and now, in spite of his age, he associates with Damon for the sake of this very thing.[18]

SOC.: What of this? Have you ever seen any wise man who was unable to make another wise in the same way as himself? For example, the man who taught you letters was wise himself and made you so and whomever else he wanted? Or not?

ALC.: Yes.

d SOC.: Having learned it from him, then, will you not be able to make another wise?

ALC.: Yes.

SOC.: And it is the same with the cithara player and the trainer?

ALC.: Certainly.

---

[18]Pythokleides and Damon were well-known teachers of music; Anaxagoras is the philosopher. Socrates himself had associated extensively with Damon (*Laches* 180c–d, 197d) and had read Anaxagoras (*Phaedo* 97c–99c).

soc.: For it is surely a fine piece of evidence that those having knowledge of something really know it, when they are able to point to another who has this knowledge.

alc.: It seems so to me at least.

soc.: Now then, are you able to tell me whom Pericles has made wise, beginning with his own sons?

e alc.: What if the two sons of Pericles were born fools, Socrates?

soc.: But your brother Kleinias?

alc.: Why should you mention that madman Kleinias?[19]

soc.: But if Kleinias is mad and the two sons of Pericles born fools, to what cause shall we attribute it that he has overlooked your being in this condition?

alc.: I suppose I am the cause for not having paid attention.

119a soc.: But tell me if there is anyone among the rest of the Athenians or foreigners, slave or free, whose becoming wiser is held to have been caused by association with Pericles, just as I can tell you of Pythodorus, son of Isolochus, and Kallias, son of Kalliades, who are held to have become wiser by association with Zeno—each of them becoming wise and famous after paying Zeno a hundred minas.[20]

alc.: By Zeus, I cannot!

soc.: All right, then, what do you have in mind regarding yourself? Will you let yourself continue in the state you are, or will you take some trouble?

b alc.: Let us take common counsel, Socrates. And indeed, I understand what you are saying, and I agree; for apart from a few, those who practice the things of the city do seem to me uneducated.

soc.: Well, what then?

alc.: If they were educated, presumably one who undertook to compete against them would have to learn and practice to face them as if they were athletes, but since they approach the things of the city as ordinary men[21] and are so little prepared, why is it necessary to go out of one's way to practice and learn? For I well know that, where

c nature is concerned, I will get the better of them by far.

[19]Cf. *Protagoras* 320a–b.

[20]This Kallias was an Athenian general who died trying to relieve Potidaea (Thucydides I 61–63); Zeno of Elea was a student of the philosopher Parmenides. Cf. the *Parmenides*, which is set in the house of Pythodorus.

[21]The term translated here "ordinary" (*idiōtēs*) can signify either a private individual as opposed to a politician or an unskilled amateur as opposed to one who possesses an art.

SOC.: Alas, excellent fellow, what a thing to say! How unworthy of your looks and the other things that are yours!

ALC.: Why, and with a view to what, do you say this, Socrates?

SOC.: I lament for you and for my love.

ALC.: Why?

SOC.: That you thought your contest to be against the human beings here.

ALC.: Against whom, then?

d SOC.: This at least is a question worthy of a man who supposes himself to be high-minded.

ALC.: What do you mean? My contest is not with them?

SOC.: If you had in mind to pilot a warship that was about to enter battle, would it be enough if you were the best among your fellow sailors with respect to skill in piloting? Or would you suppose that, while this must indeed be the case, you should look rather toward those who are truly your competitors and not, as you are doing now, toward your fellow competitors? These, indeed, you must get the

e better of to the extent that they do not think of competing against you but accept being looked down on and become fellow competitors with you against the enemy—that is, if you really have in mind to perform a deed that is noble and worthy of yourself and the city.

ALC.: But I certainly do have this in mind.

SOC.: There is much merit, therefore, in your being content if you are better than the soldiers, without looking toward the leaders of your opponents to see if you can ever become better than they, or considering and practicing with a view to them.

120a ALC.: Who are these you are speaking of, Socrates?

SOC.: Don't you know that this city of ours wages war from time to time against both the Lacedaemonians and the great king?

ALC.: What you say is true.

SOC.: Then if you intend to become a leader of this city, would you be correct in believing that your contest is with the kings of the Lacedaemonians and those of the Persians?

ALC.: I'm afraid that what you say is true.

b SOC.: No, good fellow, but it is toward Meidias the quail striker[22]

---

[22]Our MSS have "quail raiser"; Burnet reads "quail striker" with Olympiodorus. Quail striking was evidently a somewhat disreputable sport; see Aristophanes Birds 1297–99.

and others of this sort that you must look—men who undertake to
practice the things of the city even though they have, as the women
would say, a slave's hair in the soul through their unmusical
vulgarity[23] and have never shed it and have come with their barbaric
speech to flatter the city, not to rule it. These are the ones you must
look to, I say, and take no trouble over yourself, and not learn what
requires learning if you are going to compete in so great a contest,
c nor practice what needs practicing, and thus thoroughly prepare
yourself to approach the things of the city.

ALC.: What you say seems to me true, Socrates, but I would suppose
that the generals of the Lacedaemonians and the king of the Persians
are not different from the others.

SOC.: But consider, excellent fellow, what a supposition you are
making!

ALC.: Concerning what?

d SOC.: In the first place, in which way do you suppose you would take
more trouble over yourself—if you were afraid of them and supposed
them formidable or not?

ALC.: Clearly if I supposed them formidable.

SOC.: But do you suppose, then, that you will be harmed in some way
if you take trouble over yourself?

ALC.: Not at all; rather that I shall be greatly benefited.

SOC.: In this one respect, then, your supposition involves a considerable evil.

ALC.: What you say is true.

SOC.: In the second place, that it is also false you will see by considering likelihoods.

ALC.: How so?

e SOC.: Is it likely that better natures should come to be in well-born
lines or not?

ALC.: Clearly in well-born ones.

SOC.: And that those who are well endowed by nature, if they are also
brought up well, will become in this way perfect with a view to
virtue?

ALC.: Necessarily.

SOC.: Let us consider, then, by contrasting ours with theirs, whether
in the first place the kings of the Lacedaemonians and the Persians

---

[23]*Amousia*: lack of education or culture (literally, "lack of music"). Many Greek
slaves were of Asian origin and had distinctively curly hair.

seem to belong to baser lines. Or do we not know that the former are the offspring of Herakles and the latter of Achaimenes and that the lines of Herakles and Achaimenes go back to Perseus, the son of Zeus?

121a ALC.: Yes, Socrates, and ours goes back to Eurysakes, and Eurysakes' to Zeus.

SOC.: Yes, well-born Alcibiades, and ours goes back to Daedalos, and Daedalos' to Hephaestos, the son of Zeus.[24] But the lines of those men, beginning from themselves, are kings sprung from kings on back to Zeus—kings on the one hand of Argos and Lacedaemon, on the other of Persia (which they have always held and often of Asia as well, which they have now)—but we are ordinary men ourselves,

b and so were our forefathers. And if you had to display your ancestors or their fatherlands—Salamis in the case of Eurysakes, Aegina in the case of Ajax before him—to Artaxerxes, son of Xerxes, how much laughter do you suppose you would come in for? But look out lest we be dwarfed by these men both in pride of line and in upbringing. Or have you not observed how great are the things belonging to the kings of the Lacedaemonians, whose wives are kept under public guard by the ephors[25] so that as far as possible it can be ascertained

c that no king is born of any other line than the Heraklids? But the Persian king is so superior that no one harbors any suspicion that a king could be born from anyone other than himself, and hence the king's wife is protected by nothing other than fear. At the birth of the eldest son, to whom the rule belongs, there is first of all feasting throughout the king's lands for all who are ruled by him, while ever afterward on that day all of Asia feasts and offers birthday sacrifices.

d When we are born, however, as the comic poet has it, "not even the neighbors notice a great deal," Alcibiades.[26] After this the boy is raised, not by a female nurse of little account, but by eunuchs who are

[24]Socrates supposes a relationship here between his father, Sophroniscus, who had been a sculptor, and the legendary inventor of sculpture, Daedalus; cf. *Euthyphro* 11c–d. Tradition had it that the practitioners of the various arts were descended from the mythical founders of those arts.

[25]Elected magistrates who wielded most of the executive power in the Spartan regime. They usually exercised effective control over the actions of the king, whose authority was for practical purposes limited to command of the army in wartime. Later in life, while staying at Sparta, Alcibiades was supposed to have slept with the wife of one of the kings.

[26]A proverbial saying apparently deriving from one of the plays of the comic poet Plato.

reputed to be the best of those around the king. These are charged
with caring for the child from birth, and among other things see to it
that it turns out as fair as possible by shaping and straightening its
e limbs, and they are held in great honor, doing these things. When the
boys reach their seventh year, they get horses and go to those who
teach about them and begin to go hunting. When the boy has grown
to twice seven years he is taken over by those they call royal tutors;
four of these are chosen from among those mature Persians of best
reputation—the wisest, the justest, the most moderate, and the most
122a courageous. Of these the first teaches him both the lore of Zoroaster,
son of Horomazes—that is, the worship of the gods—and skill in
kingly things; the justest, to tell the truth throughout his whole life;
the most moderate, to be ruled not even by one of the pleasures, that
he may be habituated to being a free man and a real king, who is ruler
first of all of the things within himself, not their slave; while the most
courageous prepares him to be fearless and unafraid, on the grounds
b that to be afraid is to be a slave. To you, however, Alcibiades, Pericles assigned as tutor the one among his servants who was most
useless on account of age, Zopyros the Thracian. I could go through
for you the rest of the upbringing and education of your competitors,
if it were not so large a task, and, in any event, these things are
sufficient to make clear the other things that follow from them. As
for your birth, Alcibiades, and your upbringing and education, or
that of any other Athenian whatever, it is taken care of by no one, so
to speak, unless someone who happens to be your lover. But if,
c again, you wish to look to the riches, luxuries, clothes, trailing robes,
perfumed baths, retinues of numerous servants, and all the other
forms of Persian refinement, you would be ashamed for yourself
when you observe how far you fall short of them. If, again, you wish
to look to the moderation and orderliness, the coolness, even temper,
high-mindedness, discipline, courage, endurance, love of toil, love of
victory, and love of honor of the Lacedaemonians, you would con-
d sider yourself a child in all such things. And again, even if you pay
attention to wealth and suppose you are something on that account,
let us not leave this unsaid either, so that you can observe where you
stand. As regards this matter, if you wish to look into the riches of
the Lacedaemonians, you will recognize that things here fall far short
of things there. For as regards the estates they have both in their own
country and in Messene, not one of those here could rival them in
extent or excellence, or in the possession of chattels (especially of the

Helot type), or indeed of horses, or of the other grazing animals that
e are pastured in Messene.[27] But all of these things I shall let pass.
There is not as much gold and silver held in all of Greece as there is
privately in Lacedaemon; for it has been arriving there for many
generations from all the other Greeks, and often from the barbarians
123a as well, but never leaves to go elsewhere, but just as in the fable of
Aesop, where the fox speaks to the lion, of the money arriving in
Lacedaemon the tracks leading there are clear, but nowhere can one
see them leading out. So one should know very well that the men
there are the wealthiest of the Greeks in gold and silver too, and of
them the king is the wealthiest of all, for the greatest and most
frequent acquisitions of such things are by the kings, and in addition
b the Lacedaemonians pay to the kings a royal tax which is not small.
Now, the things the Lacedaemonians have, while great in relation to
Greek riches, are as nothing in relation to Persian riches and those of
their king. For I once heard from a trustworthy man—one of those
who had traveled upcountry to see the king—that he had passed
through a large and good territory of nearly a day's march which the
inhabitants call the girdle of the king's wife, and that there is another
c which is called the veil, and that many other fine and good regions are
reserved for the apparel of the wife, each of these regions having its
name from some part of her apparel.[28] So I suppose that if someone
should say to the mother of the king, Amestris, who was Xerxes'
wife—"the son of Deinomache intends to range himself against your
son, her apparel being worth perhaps fifty minas at the very most
while her son has an estate of not quite three hundred acres at Er-
chiae"—she would wonder what this Alcibiades could ever be trust-
d ing in to have the intention of competing against Artaxerxes, and I
suppose she would say that there is nothing else this man could be
trusting in to attempt this except taking trouble and wisdom, these
being the only things worthy of account among the Greeks. But if

[27]Originally an independent state, Messene had been conquered after a long struggle and incorporated into Lacedaemon, its land and population being divided among
the Spartan citizens. The Helots (who included the original inhabitants of Messene)
were publicly owned serfs who performed agricultural labor.
[28]It was a practice in some Eastern kingdoms to assign parts of the territory to
various furnishings of the queen: cf. Xenophon *Anabasis* I iv 9, Diodorus Siculus I 62,
and Herodotus II 98. In this passage Socrates mimics the word for "gentleman" when
he calls these territories "fine and good." The word he uses for the furnishings
themselves is *kosmos*, which was employed philosophically to designate the order of
the world as a whole.

she should learn that this Alcibiades is now attempting it, in the first place, before he is twenty years old, and at that is completely uneducated, and in addition to these things, in spite of his lover telling him

e   he must first learn and take trouble over himself and practice before going to compete against the king, he is unwilling, and asserts that even his present state will suffice, I suppose she would wonder and ask: "Whatever is it, then, that the lad trusts in?" If, then, we should say that it is beauty and size and lineage and wealth and nature of the soul, she would think us mad, Alcibiades, when she looked at all such things in relation to what is available to them. And I suppose that

24a Lampido, too, the daughter of Leotychides, wife of Archidamos and mother of Agis—all of whom were kings[29]—would wonder as well when she looked at what belongs to them, if you intended to compete against her son in spite of being so badly trained. And yet does it not seem shameful that the women of our enemies have a better idea what sort of people we ought to be to make the attempt against them than we do ourselves? Rather, blessed fellow, obey me and the Delphic

b   inscription "know thyself": these are our opponents, not the ones you suppose, and we will get the better of them by no other thing than by taking trouble and by art. If you fall short in these, you will also fall short in becoming renowned among the Greeks and the barbarians—for which you have a greater love, it seems to me, than anyone has ever had for anything.

ALC.: What trouble has to be taken, then, Socrates? Can you explain? For you very much seem to be speaking the truth.

c   SOC.: Yes; but let us take common counsel as to the way in which we might become as excellent as possible. For, indeed, I'm not speaking only of you when I say it is necessary to be educated, and not of myself, for I do not differ from you at all, unless it is in one respect.

ALC.: Which?

SOC.: My guardian is better and wiser than yours—than Pericles.

ALC.: Who is this, Socrates?

SOC.: God, Alcibiades—the very one who did not let me converse with you before today, and in whom I place my trust when I say that you will gain prominence through no one but me.

d   ALC.: You're joking, Socrates.

SOC.: Perhaps. But what I say is true—that we need to take trouble,

---

[29]Of Sparta.

or rather that all human beings do, but most particularly the two of us.

ALC.: It is not false in my case.

SOC.: Nor indeed in mine.

ALC.: What can we do, then?

SOC.: There must be no begging off or hanging back, comrade.

ALC.: That would certainly be unseemly, at any rate, Socrates.

e SOC.: It would. We must consider in common. Now, tell me: we assert that we wish to become as excellent as possible, do we not?

ALC.: Yes.

SOC.: In what virtue?

ALC.: Clearly in that of good men.

SOC.: Who are good in what respect?

ALC.: Obviously, in the practice of affairs.

SOC.: What sort? Those connected with riding horses?

ALC.: No indeed.

SOC.: Because we would go to skilled horsemen?

ALC.: Yes.

SOC.: Then do you mean those connected with sailing?

ALC.: No.

SOC.: Then what sort? The things practiced by whom?

ALC.: Those practiced by Athenians who are gentlemen.

125a SOC.: By "gentlemen" do you mean sensible men or men lacking sense?

ALC.: Sensible men.

SOC.: In whatever respect each is sensible, is he not good?

ALC.: Yes.

SOC.: And in whatever respect lacking sense, wicked?

ALC.: How could it be otherwise?

SOC.: Is the shoemaker sensible when it comes to making footwear?

ALC.: Certainly.

SOC.: So he is good at these things?

ALC.: Good.

SOC.: What of this? Is the shoemaker not lacking sense when it comes to making clothes?

ALC.: Yes.

b SOC.: So he is bad at this?

ALC.: Yes.

SOC.: The same man, therefore, at least according to this argument, is both bad and good.

ALC.: It appears so.

SOC.: Do you say, then, that the good men are also bad?

ALC.: No indeed.

SOC.: Then whom do you mean by the good?

ALC.: Those capable of ruling in the city, in my view at least.

SOC.: Not, surely, of ruling horses?

ALC.: No indeed.

SOC.: But rather human beings?

ALC.: Yes.

SOC.: Who are sick, then?

ALC.: No.

SOC.: But rather who are voyaging at sea?

ALC.: No, not that.

SOC.: But rather who are harvesting?

ALC.: No.

c SOC.: Those who are doing nothing or those who are doing something?

ALC.: Those who are doing something, I should say.

SOC.: What? Try to make it clear to me as well.

ALC.: Engaging in dealings with one another and making use of one another, as is our way of living in the cities.

SOC.: Then you mean the ruling of human beings who make use of human beings?

ALC.: Yes.

SOC.: Of boatswains who make use of rowers, then?

ALC.: No indeed.

SOC.: Because this virtue, at any rate, is the pilot's?

ALC.: Yes.

SOC.: Do you mean rather the ruling of human beings who play the
d aulos and who lead human beings in song and make use of choral dancers?

ALC.: No indeed.

SOC.: Because this, again, is the choral teacher's?

ALC.: Certainly.

SOC.: But then, whatever do you mean in speaking of being able to rule human beings who make use of human beings?

ALC.: I, at least, mean ruling those in the city who have a part in the regime[30] and engage in dealings with respect to one another.

SOC.: What art is this, then? It is as if I were to ask you again what I

---

[30]*Koinōnountes politeias:* active partners or participants in the political order or regime (*politeia*), i.e., "citizens" (*politai*) as distinct from aliens or slaves.

asked just now—what art makes one have knowledge of ruling those who have a part in a sailing?

ALC.: The pilot's.

e SOC.: And those who have a part in a song, as was just said, what is the knowledge that makes one rule them?

ALC.: The very one you just mentioned, that of the choral teacher.

SOC.: Now, what do you call the knowledge of those who have a part in the regime?

ALC.: Good counsel, in my view at least, Socrates.

SOC.: What of this? Does the knowledge of pilots seem to be bad counsel?

ALC.: No indeed.

SOC.: But good counsel?

126a ALC.: It seems so to me, at least where it is directed toward preserving the voyagers.

SOC.: What you say is fine. But this good counsel you speak of— toward what is it directed?

ALC.: Toward the better managing and preserving of the city.

SOC.: By the presence or absence of what, then, is it better managed and preserved? It is as if you were to ask me: "By the presence or absence of what is the body managed and preserved?" and I said that it is when health is present and disease absent. Do you too not suppose it is this way?

b ALC.: Yes.

SOC.: Again, if you were to ask me: "By the presence of what are the eyes better?" I should say in a similar way that it is when sight is present and blindness absent. And it is when deafness is absent and hearing present that the ears become better and are better tended.

ALC.: Correct.

SOC.: Then what of the city? By the presence or absence of what does it become better and is it better tended and managed?

c ALC.: It seems to me, Socrates, that it is when they have friendship for one another and hatred and factional strife are absent.

SOC.: By friendship do you mean concord or discord?

ALC.: Concord.

SOC.: Through what art, then, do cities reach concord about numbers?

ALC.: Through the art of number.

SOC.: What about ordinary persons? Is it not through the same art?

ALC.: Yes.

soc.: And does not each man also reach concord with himself?

ALC.: Yes.

soc.: Through what art does each man reach concord with himself

d concerning the relative length of a span and a cubit? Is it not through the art of measurement?

ALC.: What else?

soc.: And ordinary men with each other and cities as well?

ALC.: Yes.

soc.: What of this? Is it the same concerning weights?

ALC.: I should say so.

soc.: The concord you were speaking of, then, what is it and what does it concern, and what art provides it? And is it the same for a city and an ordinary person, both in relation to himself and in relation to others?

ALC.: It is likely, at any rate.

e soc.: What is it, then? Don't become weary of answering, but be eager to tell me.

ALC.: I suppose I'm talking about friendship and concord,[31] just as a man loving his son is in concord, and another likewise, and brother is with brother and wife with husband.

soc.: Do you suppose, then, Alcibiades, that a husband is able to reach concord with his wife concerning the spinning of wool—one who has no knowledge with one who has knowledge?

ALC.: No indeed.

soc.: Nor is there any need for it, since this at least is a womanly piece of learning.

ALC.: Yes.

127a soc.: What of this? Would a wife be able to reach concord with her husband concerning the art of infantry fighting, which she has not learned?

ALC.: No indeed.

soc.: For perhaps you would assert that this at least is a manly thing.

ALC.: I indeed would.

soc.: According to your argument, therefore, some kinds of learning are womanly and others manly.

ALC.: How could it be otherwise?

---

[31] "Concord" (*homonoia*—literally, "likemindedness") is a word often applied to political agreement; "friendship" is the conventional translation of *philia*, a term that describes both conjugal affection and the fellow feeling of citizens.

SOC.: At least in these, then, there is no concord between women and men.

ALC.: No.

SOC.: Nor friendship, therefore, if friendship is concord.

ALC.: It appears not.

SOC.: Insofar as women practice their own things, then, men feel no friendship for them.

b ALC.: It would seem not.

SOC.: Nor women for men insofar as they practice their own things.

ALC.: No.

SOC.: Cities are not well managed, therefore, when each practices his own things?

ALC.: I at least would suppose they are, Socrates.

SOC.: What do you mean? Friendship will not be present, and we asserted that cities are well governed where it exists but not otherwise.

ALC.: But it seems to me that friendship comes to exist between them just on this account—that each practices his own things.

c SOC.: It did not a moment ago. But again, what do you mean? Will friendship come to exist without concord? Or can concord come to exist concerning matters that some know of but not others?

ALC.: That is not possible.

SOC.: Do they practice just or unjust things when they practice their own things?

ALC.: Just things; what else?

SOC.: When citizens practice just things in the city, then, does friendship not come to exist between them?

ALC.: Necessarily, it seems again to me, Socrates.

d SOC.: Then whatever do you mean by the friendship or concord concerning which we must be wise and of good counsel in order that we may be good men? I haven't been able to learn either what it is or who possesses it, for sometimes it appears to exist in the same men and sometimes not, on the basis of your argument.

ALC.: But by the gods, Socrates! I myself do not know what I mean. I am afraid it has escaped me that I have been in a most shameful condition for some time.

e SOC.: You must take heart. For if you had observed at fifty that this was your condition, it would have been difficult for you to take trouble over yourself, but the age you have now reached is the one in which this ought to be observed.

ALC.: Then what should the one who observes it do, Socrates?

SOC.: Answer the questions, Alcibiades. If you do this, and god is willing—if we should put any trust in my divination—both you and I shall be in a better state.

ALC.: So we will, at least as far as my answering can achieve it.

28a SOC.: Come then, what is it to take trouble over oneself—lest it often escape us that we are not taking trouble over ourselves while supposing we are? And when does a human being do this? When he takes trouble over his own things, does he then take trouble over himself as well?

ALC.: It seems so to me, at least.

SOC.: What of this? When does a human being take trouble over his feet? Is it when he takes trouble over what belongs to his feet?

ALC.: I don't understand.

SOC.: Is there something you describe as belonging to the hand? For example, would you assert that a ring belongs to any part of a human being other than the finger?

ALC.: No indeed.

SOC.: Does footwear not belong to the foot in the same way?

ALC.: Yes.

SOC.: And clothes and coverings similarly to the whole body?

b ALC.: Yes.

SOC.: So when we take trouble over footwear, do we not then take trouble over our feet?

ALC.: I scarcely understand, Socrates.

SOC.: What of this, Alcibiades? Is there something you describe as taking trouble in the correct way in any affair whatever?

ALC.: For my part, I do.

SOC.: Is it when someone makes a thing better, then, that you speak of taking trouble correctly?

ALC.: Yes.

SOC.: What art, then, makes footwear better?

ALC.: Shoemaking.

SOC.: By shoemaking, therefore, we take trouble over footwear?

c ALC.: Yes.

SOC.: And by shoemaking also over the foot? Or by that art by which we make feet better?

ALC.: By that.

SOC.: And don't we make feet better by the same art by which we make better the whole body?

ALC.: It seems so to me, at least.

SOC.: Is this not the art of gymnastic?

ALC.: Very much so.

SOC.: By the art of gymnastic, therefore, we take trouble over the foot, and by shoemaking over what belongs to the foot?

ALC.: Certainly.

SOC.: And by the art of gymnastic we take trouble over the hand, and by the art of the ring cutter over what belongs to the hand?

ALC.: Yes.

d SOC.: And by the art of gymnastic we take trouble over the body, and by weaving and the other arts over what belongs to the body?

ALC.: By all means:

SOC.: It is by one art, therefore, that we take trouble over each thing and by another over what belongs to it?

ALC.: It appears so.

SOC.: When one takes trouble over his own things, therefore, he does not take trouble over himself.

ALC.: Not at all.

SOC.: For it is not the same art, it would seem, by which one would take trouble over himself and his own things.

ALC.: It appears not to be.

SOC.: Come now, by what sort of art would we take trouble over ourselves?

ALC.: I cannot say.

e SOC.: But this much has been agreed, at any rate—that it is not one by which we would make any of our things better but one by which we would make ourselves better?

ALC.: What you say is true.

SOC.: Now, would we ever have known what art makes footwear better if we did not know footwear?

ALC.: Impossible.

SOC.: Nor what art makes rings better if we were ignorant of a ring.

ALC.: True.

SOC.: What of this? As to what art makes better oneself, could we ever know it if we were ignorant of what we are ourselves?

129a ALC.: Impossible.

SOC.: Does it happen to be easy, then, to know oneself, and was the man who inscribed this on the temple of the Pythian a mean sort, or is it difficult and something that does not belong to everyone?

ALC.: It has often seemed to me, Socrates, that it belongs to everyone and often that it is very difficult.

SOC.: But whether it is easy or not, Alcibiades, this at any rate is the way the matter stands for us: if we know this, we can perhaps know what it is to take trouble over ourselves, but if we are ignorant, we never can.

ALC.: These things are so.

b SOC.: Come then, in what way might the self itself[32] be discovered? For in this way we might perhaps discover what we are ourselves, while as long as we are ignorant of this it will presumably be impossible for us.

ALC.: What you say is correct.

SOC.: Stop there, then, in the name of Zeus! With whom are you now conversing? Is it not with me?

ALC.: Yes.

SOC.: And I with you?

ALC.: Yes.

SOC.: Socrates, therefore, is the one conversing?

ALC.: Certainly.

SOC.: And Alcibiades the one listening?

ALC.: Yes.

SOC.: Is it not by speech that Socrates converses?

c ALC.: How else?

SOC.: To converse and to use speech you call the same thing, presumably.

ALC.: Certainly.

SOC.: But aren't the user and what he uses different?

ALC.: What do you mean?

SOC.: Just as, presumably, a shoemaker cuts with a cutting knife and a carving knife and other tools.

ALC.: Yes.

SOC.: The cutter and user, then, is one thing, what he uses to cut another?

ALC.: How could it be otherwise?

SOC.: And in this way the things with which the citharist plays the cithara, and the citharist himself, would be different?

---

[32]Or "the same itself" (*auto tauto*): the expression refers to self-identity generally. See further 130d below.

ALC.: Yes.

d SOC.: This, then, is what I was asking just now—whether the user and what he uses seem always to be different.

ALC.: They seem to be.

SOC.: Then what shall we assert of the shoemaker? That he cuts with tools only or also with his hands?

ALC.: Also with his hands.

SOC.: He uses these as well, then?

ALC.: Yes.

SOC.: Does he also use his eyes when he engages in shoemaking?

ALC.: Yes.

SOC.: But we agree that the user and what he uses are different?

ALC.: Yes.

SOC.: The shoemaker and the cithara player are, therefore, different

e from the hands and eyes with which they do their work?

ALC.: It appears so.

SOC.: Doesn't a human being also use his whole body?

ALC.: Certainly.

SOC.: But what uses and what it uses were different?

ALC.: Yes.

SOC.: A human being is different, therefore, from his own body?

ALC.: Apparently.

SOC.: Then whatever is man?

ALC.: I cannot tell you.

SOC.: But you can—at least that he is something that uses the body.

ALC.: Yes.

130a SOC.: Does anything use this other than the soul?

ALC.: Nothing.

SOC.: While ruling it?

ALC.: Yes.

SOC.: Now this, I suppose, no one would suppose to be otherwise.

ALC.: What?

SOC.: That man is one of three things.

ALC.: Of which things?

SOC.: Soul or body or both together as a whole.

ALC.: Of course.

SOC.: And yet we have agreed that what rules the body is man?

b ALC.: We have agreed.

SOC.: Does the body itself rule itself, then?

ALC.: Not at all.

soc.: For we said it is ruled.

alc.: Yes.

soc.: Then it would not be this that we are seeking, at any rate.

alc.: It seems not.

soc.: Do both together rule body, then, and is this man?

alc.: Perhaps, indeed.

soc.: It is this least of all; for if one is not a co-ruler, presumably there isn't any way both together can rule.

alc.: Correct.

c soc.: Since man is neither body nor both together, what is left, I suppose, is either that he is nothing, or if he is something, that man turns out to be nothing other than soul.

alc.: Quite so.

soc.: Is it necessary to demonstrate to you more clearly in any further way that the soul is man?

alc.: By Zeus, this seems to me quite sufficient!

d soc.: If the demonstration has been, if not precise, at least well suited, it is enough for us, for we will know the matter precisely when we discover what we just passed over because of its involving much consideration.

alc.: What is that?

soc.: What was in a way mentioned a moment ago—that we would first have to consider the self itself. As it is, we have considered, instead of the self, what each thing itself is. And perhaps this will be enough, for presumably we could not assert there is anything more dominant in ourselves than the soul.

alc.: No indeed.

soc.: And is it not fine to believe thus—that you and I are associating with one another using speeches, one soul toward the other?

e alc.: Certainly.

soc.: This, then, was what we were saying a little while ago: Socrates is conversing with Alcibiades using speech, and it is not toward your face, as it seems, that his speeches are directed but toward Alcibiades—that is, the soul.

alc.: It seems so to me, at least.

soc.: It is with the soul, therefore, that we are bid to become acquainted by the one who enjoins us to know ourselves.

131a alc.: It would seem so.

soc.: Whoever knows something of the things belonging to the body, therefore, knows his own things but not himself.

ALC.: That's so.

SOC.: Then no one among the doctors knows himself insofar as he is a doctor, nor anyone among the trainers insofar as he is a trainer.

ALC.: Apparently not.

b SOC.: And farmers and other craftsmen are very far from knowing themselves. For these apparently know not even their own things but only things even more remote than their own things in accordance with the arts they possess; for they know the things belonging to the body and by which it is tended.

ALC.: What you say is true.

SOC.: If, then, it is moderation to know oneself, none of these men is moderate by his art.

ALC.: None, it seems to me.

SOC.: On this account, then, these arts seem to be sordid and the kind of learning that does not belong to a good man.

ALC.: Certainly.

SOC.: And again, whoever tends the body tends his own things and not himself?

ALC.: I'm afraid so.

SOC.: But whoever tends money tends neither himself nor his own c things, but things even more remote than his own?

ALC.: It seems so to me, at least.

SOC.: The money-maker, therefore, no longer practices his own things.

ALC.: Correct.

SOC.: If, therefore, someone has become a lover of Alcibiades' body, he has fallen in love not with Alcibiades but with something belonging to Alcibiades.

ALC.: What you say is true.

SOC.: But whoever has fallen in love with you loves the soul?

ALC.: This appears necessary on the basis of the argument.

SOC.: The one who loves your body, will he not go away once its bloom has faded?

ALC.: It appears so.

d SOC.: But the one who loves your soul does not go as long as it proceeds toward the better?

ALC.: That's likely, at any rate.

SOC.: And I am the one who does not go but remains once the body has faded, after the others have departed.

ALC.: And it is well that you do, Socrates; don't you depart.

SOC.: Only strive to be as beautiful as possible.

ALC.: I shall strive.

e SOC.: This, at any rate, is how matters stand with you: there has never been, it would seem, a lover of Alcibiades, son of Kleinias, nor is there any, except one man, and this one cherished[33]—Socrates, son of Sophroniscos and Phaenarete.

ALC.: True.

SOC.: Did you not assert that I had barely anticipated you in approaching you—that you would have approached me first, since you wished to find out why I alone do not go away?

ALC.: It was so.

SOC.: This was the cause of it—that I was your only lover, the others being lovers of your things, and your things are fading from their

32a prime, while you are beginning to bloom. And now, if you are not corrupted by the populace of Athens and become baser, I will not give you up. For I fear most of all lest, having become a lover of the populace, you be corrupted; for many and good men among the Athenians have already had this experience. For fair of face is "the populace of great-hearted Erechtheus,"[34] but one ought to look on it without its clothes. Take the precaution, then, that I tell you of.

ALC.: Which?

b SOC.: Train first, blessed fellow, and learn what needs to be learned in order to approach the things of the city, and do not do it before, so that you may have an antidote and suffer nothing terrible.

ALC.: This seems to me well spoken, Socrates, But try to explain in what way we might take trouble over ourselves.

SOC.: We have made this much headway: what we are has been properly agreed on. We were afraid we might fail at this, and not realize we were taking trouble over something else and not ourselves.

ALC.: That is so.

c SOC.: And after this, then, we agreed that we should take trouble over the soul and look to this.

ALC.: Clearly.

SOC.: And that taking trouble over bodies and money should be handed over to others.

[33]Cf. *Odyssey* II 365.
[34]*Iliad* II 547.

ALC.: Of course.

SOC.: In what way, then, might we know this most plainly? For if we know this, it would seem, we will also know ourselves. But in the name of the gods! Do we really not understand the Delphic inscription we mentioned just now, which is so well spoken?

ALC.: What do you have in mind when you say this, Socrates?

d SOC.: I'll tell you what I suspect this inscription tells us and advises us. For there are probably not examples of it in many places but only in the case of sight.

ALC.: What do you mean by this?

SOC.: You consider it too. If, giving advice to our eye as to man, he had said "see yourself," how would we take his admonition? To look at that in looking at which the eye would see itself?

ALC.: Clearly.

SOC.: Then can we bring to mind what it is of the beings that we look

e at when we see both that and ourselves at the same time?

ALC.: Clearly, Socrates, at mirrors and things of that sort.

SOC.: What you say is correct. And in the eye with which we see there is also something of that sort of thing.

ALC.: Certainly.

133a SOC.: Have you considered that the face of one looking into the eye appears in the sight of the one opposite as in a mirror—this being what we call the pupil, a sort of image of the one looking in?

ALC.: What you say is true.

SOC.: An eye seeing an eye, therefore, and looking at that part of itself which is best and by which it sees, would in this way see itself.

ALC.: It appears so.

SOC.: But if it should look at any of the other things belonging to man or at any of the beings other than that to which it happens to be similar, it will not see itself.

b ALC.: What you say is true.

SOC.: If the eye is going to see itself, therefore, it must look at the eye, and at that place in the eye in which the virtue of the eye comes to exist, and presumably this is sight?

ALC.: It is so.

SOC.: Therefore, dear Alcibiades, if the soul too is to know itself, should it look at the soul, and above all at that place in it in which the virtue of the soul—wisdom—comes to exist, and at any other thing to which this happens to be similar?

ALC.: It seems to me, at least, Socrates.

c SOC.: Are we able to say what of the soul is more divine[35] than that which is concerned with knowing and thinking?

ALC.: We are not.

SOC.: This part of it, therefore, resembles the god,[36] and someone who looks at this and comes to know all that is divine—god and sensible thinking—would thus come to know himself also.

ALC.: It appears so.

[SOC.: Then just as mirrors are clearer than the reflection in the eye, as well as purer and brighter, so the god happens to be purer and brighter than what is best in our soul?

ALC.: It would seem so, at least, Socrates.

SOC.: In looking to the god, therefore, we shall treat him as the finest mirror, and in human things we shall look to the virtue of the soul. In this way above all, we may see and know ourselves.

ALC.: Yes.][37]

SOC.: Did we agree that knowing oneself is moderation?

ALC.: Certainly.

SOC.: Without knowing ourselves or being moderate, then, would we be able to know the things of ourselves that are good and bad?

ALC.: How could this come about, Socrates?

d SOC.: For perhaps it appears to you impossible to know that the things of Alcibiades belong to Alcibiades without knowing Alcibiades.

ALC.: Impossible indeed, by Zeus!

SOC.: Nor that our things are ours, therefore, without knowing ourselves.

ALC.: How could we?

SOC.: And if not our things, then neither would we know what belongs to our things?

ALC.: It appears not.

SOC.: Then we did not agree altogether correctly just now when we agreed that there are some who do not know themselves but know the things that belong to themselves, while others know what be-

e longs to their things. For it would seem that it belongs to one man

---

[35]One of the best manuscripts (B) reads "more intellectual."

[36]Some manuscripts (PTW) read "divine" instead of "god."

[37]The bracketed words are absent from the manuscripts and are found only in quotations of the dialogue by the late classical authors Eusebius and Stobaeus. They may have originated with Eusebius, a Christian apologist.

and one art to discern all these things—oneself, the things that belong to oneself, and what belongs to the things that belong to oneself.

ALC.: Probably so.

SOC.: Whoever is ignorant of the things belonging to himself presumably would also be ignorant of the things belonging to others in the same respects.

ALC.: But of course.

SOC.: And if of the things of others, he will also be ignorant of the things of the cities.

ALC.: Necessarily.

SOC.: Therefore one of this sort would never become a skilled political man.

ALC.: No indeed.

SOC.: Nor a man skilled in managing a household.

134a   ALC.: No indeed.

SOC.: At any rate, he will not know what he is practicing.

ALC.: Not at all.

SOC.: And one who does not know will go wrong?

ALC.: Certainly.

SOC.: And if he goes thoroughly wrong, will he not practice things badly both in private and in public?

ALC.: How could he not?

SOC.: And if he acts badly,[38] will he not be miserable?

ALC.: Exceedingly.

SOC.: What of those for whom he acts?

ALC.: These also.

SOC.: It is not possible to be happy, therefore, unless one is moderate and good.

b   ALC.: It is not possible.

SOC.: The bad among human beings, then, are miserable.

ALC.: Exceedingly.

SOC.: It is not the man who has become rich, therefore, who is relieved of misery but the man who has been moderate.

ALC.: It appears so.

SOC.: It is not, therefore, walls or warships or dockyards that the cities need, Alcibiades, if they are to be happy, nor numbers nor size without virtue.

---

[38]"Practice badly" and "act badly" both translate the expression *kakōs prattein,* which is the opposite of *eu prattein:* cf. n. 13 above.

ALC.: No, it is not.

c SOC.: Then if you are going to practice the things of the city correctly and nobly, you must give the citizens a share of virtue.

ALC.: How could it be otherwise?

SOC.: Could one give a share of something he did not have?

ALC.: How could he?

SOC.: You must first acquire virtue yourself, then, as must anyone who is going to rule and take trouble not only privately, over himself and the things belonging to himself, but also over the city and the things of the city.

ALC.: What you say is true.

SOC.: It is not, therefore, personal license and rule that you must obtain in order to act as you wish for yourself or for the city but justice and moderation.

ALC.: It appears so.

d SOC.: For if both you and the city act justly and moderately, you[39] will act in a way that is dear to the gods.

ALC.: It is likely, at any rate.

SOC.: And as we were saying earlier, you will act looking toward what is divine and bright.

ALC.: It appears so.

SOC.: But if you look there, you will behold and know both yourselves and the good things that belong to you.

ALC.: Yes.

SOC.: So you will act correctly and well?

ALC.: Yes.

e SOC.: But if you indeed act in this way, I am willing to be guarantor for your happiness.

ALC.: You are a reliable guarantor.

SOC.: But if you act unjustly, looking toward what is godless and dark, as is likely, you will practice things similar to these through ignorance of yourselves.

ALC.: It would seem so.

SOC.: But as for someone, dear Alcibiades, who has personal license to act as he wishes but lacks intelligence, what is likely to be the result for him privately and for the city? For example, what will be the result for someone who, while ill, has personal license to act as he

---

[39]Here and in what follows Socrates employs the plural "you" when speaking of Alcibiades and the city.

135a wishes and though lacking medical intelligence exercises a tyranny in which no one is able to stand up to him? Is not the most likely thing that he will be destroyed in body?

ALC.: What you say is true.

SOC.: What of this? If someone in a ship had personal license to act as seemed best to him and yet were deprived of intelligence and the virtue of the skilled pilot, do you catch a glimpse of what might happen both to him and to his fellow sailors?

ALC.: I indeed do—that all of them might well be lost.

b SOC.: Similarly, in a city and in all exercises of rule and personal license that fall short in virtue, is acting badly not the consequence?

ALC.: Necessarily.

SOC.: It is not tyranny, therefore, excellent Alcibiades, that ought to be secured either for oneself or for the city if you are to be happy, but virtue.

ALC.: What you say is true.

SOC.: But before one has virtue, it is better to be ruled, by one who is better, than to rule—for a man and not only for a child.

ALC.: It appears so.

SOC.: Is not what is better also nobler?

ALC.: Yes.

SOC.: And what is nobler is more fitting?

c ALC.: How could it be otherwise?

SOC.: It is fitting, therefore, for a bad man to be a slave; for it is better.

ALC.: Yes.

SOC.: Vice is thus something befitting a slave.

ALC.: It appears so.

SOC.: And virtue something befitting a free man.

ALC.: Yes.

SOC.: One ought to flee what befits a slave, comrade?

ALC.: Above all, Socrates.

SOC.: Do you observe now what your condition is? Befitting a free man or not?

ALC.: It seems to me I observe it all too well.

SOC.: Do you know, then, how you may escape this thing that now affects you? For let us not use the term in the case of a noble man.

d ALC.: I do.

SOC.: How?

ALC.: If you wish it, Socrates.

SOC.: This is not nobly said, Alcibiades.

ALC.: How should it be said?

SOC.: If god is willing.

ALC.: Then I say it. But in addition to these things, I want to say the following—that we will probably be changing roles, Socrates, I taking yours and you mine, for from this day nothing can keep me from attending on you, and you from being attended upon by me.

e   SOC.: Well-born fellow, my love will then be no different from a stork if after hatching in you a winged love it is tended by this in turn.[40]

ALC.: But so matters stand, and I shall begin at this moment to take trouble over justice.

SOC.: And I would wish you to continue doing so. Yet I stand in dread, not because I do not have trust in your nature, but rather because, seeing the strength of the city, I fear that it will overcome both me and you.

[40]It was widely believed (see Aristophanes *Birds* 1353–57) that older storks are fed by their offspring.

On the
Alcibiades I

STEVEN FORDE

The *Alcibiades I* was held in the greatest esteem in the Platonic school of antiquity. There was a tradition in fact that placed the dialogue at the head of all of Plato's works, as the opening to the entire corpus; hence, perhaps, the traditional subtitle, "On the Nature of Man." The neo-Platonist Iamblichus wrote that the *Alcibiades I* contains the whole philosophy of Plato, as in a seed. The Islamic sage and Platonic commentator Alfarabi concurs, saying in effect that in the *Alcibiades I* all the Platonic questions are raised as if for the first time.[1] The dialogue itself is almost kaleidoscopic in appearance because of the range of issues raised and the manner of their treatment. Questions are introduced, discussed, and dropped, often with no apparent resolution and no apparent connection with what comes before or after. Readers with exposure to other Platonic dialogues are likely to recognize each of the arguments in detail but still to come away bewildered by the dialogue as a whole. The most obvious place for us to begin interpreting the bewildering progress of the dialogue is in the dramatic situation that develops throughout.

The *Alcibiades I* is, to begin with, a very private dialogue; in it, Alcibiades and Socrates are very pointedly alone (cf. 118b). Alcibiades is rather young.[2] Socrates approaches him with the intention of influencing and educating him, and indeed, the *Alcibiades I* is al-

---

[1]Alfarabi *The Philosophy of Plato* I 1–2. For a brief discussion of the tradition in the Greek school, see Paul Friedländer, "Alcibiades Major," in his *Plato,* 3 vols. (Princeton, 1958–70), 2:231–43.

[2]The dramatic date of the dialogue is about 433 B.C. Alcibiades is scarcely twenty years old (123d); Socrates is about forty.

most unique among the dialogues of Plato in depicting the profound transformation of an interlocutor in the course of a single conversation. Yet we know that Socrates was later put to death by the city of Athens for allegedly corrupting its youth, and we are told, especially by Xenophon, that Socrates' association with Alcibiades was widely taken to be a case in point.[3] Xenophon, who takes it upon himself explicitly to defend Socrates against the charges of the city, does his best to distance Alcibiades from Socrates. The *Alcibiades I* to the contrary presents Socrates from the beginning as a lover of Alcibiades.

I

Almost the first thing that we learn from Socrates in the *Alcibiades I* is that, although he has been a lover of Alcibiades for some time, he has been prevented by his "divine sign" from speaking to Alcibiades until this moment. The divine sign—which according to both Plato and Xenophon was supposed to keep Socrates out of trouble—has given its blessing so to speak before the conversation begins. Socrates says at the end of his opening remarks that he supposes the god forbade him before because until this moment Alcibiades was too young and would not listen to Socrates (105e–106a). Indeed, the recalcitrant youthfulness of Alcibiades might be called one of the governing facts of the first half of the dialogue. Here at the beginning, Socrates is able to get Alcibiades' serious attention only with difficulty, by means of an uncharacteristic monologue in which he intrigues Alcibiades with his strangeness. Throughout the rest of the first half (roughly to 119b), Alcibiades continually threatens to stop taking Socrates' questions seriously and to answer any which way, in childish fashion, to avoid being trapped in the argument. The first half of the dialogue is almost a game of cat and mouse.

The Alcibiades who stands before us at the opening of the *Alcibiades I* is proud, even haughty. He has spurned all his needier lovers; he is the very antithesis of love. The erotic Socrates cannot help being diffident in approaching this Alcibiades. Alcibiades, he says, believes he has no need of anyone because of the greatness of his possessions. Furthermore, he charges Alcibiades with cherishing the

---

[3]Xenophon *Memorabilia* I ii 12–28, 39–47.

greatest ambition. If some god were to offer Alcibiades a choice between resting content or dying immediately if he could not hope to "acquire more," Socrates claims that Alcibiades would choose death. He would even choose death, Socrates says, if the god allowed him the rule of Europe only, without supremacy in Asia as well. We do not know whether Alcibiades had actually conceived an "Asian" ambition before this moment, since Socrates claims only that once offered the choice he would immediately take it up, but from this moment Socrates treats it as an established fact. Socrates and his nameless god appear as goads to the greatest political ambition. Precisely in attaching Alcibiades' ambition to the greatest objects, however, they bring Alcibiades implicitly under their own tutelage and authority. For the god presumably has power to grant or withhold the prizes with which he is enticing Alcibiades, and Socrates is the sole mouthpiece of this god, whom he conflates with his own divine sign here and throughout the dialogue. Socrates claims that only with his own and the god's help will Alcibiades succeed.

Socrates, with this much hold on Alcibiades' attention, is able to begin the dialogue in earnest; his first task, not an easy one, is to show the skeptical Alcibiades that he does indeed need help. He begins hypothetically from the moment, which he says is not far off, when Alcibiades will be about to ascend the speaker's platform in the Athenian assembly (106c). Socrates takes hold of Alcibiades and asks him on what he plans to advise the Athenians. The subject of their discussion, which remains the explicit theme throughout the dialogue, is thus the question of what knowledge is appropriate to a statesman, what knowledge is the knowledge connected with ordering a city and deserving of the greatest honor from it. According to the dramatic setting that Socrates supposes here, the dialogue as a whole replaces at least temporarily Alcibiades' political debut. Alcibiades for his part agrees from the start that it must be some kind of knowledge or art that entitles him to advise the city. He even agrees with Socrates' argument that such things as beauty, wealth, and noble birth, the very things Socrates said earlier he had been priding himself on, do not entitle him to advise the city and will get him nowhere. When Socrates asks him though on what subjects of political deliberation he will knowledgeably advise the city, Alcibiades says only "their own affairs" (107c). When pressed by Socrates to give a further, more substantial answer, he singles out particularly the issues of war and peace (107d).

Socrates appears to consider this answer sufficient and prepares for an inquiry into whether Alcibiades has the art pertaining to war and peace by showing Alcibiades, who has some difficulty following, what an art is as such (107d–108d). An art, according to Socrates, is the knowledge of "the better" (or more simply, the good) relevant to an activity. In the case of music at least Socrates suggests that art is divine or is connected with the gods. He then asks Alcibiades what art it is that he must know to be a proper adviser on war and peace, but Alcibiades does not know. In order to discover what this art is, Socrates suggests that they have recourse to speeches. It turns out that everyone who goes to war claims to do so justly: the art of war, Socrates concludes, must be justice (109b). Socrates ignores Alcibiades' contrary suggestion, reasonable enough in itself, that everyone's claims are based not so much on concern for the "lawful" as for a certain kind of reputation (109c), and his peculiar argument from pretexts, as it might be called, stands.

Alcibiades, who plans to advise the city brilliantly, must know the art of justice thoroughly. When Socrates asks him where he learned it, though, Alcibiades scarcely thinks he can be serious. Socrates' pursuit of the whole matter in this fashion must be a joke. Alcibiades' inclination to shrug the argument off in this way draws from Socrates his first oath: in the name of Friendship! he is serious (109d). He forces Alcibiades to admit that he has not taken the trouble to discover what justice is, because he always thought he knew. In particular, Socrates says that he often heard Alcibiades as a child, when he was playing at dice or some other game, vehemently denouncing one of his playmates for doing him an injustice, as if he had not the slightest doubt about what justice is (110b). The vehemence of Alcibiades' responses to this remark shows almost comically that his attitude toward the game and toward justice remain fundamentally unchanged since that time. We see in the first place that Alcibiades does care about justice and not only as a pretext. His notion of justice itself, however, seems rather unusual. Socrates' allusion to the dicing episode draws from Alcibiades an astonishing outburst of spiritedness and even anger; not only his defense of justice but his very idea of what it is seem to be rooted in spiritedness and love of victory. Given the fact—and we may presume it is a fact—that Alcibiades is "best," justice is giving him the victory in whatever contest is at hand. The just Alcibiades demands it and backs his demand with anger. Socrates said earlier that Alcibiades' ambition in Athens was to come before the city, display his worth, and immediately be accorded the first place (105a–b). We can now imagine that Alcibiades was likely to be rather insistent about that point.

In the present context, Socrates chooses for a second time simply to ignore Alcibiades' resistance to his argument. Alcibiades always thought he knew what justice is, therefore he would never have made the effort to discover on his own what it is (110c; cf. 109c). The unchastened Alcibiades simply returns to the argument that he was taught it—taught it, as he now says, by the many (110d–e). Socrates in response maintains that the many are ignorant, as is proven by the fact that they disagree; they disagree more violently about justice perhaps than about anything else. He points by way of demonstration to Homer (112a–b).

What Socrates says about Homer is striking for at least two reasons. To begin with, there is the fact that he uses Homer to typify the attitude of the many about justice and to prove that they do not know what it is. Then, his epitome of Homer is in itself rather surprising. From the *Odyssey* he mentions only the fight of Odysseus and the suitors over Penelope. His selectivity brings to mind the fact that the *Iliad* too, and with greater justification, could be said to be about the fight over a woman. There seems to be a suggestion that ordinary quarrels over justice are somehow erotic or are linked to erotic possession. That thought seems to indicate something like the following general view of things. Human beings desire certain objects with a passion that could be described as erotic. Their desire they take to be "just," and they are led by it to conclude that they have a right, as we would say, to the objects of their desire. Since human beings agree by and large about what is desirable, they fight over the possession of those things and hence over conflicting views of justice. Their appeals to justice may mask a certain selfish hypocrisy, but it is not a hypocrisy of which they are necessarily aware. It remains true, however, that, not having thought seriously about the question, and about what truly can be said to belong to them, they do not "know" about justice. If they had knowledge, Socrates implies, they would not fight.

Socrates' appeal to Homer, given its position in the dialogue, invites us to consider the difference between Alcibiades and the many on the question of justice. The ordinary attachment to justice revolves around the desire for certain substantial goods; Alcibiades is attached only to victory. The many desire victory but primarily as a means to the possession of goods rather than as an end in itself. Thus if, according to Socrates, the attachment of the many to justice can be called somehow erotic, Alcibiades does not seem to share that eroticism. Pure spiritedness or love of victory has no necessary reference to anything beyond victory itself, no longing for a fixed object, or even dedication to a particular contest, unless on the grounds that victory in one contest is more glorious than victory in another. It is not as such devoted to any cause.

Socrates' impeachment of the authority of the many on the question of justice completes his proof that Alcibiades must be ignorant about justice himself. Alcibiades, however, is uncowed. He now declares that the Greeks rarely deliberate about justice anyway but instead concentrate on the expedient (113d). Socrates patiently produces for Alcibiades a proof that he does not know the expedient either, because the just and the expedient are the same. The briefest way to state the core of Socrates' argument would be to say that it rests on the notion that the pursuit of justice is always "expedient" because justice, and virtue in general, is the greatest human good and hence in every case the supremely choiceworthy thing. Thus as Alcibiades readily admits, the performance of noble actions is to be preferred even to life itself. It is a false notion of expediency that takes self-preservation or gain to be the goal of human life.

With the argument on expediency Socrates finally succeeds in subduing Alcibiades. Alcibiades cannot deny that he is devoted to justice, even in the sense of self-sacrifice, and that he does not know what it is. At the conclusion of Socrates' last argument Alcibiades swears by all the gods that he no longer knows what he is saying (116e). According to Socrates this situation has come about not because Alcibiades is ignorant but because, being ignorant, he thought he knew. There is a certain suggestion that Alcibiades' initial claim to know, like the similar claims of others, was dictated by his desire to act. Human action in general carries the implicit claim that one knows what one is doing (cf. 117d). Alcibiades' ambition involved a claim to know about the most important things, hence he was caught in the greatest stupidity (118b). Socrates claims that Alcibiades himself now admits this, along with the argument, meaning to say that Alcibiades has finally taken the argument seriously to heart. The contest of the first part of the dialogue seems to be won. Accordingly, Socrates moves now for the first time to console Alcibiades: Alcibiades is by no means alone in his plight but shares it with perhaps all the political men in Athens.

It may be that hidden in Socrates' consolation is a test. If so, Alcibiades fails it miserably, in a way that jeopardizes everything that Socrates has accomplished with him. After a moment's discussion, the conclusion that Alcibiades draws from the ignorance of his competitors is that he can get by himself, and even prevail in Athens, without taking the trouble to educate himself. He threatens in effect to wallow in his ignorance and to forsake any higher hope. This draws a lament from Socrates, that Alcibiades is betraying his own worth. He is doing so in part, of course, because Socrates has been lecturing him on how far he is at this moment from doing himself justice. What Socrates must do now is establish, or reestablish, a real attachment to perfection in Alcibiades.

II

A crisis of sorts in the dialogue thus marks the beginning of a new phase in it and a new strategy on Socrates' part. Hitherto, Socrates' manner has been combative and refutative; he has practically taunted Alcibiades with paradoxical arguments that, while unconvincing, forced Alcibiades into silence. In the next section of the dialogue, consisting for the most part of a striking "royal tale,"[4] he weaves an immensely attractive picture of political success as a prize for self-perfection. He begins with an image of Alcibiades' situation in Athens: if Alcibiades were on a warship, he would not rest content with being superior to his shipmates but rather would strive to be superior to the opposing commanders (119d–e). As to his fellow sailors, he should be so superior to them that they would be content merely to range themselves beneath him and follow his command. The ship metaphor is calculated to appeal powerfully to Alcibiades and his ambition. Its bearing can be most easily grasped by contrasting it

---

[4]The "royal tale" (121a–24b) occupies a position in the dialogue that is similar to that of the myths found in other dialogues of Plato, but for rhetorical reasons it is presented by Socrates less as a fanciful creation and more as a description of realities. For that reason I have elected to call it a "tale" rather than a myth, adhering to the original sense of the Greek *mythos*.

with Socrates' more famous ship analogy in the *Republic*.[5] According to the analogy in the *Republic,* the partial intention of which is to depreciate politics and political ambition, the city is like a ship on which sailors are constantly fighting over the command, seldom or never allowing it to go to the deserving one. The conditions of ordinary politics make the rule of the best unlikely, to say the least. What Socrates suggests to Alcibiades is instead that, if he makes himself sufficiently deserving, spontaneous and uncomplaining obedience will be his from the city, allowing him, as Socrates says, to accomplish truly noble deeds, worthy of himself and of the city (119e).

Alcibiades is immediately enchanted with ths image. Socrates tells him that the kings of Sparta and Persia are the true rivals, the opposing commanders, indicated by the analogy (120a). Scarcely has he said so, however, before he abruptly and jarringly contradicts himself: Alcibiades must look not to these but to the likes of Meidias the petty demagogue, whom Socrates follows Aristophanes in comparing to a quail striker (120a–c; cf. Aristophanes *Birds* 1297–99). These are the men to whom one must look and neglect oneself, these men who still have, as the women would say, slavish hair in their souls through lack of education. Socrates' abrupt reversal of position seems to point to something like the teaching of the ship metaphor in the *Republic*. The demagogic politics of Athens, at least, makes the rule of the best more or less impossible. In accordance with his rhetorical intention with Alcibiades, Socrates does not pursue this thought. The challenge of Meidias is dropped as quickly as it was raised; entering the contest with Meidias means neglecting oneself. As a result, however, the real problem represented by Meidias is left wholly unresolved. Or rather, there is one slight hint as to how it might be resolved, namely by putting the women, who alone might know how to despise Meidias, in control of Athens.

Precisely this suggestion, unlikely as it may seem, is taken up by Socrates in his royal tale. Women, the queens of Sparta and Persia, are the most conspicuous characters in the tale. As he introduces the tale, Socrates returns emphatically to the contention that Alcibiades' competitors are the Spartan and Persian kings. Almost the first thing he says about the exemplary rule of the kings is that they control their

[5]*Republic* 488a–489a.

women admirably (121b–c). The Spartan queens, he says, are publicly guarded to guarantee their fidelity and the purity of the royal
lineage; in the case of Persia, the king himself is so superior that no
one could have any suspicions against the queen. She is guarded by
nothing but fear. The rule of the Persian king in this instance, for rule
it is, operates simply by virtue of his own overwhelming superiority,
which inspires a kind of spontaneous obedience in both queen and
subjects. The "fear" they have, since it is distinguished from the kind
of fear legal magistrates such as the ephors inspire, seems to be something akin to awe. Socrates then says that, in Persia, when the future
king is born, the subjects in the kingdom and all of Asia celebrate the
event and celebrate its anniversary forever after. From the moment of
his birth, so to speak, the figure of the Persian king has the power to
move all his subjects; all of Asia in a manner moves itself around him.
The birth of ordinary men such as Alcibiades and himself, Socrates
notes, is comically insignificant by contrast.

The education of the future king of Persia, according to Socrates, is
correspondingly splendid and culminates in a training in the four
Socratic virtues (121d–122a). There is more training in addition, he
says, but he declines to describe it and gives us a description of the
sumptuous luxury of the Persians instead (122b–c). After giving Alcibiades a parallel account of the education and wealth of the Spartans, Socrates returns to the Persian case, to relate what he once heard
from a trustworthy traveler who had been through the king's domain. He said that, on his way, he passed through many fine and
good regions that had been reserved for and named after various of
the queen's furnishings (123b–c). The word that Socrates uses to
designate each of these is *kosmos,* a term used often enough to designate at least ornamental or cosmetic furnishings but one whose primary meaning is "order" and one that in this acceptation is of great
philosophical significance. Indeed, what we learn from the trustworthy traveler whom Socrates cites is precisely that the Persian domain
is cast onto a very well-defined order; that order revolves somehow
around the person of the queen. The fact that the whole is rationally
ordered in this way seems to prompt Socrates to call the various
Persian regions "fine and good" in themselves, echoing thereby the
compound Greek word for "gentleman." A gentleman in the best
case is a man who knows statesmanship perfectly.

Socrates prefaced the story of the traveler by saying that the wealth
of the Persians was incomparably greater than the wealth of the

Spartans. Socrates' description of the Persian wealth shows that quantity is not the only measure by which the Persians are superior. In his account of the Spartan wealth, Socrates never said that it was "fine and good." In fact, he had to rely on an Aesopian inference to show how great it must be (123a). The Spartan wealth is hidden; it is held "privately."[6] The Spartan contrast especially makes us aware that the virtue of the Persian kingdom is seen precisely in its wealth, and the order given to its wealth, "publicly" or politically. We might say that in Persia the display of wealth, of land and of luxury, is the very medium in which the virtue of the regime and of the king expresses itself. Socrates draws attention to the vast number of slaves that the Spartans have (122d) but says nothing about slavery among the Persians. We already remarked that the Persians, from the queen down, seem to bow willingly to the authority of the king. The Spartan queens must instead be guarded publicly by magistrates, a system that, Socrates indicates, is not even completely secure ("as far as possible" 121b). In the light of Alcibiades' later exploits in particular, Socrates' claims about the efficacy of the Spartan system sound almost like a joke.[7]

At the conclusion of his royal tale, Socrates introduces both the Persian and Spartan queens and has them speak to Alcibiades. They are both astonished that Alcibiades, in his present state, should presume to rival their sons and husbands. According to Socrates, the queens know better than Socrates and Alcibiades how they should perfect themselves for the contest against the kings (124a). He implies that, if Alcibiades does perfect himself, he will prevail over the kings his opponents. He will rule as the Persian king rules, by awesome superiority alone, over queen and subjects. Indeed, since the Persian queen recognizes true superiority, and since that appears to be the principle of her devotion and obedience, it seems that she will give herself voluntarily to Alcibiades if he makes himself superior to her king. In effect, at the end of the royal tale, Socrates appears to make her go as far as to tell Alcibiades what he must do to win her over.

---

[6]It was something of a commonplace, and later became notorious, that the Spartans, who were forbidden by law to use anything but the cumbersome and otherwise useless currency of the city, responded by hoarding gold and silver privately and extralegally. The law directed toward keeping the Spartans virtuous by contrivance was ultimately a failure.

[7]Plutarch relates that Alcibiades, while living in exile at Sparta, seduced the wife of King Agis (*Alcibiades* 23).

The queen of Persia, as beautiful and alluring as a Cleopatra perhaps, offers herself and her domain to the most perfect man.

At the end of the royal tale Socrates declares for the first time that Alcibiades is an erotic man. He now seems to Socrates to love renown more than anyone ever loved anything (124b). Socrates has provided Alcibiades with an almost unspeakably flattering image of politics, for an ambition such as his, and Alcibiades has fallen in love with it. He has been transformed by Socrates' speech into an erotic man. There is a difference between erotic love of renown and the contentious love of victory we saw in Alcibiades in the first part of the dialogue. The latter is reminiscent of a man like Coriolanus, who indignantly insists on the honor he has merited according to the rules, so to speak. The erotic love of renown conditioned by Socrates' royal tale craves human recognition of the most subjective, even intimate kind, recognition that is both voluntary and knowing, that honors and admires a great political man on the true grounds of his greatness. Socrates portrays this as the quasi-erotic devotion of a Persian queen who knows what true political greatness is and bows to it. The royal tale begins with the vision contained in Socrates' ship metaphor but goes further to suggest that the rule of virtue or superiority extends beyond the boundaries of one city. The first practical result is to preclude war; Socrates is not telling Alcibiades to take the field against the kings of Sparta and Persia. It is as though the superiority of the perfect ship's commander inspired allegience not only in his own crew but in those of the enemy ships as well. The royal tale is the perfection of Socrates' paradoxical argument that justice is the true art of war. Indeed, the royal tale properly understood is nothing but a seductive presentation of all the Socratic paradoxes that annoyed Alcibiades throughout the first part of the dialogue: that war only proves the ignorance of the many about justice, that the city listens to and honors only the man of knowledge, and so on. The Socratic paradoxes, taken together, present statesmanship in a very attractive light.

Within the context of the dialogue as a whole, the purpose of the royal tale is to use Alcibiades' ambition to get him to care earnestly for his self-perfection. The tale is an exhortation to virtue. In the very act of showing Alcibiades the most pleasing possible political prospect, Socrates cements his subjection to a new authority, the Persian queen who as judge imposes conditions for his success. We are reminded of the way that Socrates was able to subject Alcibiades implicitly in the opening passage of the dialogue by implanting or sharpening in him a fantastic "Asian" ambition (105b–c). There the subjection was to Socrates and his god. Here Socrates declares that he and Alcibiades must engage in an urgent quest for self-perfection, the greatest help to which is Socrates' god (124b–d).

III

The remainder of the dialogue is devoted to a search for the self-perfection or virtue required by the royal tale. That search is understood from the start to be a search for the virtue or excellence of the unqualifiedly good man (124e); the good man simply, Socrates and Alcibiades agree, is the man who is able to rule (cf. 124e, 125b, et al.). The discussion here begins from the standpoint of "ruling" rather than "advising" the city and hence deals most comprehensively with the world of issues that make up politics. The "virtue" of the statesman has primarily to do with the art of properly ordering that world. The names of the ordinary virtues, in contrast, are practically absent from the first part of the discussion.

In the first section of the dialogue following the royal tale (to 127d) Alcibiades attempts, under Socrates' questioning, to define that which constitutes a healthy city and that which statesmanship should work to produce. Alcibiades proposes near the end that the task of the ruling art is to create "friendship" in the city and to banish faction and hatred from it (126c). Socrates construes "friendship" to mean concord or "like-mindedness" (*homonoia*) and concludes that it must be analogous to the like-mindedness produced among knowers by the common knowledge of some art, such as arithmetic. When Alcibiades is pressed to say what concord in the city is, he likens it to the concord among members of a family (126e). This is his final attempt to describe the character of a healthy city. Socrates himself is rather notorious for arguing that the family and the city are essentially the same, and his portrayal of royal families in the royal tale may actually have given Alcibiades this notion, but in this context Alcibiades' remark appears to be an objection to Socrates. His description of concord in the family, based on familial love, refers precisely to the nonrational elements in it, to those that are not derived from any shared knowledge or art. Socrates succeeds in refuting Alcibiades while essentially ignoring that part of his suggestion, but the suggestion itself is significant because it may interpret for us what Alcibiades' new-found erotic love of renown means to Alcibiades himself. If the renown he is looking for from the likes of the queen of Persia in his mind resembles the adulation of a wife for her husband or a mother for her son, it differs somewhat from a rational devotion based on the clear judgment that Alcibiades is best. In some respects, it is a more appealing kind of devotion, but it is more problematic as well. In particular, if the attachment of the Persian queen to her present king is of that character, she may not be so easily won away. Honor and renown in the city understood in those terms are no longer gained by simple superiority in wisdom and art. For that reason the suggestion contained in Alcibiades' appeal to the family decisively undermines the hope that Socrates was able to hold out to him in the royal tale. It also undermines Socrates' argument that Alcibiades must perfect himself in order to fulfill his ambition.

Perhaps because it jeopardizes the cherished hope Socrates has offered him, Alcibiades does not vigorously pursue his appeal to familial love. Socrates refutes him, bringing Alcibiades to admit with an emphatic oath that he does not know what he means with his talk about the city (127d). Initiative in the discussion now passes entirely to Socrates. Socrates says that, in their ignorance about the art of politics, the knowledge of which was to have constituted their own perfection, they must retreat to a prior and apparently simpler question. What is the art of self-care or of taking trouble over oneself simply? Compelled by their further ignorance, Socrates and Alcibiades will soon have to retreat to the still prior question of what they themselves are, to be cared for, and will come to the discussion of the soul. This whole progress is accomplished by Socrates in two arguments. The first one (127e–128d) deals with the question of possessions or belongings and proceeds on the supposition that the art of taking trouble over something is different from the art of taking trouble over what belongs to it. Socrates and Alcibiades attempt to ascend from the arts of caring for the things belonging to human beings to the art of caring for the human being himself, but are unable to make the last step. They are forced to address directly the question of what a human being in himself is.

If Socrates and Alcibiades do not find an answer to this question, it is difficult to know what prior or simpler question they could fall back to. All the urgency of the dialogue is in a manner focused on this point: they must not come up short (cf. 124d). Socrates begins with his first and only explicit oath to an Olympian god in the dialogue (129b; cf. 109d). In the name of Zeus, with whom is Alcibiades conversing at this moment? It is with Socrates. Both of them are using speech, just as artisans of all sorts use tools and their bodies as well. The user must be different from the thing used and so, Socrates declares, the human being in himself, the ruler and user of all these things, must be the soul. Moreover, since Alcibiades agrees that the body by no means rules itself, the human being strictly speaking must be the soul purely by itself. Socrates asks Alcibiades whether the proof has been good enough for him. Alcibiades responds "by Zeus" that it is, thereby answering after a fashion Socrates' opening prayer to Zeus (130c). On the basis of this "discovery" of the soul, the dialogue is able to reach a satisfactory conclusion, although Socrates immediately indicates that there is reason to be dissatisfied with it (130c–d). Indeed, the argument might be said to have presupposed the existence of a "hidden artisan" inside the human being rather than demonstrating it. Against the argument Socrates says that it would require an account of the "self itself" to be conclusive, a mysterious problem that might have to do with our ability to make subtle distinctions between beings precisely, such as that between body and soul.

In any case, Socrates says, it is surely a fine or beautiful thing to believe, as they were saying before, that Socrates and Alcibiades are conversing not face to face but soul with soul (130d–e). This sudden appeal to the "beauty" of the argument, coming after the remark on its insufficiency, makes us wonder whether its beauty is not what won Alcibiades to it in the first place. As we could see in the royal tale as well, a beautiful image has power in itself to carry conviction in the soul of an erotic man. There might be a suggestion in this also that Socrates' hypothesis of the soul is itself an erotically inspired one. Socrates develops the erotically most seductive side of it shortly, when he speaks of one human eye as reflecting the image of another (132d–133c). First, however, he draws Alcibiades' attention to the greatest danger he sees in Alcibiades' eroticism, namely that he may fall prey to a corrupt "love of the *demos*," or love of the people. Socrates does not make clear whether he thinks that Alcibiades is already a lover of the demos or whether he thinks that all love of the demos is corrupt in the sense intended. His statement seems to imply that corrupt love of the demos is like the reprehensible love of bodies as opposed to souls (131e–132a). The statement certainly implies that, if Alcibiades is corrupted, the Athenian demos will most likely be the cause rather than Socrates himself.

The prophylactic that Socrates recommends against the ills to which lovers of the city are subject is to see the city stripped and to train properly before undertaking to direct its affairs (132a–b). He begins by building on the hypothesis of the soul that he and Alcibiades have agreed upon, by means of an analogy to sight. Knowing oneself, he suggests, is like seeing oneself (132d). One can see oneself by looking into the eye of another human being, into the center of that eye, and finding there the image of oneself reflected. Similarly, Socrates argues, self-knowledge can be gotten by peering into the soul of another. This visual metaphor, bringing to mind as it does the soul-searching gaze of two lovers into each other's eyes, might be the erotic peak of the dialogue. It also continues the crucial project begun in the first discussion of the soul by providing a bridge between the isolated, invisible soul and the world as we know it, eventually even the political world. For according to the visual analogy as Socrates describes it, when one looks into another's eye, what one sees there is not only the image of one's eye but of one's face and even one's whole body (132e–133a). Similarly, one peering into the center of another's soul would discern not only the center of his own soul but the whole of it and indeed the whole of it in relation to the things naturally surrounding and "belonging to" it. Self-knowledge seems to include knowledge of how the parts of oneself, of soul and body and the parts of the soul within itself, are properly ordered around the rational center of the soul. This appears to be the justification for Socrates' repeated assertion that self-knowledge is moderation (131b, 133c). By the same token self-knowledge seems to provide the avenue at least to knowledge of one's proper relation to "possessions" more remote than one's body, to "belongings of one's belongings" (cf. 133d–e).

Socrates reconstructs the whole political world, so to speak, in this way, in terms of "possessions." Statesmanship is the proper ordering of the things belonging to many, just as moderation is the proper ordering of one's own most intimate belongings (133e). We are reminded of the fact that the statesmanship of the Persian king consisted in properly ordering his domain around the queen his wife, and also of the fact that according to the Persian teaching the virtue of moderation is the model for the ruling, kingly virtue (122a). The comprehensive vision that emerges from Socrates' visual analogy is that of a whole world ordered in concentric circles, so to speak, around the human soul. It is necessary to see these souls stripped of everything in order to discern what truly belongs to them and what does not, and how to order the things that do, but the art of seeing souls in themselves is precisely what Socrates and Alcibiades seem to have discovered. The first impression we receive from the concluding section of the dialogue is that Socrates and Alcibiades are on the direct path to perfect statesmanship.

Our first, sanguine impression is somewhat tarnished by the recollection that the whole argument concerning self-knowledge depends on the questionable proofs of the soul. It is also not difficult to see that self-knowledge as Socrates describes it, and the knowledge of politics derived from it, are necessary but perhaps not sufficient conditions for political success. Knowledge of the correct political order may be different from knowledge of how to implement it. Indeed, all that Socrates continually says throughout the final part of the dialogue is that, if Alcibiades is without self-knowledge and its corollary, political knowledge, he will necessarily fail. He never explicitly promises Alcibiades success on the basis of this knowledge. More than that, at the moment when Socrates begins to describe the exemplary political career that Alcibiades might have, he distances himself from Alcibiades and the city by referring to the two of them in the second person, excluding himself (cf. 134d–e and n. 39 on the text). Prior to this point, Socrates has for the most part portrayed himself and Alcibiades as men on a common quest, although there have been indications enough that Socrates does not have precisely the same ambition as Alcibiades. To mention only the most striking example, it can scarcely have escaped our notice in the royal tale that Socrates' own attitude toward the brilliant image he produced for Alcibiades was somewhat ironic, particularly when he reduced Alcibiades' contest with the Persian king to a kind of tawdry calculation of the relative value of their mothers' wardrobes and of the lands belonging to the sons themselves (123c–d). There may be a perspective from which all practical politics as such, inasmuch as it deals decisively with "possessions," appears a tawdry business.

On Alcibiades' side, we need not presume that the inconclusiveness of Socrates' argument in the last segment of the dialogue has escaped him entirely or that he took Socrates' royal tale to be a literal or even a realistic view of things. The fact is that the "idealized" vision of politics that Socrates offers is irresistibly attractive to a man of Alcibiades' ambitions and sensibilities. It would not be surprising if we found that the political ambition of the most profound political men is always nourished by something like the Socratic vision of politics, according to which human wisdom ultimately avails in politics and hence is the proper grounds of political action, while political wisdom, which is distinct from ordinary moral virtue, is somehow recognized and honored by the city as such. It would be wrong to say that there are no grounds for this conviction in practice. The drama of this dialogue indicates that, in the case of Alcibiades, the implanting of this conviction alone allows him to have his political ambition without immediately compromising his pursuit of real human and political perfection.

There is no question that, over the course of this dialogue, the character and convictions of Alcibiades undergo a great transformation. Cicero refers to a tradition that Alcibiades burst into tears when Socrates showed him how ignorant he was and implored him for help.[8] At the close of this dialogue, Alcibiades promises to become a devoted disciple of Socrates, and therefore, as Socrates reminds him, of Socrates' god as well. Finally, he says he will begin to take trouble over justice. To avoid misunderstanding, we should note that this transformation of Alcibiades comes both from a change of heart and from a change in his understanding of the political categories. The justice Socrates has been talking about, unlike the justice the many believe in, is something derived purely from the scientific art of ordering the city. His piety is similar. From the moment early in the dialogue when Socrates linked the art of music to the divine Muses, divinity and art have been closely connected. In the final passages of the dialogue, the god of which Socrates speaks is more or less explicitly identified with the scientific art to which true statesmanship looks as its source and guidance. The perfect statesman follows religiously the dictates of political science.

This is not by any means to make a sham of the piety in the *Alcibiades I*. It remains in a way the key to what Socrates is attempting to accomplish with Alcibiades in this first, propaedeutic conversation. Socrates' god is still a strict master and a restraint on Alcibiades, particularly now when Alcibiades is ignorant of the political art. From Socrates' point of view and the point of view of the dialogue, Alcibiades must remain under Socrates' tutelage, and the tutelage of

[8] *Tusculan Disputations* III 32.

Socrates' god, in order to become as good as possible. The corruption of Alcibiades would consist in his being lured away from them into recalcitrance and "impiety." Socrates has said already that he fears most that Alcibiades might be corrupted by a certain kind of love of the people (131e–132a). Other passages in the dialogue suggest that the greatest danger for Alcibiades is that he find some way to succeed or appear to succeed in politics not by knowledge and true merit but by a kind of seduction of the city, whether by beauty or wealth or family or something else. If he were to find some way to seduce the Persian queen, the rhetorical purpose of the royal tale would be completely overthrown. The fact that Alcibiades did later seduce the Spartan queen may or may not mean that he fell into that fate.

As to the city's charge that Socrates was guilty of corrupting Alcibiades, the dialogue seems to indicate that the most sober way to approach the question is by considering whether creating or sharpening an "Asian" ambition in Alcibiades in the figurative sense of the word, an ambition to rule as perfectly and be honored as greatly as Socrates' fanciful king of Persia, is a real corruption. One can imagine that, in the eyes of the Athenian democracy, it might seem so. In the concluding remark of the dialogue, Socrates expresses the fear that both Alcibiades and himself may be overcome by the strength of the city (135e). He seems to have a premonition that both he and Alcibiades will suffer similar fates at the hands of the city. Indeed, we should never forget that Alcibiades as well as Socrates was once condemned to death by the city for impiety and corruption. The city's suspicions about Socrates and about Alcibiades are similar; their condemnation of Alcibiades is a kind of image of their condemnation of Socrates' teachings about politics and virtue.

LACHES
[or, On Courage]

Translated by JAMES H. NICHOLS, JR.

Lysimachus, Melesias, Nicias, Laches,
children of Lysimachus and Melesias, Socrates

178a LYSIMACHUS: You have seen the man fighting in armor,[1] Nicias and
Laches.[2] Melesias here and I did not tell you at that time, however,
why we bade you see it together with us, but now we shall: for to
you we think we should speak frankly. Now there are some who
b ridicule such things, and if one should consult with them, they would
not say what they think; rather, they second-guess the one who is
consulting and say other things against their own opinion. But you,
we thought, were both capable of knowing and, when you knew,
would state your opinions simply, and so we took you into our

---

[1]Fighting in armor, as a professional art, was not highly reputed. The rather
ludicrous brother sophists Euthydemus and Dionysodorus practice this among other
arts of battle. See *Euthydemus* at 271d; see Paul Friedländer, *Plato,* 3 vols. (Princeton,
1958–70), 2:38.

[2]Lysimachus and Melesias were the obscure sons of famous fathers: Lysimachus of
Aristeides, known as "The Just," a general and statesman contemporary with
Themistocles; and Melesias of Thucydides, who led the aristocratic party opposed to
the democratic party of Pericles. (Melesias is mentioned by the historian Thucydides
as having been a member of the Four Hundred, an oligarchic regime that ruled Athens
briefly late in the Peloponnesian War.) Nicias was a moderate, wealthy, and prominent general and statesman. He successfully favored a negotiated peace with Sparta
(concluded in 421, perhaps close to the time at which this dialogue takes place). Later
he was appointed to lead the Sicilian expedition, an undertaking he had unsuccessfully
opposed; he died in 413, with most of the expedition, in that disaster. Laches, much
less well known, is reported by Thucydides to have served as a competent general in
several situations in the Peloponnesian War; he died in the Athenian defeat at Man-
tinea in 418.

counsel on the matters which we are about to communicate. Well
then, the following is what I have been saying so much about by way
of preface.

These are our sons. This one is his and has his grandfather's name,
Thucydides. And this one also has a name from his grandfather, my
father; for we call him Aristeides.[3] Now, it seemed to us that we
ought to take care of them as much as possible and not to do what the
many do—let them loose, when they have become lads, to do what
they want—but rather already now begin to take care of them to the
extent that we are able. So then, knowing that you too have sons, we
thought that you, if anyone, must have been concerned with how
they should be cared for so as to become best, but that, if you have
not often turned your mind to such a thing, we would remind you
that one must not neglect it and would summon you in common
with us to devote some care to our sons.

You must hear, Nicias and Laches, whence these opinions came to
us, even if it takes a little longer. Now, Melesias here and I take our
meals together, and the lads eat with us. As I said when I began the
speech, we will be frank with you. Now each of us, concerning his
own father, has many noble deeds to tell the young men, which they
accomplished both in war and in peace, managing the affairs both of
the allies and of this city, but as for our own deeds, neither of us has
any to tell. These things make us rather ashamed before them, and we
blame our fathers for letting us live a soft life, when we became lads,
while they were busy with the affairs of others. We point out these
very things to these young men, telling them that, if they neglect
themselves and do not obey us, they will be without fame, but if they
take care, they might become worthy of the names that they bear.

Now then, they declare they will obey us. We in turn are looking
into this: what should they learn or practice so as to become as good
as possible? Now, someone proposed this study to us, saying that it
would be noble for a youth to learn fighting in armor, and he praised
this man whom you have now seen putting on a display, and he
further bade us see him. It seemed necessary that we ourselves should
go to the man's spectacle and take you along with us as fellow spectators and also as counselors and partners,[4] if you wish, in the care of
our sons.

[3]It was frequent Athenian practice to name sons for their grandfathers; thus the
boys have the names, not of their obscure fathers, but of their illustrious grandfathers.
[4]The words translated "partner" and "partnership" are derivatives of *koinos,* translated "common," whence too "communicate" (179a, 180a) is derived.

180a   These are the things that we wanted to communicate to you. So now it is your part to give counsel both about this study—whether it seems it must be learned or not—and about the others if you have any study or practice to praise for a young man and to say what you will do about our partnership.

NICIAS: I for my part, Lysimachus and Melesias, praise your intention and am ready to be a partner, and I think that Laches here is too.

b   LACHES: What you think is true, Nicias. And what Lysimachus was just saying about his own father and Melesias's was very well said indeed, in my opinion—against them and us and all who are busy with the affairs of the cities. Pretty much what this man says happens to them: they are of a heedless and neglectful disposition toward both children and other private affairs. So these things that you are saying are fine, Lysimachus. I am amazed, however, that you summon us as

c   counselors on the education of the young men but do not summon Socrates here; first because he is of your deme[5] and next because he is always spending his time wherever there is any noble study or practice of the sort you are seeking for the youths.

LYS.: What are you saying, Laches? Has Socrates here indeed devoted care to some such things?

LACH.: Most certainly, Lysimachus.

NIC.: I too could tell you this no less than Laches. For he recently

d   introduced a man to me as music teacher for my son: Damon the student of Agathocles,[6] not only the most refined of men in music, but, in whatever other matters you wish, worthy to spend time with young men of that age.

LYS.: People of my age, Socrates and Nicias and Laches, no longer know the younger men, since we spend much of our time at home because of our age. But child of Sophroniscus,[7] if you too have some

e   good counsel to give to this fellow demesman of yours, you must

---

[5]The demes of Athens were the original territorial townships. In the legislation of Cleisthenes, they kept certain political functions, but membership in demes became hereditary rather than territorial, and their political importance lessened. Nonetheless, people of various demes were traditionally thought to have a certain typical character (see n. 36).

[6]Damon was a teacher of music, best known for the role he assigned to music in the formation of character (a point that Laches too has apparently at least vaguely in mind at 188d); this knowledge of his is referred to approvingly by Socrates, *Republic* 400a–c and 424c. Together with Anaxagoras, he was a teacher of Pericles.

[7]The obscure Sophroniscus was Socrates' father; he is said to have been a sculptor or stone mason.

give counsel. And you will be just: for you also happen to be a paternal friend of ours. For your father and I were always comrades and friends, and he died before having any quarrel with me. And now I am carried back by a certain remembrance of these boys' speaking recently. For these lads, in discussion with each other at home, frequently mention Socrates and praise him vehemently, yet I have never asked them if they meant the son of Sophroniscus. But children, tell me: is this the Socrates of whom you made mention each time?

CHILDREN: Most certainly, father, this is he.

LYS.: By Hera, Socrates, how well have you exalted your father, the best of men! And would that your things might belong to us and ours to you!

LACH.: Indeed, Lysimachus, do not let the man go. I for one saw him elsewhere too, exalting not only his father but also the fatherland, for in the flight from Delium[8] he withdrew with me, and I tell you that, if the others had been willing to be such as he, the city would have been upright[9] and would not then have suffered such a fall.

LYS.: Socrates, this indeed is fine praise which you are now receiving—from men worthy of being trusted and for such things as those for which they are praising you. Know well, then, that, upon hearing these things, I rejoice that you enjoy a good reputation, and be sure to consider me among those who are best disposed to you. You yourself should have come frequently to us even before and regarded us as your own, as is just. But from this day forth, now that we have recognized each other, do not fail to attend and become acquainted with both us and these younger men, so that you too may preserve our friendship. So then, you will do these things, and we shall remind you yet again hereafter; but now, what do you assert about the subject we began with? How does it seem? Does the study seem to be suitable for lads or not, learning to fight in armor?

SOCRATES: Well, Lysimachus, I for my part shall try both to give some

[8]In 424, the eighth year of the Peloponnesian War, an Athenian army was routed by a Boeotian army (the Athenians having previously seized and fortified a temple at Delium in Boeotian territory). See Thucydides IV 90–101. Alcibiades (in Plato's *Symposium* 220e–221c) describes Socrates' and Laches' retreat in a manner more laudatory of Socrates than of Laches (see n. 25).

[9]"Upright" translates *orthos*, elsewhere translated "correct." In this speech and the preceding, "exalt" translates a verb derived from *orthos* whose basic meaning is "to set straight."

counsel about these things if I can and further to do all the things you propose. But it seems to me most just, since I am younger than these men and less experienced in these matters, that I should first hear what they say and learn from them. And if I have something else to say besides what is said by them, then I should teach and persuade both you and them. So, Nicias, why doesn't either one of you speak?

e   NIC.: Well, nothing prevents it, Socrates. Now then, in my opinion this study is helpful for youths to know in many ways. For it is good that they not pass time elsewhere, in places where the young love to spend their time when they have leisure, but in this, from which they must necessarily be in better bodily condition—for it is not inferior to

182a any of the gymnastic exercises, nor does it offer less toil—and at the same time this gymnastic exercise, as well as horsemanship, most befits a free man. For only they who exercise themselves in the implements relating to war exercise themselves in that contest in which we are competitors and in those things for which the contest lies before us.

Next, this study will be of some benefit even in the battle itself, when one must fight in the ranks with many others. Its greatest benefit, however, will be when the ranks are broken and one must,

b   one on one, either pursue to attack someone who is defending himself or defend oneself even in flight from another who is attacking. One man who knows this would not suffer anything from one man, at any rate, nor perhaps from several, but in this way he would gain the advantage everywhere.

Furthermore, such a study summons one to a desire of other noble study too. For everyone who has learned fighting in armor would desire the study that comes next, concerning orders of battle,[10] and

c   when he has grasped these and sought honor in them, he would eagerly press on to the whole of what concerns generalship. Clearly now, all the studies and practices connected with these things, to which this study would lead, are noble and worth much for a man to learn and to practice.

We shall further attribute to it no small addition: this knowledge would make every man in war not a little more confident and more courageous[11] than himself. And let us not consider it dishonorable to

---

[10]"Orders of battle" translates the same word, *taxis,* translated twice in 182a as "ranks." One could call this study "tactics"; the next, translated "generalship," is *stratēgia* in Greek.

[11]The word "courageous," *andreios,* occurs here for the first time in the *Laches.* The word comes from *anēr,* meaning "man" in an emphatically masculine sense (as dis-

say—even if to someone it seems to be a rather small thing—that the
d man will also appear more graceful where he must appear more
graceful and where at the same time he will appear more terrible to
the enemies[12] through his gracefulness.

In my opinion, then, Lysimachus, as I say, one must teach the
young men these things, and I have stated the reasons for my opinion. And if Laches says something besides these things, I would hear
him with pleasure.

e LACH.: Indeed, Nicias, it is hard to say about any study at all that one
must not learn it, for it seems good to know all things. Now, as to
this business of armor: if it is a study, as the teachers assert, and of the
sort that Nicias says, one must learn it. If it is not a study, however,
but those who profess it are deceivers, or if it happens to be a study,
but not a very serious one, what need would there be to learn it?

I say these things about it with a view to the following considerations. I think that, if there were something to this, it would not have
escaped the notice of the Lacedaemonians, for whom nothing else in
83a life is a care but to seek and practice that, by learning and practicing
which they may gain the advantage over others in war. But if it had
escaped their notice, surely this has not escaped the notice of these
teachers of it, at any rate: that the Lacedaemonians are the most
serious of the Greeks about such things and that someone who was
honored for these things among them would make the most money
from others as well, just as a tragic poet who has been honored
among us. Therefore whoever thinks he does a fine job of composing
b tragedy does not go abroad and pass in a circle around Attica, putting
on a display to the other cities, but he comes straight here and,
reasonably, puts on a display to these people. But I see that these
fighters in armor consider Lacedaemon to be inaccessible sacred
ground and do not so much as set foot on it on tiptoe; they go around
it in a circle and put on a display rather for everyone else—especially
for those who would themselves agree that many are superior to
them in the things of war.

c Next, Lysimachus, I have been near no small number of these men
in real action, and I see what sort they are. And we can consider it on

---

tinguished from *anthrōpos,* "human being"); accordingly, the meaning of *andreia,*
"courage," could well be rendered "manliness." These points of language correspond
to the fact that courage is the most prominent public virtue.

[12]Nicias here uses *echthros,* a word for enemy that can apply either to private or
public enemies; all other occurrences of "enemy" in the dialogue translate *polemios,*
meaning "(public) enemy in war."

the basis of this fact too. As if on purpose, of those who have practiced this business of armor, no man has ever yet become highly esteemed in war. And yet in all other things, those who win a name for themselves come from those who have practiced each thing; but compared to others, as it seems, these have been very unfortunate indeed in this respect. And furthermore, this Stesilaus, whom you

d saw, together with me, putting on a display amid so great a crowd and saying the great things about himself that he said—I have seen him elsewhere truly putting on a finer display, albeit unwillingly.

When the ship on which he had embarked as a soldier was sailing to attack a transport vessel, he was fighting with a scythe spear—a weapon as distinguished as he himself is distinguished from others. Now then, other things are not worth telling about the man, but it is

e worth telling how the wise business of the scythe attached to the lance turned out. For as he fought, it somehow became entangled in the ship's tackle and held fast. Then Stesilaus pulled on it, wishing to free it, but was not able, and the one ship was passing by the other. So for a while he ran along on the ship, holding onto the spear. And when the one ship passed beyond the other and dragged him along,

184a holding the spear, he let the spear pass through his hand, until he was holding fast to the end of the handle. There was laughter and applause from the men on the transport vessel at the figure that he cut, and when someone threw a stone on the deck by his feet and he let the spear go, then indeed the men on the trireme too were no longer able to hold back their laughter, seeing that scythe spear hanging from the transport vessel. So perhaps there might be something to these things, as Nicias says, but what I have met with is of this sort.

b So then, as I said even at the beginning, whether it is a study but is of such little help, or whether it is not a study but they claim and pretend that it is—it is not worth endeavoring to learn it. And in my opinion, if someone cowardly thought he knew this study, he would become bolder on account of it and would be more clearly revealed for what he was. And if courageous, he would be under close watch from human beings, and if he made even a small mistake, he would

c receive great slanders; for the pretense of such knowledge evokes envy, so that unless he is distinguished from others in virtue to an amazing degree, it is not possible that someone who claims to have this knowledge should escape becoming ridiculous.

Something of this sort, in my opinion at least, Lysimachus, is the seriousness belonging to this study. But as I said to you at the beginning, you must not let Socrates here go but must beg him to give counsel on his opinion about the subject that lies before us.

d LYS.: Well, Socrates, I for my part do beg you. For in my opinion our council still needs one who will decide the issue, as it were. If these two had agreed, there would be less need of such a one. Now, however—since, as you see, Laches has asserted the opposite to Nicias—it is well to hear from you too, with which of the two men you cast your vote.

SOC.: What then, Lysimachus? Are you going to adopt whatever the greater number of us praise?

LYS.: What else would one do, Socrates?

e SOC.: And would you too, Melesias, act thus?[13] Even if, concerning your son's athletic competition, you were deliberating on how he should train, would you then obey the greater number of us or that man who happens to have been educated and to have trained under a good trainer?

MELESIAS: Most likely the latter, Socrates.

SOC.: So you would obey him rather than even four of us?

MEL.: Probably.

SOC.: Yes, for what is to be finely judged, I think, must be judged by knowledge, not by majority.

MEL.: How could it be otherwise?

185a SOC.: So then now it is necessary to examine this first, whether or not one of us is expert[14] in that about which we are deliberating. And if so, it is necessary to obey him, albeit one man, and to let the others go, and if not, to seek someone else. Or do you and Lysimachus think that what you have at stake is something small but not what happens to be the greatest of your possessions? For presumably when sons become good or the opposite, so too the whole house of the father will be governed in a manner corresponding to the sort of people the children become.

MEL.: What you say is true.

SOC.: We must therefore have much forethought for it.

MEL.: Certainly.

b SOC.: How then, as I was just saying, would we examine it, if we wanted to examine which one of us was most expert about athletic

[13]Only here does Socrates draw Melesias, son of the aristocratic Thucydides, into active participation in the conversation.
[14]"Expert," *technikos,* is derived from *technē,* translated "art" below.

competition? Would it not be he who had learned and practiced it and had also had good teachers of this very thing?

MEL.: In my opinion, at least.

SOC.: So then should we first ask what this thing is, of which we are seeking teachers?

MEL.: What do you mean?

SOC.: Perhaps it will be clearer in this way. In my opinion we have not come to an agreement from the beginning on whatever it is about which we are deliberating and examining which of us is expert (and c got teachers for this purpose) and which of us is not.

NIC.: Well, Socrates, are we not examining fighting in armor, to see whether the young men should learn it or not?

SOC.: Most certainly, Nicias. But when someone examines a drug for the eyes, to see whether he should smear it on or not, do you think that the deliberation then is about the drug or the eyes?

NIC.: About the eyes.

d SOC.: Then too, when someone examines whether or not, and when, a bridle should be put on a horse, presumably he is then deliberating about the horse, not about the bridle?

NIC.: True.

SOC.: Then in a word: when someone examines one thing for the sake of another, the deliberation happens to be about that thing for the sake of which he was examining, not about that which he was seeking for the sake of the other.

NIC.: Necessarily.

SOC.: We must therefore examine the counselor too, as to whether he is expert in the care of that for the sake of which we are examining what we are examining.

NIC.: Certainly.

e SOC.: So then, do we now assert that we are examining a study for the sake of the soul of the young men?

NIC.: Yes.

SOC.: Which of us is expert concerning the care of the soul and able to do a fine job of caring for this, and which of us has had good teachers of this, must therefore be examined.[15]

LACH.: What, Socrates? Have you never seen men become more expert in some things without teachers than with teachers?

---

[15]Here I follow Schanz's small emendation, which preserves parallelism in the two parts of the question. The MSS could be translated "Whether some one of us is expert . . ."

SOC.: Indeed I have, Laches. But you would not be willing to trust them, if they claimed they were good craftsmen, unless they could 86a show you some work of their art that was well done, either one or more.

LACH.: What you say here is true.

SOC.: Therefore, Laches and Nicias, since Lysimachus and Melesias summoned us to a consultation about their sons, being eager that their souls become as good as possible, we—if we claim we can— must show them the teachers we have had, who, first of all, are themselves manifestly good and who, furthermore, have cared for b the souls of many youths and have taught us. Or if one of us denies that he himself has had a teacher but has works of his own to tell of, he must show what Athenians or foreigners, whether slaves or free, have by general agreement become good because of him. But if none of these things is available to us, we must bid them seek other men and must not run the risk, with the sons of men who are comrades, of corrupting them and thus getting the greatest blame from the nearest relatives.

c   Now then, I, Lysimachus and Melesias, am the first to say about myself that I have not had a teacher in this. Yet I have desired the thing, at any rate, starting from my youth. But I do not have the wages to pay sophists, the only ones who proclaim themselves able to make me noble and good,[16] and I myself, in turn, am as yet still unable to discover the art. But I would not be amazed if Nicias or Laches has discovered or learned it, for they are both more powerful than I in money, so as to learn it from others, and at the same time older, so as already to have discovered it. Indeed, to me they seem d able to educate a human being; for they would never make fearless declarations about good and bad practices for a youth, unless they trusted themselves to have adequate knowledge. So in other respects I, for one, trust them, but I was amazed that they disagreed with each other.

I in turn, then, beg this of you, Lysimachus. Just as Laches recently admonished you not to let me go but to question me, so I now summon you not to let Laches or Nicias go but to question them, e saying that Socrates denies that he understands the affair and is capa-

---

[16]"Noble and good" translates *kalos* (always translated either "noble" or "fine") and *agathos;* the two words together are a standard formula meaning something like a complete gentleman. The phrase was also used by the party of the nobles or gentlemen to distinguish themselves from common folk.

ble of judging which of you speaks truly, for he has neither discovered nor learned anything about such things. Each of you, Laches and Nicias, tell us with what man who is terribly clever[17] concerning the rearing of the young you have associated and whether you know through having learned from someone or through discovering for 187a yourselves, and if you learned, who is the teacher of each of you and what other people are expert in the same art with them—in order that, if you do not have leisure on account of the affairs of the city, we may go to them and persuade them with gifts or favors or both to take care both of our children and of yours so that they will not put their ancestors to shame by becoming base. If, on the other hand, you yourselves have discovered such a thing, give an example of what others you have already taken care of and made noble and good b instead of base. For if you are now beginning to educate for the first time, you must watch out lest the dangerous risk that is run should be not with some Carian[18] but with your sons and with the children of friends and lest what is said in the proverb should simply happen to you—to begin pottery on a wine jar.[19] Say, then, which of these do you assert or deny is applicable and appropriate to you?

Inquire about these things from them, Lysimachus, and don't let the men depart.

c LYS.: In my opinion at least, men, what Socrates says is fine. Whether you wish to be questioned and to give an account about such matters, you yourselves must know, Nicias and Laches. For clearly Melesias here and I would be pleased, if you should be willing to go through in speech all the things that Socrates is asking. Indeed I began at the start by saying that we summoned you into consultation because we thought you had most likely been concerned about such things, es- d pecially since your children, just like ours, are pretty much of an age to be educated. So then, if you do not disagree, speak and examine in common with Socrates, giving and receiving an account from each other. For this too that he says is good, that we are now deliberating

---

[17]The word *deinos,* here "terribly clever," comes from the root *deos,* meaning "fear"; in its more basic meaning, *deinos* has been translated "terrible."

[18]Because the Carians, a people of southwestern Asia Minor, were often used as mercenary soldiers, it became proverbial to speak of a Carian as a *corpus vile* on which to try something dangerous. The same phrase is used in *Euthydemus* at 285b–c.

[19]A wine jar was a large and difficult work of pottery; the beginner should start with something smaller and simpler. The same saying is mentioned by Socrates in the *Gorgias* at 514e.

about the greatest of our things. But see whether it seems that we should act thus.

NIC.: Lysimachus, you seem to me truly to know Socrates only from his father and not to have associated with him except when he was a child if, perchance, following along with his father, he kept company with you among fellow demesmen, either in a temple[20] or in some other gathering of the demesmen. But since he has become older, you have clearly not happened to meet with the man.

LYS.: Why so, in particular, Nicias?

NIC.: You do not seem to me to know that whoever is very close to Socrates in speech—as if in kinship—and keeps him company in discussion, even if he has earlier begun a discussion about something else, must of necessity not stop but be led around in speech by this man until he falls into giving an account of himself, the way he now lives, and the way he has lived his past life; and that, when one falls into this, Socrates will not let him go before he puts all these things well and nobly to the test. I am accustomed to this man and know that it is necessary to suffer these things from him, and furthermore I know well that I myself will suffer these things. For I rejoice, Lysimachus, at keeping the man company, and I think it is no bad thing to be reminded of what we have done or are doing that is not noble; rather, he must necessarily be more forethoughtful for his life afterward who does not flee these things but is willing and deems it worthwhile, in accordance with Solon's saying,[21] to learn as long as he lives and does not think that an old age possessed of intelligence will come forward of itself. For me, then, it is nothing unaccustomed or unpleasant to be put to the test by Socrates, but for a long time I have pretty much known that, with Socrates present, our speech would be not about the lads but about ourselves. As I am saying, then, for my part nothing prevents passing time with Socrates however he wishes, but see how Laches here stands concerning such a thing.

LACH.: My situation concerning speeches is simple, Nicias—or if you wish, it is not simple but double. For I might seem to someone to be a lover of speech and, in turn, a hater of speech. Whenever I hear a man

[20]The same word here translated "temple" was translated "sacred ground" at 183b.
[21]Solon (ca. 640–560), the famous Athenian legislator and one of the "Seven Sages," expressed his wisdom in poetry. Nicias refers to a line of elegiac poetry that has come down to us: "I grow old ever learning (or being taught) many things." Socrates criticizes the validity of this saying in *Republic* 536d.

discussing virtue or some wisdom who is truly a man and worthy of
d the speeches that he is uttering, I rejoice extraordinarily upon seeing
that the speaker and the things said are suitable and harmonious with
each other. And in my opinion such a one is altogether musical: he has
tuned himself to the finest harmony, not on the lyre or instruments of
play, but[22] really to live his own life as a concord of speeches in relation
to deeds—not in the Ionian, I think, or the Phrygian or Lydian but
simply in the Dorian, which is the sole Greek *harmonia*.[23] When such a
e one gives voice, therefore, he makes me rejoice and seem to anyone to
be a lover of speech, so eagerly do I accept from him the things said,
but he who does the contrary of this man pains me, all the more the
better he seems to speak, and makes me seem to be a hater of speech.

I am not experienced in Socrates' speeches, but, it seems, I for-
189a merly had experience of his deeds, and there I found him to be
worthy of noble speeches and of complete frankness. So then, if he
has this as well, his wishes are mine, and I would be scrutinized by
such a one with great pleasure and would not be vexed at learning,
but I too accede to Solon's saying, with the addition of only one
thing: for I am willing in growing old to be taught many things but
only by worthy men. Let this be conceded to me, that the teacher
himself be good, so that I am not revealed to be a poor learner by
learning without pleasure, but it is no concern to me if the teacher is
b younger or is not yet a man of reputation or anything else of that sort.
To you, then, Socrates, I give the command both to teach and to
refute me however you wish and to learn whatever I, in turn, know.
Thus do you stand with me, from that day when you shared the
danger with me and gave of your own virtue proof which he who is
to give proof justly must give. Say, then, whatever is dear to you,
taking no account of our age.
c soc.: We shall not blame you, it seems, for not being ready both to
consult and to examine together.
lys.: Indeed the work is ours, Socrates; for I, at least, put you down
as one of us. Therefore examine in my place, on behalf of the young
men, what we need to inquire of these men, and give counsel in
discussion with them. For on account of age I now forget many
things that I intend to ask, and furthermore I do not remember what I

[22]The translation follows Schantz's emendation, which drops a second "has tuned
himself" found in the MSS.
[23]For the particular features of Greek music involved here, see the Editor's
Introduction.

d hear very well, if other speeches come up in between. Therefore
speak and go through what we proposed among yourselves; I shall
listen and, having heard, will then with Melesias here do what seems
good to you.

soc.: Nicias and Laches, we must obey Lysimachus and Melesias.
Perhaps it is not bad that we ourselves should also scrutinize such
things as those we endeavored to examine just now—what teachers
e of such education have we had or what others have we made better.
But I think that an examination of the following sort would also lead
to the same thing and would start somewhat more from the beginning. For if we happen to know, about anything whatever, that
which, when present in something, makes that thing in which it is
present better, and if we are furthermore able to make it be present in
that thing, it is clear that we know this very thing concerning which
we would be counselors as to how someone might obtain it in the
easiest and best fashion. Now then, perhaps you do not understand
what I mean, but you will understand[24] more easily as follows.

190a   If we happen to know that sight, when present in eyes, makes
those eyes in which it is present better, and if we are furthermore able
to make it be present in eyes, it is clear that we know what sight itself
is, concerning which we would be counselors as to how someone
might obtain it in the easiest and best fashion. For if we do not know
even this thing—what sight is or what hearing is—we would hardly
be counselors worthy of mention and doctors concerning either eyes
b or ears, as to the way in which someone might obtain hearing or sight
in the finest manner.

LACH.: What you say is true, Socrates.

soc.: So then, Laches, are these two now summoning us to a consultation on the way in which virtue, through being present in their
sons, might make their souls better?

LACH.: Certainly.

soc.: Therefore must this, at least, be available already: to know what
virtue is? For presumably if we did not at all know even what virtue
c happens to be, in what way would we be counselors of this for
anyone, as to how he might obtain it in the finest manner?

LACH.: In no way, in my opinion at least, Socrates.

[24]The verb *manthanō* has usually been translated "learn." Here (and in 191e, twice in
194d, and in 196a) it is "understand." The related noun *mathēma* has been translated
"study" (e.g., several times in Laches' first long speech); it also can mean "learning,"
"science" (especially mathematical), "knowledge."

SOC.: We therefore assert, Laches, that we know what it is.

LACH.: We assert it indeed.

SOC.: And therefore, since we know it, we could doubtless state what it is.

LACH.: Why not?

SOC.: Let us not, however, best of men, examine the whole of virtue straightaway; for the work would perhaps be rather much. But let us first see about some part, whether we are in a capable condition for
d   knowing, and most likely the examinination will be easier for us.

LACH.: Well, let us do thus, Socrates, as you wish.

SOC.: What, then, of the parts of virtue should we choose? Or should it clearly be what the learning about armor seems to aim at? To the many it seems, presumably, to aim at courage—isn't that so?

LACH.: Indeed it does seem so.

SOC.: Let us then first undertake this, Laches, to state what courage is.
e   Then after this we shall also examine in what way it might be present in young men, to the extent that it can be present from practices and studies. But try to state what I am saying—what courage is.

LACH.: By Zeus, Socrates, it is not hard to state. For if someone should be willing to remain in the ranks and defend himself against the enemies and should not flee, know well that he would be courageous.

SOC.: You speak well, Laches. But perhaps, by not speaking distinctly, I am to blame for your answering, not what I intended when I asked, but something else.

LACH.: What do you mean by this, Socrates?

191a   SOC.: I shall explain if I am able. This man of whom you speak, who remains in the ranks and fights the enemies, is presumably courageous.

LACH.: So at least do I assert.

SOC.: And so do I. But then what about this one, who fights the enemies, not while remaining, but while fleeing?

LACH.: How so, fleeing?

SOC.: Just as the Scythians, for instance, are said to fight no less while fleeing than while pursuing,[25] and Homer, praising the horses of
b   Aeneas, declared somewhere that they knew how to "pursue and to

---

[25]Socrates, in reminding Laches that one can be courageous while fleeing, tactfully refrains from mentioning his and Laches' behavior in defeat at Delium; thus, too, Socrates broadens Laches' tactical horizons.

flee very swiftly hither and thither."[26] And he lauded Aeneas himself for this, for the knowledge of flight, and said that he was a "counselor of flight."[27]

LACH.: And that is fine, Socrates, for he was speaking about chariots, and what you are talking about is the Scythian horsemen. Their cavalry does fight thus, but the heavy-armed soldiery, of the Greeks at least, fights as I am saying.

c SOC.: Except, perhaps, Laches, for that of the Lacedaemonians. For they claim that at Plataea, when the Lacedaemonians were up against the troops who carried wicker shields, they were not willing to remain and fight against them but fled, and when the Persians' ranks were broken, they turned around to fight, just like horsemen, and thus won victory at the battle there.

LACH.: What you say is true.

SOC.: This, then, is what I was just saying, that I am to blame for your not giving a fine answer, because I did not ask in a fine manner. For I

d wished to inquire of you about not only those who are courageous in the heavy-armed soldiery but also those in the cavalry and in every form of warfare, and not only those in war but also those who are courageous in dangers at sea, and those who are courageous toward sickness and poverty or even toward politics, and yet further not only those who are courageous toward pains or fears but also those who

e are terribly clever at fighting against desires or pleasures, whether remaining or turning around in retreat—for there are presumably some courageous people, Laches, in such things too.

LACH.: Very much so indeed, Socrates.

SOC.: So then all these men are courageous, but some possess courage in pleasures, some in pains, some in desires, and some in fears, and others, I think, possess cowardice in these same things.

LACH.: Certainly.

SOC.: What in the world is each of these? This is what I was inquiring. So try again to say, first about courage: what is it that is the same in all these? Or do you not yet fully understand what I mean?

---

[26]*Iliad* V 223 and VIII 107. The Homeric "to flee," *phebesthai,* also carries connotations of fear or fright. (Socrates' earlier "fleeing," *pheugō,* is the more common word in Attic Greek.)

[27]At *Iliad* V 272, this epithet may apply either to Aeneas or to his two horses, depending on which reading one accepts; at VIII 108 it clearly applies to Aeneas. The word "flight," *phobos,* also means fear or fright. Socrates turns Homer to his own purpose: in the *Iliad* the epithet seems rather to mean "counselor of fright" (viz., striking terror into his enemies).

LACH.: Not altogether.

192a SOC.: I mean it thus: just as if I were asking what speed is, which happens to exist for us in running and playing the cithara and speaking and learning and many other things, and we possess it—where it is worth speaking about—pretty much in the actions of hands or legs or mouth and voice or thought. Isn't this what you too say?

LACH.: Certainly.

SOC.: Then if someone should ask me, "Socrates, what do you say

b this is, which in all things you name swiftness?" I would say to him that I for one call swiftness the power of accomplishing many things in a short time, in respect of voice and running and all other things.

LACH.: What you would say is correct, at any rate.

SOC.: Then you in turn try, Laches, to speak of courage in this way: what power is it that is the same in pleasure and in pain and in all those things in which we were just now saying it exists, and that is therefore called courage?

LACH.: In my opinion, then, it is a certain steadfastness[28] of the soul,

c if one must say about courage what it is by nature in all cases.

SOC.: Indeed one must, at least if we are to answer for ourselves what is asked. Now then, it looks this way to me at least: not quite all steadfastness, I think, appears to you to be courage. I make that conjecture from this: I pretty much know, Laches, that you hold courage to be among the altogether noble things.

LACH.: Know well, then, that it is among the noblest.

SOC.: So then, is steadfastness accompanied by prudence noble and good?

LACH.: Certainly.

d SOC.: And what about it accompanied by folly? As the opposite of this, isn't it harmful and evildoing?

LACH.: Yes.

SOC.: Will you then assert that such a thing, which is evildoing and harmful, is something noble?

LACH.: It would certainly not be just, at any rate, Socrates.

SOC.: You will therefore not agree that steadfastness of this sort, at any rate, is courage, since it is not noble, and courage is a noble thing.

LACH.: What you say is true.

---

[28]"Steadfastness," *karteria,* comes from *kratos* (*kartos* in Ionic and Epic), meaning "strength." Twice in 193d and once in 194a, Socrates uses a variant form, *karterēsis,* that I have also translated "steadfastness."

SOC.: Prudent steadfastness, therefore, would be courage, according to your argument.

LACH.: It seems so.

e SOC.: Let us now see: prudent in what respect? Or is it with respect to all things both great and small? For example, if someone is steadfast in spending money prudently, knowing that having spent he will possess more, would you call this one courageous?

LACH.: By Zeus, not I!

SOC.: What if some doctor, when his son or someone else has an

193a inflammation of the lungs and begs to be given drink or food, didn't bend but was steadfast?

LACH.: This is not it either, in any way at all.

SOC.: How about a man in war who is steadfast and willing to fight, calculating prudently and knowing that others will come to his aid, that he will be fighting against fewer and inferior men than those he is with and further that he holds stronger ground? Would you assert that this man who is steadfast with such prudence and preparation is more courageous than one in the opposite camp who is willing to remain standing his ground and to be steadfast?

b LACH.: In my opinion, at least, it is the one in the opposite camp, Socrates.

SOC.: But surely the steadfastness of this one is more foolish, at any rate, than that of the other.

LACH.: What you say is true.

SOC.: And you will therefore assert that the one who is steadfast with knowledge of horsemanship in a cavalry battle is less courageous than the one without knowledge.

LACH.: In my opinion, at least.

SOC.: And so is the one who is steadfast with the art of the sling or of the bow or some other art.

c LACH.: Certainly.

SOC.: And those who are willing to be steadfast in going down into a well and diving, not being terribly clever in this work, or in some other such work—you will then assert that they are more courageous than those who are terribly clever in these things.

LACH.: For what else would one say, Socrates?

SOC.: Nothing, at least if that is how one thought.

LACH.: Well, I do indeed think so.

SOC.: And yet such ones, Laches, presumably run the risk and are steadfast more foolishly, at any rate, than those who do the same thing with art.

LACH.: It looks that way.

d SOC.: Wasn't foolish daring, and steadfastness, revealed to us in what preceded to be shameful and harmful?

LACH.: Certainly.

SOC.: And courage was agreed to be something fine.

LACH.: Yes, it was agreed.

SOC.: But now in turn we assert to the contrary that that shameful thing, foolish steadfastness, is courage.

LACH.: We seem likely to.

SOC.: In your opinion, then, is what we are saying fine?

LACH.: By Zeus, Socrates, not in my opinion.

SOC.: Then you and I, Laches, according to your speech, are presum-
e ably not harmoniously tuned to the Dorian; for in our case, deeds are not in concord with speeches. For in deed, it is likely, someone would declare that we partake in courage, but in speech, I think, he would not, if he now heard us discussing.

LACH.: What you say is very true.

SOC.: What then? Does it seem a fine thing for us to be in this condition?

LACH.: Not in any way at all.

SOC.: So then, do you wish us to obey what we are saying, at least in this respect?

LACH.: In what sort of respect and obeying what?

194a SOC.: The speech that bids us to be steadfast. So if you wish, let us too remain persistent and be steadfast in the search, in order that courage herself not ridicule us, because we do not seek her courageously, if perhaps steadfastness itself is often courage.

LACH.: I am ready, Socrates, not to desist. And yet I am unaccus-tomed to such speeches. But a certain love of victory in regard to
b what has been said has taken hold of me, and I am truly irritated, if I am unable to say what I thus perceive in my mind. For in my opin-ion, at least, I do perceive in my mind what courage is, and I don't know how it just now fled away from me, so that I didn't grasp it in speech and say what it is.

SOC.: Then surely, friend, the good hunter must pursue and not give over.

LACH.: Yes indeed, by all means.

soc.: So do you want us to summon Nicias here too to the hunt if he is in some respect more resourceful than we?

lach.: I do; why not?

c   soc.: Come then, Nicias, if you have some power, come to the aid of your friends, men who are storm-tossed in speech and at a loss. For you see how our affairs are at a loss. By saying what you consider courage to be, deliver us from perplexity[29] and securely establish in speech what you yourself perceive in your mind.

nic.: Well then, you have for a long time seemed to me, Socrates, not to be giving a fine definition of courage; for you are not using this fine thing that I have heard you say formerly.

soc.: What sort of thing, Nicias?

d   nic.: I have often heard you say that each of us is good in those things with respect to which he is wise and bad in those with respect to which he is unlearned.

soc.: What you say, Nicias, is true indeed, by Zeus!

nic.: So then, if the courageous man is good, clearly he is wise.

soc.: Did you hear, Laches?

lach.: I did, and I do not particularly understand what he is saying.

soc.: But I seem to understand, and the man seems to me to be saying that courage is a certain wisdom.

lach.: Wisdom! Of what sort, Socrates?[30]

e   soc.: Are you then asking him this?

lach.: I am.

soc.: Come then, Nicias, tell him what kind of wisdom courage would be, according to your account. For presumably it would not be the art of the aulos.

nic.: Not at all.

soc.: Nor the art of the cithara.

nic.: Indeed not.

soc.: But then what, or of what, is this knowledge?

lach.: You are questioning him very correctly indeed, Socrates; and let him say what he asserts it is.

---

[29]"Perplexity," *aporia,* means literally "lack of resources"; the closely related verb and adjective have been rendered "(be) at a loss" in this same paragraph.

[30]Literally, Laches asks, "What sort of wisdom?" The phrase, frequent in comedy, also has the force of an exclamation of disbelief—perhaps "Wisdom, my foot!" (So, in *Euthydemus* 291a, does Crito exclaim his disbelief that Ctesippus stated a Socratic-sounding argument.)

195a   NIC.: This, Laches, is what I say it is: the knowledge of terrible and of confidence-inspiring things, both in war and in all other things.

LACH.: How strange are the things he says, Socrates!

SOC.: With a view to what did you say this, Laches?

LACH.: To what? Wisdom is doubtless distinct from courage.

SOC.: Nicias certainly does not say so.

LACH.: Indeed not, by Zeus, and that is why he is talking rubbish!

SOC.: Then let us teach him, let us not revile him.

b   NIC.: No, Socrates, but in my opinion Laches desires that I too be revealed to be talking nonsense, because he himself was just now revealed as such.

LACH.: Most certainly, Nicias, and I shall try, at least, to prove it. Indeed you are talking nonsense, since—to begin with—in the case of illnesses, do not doctors know the terrible things? Or in your opinion do courageous men know? Or do you call doctors courageous?

NIC.: Not in any way at all.

LACH.: Nor indeed farmers, I think. And yet these doubtless know the things that are terrible in farming, and all the other craftsmen

c   know the things that are terrible and confidence inspiring in their own arts. But they are none the more courageous for it.

SOC.: What in your opinion is Laches saying, Nicias? He does seem to be saying something.

NIC.: He is indeed saying something but not something true.

SOC.: How so?

NIC.: Because he thinks doctors know something more about the sick than what is healthful and unwholesome. But doubtless they know only this much.[31] But whether it is terrible for someone to be healthy rather than to be sick—do you believe, Laches, that doctors know this? Or do you not think that it is better for many not to get up from

d   an illness than to get up? Say this: do you assert that it is better for all to live and not better for many to die?

LACH: This, at least, I do think.

NIC.: So then do you think the same things are terrible for those for whom it is profitable to die as for those for whom it is profitable to live?

LACH.: No, I don't.

---

[31]In the first of the two preceding sentences, I follow Badham's emendation; the MSS read "know something more about the sick than to say what sort of thing the healthful is, and the unwholesome." In the next, I follow Hermann; the MSS might be translated "They doubtless know only something like this much."

NIC.: But do you give the knowing of this to doctors or to any other craftsman, besides the knower of terrible and not terrible things, whom I call courageous?

SOC.: Do you fully perceive in your mind, Laches, what he is saying?

e LACH.: I do: he is calling diviners courageous. For who else will know whether it is better for someone to live or to die? And you, Nicias, do you agree that you are a diviner or neither a diviner nor courageous?

NIC.: What? Now do you think it belongs to a diviner to know the terrible and the confidence-inspiring things?

LACH.: I do, for to whom else?

NIC.: Much more to him whom I say, best of men. For the diviner must know only the signs of the things that will be—whether death 196a or illness or loss of property will come to someone or victory or defeat either in war or in some other competition. But whether it is better for someone either to suffer or not to suffer these things—why does it belong to the diviner to judge rather than to anyone else at all?

LACH.: Well, I do not understand, Socrates, what he wants to say, for he does not make clear that either the diviner or the doctor or anyone else is the man whom he says to be courageous—unless he is saying b that it is some god. So then, Nicias appears to me unwilling nobly[32] to agree that he is talking nonsense, but he turns around this way and that, concealing his own perplexity. And yet we could also, you and I, have turned around in such ways just now, if we wanted not to seem to say things that contradicted ourselves. Well then, if our speeches were in a law court, there would be some reason to do these things, but now, in an association of this sort, why should someone adorn himself in vain with empty speeches?

c SOC.: In my opinion too, there would be no reason, Laches. But let us see if Nicias doesn't think he is saying something and not saying these things for the sake of a speech. So let us inquire of him more clearly what in the world he perceives in his mind. And if he is revealed to be saying something, we shall accede to it, and if not, we shall teach him.

LACH.: If you wish to inquire, Socrates, you inquire then. I have perhaps inquired sufficiently.

SOC.: Well, nothing prevents me, for the inquiry will be a common one on behalf of me and you.

---

[32]Elsewhere, "noble" always translates *kalos;* here only it translates *gennaios,* which is derived from words for, and emphasizes, birth or descent (cf. *generosus* in Latin).

LACH.: Most certainly.

d soc.: Tell me then, Nicias, or rather tell us; for Laches and I are sharing the argument in common. Do you assert that courage is the knowledge of terrible and confidence-inspiring things?

NIC.: I do.

soc.: And it does not belong to every man to know this, when neither doctor nor diviner knows it nor is courageous, unless he has acquired this very knowledge in addition. Weren't you saying this?

NIC.: Yes, that's it.

soc.: According to the proverb, therefore, it really is the case that not every sow would know it or be courageous.[33]

NIC.: Not in my opinion.

e soc.: It is clear, Nicias, that you at any rate don't trust the Crommyonian sow[34] to be courageous either. I do not say this as a joke, but I think it is necessary for someone who says these things not to admit the courage of any wild animal or else to concede that some wild animal is so wise that, he must assert, a lion or leopard or some boar knows things that few among human beings know because of their being hard to know. But he who posits courage as what you posit must of necessity assert that lion and deer and bull and monkey are by nature alike as regards courage.

197a LACH.: By the gods, what you say is good, Socrates! And answer us this truly, Nicias: do you assert that these wild animals, which we all agree are courageous, are wiser than we, or contradicting us all, do you dare not to call them courageous either?

NIC.: Well, Laches, I for my part call either wild animals or anything else that does not fear terrible things on account of ignorance not courageous but fearless and stupid. Or do you think that I also call all b children courageous, who are afraid of nothing on account of ignorance? I think, rather, that the fearless and the courageous are not the same thing. I think that a very few people have a share in courage and forethought, whereas very many—among men and women and children and wild animals—have a share in boldness and daring and

[33]According to the scholiast, the proverb was applied to something so easy and well known that "even the most ignorant animals understand it fully" (W. C. Greene, *Scholia Platonica* [Haverford, Pa., 1938]).

[34]The sow of Crommyon was a fierce beast slain by Theseus, the legendary national hero of Athens, who is best known for having killed the dread Minotaur on Crete (thus freeing Athens from sending a yearly tribute of youths and maidens) and unifying the several communities of Attica into one political community centered on Athens.

fearlessness with lack of forethought. So then, these things that you
c and the many call courageous, I call bold, and I call courageous the
prudent things about which I am talking.

LACH.: You see, Socrates, how well this fellow here adorns himself—
as he thinks—in speech. He endeavors to deprive those whom all
agree to be courageous of this honor.

NIC.: No, I don't, Laches, but have confidence, for I assert that you
are wise, and Lamachus[35] too, if indeed you two are courageous—
and numerous other Athenians as well.

LACH.: I shall say nothing to this, though I have things to say, lest you
assert that I am truly an Aixonean.[36]

d SOC.: Don't say it, Laches. For in my opinion you have not noticed of
this man that he has received this wisdom from our comrade Damon,
and Damon keeps company a good deal with Prodicus,[37] who, of the
sophists, seems to distinguish such terms[38] in the finest manner.

LACH.: It is indeed fitting for a sophist, Socrates, to contrive such
subtleties rather than a man whom the city deems worthy to be its
leader.

e SOC.: Yet it is surely fitting, blessed man, for him who is leader of the
greatest things to partake in the greatest prudence. Now, Nicias in
my opinion is worthy of examination, as to what in the world he
looks to when he assigns this name, courage.

LACH.: Well then, examine him yourself, Socrates.

SOC.: I am going to do this, best of men. Do not think, however, that
I am letting you go from partnership in the argument, but turn your
mind to it and join in examining what is said.

LACH.: Let it be so, if it seems that it must.

198a SOC.: It does seem so. Now you, Nicias, tell us again from the beginning. Do you think that at the beginning of the argument we were
examining courage by examining it as a part of virtue?

[35]An Athenian general, of the prowar party. He was later to be appointed, with
Nicias and Alcibiades, to lead the Sicilian expedition that set forth in 415. He favored
an energetic and aggressive policy; after the recall of Alcibiades and the death of
Lamachus, Nicias' cautious policy prevailed, with disastrous results.

[36]The scholiast explains that people of the deme Aexone were lampooned in come-
dies as being abusive in speech (*blasphēmos*). (See n. 5.)

[37]Socrates frequently mentions Prodicus as a maker of fine distinctions in the search
for correct terminology. For instance, see *Charmides* 163d; *Cratylus* 384b; *Euthydemus*
277e and 305c; and *Protagoras* 315e, 337a–c, 339e–341e, 358a–e; sometimes, to be
sure, Socrates seems ironical in his praise of Prodicus.

[38]More literally (and so translated elsewhere) "names," which according to the
Seventh Letter are the first element in the knowledge of something (342b).

NIC.: Certainly.

SOC.: So then, when you gave this answer, did you too take it as a portion, there being other parts as well, which all together are called virtue?

NIC.: How else?

SOC.: Do you therefore say that these are what I say? I call them, in addition to courage, moderation and justice and some other such things. Don't you too?

b NIC.: Most certainly.

SOC.: Stop there, for we agree on these things, and let us now examine the terrible and the confidence-inspiring things so that you do not believe some things while we believe others. We shall explain to you, therefore, what we believe, and if you do not agree, you shall teach us. We believe that the things that cause fear are terrible and the things that do not cause fear are confidence inspiring and that fear is caused not by past nor present evils, but by those that are expected, for fear is the expectation of future evil. Don't you also think so, Laches?

LACH.: Very much so indeed, Socrates.

c SOC.: Well then, you hear our positions, Nicias: we assert that future evils are terrible and future nonevils or goods are confidence inspiring. Do you speak in this or in some other way about these things?

NIC.: This is what I say.

SOC.: And is it the knowledge of these things that you call by the name of courage?

NIC.: Exactly.

SOC.: Let us examine yet a third thing, as to whether you and we share the same opinion.

NIC.: What sort of thing is this?

d SOC.: I shall explain to you. It seems to me and to this man here that, in regard to things of which there is knowledge, there is not one knowledge about that which has come into being, which knows in what way it has come into being, and another about the things that are coming into being, as to the way in which they are coming into being, and another about the way in which what has not yet come into being would come into being in the finest manner and will come into being; rather, it is the same knowledge. For example: in regard to the healthful, for all times no other knowledge than medicine, which is one, oversees the things that are coming into being and those that have come into being and those that will come into being, as to e how they will come into being. And again, in regard to the things that by nature grow from the earth, farming does likewise. And as for the things relating to war, doubtless you yourselves would bear witness that generalship uses forethought in the finest manner in other respects and also concerning what is going to be, and it thinks that it must not serve, but rule, divination, on the grounds that it has

99a finer knowledge of the things relating to war, both those that are coming into being and those that will come into being. And the law ordains thus, not that the diviner rule the general, but that the general rule the diviner. Shall we make these assertions, Laches?

LACH.: We shall.

SOC.: What then, Nicias? Do you assert with us that, in the case of the same things, the same knowledge understands the things that will be and those that are coming into being and those that have come into being?

NIC.: I do, for this is my opinion, Socrates.

b SOC.: And then, best of men, courage is the knowledge of terrible and confidence-inspiring things, as you assert, isn't it?

NIC.: Yes.

SOC.: And terrible and confidence-inspiring things have been agreed to be on the one hand future goods and, on the other, future evils.

NIC.: Certainly.

SOC.: And of the same things, the knowledge is the same, both of things future and of things in all conditions.

NIC.: This is so.

SOC.: Courage is therefore not knowledge only of terrible and confidence-inspiring things. For it understands not only about future goods and evils but also about those that are coming into being and

c that have come into being and that are in all conditions, just like the other knowledges.

NIC.: It seems so, at least.

SOC.: You therefore gave us as your answer, Nicias, a part of courage—about a third. Yet we asked you what the whole of courage was. And now, as it seems, according to your argument, courage is not knowledge only of terrible and confidence-inspiring things, but,

d as your argument now runs, courage would be the knowledge about pretty much all goods and evils and in all conditions. Is it in turn to be changed thus, or what do you say, Nicias?

NIC.: Yes, in my opinion, Socrates.

SOC.: So then, in your opinion, demonic man, would such a one lack

anything of virtue if indeed he knew how all good things, in all ways, come into being and will come into being and have come into being and all bad things in the same way? And do you think that this one would be in need of moderation or justice and piety—he to whom alone it belongs, as regards both gods and human beings, to be
e thoroughly on his guard for the terrible things and for those that are not, and to provide himself with the good things, through his knowing how to associate with them correctly?

NIC.: In my opinion, Socrates, you are saying something.

SOC.: Therefore, Nicias, what you are now saying would be not a portion of virtue but virtue entire.

NIC.: It seems so.

SOC.: And surely we were asserting that courage is one of the portions of virtue.

NIC.: We were indeed.

SOC.: And what is now said does not look like it.

NIC.: It seems not.

SOC.: Therefore, Nicias, we have not found what courage is.

NIC.. It looks as if we haven't.

LACH.: And I at any rate really thought, Nicias my friend, that you
200a would discover it, since you thought contemptuously of me as I answered Socrates; I had very great hope that, with the wisdom from Damon, you would discover it.

NIC.: Very well, Laches; you think that it is no longer any matter that you yourself were recently revealed to know nothing about courage, but if I too shall be revealed as another such, you look toward this, and it will no longer make a difference to you, it seems, that you together with me know nothing of the things of which it befits a man
b who thinks he is something to have knowledge. In my opinion, then, you do something that is truly human: you look not toward yourself but toward others. And I think that I have now spoken suitably on the things that we were talking about, and if something of them has not been adequately said, I shall correct it later both with Damon—whom you presumably think fit to ridicule, and that though you have never seen Damon—and with others. And when I have securely established these things for myself, I shall teach even you, and shall
c not begrudge it, for in my opinion you are in very great need of learning.

LACH.: Well, you are indeed wise, Nicias. But nevertheless I counsel

Lysimachus here and Melesias to bid you and me farewell, as regards the education of young men, and not to let this Socrates go, as I was saying from the beginning. And if my children were of an age, I would do these same things.

d   NIC.: I too accede to these things—if Socrates is willing to take care of the lads, to seek no one else. Indeed I would turn Niceratus over to this man with the greatest pleasure if he were willing. But on each occasion he recommends others to me whenever I make some mention of this to him and is himself unwilling. But see, Lysimachus, if Socrates would heed you somewhat more.

LYS.: It would be just, Nicias, since I too would be willing to do many things for this man, which I would not be willing to do for very many others. What do you say, then, Socrates? Will you pay some heed and join in our zeal for the lads to become as good as possible?

e   SOC.: This would indeed be a terrible thing, Lysimachus, to be unwilling to join in someone's zeal to become as good as possible. So then, if in the discussions just now I had been revealed to know and these two not to know, it would be just to summon me most of all to this work, but now, however, we were all alike at a loss. So then why, and which of us, should someone choose? In my own opinion, then, none of us. But since these things are so, examine whether I seem to you to give some counsel. For I assert, men—and the speech is not one to be divulged—that we must all seek in common as good a teacher as possible, most of all for ourselves, for we are in need, and then for the lads too, sparing neither money nor anything else. But I do not counsel that we let ourselves be in the condition we are now

b   in. And if someone ridicules us, because at our age we think it worthwhile to frequent teachers, in my opinion we must put forward Homer, who said that "it is not good for shame to be present in a needy man."[39] And so, bidding farewell to anyone who will say something, let us in common take care of ourselves and of the lads.

c   LYS.: What you say, Socrates, pleases me. And I am willing to learn with the lads—most zealously by as much as I am oldest. Now, do

[39]*Odyssey* XVII 347. Telemachus, looking upon his father Odysseus disguised as an old beggar, speaks these words to his swineherd, whom he sends to give food to the seeming stranger. Socrates uses the same quotation in the *Charmides* (at 161a); in that context, more than here, one might think of "the accuser" in Xenophon's *Memorabilia*, I ii 56, who said that Socrates used the most wicked passages of the most reputed poets to teach his associates to be evildoers and tyrannical.

this for me. Do not fail to come to my house tomorrow at dawn so that we may deliberate on these same things. As for now, let us break up our conversation.

soc.: Well, Lysimachus, I shall do these things and shall come to you tomorrow if god is willing.

Introduction to
the *Laches*

JAMES H. NICHOLS, JR.

Three questions concerning the *Laches* as a whole can hardly fail to strike the reader. Everyone knows that the *Laches* is about courage: why, then, is fully half of the dialogue devoted to other matters before Socrates clearly formulates the question of what courage is? Second, Nicias is more famous, more cultivated, and more fully acquainted with Socrates than Laches is: why, then, did Plato name the dialogue for Laches? Finally, the dialogue is one of those called "aporetic," which do not state a clear answer to the principal question raised: what, then, can we learn from it about courage? The present essay seeks to suggest some ways of interpreting the *Laches* by reflecting on these three questions.

Plato apparently devotes the dialogue's first half to questions other than what courage is for two interrelated purposes: to situate the question of courage within the larger context of questions about education to virtue and to provide the reader with a more fully developed dramatic representation of the characters of the dialogue than the second half alone presents.

The broader questions about education to virtue are less explicitly discussed (except briefly by Socrates near and at the end of this first half) than depicted through the characters and their situations, purposes, and speeches. Lysimachus presents a remarkable statement about himself and Melesias: they recognize and frankly state that their own lives are distinguished by no noble deeds like those of their illustrious fathers; they are unworthy of their ancestry (and hence feel shame before their sons), but they seek to cause their own sons to turn out worthy of their grandfathers' names. No one present ventures to suggest that Lysimachus and Melesias have in any way judged themselves too harshly. They attribute their own shortcomings wholly to defective education; too occupied with public affairs, their fathers neglected them and let them live a soft life.

But is education to blame for their lack of virtue? It might be, but other causes may well be involved. In particular, a crucial cause of virtue (which Lysimachus seems to equate with what produces noble deeds and hence fame) is doubtless nature, natural endowment, natural capacity. Laches seems aware of this point; later on (185e), concerning the broad issue of caring for the soul, he asks Socrates whether he has never seen men become more expert without teachers than with them, and Socrates, of course, agrees. It is readily understandable (and all too human) that Lysimachus prefers to blame his father for neglect rather than to examine whether he himself might not simply have a worse natural endowment than his father's, and this limitation of this thinking does serve to strengthen his praiseworthy resolve, with which no one could find fault, to seek out the best education possible for his son. But at the same time, Lysimachus implicitly maintains the contradictory notion that nature (as birth, descent) does make a difference; only some such notion makes intelligible the expectation that one should live up to one's ancestry.

Socrates' last utterance in this half of the dialogue underlines the question posed by Lysimachus' character and situation. Finally asking Laches to state what courage is, Socrates suggests that later on they might "examine in what way it might be present in young men, to the extent that it can be present from practices and studies." But to what extent is that? This question Melesias and Lysimachus, speaking as though only education made a difference, prefer not to face. On another occasion (*Meno* 94a–e), however, in their absence, Socrates *does* address it. Talking with Anytus (who was later to prosecute him for corrupting the young and for impiety) about whether virtue is teachable, Socrates uses Lysimachus and Melesias as examples to convince him that it is not. Against Lysimachus' claim here, Socrates asserts that Aristeides did give him the finest education among Athenians, in those things of which there are teachers, but, Socrates asks, did that make him a better man? "You see what sort he is." Socrates further argues that Thucydides too educated his sons, and since he would not have passed over the obviously most important thing, virtue, one must entertain the possibility that virtue is something unteachable.

The question of the relative efficacy of nature and of education in endowing men with virtue, while not explicitly discussed, is thus powerfully presented to the reader of the *Laches*. It has, furthermore, a continued bearing on what follows. When Nicias argues that the study of fighting in armor can make a man more courageous, he is maintaining that this virtue can to a significant degree be taught. When Laches denies it, and when he later defines courage as steadfastness of soul, he seems rather to take courage or cowardice as something given, a consequence—or better, manifestation—of the kind of man one is. He does not quite state that courage exists by nature, but he is the first to use a word connected to nature (192c), and he uses it precisely in connection with courage. In contrast, Nicias' definition of courage as a type of knowledge again suggests that it is teachable. The *Laches* does not answer this question of the relative importance of nature and education, but by showing different kinds of characters who choose to stress exclusively one or the other, it reveals much of the human significance of different positions on the question.

The first half of the dialogue also makes possible a fuller representation of the characters of Laches and Nicias. As soon as they have both acceded to Lysimachus' request for counsel, the differences begin to emerge. Laches agrees with the blame that Lysimachus has assigned to his own father, says it applies to all who are busy with the city's affairs, and extends the charge of neglect beyond children to "other private affairs." He can accept such blame cheerfully because he does seem to consider city and fatherland to be nobler concerns than private affairs, as becomes clear from his praise of Socrates (181a–b and 188e–89a). Nicias, by contrast, is not neglectful of things private: we learn at once that at Socrates' recommendation he has engaged Damon as teacher for his son, and as for other private affairs, Nicias was very wealthy. In his last speech to the doomed Athenian expedition in Sicily, as reported by the historian Thucydides, Nicias refers to his previous good fortune "both as regards private life and in other things" (VII 77.2). Laches is a very public man; for Nicias, despite his public career, private concerns come first.

The same difference finds expression in their respective speeches for and against the study of fighting in armor. Nicias says that the knowledge would be of greatest benefit when the ranks are broken and the contest is one on one; he emphasizes the individual's skill on his own. Laches, in contrast, emphasizes what is public and collective (thus, in his first halting attempt to define courage, he says that one who remains fighting in the ranks and does not flee is courageous). In his rejection of the study in question, he emphasizes ridicule and slander—means by which the community conveys and inculcates its standards of public respectability.

Certain other differences between Nicias and Laches emerge from these long speeches on fighting in armor. Nicias manifests the Athenian trait of openness to novelty; Laches, in contrast, expresses respect for the Lacedaemonians' attainments in war, and appeals to their expertise to support rejection of this study. Nicias is in some vague sense more intellectual, fond of arts and studies; he praises the consequences of the study of fighting in armor theoretically or in principle, with no concrete evidence. Laches, in contrast, appeals to facts: that the teachers of the study avoid the expert Lacedaemonians, that none has won fame in war, that he himself has seen one make a fool of himself. Nicias thinks that this skill would make a man more courageous; Laches thinks it will lure a coward into actions where he will be revealed for what he is and will bring a courageous man only envy.

Finally, Nicias' and Laches' attitudes toward continuing the discussion under Socrates' guidance differ. Nicias claims familiarity with Socrates' way of conducting a discussion and considers it beneficial; he also describes the experience as "suffering these things" from Socrates and being reminded of what one has done that is not noble. The whole experience appears to be something painful that one perhaps should not always flee, and when Nicias expresses concern that this kind of discussion may not suit Laches, one feels that Nicias might like Laches to get him off the hook by declining to continue the conversation. But Laches, though unaccustomed to Socratic speaking, is willing to participate, since Socrates measures up to the standard that Laches holds to be crucial: his deeds prove him to be good enough to speak about noble things. In contrast, Laches is pained by people like Stesilaus (the teacher of fighting in armor) and other sophists, who are not in their own deeds worthy of the speeches they make. Whereas Nicias appears open to sophists, Laches finds them tiresome and ridiculous boasters. (In this he differs from Anytus in the *Meno,* who divines[1] that the sophists are dangerous corrupters and feels anger toward them.)

---

[1]Socrates calls Anytus a diviner, *Meno* 92c.

Why did Plato name the dialogue for Laches rather than for Nicias? At first sight, the choice is surprising. Not only is Nicias more famous by far, he also seems in many ways closer to Socrates. Like Socrates, he is concerned with education, open to new ideas, and receptive to the knowledge that may be available from sophists. He is familiar with Socratic conversations, seeks Socrates' guidance on education, and frames a definition of courage that sounds quite Socratic, on the basis of something he has often heard Socrates say. At the end of the aporetic discussion of courage, Nicias indicates that he will seek to remedy the deficiency of his definition and justly notes that Laches is quite unconcerned about the inadequacy of his own definition (now that Nicias has ended up in the same boat).

Upon closer examination, however, Laches seems ultimately to be closer to Socrates, especially in regard to courage, and Nicias to have the more grievously flawed character. Some support for this assertion is already apparent from the depiction of characters in the first half of the dialogue. Though Nicias is more familiar with Socrates, Laches brings Socrates into the discussion, and as noted earlier, Laches seems more eager than Nicias for the conversation to continue. Laches' concern that a man's speeches and deeds go together to form a harmonious whole reflects a real seriousness of character that is somehow Socratic, even though his holding deeds to be more important than speeches (arguments, reasonings) is doubtless un-Socratic. In contrast, Nicias' intellectual sophistication at first appears Socratic but ultimately proves to be shallow. To take an example from near the end of the dialogue, when Nicias is refuted, he thinks he has nonetheless spoken suitably and will easily patch up his definition with Damon's help; he seems to have no notion that the problem reflects a serious weakness in his own character and understanding. Finally, both Laches and Socrates neglect private affairs[2] because of their respective more serious concerns, whereas Nicias pays great attention to his private affairs.

Added support for my assertion emerges in the dialogue's latter half, where, as one would expect, the strengths and weaknesses of the definitions given correspond in a revealing manner to the characters who give them. Laches' second definition of courage as steadfastness of soul proves to be inadequate: he considers courage to be a good thing; Socrates leads him to accept that good things are accompanied by prudence rather than folly; but his real view of what the core of

---

[2]For Laches, see 180b; for Socrates, *Apology* 23b–c, 31b–c, 36b.

courage truly is, as Socrates draws it out into the light, has no connection with prudence. Though inadequate, Laches' definition is not
misleading and indeed captures something crucial to courage: Socrates himself (at 194a) suggests that perhaps steadfastness is often
courage, and in the *Gorgias* (507b) Socrates indicates that it belongs to
the courageous man "to abide and be steadfast where he ought."

Laches frames this second definition in response to Socrates' questions and examples, in accordance with which he must define courage
so broadly as to cover its manifestations in warfare, navigation, sickness, poverty, and politics, and not only toward pains or fears but
also toward desires or pleasures (that is, Socrates' question points
toward a definition that would include what is ordinarily called moderation). What Laches considers primary to courage, however, is
clear from his first definition: the courageous man stays in the ranks
and fights instead of fleeing. These definitions together with traits of
Laches' noted earlier—the overriding value he places on duty to city
or fatherland, his manifest concern with honor and ridicule, his very
public character—make it apparent that Laches has a commonsense,
political conception of courage. In the *Republic,* Socrates distinguishes
political courage from courage that could be given a finer treatment
(which for convenience I shall call philosophic courage); he defines
political courage as "power and preservation, through everything, of
the right and lawful opinion about what is terrible and what not."
Laches' courage is of this sort: it rests on preserving the opinion that
ridicule and disgrace, above all for not bravely fighting for the city,
are more terrible than the risk of death.

One other aspect of Laches' notion of courage emerges in subsequent discussion of Nicias' definition. Laches believes that such animals as boars and lions do have courage—courage can exist on a
subhuman, brute level. One may well decide, with Nicias, to withhold the name "courage" in such instances in order to save it for fully
human courage (accompanied by reason), but this aspect of Laches'
notion nonetheless points to an important truth about human courage. A necessary condition of what we ordinarily recognize as courage is a certain natural disposition or temper—whether boldness,
confidence, steadiness, perseverance, spiritedness, or some combination—that is or provides the strength or steadfastness by which one
can in fact stand firm against dangers. I shall call this necessary condition a natural temper of bravery. Without a sufficient degree of this
temper, one may reason well on what one should do but succumb
nonetheless to an irresistible urge to flee.

In contrast, Nicias' more sophisticated definition of courage as knowledge of terrible and confidence-inspiring things sounds more philosophic than Laches', but it too proves inadequate. Furthermore, it is misleading, and the character of its defect corresponds to the profound defectiveness of Nicias with regard to courage.

Laches' imperfect attempt to refute Nicias points in the direction of the basic problem with Nicias' definition (and with Nicias). Laches thinks courage has nothing to do with knowledge. He gives the examples of doctors and farmers, who in their respective fields know the terrible and confidence-inspiring things, but this knowledge does not make them courageous. Nicias agrees but saves his definition by maintaining that, while doctors know what produces sickness and health, they do not as doctors know what is truly terrible or the opposite—for example, whether it is better for a given patient to get well or to die. Laches, remaining well within the limits of ordinary common sense, supposes that Nicias must mean that doctors, for instance, lack this knowledge because, like most people, they do not know what will befall their patient in the future; accordingly, he derisively concludes that Nicias must think that diviners are the courageous men. Nicias denies this in the same way that he earlier denied such knowledge to the doctor; thus he seems at first to raise genuinely philosophical issues about what truly is good for a human being. Laches, however, does not see his way through to such profound issues; he simply feels irritation at Nicias, who he thinks is basely wriggling out of admitting his error.

Nicias defeats Laches in debate here, but Laches' point about diviners is truly revealing of Nicias. To state Nicias' flaw most simply: he is in fact superstitious; as Laches' derision suggests, he is overly given to following the counsels of diviners. Thucydides himself makes this observation in reporting Nicias' last great error of the Sicilian expedition.[3] The Athenians have failed to make a breakthrough in their attempt to besiege Syracuse. Their position can only get worse, and Demosthenes (who brought reinforcements and had correctly urged taking the offensive without delay) now favors abandoning the invasion and sailing home. Nicias opposes going home, among other reasons because of his fear that the Athenians will condemn the generals to death for abandoning the expedition; he would prefer to die at the hands of the enemies (Nicias thus displays a lack of

---

[3]Thucydides VII 42–50. Plutarch's *Nicias* discusses his concern with diviners in considerable detail.

courage in politics, and his private concern wins out over the public interest of Athens). As the situation of the Athenians deteriorates still further, Nicias finally agrees to withdraw, but an eclipse of the moon takes place, and he insists on following the diviners' belief that they must not move for thrice nine days. The possible moment of successful escape is thus lost, and the Athenians soon meet with complete ruin. Lest Laches' mention of diviners be insufficient to prompt the reader to these reflections, Plato has Socrates make a point that reminds one still more powerfully of Nicias' subsequent fate and its significance for understanding his character. Socrates affirms that generalship is *the* knowledge of war, finer than divination; the law therefore embodies reason in ordaining, "not that the diviner rule the general, but that the general rule the diviner." Socrates turns to Laches for confirmation of this assertion; Nicias utters no objection, but his later actions in Sicily reveal that he really holds to the very opposite ordering of generalship and divining.

The significance of these facts about Nicias is brought to light by Socrates' manner of refuting him. Nicias has defined courage as knowledge of terrible and confidence-inspiring things; these Socrates shows, are future goods and evils. No knowledge (or science), however, deals with future things alone; in any area, it is the same knowledge that deals with past, present, and future. The knowledge that Nicias has called courage, therefore, cannot exist. And if Laches' hunch is correct that Nicias has really defined divination rather than courage, divination as knowledge of the future only, to which Nicias later subordinates what should have been his better knowledge as general, can also not exist. (Interestingly, Homer says of the Greek diviner Chalchas that he "knew the things that are and the things that will be and the things that were before" [e.g., at *Iliad* I 70]; but Nicias is no more up to the level of Homeric wisdom than to that of Socratic.) Nicias is therefore compelled by Socrates' questioning to expand his definition so that it becomes knowledge of past, present, and future goods and evils, but then he has defined virtue entire rather than courage as a part of virtue and is refuted on that point.

Nicias defines courage as a knowledge that one might, with Laches, confuse with divination but that upon examination proves unable as defined to exist as knowledge at all. This error has decisive significance for our understanding of Nicias' character; it points beyond the seemingly philosophical surface of Nicias' sophistication to his real concerns, which are in no sense philosophical. The emphasis in his definition of courage, as Socrates investigates it, is not on anything that would strike most people (including, of course, Laches) as belonging to courage but on forethought, taking care for the future. Nicias' deepest trait is anxiety about future events. He does not, despite superficial appearances, raise philosophical questions about what things are truly good and bad for human beings; his cautious and anxious forethoughtfulness, within the horizon of common judgments of good and bad, seeks to find security through knowledge of the future. Laches is profoundly right in deriding Nicias for identifying courage with divination: Nicias wants refuge from the dangerous uncertainties of the future. He seeks knowledge of future events as a substitute for courage. But such knowledge, which could be thought to make courage unnecessary, does not exist, and indeed courage is needed above all to enable us to act as we should in the face of an uncertain future.

In the process of compelling Nicias to expand his definition to make it compatible with the character of genuine knowledge, Socrates underlines the thoroughly unphilosophic character of Nicias' concerns. Socrates uses mainly the verb "to come into being" or "to become" (*gignesthai*) instead of the verb "to be" (*einai*). Elsewhere (as in the treatment of philosophers in the *Republic,* V–VII) Socrates develops the distinction between the realm of being, to which genuine philosophic knowledge is directed, and the realm of becoming or of coming into being and passing away, with which the ordinary opinions of nonphilosophers are mainly concerned. The distinction is not elaborated here but is presupposed and alluded to. Concluding a section of the argument against Nicias, Socrates asserts that, if it is knowledge, courage must understand "not only about future goods and evils, but also those that are coming into being and that have come into being *and that are in all conditions,* just like the other knowledges" (199b–c, emphasis added). Those things that are "in all conditions" include, beyond those that come into being in the past, present, or future, the things that most truly *are,* that are permanent, eternal—that is, the ultimate intelligible objects of the philosopher's search for knowledge. These, the conversation makes clear, do not figure in Nicias' conception of knowledge. His concerns are with past, present, and above all future events, toward which he looks with anxious forethought.

Near the end of the *Euthydemus,* Socrates talks with Crito about certain teachers of speaking in law courts. They partake moderately of philosophy and moderately of politics and believe they are wisest

of all, superior to both philosophers and statesmen. If both philosophy and politics are bad, the claim of these men may well be true. But
if (as seems likely) philosophy and political action are both good
things and each aims at something different from the other, Socrates
says, those who are in between and partake of both are in fact inferior
to either philosopher or statesman.

The ordering of the three principal characters of the *Laches,* in
relation to courage, is parallel to this ordering of philosophy, politics,
and rhetoric suggested by the *Euthydemus.* Both Socrates and Laches
have courage, as their conduct together in the battle of Delium shows
and as Socrates suggests someone would declare on the basis of their
deeds (193e), but each has a different kind. Laches' courage, we have
seen, has a decidedly political character and rests, I would surmise, on
a generous allotment to him by nature of a temper of bravery. Socrates, on the other hand, has philosophic courage. Nicias falls in
between. He shares with Laches a public career as general but lacks
Laches' thoroughly public, political character (and also appears unen-
dowed with a natural temper of bravery). His openness and
thoughtfulness move him toward Socrates but without any real
change in fundamental orientation; his concerns do not become philosophic. While it may well be too simple to say with Plutarch that
Nicias is cowardly, Plato surely represents him as being of inferior
and more dubious courage than either Laches or Socrates.

Since the *Laches* ends without an explicit answer to the question of
what courage is, the reader is left with depictions of two kinds of
courageous men and of a third man in between who falls short in
courage. Concerning Laches' political courage, perhaps enough has
already been said; let us recall, however, one crucial problem: courage as he understands it has no necessary connection with reason-
ableness. Nicias' definition of courage as knowledge associates courage with reason: he does not, however, carry his thinking through to
a thoroughly rational position that one could call philosophic, yet
along the way his thoughts on courage lose sight of basic features that
anyone of common sense would identify. Plato presents Socrates'
courage, in contrast, as philosophical. The drunken but perceptive
Alcibiades notes the difference between Socrates' courage and Laches'
in the flight from Delium (*Symposium* 221b): he says not that Socrates
was more courageous but that he surpassed Laches in being *em-
phron*—"in possession of his mind" (or "having his wits about
him"). Unlike Laches, Socrates is not moved most deeply by pa-
triotism, love of honor, and fear of shame or ridicule to courageous

actions; rather, his courageous actions are made possible by his philosophic thinking. He has followed the rational direction in which Nicias' definition points through to a philosophical standpoint that is radically different from ordinary human concerns. As philosopher, Socrates is most deeply concerned with the search for permanent truths, with knowing those eternal entities that are truly intelligible. From the standpoint of such concerns, the world of becoming, of human events, of the things that are of primary concern to most men (including both Nicias and Laches), assumes a lower order of importance. Socrates sees and accepts the unavoidable role of chance or fortune in the world: he can recognize uncertainty and act reasonably in the face of uncertain dangers without the support of limited opinions such as those of Laches and without seeking delusory assurance through the divination so dear to Nicias or through any other spurious knowledge of the future.

One remaining problem must be addressed. Nicias' definition, once broadened, is refuted because it then appears to designate all of virtue, not courage as a part of virtue. Is not what I have said about Socrates' philosophic courage open to the same objection?

This objection raises the whole problem of the relation between the parts of virtue and virtue as a whole. This problem pervades the *Laches*. Lysimachus is concerned with education as a whole but is sent to inspect (at most) a small part, fighting in armor. Socrates emphasizes that their deliberation must be about the whole well-being of the soul, but then he singles out a part: courage. His questions lead Laches toward a broad definition of courage (such, e.g., as to include moderation and prudence). Next, Socrates first shows that Nicias' definition has grasped only a part of courage—about a third. But finally, when Nicias' definition is adequately broadened, Socrates refutes it by showing that it would be the whole of virtue, and not the part—courage—that they were seeking. This same problem occurs elsewhere in Plato. As in the *Laches,* the search for a particular virtue (moderation in the *Charmides,* for example, or justice in the *Republic*) seems to lead by dialectical necessity toward knowledge; and conversely, the lover of knowledge (the philosopher, as characterized for example in the *Republic*) is seen necessarily to be endowed with the other virtues.

So central a question, which runs through so many of the dialogues, cannot be fully answered here. Let us nonetheless cite a crucial passage from the *Republic,* to use in clarifying the question as presented by the *Laches*. Having spoken of the fundamental intellectual virtue of the soul, here named prudence, Socrates continues as follows: "Therefore, the other virtues of a soul, as they are called, are probably somewhat close to those of the body. For they are really not there beforehand and are later produced by habits and exercises, while the virtue of exercising prudence is more than anything somehow more divine, it seems."[4] The fundamental virtue of a soul may be called knowledge, prudence, or wisdom. For convenience, let us call it intellectual virtue. The perfect development of any of the virtues (that is, any part of virtue entire, such as courage) does somehow require this fundamental intellectual virtue, for without it, a "virtue" such as courage may be foolish, harmful, and thus not truly virtue. Courage and the other parts of virtue are not, however, simply identical with intellectual virtue, because we humans are complex beings, compounded of soul and body, faced with varying situations in life (such as the danger of death, which is either the annihilation of our being or the separation of soul and body). The particular parts of virtue (the virtues, like courage) are particular modes of applying intellectual virtue in different situations and with regard to different aspects of our complex being. What I have called philosophic courage does require intellectual virtue, but *as courage* it requires also something else, which I have called a natural temper of bravery.[5]

Laches has such a temper; in place of philosophic intellectual virtue, he has certain emphatically *political* opinions; in consequence, he has a kind of courage that is the steadfastness of soul by which he can persevere in the face of uncertain dangers. Nicias, I believe we are meant to conclude, has less of this natural temper of bravery than either Laches or Socrates; he also has neither the philosophic stance of Socrates nor the political opinions of Laches; in consequence, he is filled with anxiety about the future and seeks the spurious assurance of divination. Socrates' philosophic courage combines intellectual virtue with a natural temper sufficiently brave to enable him to persevere in reasonable action despite full awareness of uncertainty and danger. Indeed, as Socrates suggests to Laches, courage as steadfastness of soul is required for the very search for genuine knowledge. Without such courage, one may refuse to see the truth about the situation and take refuge instead in divination.

---

[4]Allan Bloom, trans., *The Republic of Plato* (New York, 1968), 518d–e.
[5]The passage cited from the *Republic* suggests that this temper can be to some extent produced, and certainly enhanced and cultivated, by habits and exercises.

LESSER HIPPIAS
[or, On the Lie]

Translated by JAMES LEAKE

Eudicus, Socrates, Hippias

363a EUDICUS: But you, Socrates, why are you silent after Hippias has made an exhibition[1] of such great things? Why do you not either join in praising any of the things that were said, or even refute something, if it does not seem to you to have been finely spoken? Especially since we alone are left who would particularly make claim to share in the pursuit of philosophy.

b SOCRATES: Indeed, Eudicus, there are some things, among those Hippias just now said about Homer, that I would ask him about with pleasure. For I used to hear from your father, Apemantus, that the *Iliad* of Homer is a more beautiful [noble] poem than the *Odyssey,* and more beautiful [noble] in the measure that Achilles is a better man than Odysseus; for he asserted that of these poems the one was composed about Odysseus, the other about Achilles. I would with pleasure inquire about that, then, if Hippias is willing—what his opinion

c is of these two men and which he asserts to have been better, for he has exhibited to us many other things of every kind both about other poets and about Homer.

EUD.: But it is clear that Hippias will not begrudge you an answer if

[1]*Epideiksis* ("exhibition," "declamation," "display"). Sophists such as Hippias were accustomed to make such long elaborate speeches for purposes of displaying their wisdom. Socrates contrasts it with his own humble art of asking questions or conversing, which he calls dialectics. Cf. 364d1–3, 373a1–3; *Meno* 75c8–d7; *Republic* 338a3–b9.

you ask him something. Is it not so, Hippias? If Socrates asks you something, will you answer? Or what will you do?

HIPPIAS: I would certainly be acting strangely, Eudicus—I, who al-
d ways come up from my home in Elis to Olympia to the solemn assembly of the Greeks when the Olympic festivals are held, and there present myself in the temple to speak on whatever anyone may wish from among those things I have prepared for exhibition and to answer whatever anyone who wishes should ask—were I now to flee the questioning of Socrates.

364a SOC.: Blessed indeed, Hippias, is your experience, if at each Olympiad you have reached the temple being so hopeful about your soul with respect to wisdom, and I would marvel if any of the athletes concerned with the body comes there to contend as fearlessly and confidently trusting in his body as you assert you do in your mind.

HIP.: It is fitting, Socrates, that I should have experienced this; for since I began contending for victory at Olympia, I've never yet met anyone better than I am in anything.

b SOC.: It is a fine thing indeed you're saying, Hippias—that your reputation is a monument of wisdom both for the city of the Eleans and for your parents. But whatever do you say to us about Achilles and Odysseus? Which do you assert is better and in what respect? For when there were many of us inside, and you were making your exhibition, I was left behind by the things you said. I hesitated to question you, both because there was a large crowd inside, and lest I interfere with your exhibition through my questioning, but now, since there are fewer of us and Eudicus here bids me to ask, speak out
c and teach us clearly, what were you saying about these two men? How were you distinguishing them?

HIP.: I'm certainly willing, Socrates, to explain to you still more clearly than before what I have to say about these men as well as others. I assert that Homer represented Achilles as the best[2] man of

---

[2]The Greek word here, *aristos* ("bravest," "best"), is the superlative of *agathos* ("brave," "good"). The primary meaning of this crucial word in Homer is "brave." As one sees from the case of Achilles above all, however, the heroes believe that to be brave and fight in the forefront of the battle with ardor is to be good simply, to do what is right. The expectations connected with such actions become apparent when honor is denied, as in the "baleful wrath" of Achilles and his demand that he be honored for his goodness by Zeus. He even comes to doubt whether brave action is the core of goodness (see *Iliad* IX 313ff.).

those who came to Troy, Nestor as the wisest, and Odysseus as the most versatile.[3]

SOC.: My, my, Hippias! Please, would you do me a favor such as the following—do not laugh at me if I should have difficulty understanding what is said and often raise questions? Instead, try to answer me gently and calmly.

HIP.: It would indeed be shameful, Socrates, if I, who educate others in these very things and think I am worthy to take money for this, should not myself be indulgent and answer gently when questioned by you.

SOC.: What you say is very fine. Now, when you asserted that Achilles has been represented as the best, I seemed to understand what you were saying, and also when you asserted that Nestor was the wisest, but when you said that the poet has represented Odysseus as the most versatile, in this case, to tell you the truth, I absolutely do not know what you are saying. Tell me, then, and perhaps I will understand it better this way: has Achilles not been represented by Homer as versatile?

HIP.: No indeed, Socrates, but as most simple.[4] For example, in "The Prayers,"[5] when he represents them conversing with one another, he has Achilles say in reply to Odysseus:

[3]The Greek word is *polytropōtatos*, superlative of the Homeric epithet of Odysseus, *polytropos*. In the *Odyssey* it appears twice and seems to mean "much turned," "much wandering" (I 1, X 330). The other, more common epithets of Odysseus—*polymētis* ("crafty," "shrewd"), *polymēchanos* ("much contriving"), *poikilomētēs* ("with versatile mind"), *polyphrōn* ("very sagacious")—seem to color the meaning "versatile" given the word by Hippias and some modern editors (e.g., Merry and Riddell). Liddell and Scott insist that in Homer the word means not "versatile" but "much traveled." I translate it as "versatile" in accordance with Hippias' interpretation (cf. 365b5).

[4]Burnet inserts here in the Greek "and most truthful," as had Stephanus before him, following an inferior manuscript. Stallbaum gives a sensible explanation, in his note on this passage, for regarding these words as a gloss introduced from the sequel by some literal-minded scholar and for following the better manuscripts. I have done so in omitting these words, which Hippias brings forth later in his interpretation.

[5]"The Prayers" was the ancient name (cf. *Cratylos* 428c) of the central scene in the *Iliad* where Odysseus, Ajax, and Phoenix were sent as an embassy by the chiefs of the Greeks in the name of Agamemnon to appease Achilles' anger. Odysseus spoke first. In an adroit speech he tried to induce the hero to rejoin the Greek forces who, far from taking Troy, were in danger of losing their very ships to the Trojans since Achilles had withdrawn from the battle. Odysseus flattered Achilles and promised him gifts and honors. The verses here cited, *Iliad* IX 308–14, were taken from Achilles' response, in which he rejects the offer, still angry, having come to doubt the conven-

365a   Son of Laertes, sprung from Zeus, much-devising Odysseus,
One surely must speak out without regard to consequences,
Just as I am going to do and as I think it will be fulfilled;
For that one is hateful to me as the gates of Hades

b   Who hides one thing in his mind but says something else.
But I will speak, as it is also going to be fulfilled.

In these verses he shows clearly the manner of each man, how
Achilles was both truthful and simple, Odysseus both versatile and
lying, for he represents Achilles speaking these verses to Odysseus.
SOC.: Now, Hippias, I am perhaps beginning to understand what you
are saying; you are saying that the versatile man is a liar, at least as it
appears.

c   HIP.: Precisely, Socrates. For Homer has represented Odysseus as this
sort of man in many places both in the *Iliad* and in the *Odyssey*.
SOC.: Apparently, then, it seemed to Homer that the truthful man is
one sort and the liar another, and they are not the same.
HIP.: How could it not have seemed so, Socrates?
SOC.: And does it seem so to you yourself as well, Hippias?
HIP.: Most certainly! For indeed it would be a strange thing if it were
not so.

d   SOC.: Well, let us leave Homer aside, since it is impossible to ask him
what he was thinking when he composed these verses anyway, but
since you are evidently taking upon yourself the responsibility, and
you agree with these things you assert Homer said, answer on behalf
of Homer and yourself in common.
HIP.: So be it; just ask briefly what you want.
SOC.: Do you say that liars are incapable[6] of doing anything, like sick
men, or are they capable of doing something?
HIP.: I, for my part, say that they are very capable of doing many
things and particularly of deceiving people.

e   SOC.: Apparently, then, they are capable, according to your argument, as well as versatile, or not?

---

tional notion of virtue or heroism. Hippias drops verse 311, "That you may not keep
moaning one after another, sitting beside me." In verse 310 he changes our text of
Homer from "as I think" to "as I am going to do," and in verse 314 he changes "as it
seems to me to be best" to "as it is also going to be fulfilled," apparently to underline
Achilles' certainty.

[6]Here and in the following exchanges, the words rendered "incapable" and "capable" might also be rendered "lack the power" (or "are powerless") and "have the
power" (or "are powerful").

HIP.: Yes.

SOC.: Are they versatile and deceiving by foolishness and imprudence or by unscrupulous wickedness and a certain prudence?

HIP.: By unscrupulous wickedness, most certainly, and by prudence.

SOC.: Apparently, therefore, they are prudent.

HIP.: Yes, by Zeus—too much so!

SOC.: And since they are prudent, do they not know what they are doing, or do they know?

HIP.: They know very well; that is why they do evil.

SOC.: And since they know what they know, are they ignorant or wise?

HIP.: They are surely wise, at least with respect to this very thing: deceiving thoroughly.

366a SOC.: Stop there. Let us recollect what it is you are saying. You assert that liars are capable, prudent, knowing, and wise in those things in which they are liars.

HIP.: I do assert it.

SOC.: And that the truthful and the liars are different and most opposite to one another?

HIP.: I say these things too.

SOC.: Come, then: some of the capable and wise, apparently, are the liars according to your argument.

HIP.: Certainly.

b SOC.: Now, when you say the liars are capable and wise in these very things, are you saying they are capable of lying if they should wish to or that they are incapable with respect to these things about which they lie?

HIP.: I say they are capable.

SOC.: To sum up, then, the liars are the wise and capable of lying.

HIP.: Yes.

SOC.: Therefore, a man incapable of lying and ignorant would not be a liar.

HIP.: That's so.

c SOC.: But each one is capable who does what he wishes when he wishes. I am not speaking of one who is prevented by sickness or such things; I simply mean someone who is in the situation you are in with regard to the power of writing my name whenever you wish— that is what I mean. Or do you not call one who is in such a condition "capable?"

HIP.: Yes.

soc.: Now tell me, Hippias, are you not experienced in calculations and in the art of calculating?

hip.: Most certainly, Socrates.

soc.: If, then, someone were to ask you how great a number is three times seven hundred, could you not say the truth about this most swiftly of all and most precisely, if you wished?

d hip.: Surely.

soc.: And is that because you are most capable and wisest in these matters?

hip.: Yes.

soc.: Are you then only wisest and most capable, or are you also best in those matters in which you are most capable and wisest, that is, in matters of calculation?

hip.: I am of course also best, Socrates.

e soc.: You would then most capably speak what is true about these things? Or not?

hip.: I at least suppose I would.

soc.: But what of lies about these same matters? And as before, answer me in a well-born and magnificent way, Hippias. If someone asked you how much is three times seven hundred, could you lie most precisely, and could you always speak lies in the same respects about these things if you wished to lie and never answer the truth, or

367a would one ignorant in calculations be more capable of lying than you if he wished? Or would the ignorant one involuntarily speak the truth many times if he should chance upon it through not knowing, though he might wish to speak lies, whereas you, the wise man, would always lie in the same respects, at least if you were to wish to lie?

hip.: Yes, that's the way it is, just as you say.

soc.: Is the liar then a liar only about other things but not about number, and would he not lie in counting?

hip.: Oh, yes, he would, by Zeus, he would lie about number as well!

soc.: Should we then regard this too as established, Hippias, that a certain sort of human being is a liar about calculation and number?

b hip.: Yes.

soc.: And who would this be? Must it not belong to him to be capable of lying, if he is going to be a liar, as you just now agreed? For if you remember, it was said by you that he who is incapable of lying would never become a liar.

hip.: I do remember; that was said.

soc.: Then did you not just now appear as one most capable of lying about calculations?

hip.: Yes; this too was said, at least.

c soc.: Are you, therefore, also most capable of speaking truth about calculations?

hip.: Surely.

soc.: Then isn't the same man most capable of speaking lies and truths about calculations? And this is the one who is good at these things, the expert calculator.

hip.: Yes.

soc.: Who then, Hippias, becomes a liar about calculation other than one who is good? For the same man is also capable, and this man is truthful as well.

hip.: It appears so.

soc.: Do you see, then, that the same one is a liar and truthful about
d these things, and the truthful is no better than the liar? For indeed he is the same man, and he does not possess characteristics which are most opposite, as you supposed just now.

hip.: He does not appear to, at least here.

soc.: Do you wish us, then, to consider it elsewhere as well?

hip.: If you like.

soc.: Then are you not also experienced in geometry?

hip.: I am.

soc.: Well, then, is it not this way in geometry as well? Is the same one most capable of lying and speaking the truth about geometrical figures—that is, the expert in geometry?

hip.: Yes.

e soc.: Is anyone else good in these things other than this one?

hip.: No other.

soc.: Accordingly, is not the good and wise geometer most capable, at least, with respect to both? And if anyone else could be a liar about geometrical figures, it would be he, the one who is good? For this one was capable of lying, while the bad one was incapable of it, so that he would not become a liar who is unable to lie, as has been agreed.

hip.: These things are so.

soc.: Yet further, let us also investigate the third man, the astrono-
368a mer, in whose art you think you are still more knowledgeable than in those taken up before. Do you not, Hippias?

hip.: Yes.

soc.: Are not these things also the same in astronomy?

HIP.: It is likely, at least, Socrates.

SOC.: In astronomy too, therefore, if anyone is a liar, the good astronomer—that is, the one who is capable of lying—will be a liar. For it will not be the one who is incapable, for he is ignorant.

HIP.: It appears so.

SOC.: In astronomy as well, therefore, the same one will be truthful and a liar.

HIP.: Apparently.

b SOC.: Come then, Hippias, consider freely in this way in the case of all the sciences whether matters are anywhere in a condition other than this: you are altogether the wisest of all human beings in the greatest number of arts, as I once heard you boasting, when you yourself narrated your extensive and enviable wisdom in the marketplace beside the banking tables. You asserted that you had once come to Olympia, having all you had about your body as your own works: first, that the ring you were wearing (for you began with that) was

c your work, since you knew how to cut rings, and that another signet too was your work, and a scraper and an unguent bottle, all of which you yourself made; then you said that you had cut from leather the footwear you were wearing and that you had woven your outer clothing and your tunic, and then, what seemed most unusual[7] to all and a display of the greatest wisdom, was when you said the belt of your tunic, which you were wearing, was like the very expensive Persian ones and that you had plaited this yourself. In addition to these things, you said that you came having poems—epic verses,

d tragedies, dithyrambs—and many speeches of all sorts in prose. And you said that you came with knowledge, distinguished from that of others, concerning the arts of which I have just spoken, and about rhythms, harmoniae, correctness of letters, and very many other things in addition to these, as I remember. And further, I forgot your artful device (as it seems) for remembering, in which you suppose

e you are most splendid, and I suppose I have forgotten very many other things. But as I say, look both at your own arts (for they are sufficient) and at those of others, and tell me if anywhere you can find, from among those things to which you and I have agreed, where one is truthful and another—a separate one, not the same—is a liar. Consider this in the case of whatever wisdom you wish, or

---

[7] *Atopōtaton* can mean "most absurd."

369a whatever unscrupulous wickedness, or whatever you are pleased to name it. But you will not find it, comrade—for it does not exist. But speak up!

HIP.: Nothing occurs to me Socrates, at least not offhand.

SOC.: Nor will it, as I suppose; but if I am speaking the truth, remember what results from our argument, Hippias.

HIP.: I don't understand very well what you're saying, Socrates.

SOC.: That is perhaps because you are not now using your artful device for remembering—for it is clear that you do not suppose you need it. But I will remind you. Do you know that you asserted

b Achilles was truthful, while Odysseus was a liar and versatile?

HIP.: Yes.

SOC.: Now then, do you perceive that the same man has come to light as being both truthful and a liar, so that if Odysseus was a liar, he becomes also truthful, and if Achilles was truthful, he becomes also a liar, and these men are not different from one another or opposite but similar?

HIP.: Socrates, you are always weaving arguments of this sort. You pick out whatever is most difficult in an argument and hold onto this,

c making fast your grip on small details and not contending with the whole matter which the argument concerns. For even now, if you wish, I will display to you in an ample speech with many proofs that Homer represented Achilles as better than Odysseus and not a liar, while he represented the latter as treacherous, frequently lying, and worse than Achilles. If you wish, you may counter argument with argument, to the effect that the other is better, and these people here will know more fully who speaks better.

d SOC.: Hippias, I certainly do not dispute that you are wiser than I, but I am always accustomed to pay attention whenever someone says something and especially when the speaker seems to me to be wise. And since I desire to learn what he is saying, I question him thoroughly and consider again and compare the things said, so that I may understand. If the one speaking seems to me to be of little account, neither do I ply him with questions, nor is what he says of concern to me. And you will know from this which ones I hold to be wise. For

e you will find me being indefatigable about the things said by one of that sort, questioning him so that by understanding I may be benefited in some way. For even now I have been reflecting as you were speaking, that in the verses you just now spoke, where you show

Achilles speaking to Odysseus as to one who is an imposter,[8] it seems
370a to me to be strange, if you speak the truth, that Odysseus, the versatile, is nowhere shown to be a liar, while Achilles is shown to be
someone versatile, according to your argument; at any rate, he lies.
For though he begins by speaking verses which you also just now
spoke—

> For that one is hateful to me as the gates of Hades,
> Who hides one thing in his mind but says something else,

b a little later he says he would not be persuaded by Odysseus and
Agamemnon, nor would he remain at all in Troy, but as he says:

> Tomorrow, when I have performed the sacrifices to Zeus and
>   all the gods,
> Having loaded well the ships after I have drawn them down to
>   the sea,
> You will see if you want to, and if indeed these things concern
>   you,
> My ships sailing very early on the fishy Hellespont,
c > And in them the men eager to row:
> And if the glorious Earth-shaker[9] should give a fair voyage
> I would arrive at rich-soiled Phthia on the third day.[10]

Moreover, before these things, when railing against Agamemnon, he
said:

> Now I am going to Phthia, since surely it is much better
> To go home with the curved ships, nor do I think
d > I will draw full draughts of wealth and riches for you, since
>   I am dishonored here.[11]

Though he says these things once before the entire army and once
before his own comrades, nowhere is he seen to have prepared or
tried to drag down the ships to sail back home; rather, he shows quite
a well-born contempt of speaking the truth. Now I, Hippias, have
been questioning you from the beginning because I am at a loss as to

---

[8]*Alazona* ("imposter," "false pretender," "boaster").
[9]Homeric epithet of Poseidon, god of the sea and earthquakes.
[10]*Iliad* IX 357–63.
[11]*Iliad* I 169–71. Socrates changes the word "better" from *pherteron,* meaning "better" or "braver," to *lōion,* which means only "better."

e   which of these two men was represented as better by the poet, holding that both are excellent and that it is hard to distinguish which one
might be better with regard both to lying and truth and to the rest of
virtue; for in this respect too both are quite similar.

HIP.: That is because you do not examine it in a noble manner,
Socrates. For where Achilles lies, it is evident that he is lying not out
of design but involuntarily, since he was compelled on account of the
misfortune of the army to stay behind and bring aid, but the lies of
Odysseus are voluntary and from design.

SOC.: You are deceiving me, dearest Hippias, and are yourself imitating Odysseus!

371a HIP.: By no means, Socrates! But what is it you are saying and with a
view to what?

SOC.: Because you assert that Achilles did not lie from design; yet he
was such a cheat and a designing plotter in addition to his imposture,
as Homer has represented him, that he appears to be so much more
prudent even than Odysseus with regard to easily escaping detection
as an imposter that right in the presence of the latter he dared to
contradict himself and escaped detection by Odysseus. At any rate, it
b   is evident that Odysseus says nothing to him that shows he perceived
he was lying.

HIP.: What are these things you speak of, Socrates?

SOC.: Do you know that after he has affirmed to Odysseus that he
would sail away at dawn, he does not again assert that he will sail
away when he speaks to Ajax but says something else?

HIP.: Now where is this?

SOC.: In the verses where he says—

> Indeed I will not take thought of bloody war
c > Until divine Hector, the son of prudent Priam,
> Comes to the huts and the ships of the Myrmidons
> Killing the Argives, to burn up the ships with blazing fire;
> But at my tent and my dark ship
> I think Hector himself will be stopped though eager for battle.[12]

d   Well then, Hippias, do you think the son of Thetis, who was educated by the most wise Cheiron, could have been so forgetful as to

[12]*Iliad* IX 650–55. Several words quoted by Socrates are different from the text of
Homer that has come down to us. In verse 653 he uses the word "burn in blazing fire"
where Homer has "burn in smouldering fire," and in verse 654 he replaces "indeed"
with a word emphasizing Hector "himself."

affirm to Odysseus that he would sail away but to Ajax that he would remain, when just a little before he had railed against imposters with the most extreme abuse; do you think he was not a designing plotter who believed Odysseus was someone of primitive simplicity whom he could get the better of precisely by such artful contriving and lying?

HIP.: It does not seem so to me, at least, Socrates; rather, with regard
e to these things too it was his guilelessness[13] that led him to say different things to Ajax than to Odysseus. When, however, Odysseus speaks the truth he always speaks by design, and whenever he lies it is the same.

SOC.: Then it looks as if Odysseus is, after all, better than Achilles.

HIP.: Not at all, surely, Socrates.

SOC.: What? Did not those who lie voluntarily just now come to light as better than those doing so involuntarily?

372a HIP.: And how, Socrates, can those who are voluntarily unjust, who have voluntarily plotted and done evil, be better than those who do so involuntarily, when for the latter there seems to be much forgiveness—when someone unknowingly acts unjustly or lies or does some other evil? And the laws, surely, are much more harsh toward those who do evil voluntarily and lie than toward those who do so involuntarily.

b SOC.: Do you see, Hippias, that I speak the truth, when I say that I am indefatigable in questioning the wise? And I run the risk of having only this one good thing, all else that I have being of little account. For as to the actual condition of things I am baffled, and I do not know how they stand. I find it a sufficient proof of this that when I am together with one of you who are highly reputed for wisdom and to whose wisdom all Greeks bear witness, it is evident that I know nothing; for nothing, so to speak, seems the same to me as it does to
c you, yet what greater proof of ignorance is there than when someone differs with wise men? But I have this one marvelous good which preserves me: I am not ashamed to learn, but I inquire and I question and I am very grateful to the one who answers, and I have never

---

[13]I follow the reading of the better manuscripts, T and W, *euētheias* ("guilelessness," "integrity," "simplicity") rather than Burnet's choice of *eunoias* ("kindness"), which is found in a solitary and less authoritative manuscript, F. The better attested reading makes more sense in the argument. It is not Achilles' kindness and complaisance to the other chiefs that explains his contradictions. Rather, he is uncertain of himself; he doubts his course of action and "guilelessly" speaks out directly whatever he thinks even though he is in the process of changing his mind.

deprived anyone of gratitude. For I have never denied it when I learned something, pretending that what I had learned was my own discovery; instead, I praise the one who taught me as a wise man and
d   proclaim what I learned from him. And indeed, with regard to what you are now saying, I do not agree with you, but I differ very strongly, and I know well that this happens because of me—because I am the sort that I am, not to say anything greater of myself. For to me it appears, Hippias, that all is the opposite of what you say it is— that those who harm human beings, who do injustice, lie, deceive, and go wrong voluntarily rather than involuntarily are better than those who do so involuntarily. Sometimes, however, the opposite of these things seems to me to be the case, and I vacillate about these
e   things—clearly because I do not know. But at the present a sort of seizure has overtaken me, and those who voluntarily go wrong about something seem to me to be better than those who do so involuntarily. I blame the previous arguments as causes of my present experience—of making it appear at present that those who do each of these things involuntarily are more good-for-nothing[14] than those who do so voluntarily. Do me a favor, then, and do not begrudge to heal my
373a soul; for be assured you will do me a greater good by giving my soul rest from ignorance than my body from disease. But if you wish to speak a long speech, I warn you in advance that you would not cure me—for I could not follow; but if you wish to answer me just as before, you will benefit me very much, and I do not suppose you yourself will be harmed. And I might justly call for your help, son of Apemantus, for you stirred me up to converse with Hippias: now, if Hippias does not want to answer me, ask him on my behalf.
b   EUD.: I do not suppose, Socrates, that Hippias will need our request. For his initial statements were not of this sort, but he said he would flee the questioning of no man. Is it not so, Hippias? Was not this what you said?

HIP.: I did. But Eudicus, Socrates always causes confusion in the argument and seems to want to make trouble.

SOC.: Hippias, best of men, it is not voluntarily, at any rate, that I do

---

[14]*Ponēros* ("useless," "worthless," "good for nothing"; also "morally depraved" or "wicked"). I have chosen to translate the word "good for nothing" to preserve something of the ambiguity of the argument. Socrates seems to use the word in a primarily "technical" sense as meaning "worthless," whereas Hippias seems to understand the argument as primarily moral: the one who voluntarily does evil is "wicked" or "depraved." Both senses are present in "good for nothing."

this—for I would be wise and tricky, according to your argument—but involuntarily, so please forgive me, for you assert that whoever makes trouble involuntarily ought to have forgiveness.

c EUD.: By no means do otherwise, Hippias, but for our sake and for the sake of your initial statements, answer what Socrates asks you.

HIP.: I will answer, then, as long as you request it. Ask whatever you wish.

SOC.: I certainly desire very much, Hippias, to investigate fully what has just now been spoken of—whether those are better who go wrong voluntarily or those who do so involuntarily. I think we would most correctly approach our investigation as follows. Now answer: do you call a certain one a good runner?

d HIP.: I do.

SOC.: And a certain one bad?

HIP.: Yes.

SOC.: And is not one who runs well good, while one who runs badly is bad?

HIP.: Yes.

SOC.: And does not he who runs slowly run badly, while he who runs quickly runs well?

HIP.: Yes.

SOC.: In a race, therefore, and in running, is quickness good and slowness bad?

HIP.: What else should it be?

SOC.: Which, then, is the better runner, he who voluntarily runs slowly or he who does so involuntarily?

HIP.: He who does so voluntarily.

SOC.: And isn't running doing something?

HIP.: Doing something, certainly.

SOC.: And if it is doing something, is it not also effecting something?

e HIP.: Yes.

SOC.: Does he who runs badly effect what is bad and shameful in a race?

HIP.: What is bad; how could he not?

SOC.: He who runs slowly runs badly?

HIP.: Yes.

SOC.: Does not the good runner voluntarily effect this bad and shameful thing, while the bad one does so involuntarily?

HIP.: It seems so, at any rate.

soc.: In a race, then, is the one who effects what is bad involuntarily
374a more good-for-nothing than he who does so voluntarily?

hip.: In a race, at any rate.

soc.: What about in wrestling? Which is the better wrestler, he who
voluntarily falls, or he who does so involuntarily?

hip.: He who does so voluntarily, as it seems.

soc.: Is it more good-for-nothing and more shameful in wrestling to
fall or to throw one's opponent?

hip.: To fall.

soc.: In wrestling, too, therefore, the one who voluntarily effects
what is good-for-nothing and shameful is a better wrestler than the
one who does so involuntarily.

hip.: Apparently.

soc.: What about every other use of the body? Is not he who is better
with respect to his body able to effect both—what is strong as well as
b what is weak and what is shameful as well as what is noble—so that,
whenever he who is better in body effects what is good-for-nothing
with respect to the body, he effects it voluntarily, while he who is
more good-for-nothing does so involuntarily.

hip.: It appears so also in matters of strength.

soc.: What about gracefulness, Hippias? Is it not characteristic of the
better body to assume voluntarily the shameful and good-for-nothing postures, while it is characteristic of the more good-for-nothing
body to do so involuntarily? Or how does it seem to you?

hip.: Just so.

c soc.: As for gracelessness, therefore, if voluntary, it is associated with
the virtue, if involuntary, with the good-for-nothingness of the
body.

hip.: It appears so.

soc.: What do you say about the voice? Which do you assert is better,
the one that voluntarily sings out of tune or the one that does so
involuntarily?

hip.: The one that does so voluntarily.

soc.: The one singing out of tune involuntarily is the more wicked?

hip.: Yes.

soc.: Would you prefer to possess what is good or what is bad?

hip.: What is good.

soc.: Then would you prefer to possess feet that limp voluntarily or
involuntarily?

d HIP.: Voluntarily.

SOC.: Is not a limp good-for-nothingness and gracelessness of the feet?

HIP.: Yes.

SOC.: What of this? Is not dullness of sight good-for-nothingness of the eyes?

HIP.: Yes.

SOC.: Which eyes would you prefer to possess and which to be in the presence of? Those with which one voluntarily sees dully and sees incorrectly or those with which one does so involuntarily?

HIP.: Those with which one voluntarily does so.

SOC.: Then do you believe that those of your own things that voluntarily effect what is good-for-nothing are better than those that do so involuntarily?

HIP.: Yes, with respect to these kinds of things at least.

SOC.: Then one argument comprehends all things such as ears, nose,
e mouth, and all the senses: those that involuntarily effect what is bad are not to be possessed, since they are good-for-nothing, while those that voluntarily do so are to be possessed, since they are good.

HIP.: It seems so to me, at least.

SOC.: What of this? A partnership with which sort of tools is better, those with which one voluntarily effects what is bad or those with which one does so involuntarily? For example, is a rudder with which one will involuntarily steer badly better or one with which one will do so voluntarily?

HIP.: One with which one will do so voluntarily.

SOC.: Is it not the same with a bow, a lyre, auloi, and all other things?
375a HIP.: What you say is true.

SOC.: What of this? Is it better to possess the soul of a horse with which one will voluntarily ride badly or involuntarily?

HIP.: That with which one will do so voluntarily.

SOC.: Then it is better.

HIP.: Yes.

SOC.: With the better horse's soul, therefore, one would do voluntarily the good-for-nothing works of this soul but with the soul of the good-for-nothing mare involuntarily.

HIP.: Very much so.

SOC.: And so also in the case of a dog and all other animals?

HIP.: Yes.

SOC.: What of this, then? For a human being who is an archer, is it

better to possess a soul which voluntarily goes wrong and misses the
b target or one which does so involuntarily?

HIP.: One which does so voluntarily.

SOC.: And this very one is better for archery?

HIP.: Yes.

SOC.: A soul which involuntarily goes wrong is, therefore, more
good-for-nothing than one which does so voluntarily?

HIP.: In archery, at least.

SOC.: What about medicine? Is not he who willingly effects what is
bad with regard to bodies more skilled in medicine?

HIP.: Yes.

SOC.: This [soul] is accordingly better in this art than one not skilled
in medicine?

HIP.: It is better.

SOC.: What of this? In the case of [the soul] that is more skilled at
playing the cithara and the aulos and everything else connected with
c the arts and sciences, is not the one better which voluntarily effects
evil and shameful things and goes wrong, while the more good-for-
nothing one does so involuntarily?

HIP.: Apparently.

SOC.: But presumably we would prefer to own the souls of slaves that
voluntarily go wrong and effect evil, rather than those which do so
involuntarily, on the ground that they are better in these matters.

HIP.: Yes.

SOC.: What of this? Would we not wish to possess our own [soul] in
as good a condition as possible for these matters?

d HIP.: Yes.

SOC.: Will it be better if it effects evil voluntarily and goes wrong or if
it does so involuntarily?

HIP.: It would, however, be a terrible thing, Socrates, if those doing
injustice voluntarily are to be better than those doing so involuntarily.

SOC.: But surely they appear to be, at least from what has been said.

HIP.: Not to me.

SOC.: But I supposed, Hippias, that they appeared so to you too.
Answer once again: is not justice either (1) a certain capacity or
knowledge or (2) both? Or isn't it necessary that justice should be at
least one of these?

e HIP.: Yes.

SOC.: Then if justice is a capacity of the soul, is not the more capable soul more just? For one of this sort seemed in some way better to us, best of men.

HIP.: It appeared so.

SOC.: But what if it is knowledge? Is not the wiser soul more just and the more ignorant more unjust?[15] But what if it is both? Is not the one having both, knowledge and capacity, more just, while the more ignorant is more unjust? Is it not necessary that it should be so?

HIP.: It appears so.

376a SOC.: Now the more capable and wiser [soul] came to sight as better and as more capable of doing both what is noble and what is shameful with regard to all that it effects?

HIP.: Yes.

SOC.: Therefore, whenever it effects shameful things, it effects them voluntarily through capacity and art, but these things are evidently characteristics of justice, either both or one of them.

HIP.: Apparently.

SOC.: And to do injustice at least is to do what is bad, while not to do injustice is to do what is noble.

HIP.: Yes.

SOC.: And will the more capable and better soul not do injustice voluntarily—at least whenever it does injustice—while the more worthless will do so involuntarily?

HIP.: It appears so.

b SOC.: And is not the good man the one who has the good soul, while the bad is the one who has the bad soul?

HIP.: Yes.

SOC.: Well then, it is characteristic of a good man to do injustice voluntarily, while it is characteristic of a bad man to do so involuntarily, if, that is, the good man has a good soul.

HIP.: But surely he does have one.

SOC.: Well then, he who voluntarily goes wrong and does what is shameful and unjust, Hippias, if indeed there is any such person, would be no other than the good man.

HIP.: I cannot agree with you in this, Socrates.

SOC.: Nor I with myself, Hippias. But this appears now, at any rate,

c as the necessary result of the argument. As I said before, however, I

[15]There is no manuscript authority showing that Hippias answered this question. Perhaps this is not surprising, since his lack of understanding of it is at the crux of his disagreement with Socrates throughout the dialogue. Burnet, following recent editors, attributes to Hippias a "Yes" here.

vacillate[16] back and forth about these things, and they never seem the same to me. And it is nothing marvelous that I should vacillate, or any other ordinary man. But if you who are wise will also vacillate, this is a terrible thing for us as well, if we shall not cease from our vacillation even after we have come to you.

[16]*Planein* ("to lead astray") means, in the passive, "to wander." Hence it comes to mean "to wander in mind," "to be at a loss," "to vacillate." Cf. the *Greater Hippias* 304c and note 44 to the translation of that dialogue.

Introduction to the
Lesser Hippias

James Leake

The major interlocutor of Socrates in this dialogue is Hippias, one of the most renowned sophists at the end of the fifth century. His fellow citizens at Elis, the small city in the northwestern Peloponnese, chose him on numerous occasions to represent their interests on diplomatic missions, especially to Sparta. Thanks to an exceptional memory and an astonding faculty of assimilation, he had become acquainted with all the arts and sciences of his time. Indeed, he seems to identify wisdom with *polymathia,* or "much learning." His vanity is an important subterranean theme in this dialogue, where Socrates delicately unmasks it. He seems to share conventional moral scruples and appears to be morally outraged by Socrates' arguments in this dialogue. Other conversations between him and Socrates are to be found in the *Greater Hippias* in this volume and in Xenophon's *Memorabilia* (IV iv 5–25).

Eudicus is the first speaker. Nothing is known of him other than what can be inferred from this dialogue and the one passage in the *Greater Hippias* where he is mentioned. In that passage, Hippias tells Socrates that he intends to pronounce an epideictic speech on the subject of noble pursuits, which he will illustrate with reference to the heroes of the Trojan war. Hippias claims that Eudicus, the son of Apemantus, requested it (*Greater Hippias* 286b7). Hippias then invites Socrates to the speech, which is to take place three days after their encounter in the *Greater Hippias*. This speech sounds like the speech that immediately precedes the conversation represented in the *Lesser Hippias*.

Eudicus claims to share in the philosophic way of life, as we learn from his first speech, and he is particularly interested in the opinion of Socrates. It also appears that he is well disposed toward Hippias, perhaps even an admirer. He had been the one to request that Hippias make his display. He seems to be on the lookout to protect Hippias' reputation.

Eudicus initiates the conversation of the *Lesser Hippias* by asking Socrates why he does not question Hippias after he "has made so great an exhibition." The topic of the speech was Nestor's response to a question of the son of Achilles, who asked Nestor "what sort of noble pursuits a young man should practice so that he might become most highly reputed." According to Hippias, Nestor laid down for him "all sorts of lawful practices and very noble ones."

Like Books III and X of the *Republic,* and the *Ion,* this dialogue presents a Socratic conversation that focuses on the poems of Homer. Prodded by Eudicus, Socrates asks Hippias which of Homer's heroes, Achilles or Odysseus, is the better man. Hippias, like most Greeks (cf. 363b1–5), sees no problem here. Achilles is clearly the best of those who went to Troy. He is the truly virtuous hero. Odysseus is, according to Hippias, merely "versatile." Pressed by Socrates to explain himself, Hippias replies that the predominant characteristic of Odysseus in the Homeric poems is his deceitfulness. This quality is enough to disqualify him from being the best man, or even a virtuous man, in the eyes of the moral Hippias. Socrates induces Hippias to join him in an investigation of whether the ability to lie plausibly is not an art in which even the most truthful man need share. After some comic raillery at the expense of the pretentious and vain Hippias, the first section of the dialogue concludes with Hippias reluctantly agreeing to Socrates' demonstration that the truthful man and the liar are one and the same. Applications to Homer follow. The teaching seems to apply to Odysseus better than to Achilles. In the second major section, Socrates proves, to Hippias' dismay, that to do injustice voluntarily, if ever, is the mark of a good man with a good soul, while to do so involuntarily is the mark of a bad man with a bad soul. Socrates confesses that this conclusion is disquieting to him and that he—an ordinary man—had hoped to get help from Hippias, who claimed to be wise. The dialogue seems to end without a teaching, but let us investigate it more closely and see what one can learn.

To begin with, one must never forget that Socrates has asked Hippias to compare and judge between Achilles and Odysseus. All the arguments have some ultimate relevance to the *Iliad* and the

Odyssey. The dialogue abounds in observations in light of which one can make fascinating discoveries in reading both epics.

Hippias believes that Achilles is "the best man of those who came to Troy" (364c5–6). He explains that Achilles is "truthful and simple" (365b4). The simplicity of the noble Achilles becomes apparent in the quotation Hippias chooses to illustrate his character. There Achilles denounces liars in the strongest terms. He also says three times that what he says will be completed or fulfilled. Achilles' hatred of lying accompanies his perception of his great strength as unopposed by forces beyond his control. One might well say, as Hippias does, that this is simplicity. If we turn to the *Iliad* we find that the terrific wrath of Achilles arises from a sense of disappointment that his virtue does not bring him honor; that disappointment takes on ultimately theological or cosmic proportions. Achilles is acknowledged by the Greeks at Troy to be the best man because he is strong and good and because he takes virtue so seriously and is willing to strive his utmost to perform it. But Achilles' willingness to strive his utmost is based on the assumption that he does what is right: that men acknowledge, and ultimately Zeus supports, virtue. He believes, at the outset of the poem, that the mark of this divine support of virtue is the honor in which he—the best man—is held. Thus he becomes extremely angry when Agamemnon dishonors him by depriving him of his girl. Whether this view is tenable is Homer's great question throughout the *Iliad*.

The passage Hippias has chosen in order to illustrate Achilles' character comes at the beginning of the great speech in which he rejects Agamemnon's embassy of reconciliation (*Iliad* IX 307–429). In that speech Achilles expresses the gravest doubts as to the correctness or the goodness of the virtue to which he had been hitherto devoted. But even there, as we see in the passage that Hippias quotes, Achilles remains simple or straightforward because he perceives himself as fundamentally strong: "But I will speak as I think it is going to be fulfilled." To be a liar one must recognize that there are limits to one's power to effect what one regards as good. To regard lying as morally defensible or necessary to bring about the good, one must recognize that the good is of limited efficacy—not simply triumphant in human affairs or the cosmos. Homer represents "the versatile" Odysseus as somehow aware of this, and Socrates devotes himself in the remainder of the dialogue to breaking down Hippias' moral scru-

ples to this "Odyssean" view (365c7, 369c2–5, 375d3–4)—a view
that Socrates apparently shares (371d8–e6).

Odysseus, like the philosophers in the *Republic,* finds it necessary
to lie on occasion. Hippias singles out lying as the most distinguishing characteristic of Odysseus in both the *Iliad* and the *Odyssey*
(365c1–2). The dialogue thus presupposes that we should be thoroughly familiar with both epics. Socrates suggests that this capacity
to lie and the overall view on which it is based might even make
Odysseus a better, that is, deeper, man than Achilles. Briefly then,
under what circumstances does Homer represent Odysseus as lying?

Most famous of all his deceits is the strategem of the Trojan horse
(*Odyssey* VIII 492–520), which enabled the Greeks to take Troy after
they had unsuccessfully besieged it for ten years. Previously, when
the absence of Achilles and the pursuit of Hector and the Trojans had
reduced the Greeks to the utmost straits, he went on a spying expedition by night with Diomedes to learn the Trojan plans. They inter-
cepted, interrogated, and killed Dolon, then slew Rheseus and his
men by stealth and stole their beautiful horses (*Iliad* X). These are all
deceits practiced on enemies. While one can say they are generally for
the common good, it is not the kind of face-to-face fighting in which
Achilles exulted. In the *Odyssey* Odysseus discovers frequent occasions in which it is possible for him to succeed only by lying. He
cunningly tells the Cyclops, who holds him prisoner, that his ship has
been wrecked to prevent the Cyclops from going to it and destroying
both it and his other companions (*Odyssey* IX 283–86). If Odysseus
had not lied, he and all his men would have helplessly died a horrible
death at the hands of the mighty, implacable Cyclops. Odysseus
escapes the Cyclops by the strategem of blinding him and cunningly
calling himself "No-man," so the other Cyclopes do not pursue him.
He deceives his crew when what is needed for the survival of the ship
is fraught with danger to individuals (*Odyssey* XII 223–25, 245–59).
Here as a leader he chooses the only policy that can possibly save the
whole ship, though some must die through it. He does not ask the
men to sacrifice for the common good, for he judges that they would
not and that the vessel would be lost. He hides the truth from them.
Above all, we see him as a consummate liar in the latter part of the
Odyssey where, having lost all his companions, he is particularly
exposed. While arranging, incognito, to repossess himself of his
household, long since in the hands of the hostile suitors of his wife, he

lies to his patron goddess, Athena, to the swineherd Eumaeus, to his wife, Penelope, and to Euryclea, his old nurse (*Odyssey* XIII 253–338; XIV 191ff.; XIX 165ff., and 381–85). Odysseus lends plausibility to his lies by masterfully interweaving them with true observations drawn from his rich store of thoughtful observations of the multiplicity and unity at the heart of things. To be a liar as Odysseus was, one must be experienced, prudent, and of an enduring toughness. One must be aware of one's own limits and of the limits of others. One must know how to appeal to others and understand just the right approach for getting them to do what is necessary. To be a consummate liar means to know what is necessary and to know the souls of those who must contribute to accomplish it. To be a consummate liar is the aspect of being wise that consists in using and helping others. Lying is a necessary part of the art of politics or ruling insofar as it enables one to deal with those who are incapable of listening to reason—whether they are enemies or friends made incompetent through passion or lack of the natural endowment necessary to see what is good. Lying is a part of the wisdom that is so reasonable that it is not and cannot be all-powerful. A favorable view of lying is the necessary concomitant of a recognition of the limits of reason. We see it in Homer, and we will see it in Plato. One should not forget that, though Odysseus comes home through his wisdom, Homer does not represent him as happy—he loses his ship and comrades, and his whole life in the *Odyssey* is a succession of sorrows.

Lying, the art of great Odysseus, and its underlying assumptions are the theme of the *Lesser Hippias*. In the first dialectical section of the dialogue, Socrates undertakes to prove that the liar and the truthful man are one and the same. Hippias objects that this would be "terrible"—it seems to him to undermine the fundamental moral distinctions. The liars of whom Socrates speaks are a very high type—men of the caliber of Odysseus. He identifies them as capable, prudent, knowing, and wise in those respects in which they lie (366a3–4). They are accordingly able to do as they wish with human beings—using lies or truth as is appropriate, according to the circumstances. They lie or tell the truth as they wish and when they wish: Socrates is concerned with conscious action taken in full awareness of the consequences, not with the fibs of the inept, which seek to avoid unpleasant consequences one has brought upon oneself (366b7–c4). Accordingly, in the second half of this section, Socrates argues that speaking the truth or lying are both aspects of an art, and he who does one best will do the other best. He argues similarly in the *Republic* that if the justest man is best at guarding deposits, he will also be the best thief, and the best doctor will also be the best poisoner (*Republic* 333e1–34b5). In the *Lesser Hippias,* he compares the unnamed art to three particularly accurate arts that are contemplative, although they can be applied to practical matters for good or bad. These arts are calculating, geometry, and astronomy. He who is best at each art is also best at deceiving in it. The unnamed art of which lying is one aspect may be philosophy. We suggest that this passage may be elucidated by the section of the *Republic* in which Socrates speaks of the lies the philosophers might need to rule. There he argues that human beings hate the lie about "the most sovereign things" most of all, yet lies are necessary for ruling. Lies are useful and necessary in the hands of the wise under the following circumstances: against enemies, as a preventive like a drug for friends when from madness or stupidity they are bent on harming themselves or others, and in the telling of tales or myths because one doesn't know the truth about the first principles of things—in all these circumstances the wise man needs lies to deal with those who cannot endure the truth (*Republic* 382a1–e6, 331c). The unstated assumption on which Socrates bases his argument for the utility and necessity of lies is the hardness of the truth and the irrefrangible proneness of most men to live under the protective limitations of illusion or belief. The very best city, ruled by philosophers, nevertheless needs a "noble lie" to deceive and improve the majority of its citizens (*Republic* 413a–415d, 459c, and 377a). The fundamental problem to which Socrates points is that most men love themselves better than they love justice. Therefore certain lies are necessary to strengthen the claim of justice upon them. He does not think that such men can be changed.

The conclusion of this first section of the *Lesser Hippias* is, then, that the consummate liar is also the most capable of speaking the truth. This conclusion is succeeded by a comic interlude in which Socrates claims, reasonably enough, that if Odysseus is a liar he must be truthful, and, less reasonably, that if Achilles is truthful he must be a liar. The second assertion forms the basis of an elaborate jeu d'esprit that shows more that Achilles vacillates rather than resign himself to his doubts about virtue, though Socrates claims it shows that he lies. Though he comes to doubt that the life of virtue and glory is right, Achilles cannot quite bring himself to draw the final consequences of his doubt—to abandon Troy and the opportunity for glory and go home—though he threatens to do so from time to time. This wavering forms the grounds for Socrates' assertion that Achilles lies. Hippias defends his view that Achilles is best, and that the best man would never lie, by distinguishing between voluntary and involuntary lies. When Achilles lies it is inadvertent, whereas "when Odysseus says the things that are true, he always speaks by design, and whenever he lies, it is the same" (371e2–3). Socrates replies that it seems, then, that Odysseus is better than Achilles. Those who lie voluntarily are better than those who lie involuntarily. In the subsequent section of the dialogue, Socrates propounds this view.

Why does Socrates argue that to commit a wicked or unjust act voluntarily is better than to do so involuntarily? We suggest that one might begin to understand him in light of the preceding argument. To possess knowledge or some capability enables one to act for good or evil. Socrates taught that all men love the good and no one does evil voluntarily (*Meno* 77b6–78b2; cf. *Republic* 517b6–c6). To possess the capability to do good, perhaps one must *necessarily* possess the capability to do evil (375e9–76a1). Could it be that Socrates is especially concerned to establish this point in the dialogue? Socrates concludes by remarking that he hesitates to accept the conclusions of his reasoning. He seems to concede that Hippias may have had some grounds for his reluctance all along. Elsewhere he amplifies the argument of this dialogue in two ways. He argues that no one does evil voluntarily—so that, the more the capability to do evil is not exercised, the better the soul (*Meno* 77b6–78b2 and context). He also remarks on the crucial importance of education and the quality of the regime, above all for the best-endowed souls, for without adequate education they are capable of greater evil than the more ordinary ones (*Republic* 491b6ff.). These aspects of the Socratic understanding are not developed in the *Lesser Hippias*. It emphatically develops the point that art, knowledge, and capability are in themselves adaptable to good or evil. The man who handles them best is he who knows what he is doing. Thus the "versatile" Odysseus is a better man than the "simple" Achilles. To verify this conclusion one must compare the *Iliad* with the *Odyssey* and Homer as a whole with Plato as a whole.

GREATER HIPPIAS
[or, On the Beautiful]

Translated by David R. Sweet

Socrates, Hippias

81a SOCRATES: Hippias, the beautiful and wise, how long a time it's been for us since you have alighted at Athens![1]

HIPPIAS: Yes, for I've had no leisure, Socrates. For whenever Elis has to conduct some business with any of the cities, she always comes to me first among her citizens when she chooses an envoy; she considers

b me to be a most able judge and reporter of whatever speeches are made by each of the cities. Therefore I've often gone as envoy to other cities but most often and regarding the most numerous and important matters I've gone to Lacedaemon. For this reason—in answer to your question—I don't come frequently to this area.

SOC.: Such a thing it is indeed, Hippias, to be a truly wise and perfect man! For in private, when you receive great sums of money from the

c young, you are able to give them still more help than you receive, and again, in public, you are able to benefit your city as one ought if he is not to be looked down on but is to be highly reputed among the many. And yet, Hippias, whatever is the cause that those men of the past whose names are said to be great in regard to wisdom—Pittacus, and Bias, and the associates of Thales the Milesian and those still later down to Anaxagoras[2]—either all or most of them apparently held themselves back from political activities?

---

[1]If the dramatic date of the dialogue is 420 (see introduction), and if Hippias' previous visit was on the occasion of the *Protagoras* (perhaps 433–32), then as many as twelve years have passed.

[2]Pittacus of Mytilene, Bias of Priene, and Thales of Miletus all lived in the late seventh or early sixth centuries B.C. and were numbered among the traditional Seven

HIP.: What else do you suppose, Socrates, other than that they lacked
d the power and were unable by prudence to succeed at both the common and the private?

SOC.: Then, by Zeus, just as the other arts have progressed and in
comparison with the craftsmen of today those of the past are poor,
are we to assert that so too your art, that of the sophists, has progressed and that those among the ancients who were concerned with
wisdom were poor compared with you?[3]

HIP.: Yes indeed, you speak very correctly.

SOC.: So, Hippias, if Bias should come to life for us again now, he
282a would be laughable compared with you, just as the sculptors maintain that if Daedalus[4] was born now and produced works such as
those from which he has acquired his name, he would be ridiculous.

HIP.: That is so, Socrates, just as you say. I myself, however, am
accustomed to praise the men of the past and our predecessors both
sooner and more so than I do the men of today, since I take heed of
the envy of the living and I fear the wrath of the dead.

b SOC.: You do beautifully, Hippias, in your use of terms and in your
thinking, it seems to me.[5] And I can bear witness for you that what
you say is true and that really your art has progressed in regard to
having the power to practice public affairs along with private ones.
For Gorgias,[6] the sophist from Leontini, came here in a public capaci-

---

Sages of Greece. For other references to them, see *Republic* 335e, *Theaetetus* 174a, and
esp. *Protagoras* 339d–347a. For evidence that they did not completely hold back from
political activities, see Herodotus I 27, 170; Cicero, *Republic* I 12; and Diogenes
Laertius' biographies of them. Anaxagoras of Clazomenae (ca. 500–ca. 428) a pre-
Socratic philosopher and friend of Pericles, spent part of his life at Athens, where he
was charged with impiety but fled. Among Platonic references to him, see particularly *Phaedo* 97b–99c.

[3]The "you" and "your" in these instances are plural, as are "you" in 282a, "your
art" in 282b, and "what happened to you" in 283a.

[4]One of the stories told of the artisan Daedalus is that his statues moved. See
Euthyphro 11c–e, 15b; *Alcibiades I* 121a; *Meno* 97d–e.

[5]Socrates is presumably referring to the beautiful way in which Hippias has just
expressed himself. Hippias' use of balanced phraseology reinforced in the Greek by
rhymed elements is characteristic of the rhetorical style of Gorgias. But the verb "to
use terms" (*onomazein*) literally means "to name." Consequently Socrates may also
mean that Hippias does beautifully in naming the men of the past and in praising them
for the reasons that Hippias has just stated.

[6]The most famous visit of Gorgias to Athens was his first one in 427 when he
amazed and delighted the Athenians with his rhetorical style. For a sample of this
style, see the end of Agathon's speech in the *Symposium* 197d–e and Socrates' response
to it, 198b–c.

ty as an envoy from his home because he was the most able of the Leontines in the practice of the affairs of the community, and before the people he seemed to speak excellently, while privately, by making exhibition speeches[7] and associating with the youth, he earned
c and took out of this city here great sums of money. And if you wish, our comrade, Prodicus,[8] has often gone elsewhere in a public capacity, but on the last occasion when he came here recently from Ceos in a public capacity and spoke before the Council,[9] he was very highly reputed, while privately, by making exhibition speeches and associating with the youth, he received a wonderful amount of money. But none of those men of the past ever thought it worthy to earn money
d as a wage or to make exhibitions of his own wisdom before all sorts of human beings—so naive were those men and so unaware of how great the worth of money is. Yet each of these two has earned more money from wisdom than any other craftsman from any art whatsoever. And even before them Protagoras[10] did too.

HIP.: Why, Socrates, you know none of the beautiful things about this. For if you knew how much money I have earned, you would be filled with wonder. I omit the other occasions, but once I went to
e Sicily while Protagoras was residing there and was in high repute, and although he was older and I much younger, in a short time I earned much more than 150 minas; indeed from one very small place, Inycum,[11] more than 20 minas. And when I came home, bringing

---

[7]"Exhibition speeches" translates *epideixeis*. In the later fifth century these were ceremonial orations, as distinguished from speeches given before judicial or legislative bodies. The sophists used *epideixeis* to demonstrate their skills. Later in the dialogue Hippias invites Socrates to listen to one such speech of his (286a–c), the very speech that he has presumably just finished giving when the *Lesser Hippias* begins. Similarly, Gorgias has just given an *epideixis* at the beginning of the *Gorgias*. Other examples in Plato are Protagoras' myth (see *Protagoras* 320b8, c1, 3) and the funeral oration of Aspasia in the *Menexenus*.

[8]Prodicus appears often in the dialogues. See esp. *Protagoras* 315c–316a, 337a–c, where Socrates represents himself as a pupil of Prodicus (341a4). Prodicus was particularly famous for the correct definition of words.

[9]The Athenian Council (*Boulē*) was made up of 500 members, 50 from each of the ten tribes, who held office for one year and prepared business for the Assembly.

[10]Protagoras of Abdera, among the most famous and influential of the sophists, lived for some seventy years during the fifth century. He was the author of the view that "man is the measure of all things." Much of what is known about him rests on the evidence of Plato, especially in the *Protagoras*.

[11]There are very few ancient references to the town of Inycum. Even its location in Sicily is in dispute, but Pausanias (7.4, 5) mentions it as the place where Daedalus found refuge when he made his winged escape from Crete and Minos.

this, I gave it to my father, so that he and the other citizens were filled with wonder and completely astonished. Why, I almost suppose that I have earned more money than any other two sophists—whichever ones you wish.

283a   SOC.: It is a beautiful thing, Hippias, that you say, and a great proof of how much both your own wisdom and that of the human beings of today differ from the ancients. For according to your argument, the ignorance of our predecessors[12] is great, since what happened to Anaxagoras, people say, is the opposite of what happened to you. For although a great deal of money was left to him, he neglected it and lost it all—so unintelligent he was at exercising his wisdom.[13] And they say other things of this sort also about other men of the past. So this proof which you have revealed seems to me to be a beautiful one

b   regarding the wisdom of men of today compared with our predecessors, and it seems to many that the wise man himself must be wise especially for himself. The mark of this is, of course, whoever has earned the most money. Let that be enough on this subject. But tell me this, from which of the cities you have gone to have you yourself earned the most money? Clearly, is it not from Lacedaemon, where you have also gone the most often?

HIP.: No, by Zeus, Socrates.

SOC.: What do you mean? There you have earned the least?

c   HIP.: Indeed, nothing at all, ever.

SOC.: A marvellous thing you are saying and wondrous, Hippias! Now, tell me. Isn't your wisdom the sort that makes those who associate with it and learn it better in regard to virtue?

HIP.: Very much so, Socrates.

SOC.: Then you were able to make the sons of the Inycinians better, but those of the Spartans you lacked the power to?

HIP.: Far from it.

---

[12]In the MSS, following *tōn gar proterōn* ("for . . . of our predecessors"), are the words *peri Anaxagorou legetai* ("said about Anaxagoras"). This comment is probably a marginal gloss explaining that "predecessors" refers to Anaxagoras. At some point the gloss entered the text, but the editor Stallbaum removed it, and later editors tend to follow his example. If one were to admit the phrase, the translation would be "For, according to your argument, the ignorance of our predecessors in the circle of Anaxagoras is said to be great."

[13]The Greek phrase *anoēta sophizesthai* perhaps contains a reference to Anaxagoras' doctrine of *nous*, or "mind" (see *Phaedo* 97b–99c), and can be translated "so *mindless* was he at being wise."

soc.: Do the Sicilians then desire to become better but not the Lacedaemonians?

d hip.: By all means, Socrates, the Lacedaemonians do too.

soc.: Was it then from lack of money that they avoided your company?

hip.: Of course not, since they have enough of it.

soc.: Why would it be then that, though they were desirous and had money and though you had the capacity to help them very greatly, they didn't send you away full of money? Surely it wasn't this, was it, that the Lacedaemonians could educate their own children better than you? Or are we to assert that this is so, and do you concede it?

e hip.: In no way whatsoever.

soc.: Then were you not able to persuade the youth in Lacedaemon that, if they associated with you rather than with their own people, they would progress further toward virtue? Or did you not have the capacity to persuade their fathers that, if they had any concern for their sons, they ought to hand them over to you rather than to take care of them themselves? For presumably they did not begrudge that their own children become the best that they could.

hip.: No, I don't suppose they begrudged this.

soc.: Yet surely Lacedaemon has good laws.

hip.: How not?

84a soc.: And in cities that have good laws virtue is most honored.

hip.: Certainly.

soc.: And you among human beings know how to hand this down most beautifully to someone else.

hip.: Very much so, Socrates.

soc.: Then would not he who knows most beautifully how to hand down horsemanship be especially honored and receive the most money at Thessaly in Greece and wherever else they are serious about this?

hip.: That is likely.

soc.: So will not he who has the capacity to hand down the most

b worthy teachings for virtue be honored and earn the most money, if he should wish to, especially at Sparta and in any other of the Greek cities which have good laws? Or do you suppose, comrade, this will take place rather in Sicily and in Inycum? Are we to believe this, Hippias? For if you bid us, we must believe it.

hip.: No, Socrates, for it is against ancestral tradition for the Lacedaemonians to change their laws or to educate their sons contrary to what is customary.

SOC.: How do you mean? That it is against ancestral tradition for the
c Lacedaemonians to act correctly rather than to make mistakes?

HIP.: No, I wouldn't say so, Socrates.

SOC.: Then wouldn't they be acting correctly by educating their youth in a better way and not a worse one?

HIP.: Yes, correctly, but it is not lawful for them to employ a foreign education. For know well, if anyone else had ever received money there for an education, I would have received by far the most—at least they enjoy listening to me, and they praise me—but as I say, that is not the law.

d SOC.: Do you say that law, Hippias, is harmful to a city or helpful?

HIP.: It is set down, I suppose, for the sake of helping, but yes, sometimes it harms if the law is set down badly.

SOC.: What then? Do not those who set down the law set it down as a very great good for a city? And without this, isn't it impossible to live under good laws?

HIP.: What you say is true.

SOC.: Whenever, then, those who undertake to set down the laws mistake what is good, do they mistake what is lawful and law, or what do you mean?

e HIP.: In precise speech, Socrates, this is so. Human beings, however, are not accustomed to use words this way.

SOC.: Those who know, Hippias, or those who do not know?

HIP.: The many.

SOC.: Are these, the many, those who know the truth?

HIP.: Of course not.

SOC.: Instead, presumably, those who know consider that, in truth, for all human beings the more beneficial is more lawful than the less beneficial, or don't you concede this?

HIP.: Yes, I concede that they do, in truth, at any rate.

SOC.: Then is it not so, and does it not hold just as those who know consider that it does?

HIP.: Certainly.

285a SOC.: And for the Lacedaemonians, as you assert, it is more helpful to be educated by your education, though it is foreign, than by the local one.

HIP.: And I say what is true.

SOC.: Yes, for you also say this, don't you, Hippias, that the more helpful things are more lawful?

HIP.: Yes, I said it.

SOC.: So, according to your argument, for the sons of the Lacedaemonians it is more lawful to be educated by Hippias, and less lawful to be educated by their fathers, if they really will be helped more by you.

HIP.: But they will indeed be helped, Socrates.

b SOC.: So the Lacedaemonians break the law by not giving you gold and turning their own sons over to you.

HIP.: I concede this, for you seem to me to be stating the argument to my advantage, and there is no need for me to oppose it.

SOC.: Then, comrade, we find the Laconians to be lawbreakers, and to be so in the most important matters, though they seem to be the most law-abiding. But before the gods, Hippias, what sorts of things *do* they praise you for and enjoy hearing? Clearly, isn't it those things

c which you know most beautifully, matters concerning the stars and events in the heavens?

HIP.: In no way whatsoever. These things they don't even put up with.

SOC.: Well, do they enjoy hearing anything about geometry?

HIP.: Not at all, since many of them, so to speak, don't even know how to count.

SOC.: So they are far from putting up with you when you make exhibitions regarding calculations, at any rate.

HIP.: Far indeed, by Zeus.

SOC.: But of course, it's those things, isn't it, which you among

d human beings know how to distinguish most precisely—what pertains to the power of letters and syllables and rhythms and harmonies?

HIP.: Harmonies and letters indeed, my good man!

SOC.: But what is it then that they are pleased to hear from you and that they praise you for? Tell me yourself, since I'm not finding it out.

HIP.: What pleases them most, Socrates, is to hear about the generations of heroes and of human beings and the founding of cities, how in ancient times they were settled, and, in sum, the entire account of

e ancient things. Consequently, because of them I have been compelled to learn completely and to practice thoroughly all of these sorts of things.

SOC.: Yes, by Zeus, Hippias, and you are lucky that the Lacedaemonians do not enjoy it if someone lists for them our archons beginning from Solon.[14] Otherwise you would have trouble learning them completely.

HIP.: How so, Socrates? If I hear fifty names just once, I recollect them.

SOC.: What you say is true, but I was not thinking of the fact that you possess mnemonic skill. Therefore I think it likely that the Lacedaemonians enjoy you because you know many things, and they use you as children use old women to tell them stories in a pleasant way.

286a

HIP.: Yes, by Zeus, Socrates, and just recently I gained a great reputation there regarding beautiful pursuits by describing in detail what a young man ought to pursue. For I have an altogether beautifully constructed speech about these pursuits which is well composed in various ways, especially in its choice of words. The ostensible occasion for the speech and the beginning of it is something like this. When Troy was captured, the speech recounts how Neoptolemus asked Nestor[15] what sorts of pursuits were beautiful, pursuits that would make a young man who practiced them most highly reputed. After this Nestor speaks and proposes to him very many things that are lawful and altogether beautiful. This speech I gave there as an exhibition, and the day after tomorrow in Pheidostratus' school I am also going to exhibit it here, as well as many other things worth hearing, because Eudicus the son of Apemantus[16] has asked me to. So be there yourself, and bring others who are able, when they hear, to judge what is said.

b

c

SOC.: So it will be, if God is willing, Hippias. For the moment, however, give me a brief answer about it, since you have reminded me opportunely.[17] Recently, best of men, someone threw me into

[14]The principal magistrates at Athens were called archons. Eventually there were nine of them. They held office for one year, and one of them, the eponymous archon, gave his name to the year. Socrates refers to the list of these eponymous archons.

[15]In the *Iliad,* Nestor, the king of Pylos, is too old to fight. His role is to give the Greeks the counsels of age. Hippias considers him to be the wisest of those who went to Troy (*Lesser Hippias* 364c). Neoptolemus, the son of Achilles and Deidamia, figured prominently in the fall of Troy. See Odysseus' description of him to Achilles' shade in Hades (*Odyssey* XI 504–40).

[16]See note on *epideixis* 282b. For Eudicus and Apemantus, see *Lesser Hippias* 363a–c. Nothing is known of Pheidostratus.

[17]The Greek phrase *eis kalon* is a colloquialism meaning "opportunely," but if translated literally, the passage also reads, "since you have reminded me of 'beautiful.'"

perplexity during an argument, when I was censuring some things as ugly and praising others as beautiful. He asked somewhat as follows, and very insolently, "Tell me, Socrates," he said, "from where do
d   you know what sorts of things are beautiful and ugly? For, come now, could you say what the beautiful is?" And I, because of my poverty, was perplexed, and I could not answer him properly. Then when I left his company, I was angry at myself and reproached myself, and I vowed that as soon as I chanced upon one of you wise men, after listening and learning and practicing thoroughly, I would go back to the one who asked the question to do battle again over the argument. So now, as I was saying, you have come upon "beautiful." Teach me sufficiently what is the beautiful itself, and in your answer, try to speak as precisely as possible so that I won't be refuted a second time and again be laughed at. For you, of course, know plainly, and this would presumably be a small piece of learning among the many things that you know.

e   HIP.: Small indeed, by Zeus, Socrates, and worth nothing, so to speak.

SOC.: Then I shall learn it easily, and no one will refute me hereafter.

287a   HIP.: No one indeed. For otherwise my business would be a poor and ordinary one.[18]

SOC.: By Hera, you speak well, Hippias, if we shall subdue the man. But would I be a hindrance if, in imitation of him, I were to object to your arguments as you answer, in order that you might give me as much practice as possible? For I am rather experienced in objections, so if it makes no difference to you, I wish to raise objections in order that I may learn more firmly.

b   HIP.: Well, make your objections, since, as I was just saying, the question is not a big one. Why, I could also teach you to answer things much more difficult than this so that no human being would have the power to refute you.

SOC.: Ah, how well you speak. But come, since even you bid me to, I will become that man as much as I can and try to ask you questions. For if you should exhibit to him this speech which you mention, the one about the beautiful pursuits, he would listen to it, and once you

[18]"Ordinary" in the Greek is *idiōtikon,* a word that refers to a person who is an amateur and not a professional in terms of having developed a skill (see, e.g., *Protagoras* 312b). A literal translation, however, of *idiōtikon* would contain the root "private," which is an important word elsewhere in the dialogue and is the term used in contrast to "common" and "public."

had stopped speaking, he would ask about nothing else sooner than

c about the beautiful—for this is a certain custom of his—and he would say, "Stranger from Elis, isn't it by justice that the just are just?" So answer, Hippias, as if he were asking.

HIP.: I shall answer that it is by justice.

SOC.: "Isn't this, justice, something?"

HIP.: Very much so.

SOC.: "Isn't it also by wisdom that the wise are wise and by the good that all good things are good?"

HIP.: How not?

SOC.: "And by these things as things that exist, for surely not by them as things that do not exist."

HIP.: As things that exist, to be sure.

SOC.: "Then aren't also all beautiful things beautiful by the beautiful?"

d HIP.: Yes, by the beautiful.

SOC.: "By it as something that exists?"

HIP.: As something that exists. For what else is it going to be?

SOC.: "Then tell me, stranger," he will say, "what is this, the beautiful?"

HIP.: Doesn't the one who asks this, Socrates, want to inquire what is beautiful?

SOC.: To me it seems not thus but rather what is the beautiful, Hippias.

HIP.: And in what does this differ from that?

SOC.: Does it seem no different to you?

HIP.: It doesn't, for there is no difference.

SOC.: Well, to be sure, clearly you know more beautifully. But nonetheless, my good man, observe. For he is asking you not what is

e beautiful but what is the beautiful.

HIP.: I understand, my good man, and I shall answer him what is the beautiful, and I shall never be refuted. For, Socrates, know well, if the truth must be said, a beautiful maiden is beautiful.

SOC.: By the dog,[19] Hippias, at least you've answered beautifully and

288a reputably. If I give him this answer, shall I have answered what was asked and done so correctly, and shall I never be refuted?

HIP.: Yes, Socrates, for how could you be refuted about a thing that

---

[19]This is a favorite oath of Socrates. The dog apparently is Anubis, the Egyptian god (see *Gorgias* 482b5). See Eva Brann, "The Music of the *Republic*," *Agon* 1:1 (1967):4.

seems so to everyone and with regard to which everyone who hears you will bear witness that you speak correctly?

SOC.: Well then. Certainly they will. Come then, Hippias, let me repeat to myself what you are saying. He will question me in some such way as this. "Come, Socrates, answer me. All these things that you assert are beautiful would be beautiful if the beautiful itself is what?" Shall I indeed say that if a beautiful maiden is beautiful, there is something on account of which these things would be beautiful?

b   HIP.: Do you suppose, then, that he will still attempt to refute you on the grounds that what you say is not beautiful or that, if he does attempt to, he will not be ridiculous?

SOC.: That he will attempt to, my wonderful fellow, I know well. But when he makes the attempt, the attempt itself will show whether he will be ridiculous. I am willing to tell you, however, what he will say.

HIP.: Do tell me.

SOC.: "How sweet you are, Socrates," he will say. "But a beautiful mare, isn't she beautiful, the one that even the god praised in his
c   oracle?"[20] What shall we say, Hippias? Shouldn't we say that the mare, the beautiful one, at least, is beautiful? For how could we dare to deny it by claiming that the beautiful is not beautiful?

HIP.: What you say is true, Socrates, since the god has surely spoken this correctly. For among us there are very beautiful mares.

SOC.: "Well, then," he will say. "What about a beautiful lyre? Isn't it beautiful?" Shall we say so, Hippias?

HIP.: Yes.

SOC.: Then after this he will say—I know rather well by conjecturing from his character—"You best of men, what about a beautiful pot? Isn't it beautiful, then?"

d   HIP.: Socrates, who is the fellow? How uneducated he is who dares to use low words this way in a dignified business!

SOC.: Such he is, Hippias, not elegant but vulgar, taking thought for nothing else but the truth. Nonetheless, the man must be answered, and I shall go ahead of you in making a declaration. Suppose the pot had been molded by a good potter, smooth and round and beautifully fired, like some of those beautiful pots with two handles, those which

---

[20]Commentators suppose that this oracle is one that Apollo gave in response to some Megarians when they asked him who were better than they. His answer was: "Of all the earth, Pelasgian Argos is better, Thracian mares and Lacedaemonian women."

hold six choes,[21] very beautiful ones. If he should ask about this sort
e of pot, we would have to agree that it is beautiful. For how could we
assert that a thing that is beautiful is not beautiful?

HIP.: We could in no way, Socrates.

SOC.: Then he will say, "Isn't even a beautiful pot beautiful?" Answer.

HIP.: Well, Socrates, so it is, I suppose. Even this utensil is beautiful
when it is beautifully made, but as a whole it is not worthy to judge it
as being beautiful compared with a mare and a maiden and all the
other beautiful things.

289a SOC.: Well, then. I understand, Hippias. When he asks these questions, this is how one ought to contradict him: "O human being, you
do not recognize that the saying of Heracleitus applies well here, that
'the most beautiful ape is ugly in comparison with the class of humans,'[22] and the most beautiful pot is ugly in comparison with the
class of maidens, as Hippias the wise asserts." Isn't it so, Hippias?

HIP.: Certainly, Socrates, you have answered correctly.

SOC.: Listen, then, for I know well that he will say after this, "What
then, Socrates? If someone should compare the class of maidens with
b the class of gods, won't the same thing happen to him as when that of
pots is compared with that of maidens? Won't the most beautiful
maiden appear ugly? Or doesn't Heracleitus, whom you introduce,
also say this, that 'the wisest human being, in comparison with a god,
will appear an ape both in wisdom and in beauty and in all other
respects'?"[23] Shall we agree, Hippias, that the most beautiful maiden
is ugly in comparison with the class of gods?

HIP.: Yes, for who would contradict this, Socrates?

c SOC.: Well, if we agree to these things, he will laugh and say "Socrates, do you then remember what you were asked?" "I do," I shall
say. "It was: whatever is the beautiful itself?" "Next," he will say,
"although you were asked about the beautiful, do you give as an
answer a thing which, as you yourself affirm, happens to be no more
beautiful than ugly?" Shall I say, "It seems likely," or what, my
friend, do you advise me to say?

---

[21]Six choes are somewhat more than four gallons.

[22]Diels-Kranz, *Die Fragmente der Vorsokratiker*, Heracl. 82. Diels-Kranz and most
editors read Bekker's emendation of *anthrōpōn* for the MSS *alloi*. If the MSS reading is
retained, translate: "the most beautiful of apes is ugly in comparison with another
class."

[23]Diels-Kranz, *Die Fragmente der Vorsokratiker*, Heracl. 83.

HIP.: I advise just that. For, of course, in saying that in comparison with gods the human class is not beautiful, he will say what is true.

SOC.: "If I had asked you from the beginning," he will say, "What is
d both beautiful and ugly, and if you had given me the answers that you do now, you would have answered correctly, wouldn't you? But does it still seem to you that the beautiful itself, by which all other things are adorned and appear beautiful whenever this form[24] becomes present,[25] is a maiden or mare or lyre?"

HIP.: Well, of course, Socrates, if this is what he's seeking, it is the easiest thing of all to tell him what the beautiful is by which all other things are adorned and made to appear beautiful whenever it becomes
e present. So he is a most naive human being, and he has no expertise concerning beautiful objects. For if you tell him that this "beautiful" which he is asking about is nothing other than gold, he will be perplexed, and he won't attempt to refute you. For we all know, of course, that, wherever this becomes present, even if a thing previously appeared ugly, it will appear beautiful once it has been adorned with gold.

SOC.: You have no experience, Hippias, of how unyielding the man is and how he accepts nothing easily.

HIP.: What does that matter, Socrates? For he must of necessity accept
290a what is said correctly, or if he doesn't accept it, he must be ridiculous.

SOC.: As to this answer, best of men, not only will he not accept it, but he will certainly also mock me, and he will say, "You deluded one, do you suppose that Phidias[26] is a bad craftsman?" And I suppose I shall say, "Not in any way whatsoever."

HIP.: Yes, and you will speak correctly, Socrates.

SOC.: Correctly indeed. Accordingly, when I agree that Phidias is a
b good craftsman, that fellow will say, "Next, do you suppose that Phidias did not recognize this 'beautiful' which you speak of?"

And I shall say, "Why in particular do you ask?"

"Because," he will say, "he made the eyes of Athena not of gold, nor the rest of her face, nor her feet, nor her hands—if in fact by

---

[24]"Form" here and in 298b translates the Greek *eidos*. See note on 297b.

[25]The Greek verb translated "becomes present" is *prosgignesthai,* which occurs here and in 289e, 290b, and 292d. This verb as well as *proseinai* and *pareinai* (both translated "to be present") and *paragignesthai* (translated "to become present") are all used to indicate the way in which a form is related to the phenomena that it informs.

[26]Phidias, the fifth-century Athenian sculptor, was a key artist in Pericles' building program. In the discussion that follows, Socrates refers to one of his most famous works, the chryselephantine cult statue of Athena that stood in the Parthenon.

being of gold they were going to appear most beautiful—but rather of ivory. Clearly he made this mistake from ignorance, since he did not recognize that gold, of course, is what makes all things beautiful wherever it becomes present." What then are we to answer him when he says this, Hippias?

c   HIP.: Nothing difficult. For we shall say that he made them correctly, since ivory too, I suppose, is beautiful.

SOC.: "Then for what reason," he will say, "did he not make also the middle parts of her eyes of ivory but of stone, finding stone that was as similar as possible to ivory? Or is stone too—that is, beautiful stone—beautiful?" Shall we affirm it, Hippias?

HIP.: We shall affirm it indeed, at least whenever stone is fitting.

SOC.: "But whenever it is not fitting, is it ugly?" Shall I agree or not?

HIP.: Agree, at least whenever stone is not fitting.

d   SOC.: "What then?" he will say. "Do not ivory and gold, you wise one, whenever they are fitting, make things appear beautiful, but whenever not, ugly?" Shall we deny it, or shall we agree with him that he speaks correctly?

HIP.: We shall agree at least to this, that whatever is fitting to each thing makes each thing beautiful.

SOC.: "Then," he will say, "whenever someone boils the pot that we were just speaking of—the beautiful one, full of beautiful soup—which of the two is fitting for it, a ladle of gold or of fig wood?"

e   HIP.: Heracles! Such a fellow you speak of, Socrates! Don't you wish to tell me who he is?

SOC.: No, if I told you his name, you wouldn't recognize it.

HIP.: Well, at least I recognize now that he is someone ignorant.

SOC.: He is very captious, Hippias. Nevertheless, what shall we say? Which of the two ladles is fitting for the soup and the pot? Clearly the one of fig wood? For presumably it makes the soup more flavorful, and at the same time, comrade, you would not shatter the pot for us and spill the soup, extinguishing the fire and depriving those who are about to dine of a very noble dish. But that golden ladle would do all

291a these things. So it seems to me that we must say that the fig-wood one is more fitting than the golden one unless you say something else.

HIP.: No, for it is more fitting, Socrates. However, I at least wouldn't converse with the fellow when he asks such things.

SOC.: Yes, that would be correct, my friend, since it wouldn't be fitting for you to be filled up with such words, you who are dressed so beautifully and wear such beautiful shoes and are so highly reputed

for wisdom among all the Greeks. But for me it is no trouble to
b mingle with the fellow. So teach me beforehand, and answer for my
sake. "Now if the fig wood one is more fitting than the gold one,"
the fellow will say, "wouldn't it also be more beautiful? For in fact,
Socrates, you have agreed that the fitting is more beautiful than the
not fitting." Shouldn't we agree, Hippias, that the fig-wood one is
more beautiful than the gold one?

HIP.: Do you wish me to tell you, Socrates, what to say the beautiful
is in order to release yourself from many arguments?

c SOC.: Certainly. Not, however, until you tell me which of the two
ladles that I was just speaking of I should answer is fitting and more
beautiful.

HIP.: Well, if you wish, answer him that it is the one made out of fig
wood.

SOC.: Now then, say what you were just about to say. For by this
answer, if I say that the beautiful is gold, it seems likely to me that
gold will not appear as being more beautiful than fig wood. But now,
again, what do you say the beautiful is?

d HIP.: I shall tell you. You seem to me to be seeking to answer that the
beautiful is some sort of thing that will never appear ugly to anyone
anywhere.

SOC.: Certainly, Hippias, and now you comprehend beautifully.

HIP.: Listen then. If anyone is able to contradict this, be sure to declare
that I have no expertise in anything at all.

SOC.: Speak then, as quickly as possible, before the gods.

HIP.: I say, then, that always, for everyone and everywhere, it is most
beautiful for a man who is wealthy, healthy, and honored by the
Greeks, having arrived at old age and having celebrated beautifully
e the funeral of his parents after they have come to their end, to be
beautifully and magnificently buried by his own offspring.

SOC.: Hurrah, hurrah, Hippias! How wonderfully and grandly and
how worthily of yourself you have spoken! And by Hera, I admire
you because you seem to me to be bringing aid with good intentions,
to the extent that you are able! Even so, we are not hitting the man,
but now, know well, he will laugh at us most of all.

HIP.: A wicked laugh, Socrates. For when he has nothing he can say
against this and yet laughs, he will laugh at himself and himself be
laughed at by those present.

292a SOC.: Perhaps this is so. Perhaps, however, for this answer, at least, as
I prophesy, he will probably not only laugh at me.

HIP.: Well, what else?

SOC.: If he happens to have a staff and if I don't escape him by fleeing, he will very well try to land it on me.

HIP.: What do you mean? Is the fellow some sort of master of yours, and if he does this, won't he be sorry and have to pay a penalty? Or
b isn't your city just? Does it instead allow the citizens to beat each other unjustly?

SOC.: In no way does it allow this.

HIP.: Then he will pay a penalty, at least if he beats you unjustly.

SOC.: It doesn't seem unjust to me, Hippias, at least not if I give this answer, but just; so it seems to me at any rate.

HIP.: Then it seems so to me as well, Socrates, if in fact you yourself suppose it is.

SOC.: Shall I also tell you why I myself suppose I would be justly beaten if I were to give this answer? Will you too beat me without a trial, or will you accept an account?
c HIP.: I shall, for it would be terrible, Socrates, if I shouldn't accept one. But how do you mean this?

SOC.: I shall tell you, in the same manner as I did just now, by imitating him, in order that I not use the sorts of expressions toward you that he will to me, ones both difficult and outlandish. For know well, he will say, "Tell me, Socrates, do you suppose that someone receives blows unjustly who, in singing such a dithyramb[27] so unmusically, has sung very far away from the question?" "How so?" I shall say. "How?" he will say. Aren't you able to remember that I
d was asking about the beautiful itself which inheres in everything in which it becomes present such that that thing is beautiful—stone and wood and human and god and every activity and all learning? For I am asking, human being, what beauty itself is, and I have no more power to make myself heard by you than if you were a stone sitting beside me, and a millstone at that, having neither ears nor brain." If, then, I took fright and said the following in response to these things,
e wouldn't you be irritated, Hippias? "But Hippias affirmed that this is the beautiful. And yet I was asking him, just as you are me, what is beautiful for all and always." What then do you say? Won't you be irritated if I say these things?

HIP.: At any rate, I know well, Socrates, that what I said is beautiful for all and will seem so, too.

---

[27]The dithyramb was a choral hymn in honor of Dionysus.

soc.: "Will it also be so in the future?" he will say. "For presumably the beautiful, at least, is always beautiful."

hip.: Certainly.

soc.: "Then was it also so in the past?" he will say.

hip.: It was also so in the past.

soc.: "As regards Achilles,28 too," he will say, "did the stranger from Elis affirm that it was beautiful to be buried later than his forebears, and for his grandfather Aeacus, and for the others, who have been born from gods, and for the gods themselves?"

hip.: What's this? Throw him to the blessed!29 *These* questions of the fellow, Socrates, are not even respectful.30

soc.: What then? Is it not also quite disrespectful to affirm that these things are so when someone else asks?

hip.: Perhaps.

soc.: "Perhaps, then, you are this person," he will say, "who affirms that for everyone and always it is beautiful to be buried by one's offspring and to bury one's parents. Or isn't Heracles31 too included among everyone as well as all those whom we were speaking of just now?"

hip.: But I at least wasn't saying that it was so for the gods.

soc.: "And not for the heroes either, as seems likely."

hip.: Not for those at least who were children of the gods.

soc.: "But for those who weren't?"

hip.: Certainly.

soc.: "Then, according to your argument again, as it appears, for Tantalus among the heroes and for Dardanus and for Zethus it is terrible and impious and ugly, but for Pelops32 and the others who were born this way it is beautiful."

hip.: To me at least it seems so.

soc.: "Then it seems to you," he will say, "though you denied it just now, that for one who has buried his forebears to be buried by his

---

28Achilles' parents were the mortal Peleus and the immortal Thetis. His grandfather Aeacus' parents were Zeus and the island nymph Aegina.

29This phrase seems to be a euphemistic substitution for the phrase "throw him to the crows" or perhaps for "throw him into Hades."

30The Greek for "respectful" here is *euphēma,* and for "disrespectful" (just below), *dysphēmon.* These terms refer specifically to words of good and ill omen, i.e., to those that may be used in a religious context and those that may not.

31Heracles' parents were Zeus and Alcmene.

32Tantalus, Dardanus, and Zethus were all sons of Zeus, while Pelops was the son of Tantalus.

c offspring is ugly sometimes and for some. And it is still more impossible, as seems likely, that this become and be beautiful for all, so that the same thing has happened to this answer as happened to those previous ones, the maiden and the pot, and even more laughably it is beautiful for some but not beautiful for others. And not yet even today, Socrates," he will say, "are you able to answer what is being asked about the beautiful, namely, what it is." These things and their like he will reproach me with justly, if I answer him in this way.

d Now, for the most part, Hippias, he converses with me more or less in this way. But sometimes, as though pitying me for my inexperience and lack of education, he himself makes a suggestion for me by asking if the beautiful seems to me to be such and such a thing and so too as regards whatever else he happens to be inquiring about and which the argument concerns.

HIP.: How do you mean this, Socrates?

SOC.: I shall tell you. "O daemonic Socrates," he says, "stop giving these sorts of answers in this way—for they are exceedingly naive

e and easily refuted—but consider whether some such thing as the following seems to you to be beautiful, which we even now caught hold of in your answer, when we were saying that gold is beautiful for those things for which it is fitting, and it is not for those for which it isn't, and so on in the case of all the other things for which this is present.[33] So consider whether this very thing, the fitting, and the nature of the fitting itself, happens to be the beautiful." Now, I for my part am accustomed to assent to such things every time—for I don't have anything to say—but does it seem to you at any rate that the fitting is beautiful?

HIP.: By all means, of course, Socrates.

SOC.: Let's consider it, so that we aren't deceived in some way.

HIP.: Yes, it ought to be considered.

294a SOC.: See then. Do we say the fitting is that which, when it becomes present, makes each of those things in which it is present *appear* beautiful or that which makes them *be* so or neither of these?

HIP.: To me at least it seems so.

SOC.: Which of the two?

---

[33]"This" is ambiguous in the Greek. In view of what precedes, "this" seems to refer to "gold," but in view of what follows, it seems to refer to "the fitting." "Is present" renders the Greek verb *proseinai*. See note on 289d.

HIP.: That which makes them appear beautiful.[34] Just as, whenever someone puts on a cloak or sandals that are suitable, even if he is laughable, he appears more beautiful.

SOC.: Then if the fitting does make things appear more beautiful than they are, wouldn't the fitting be a deception concerning the beautiful? And this wouldn't be what we are seeking, would it, Hippias? For b presumably we were seeking that by which all beautiful things are beautiful. It is just like that by which all large things are large, namely that which exceeds, because by this all large things are so, and even if they do not appear so but are in excess, it is necessary for them to be large. So too, we say, what would the beautiful be by which all c beautiful things are so, whether they appear so or not? It wouldn't be the fitting, because this makes things appear more beautiful than they are, according to your argument, but does not allow them to appear such as they are. But we must try to say what that is which makes them be beautiful, as I said just now, whether they appear so or not. For this is what we are seeking, if in fact we are seeking the beautiful.

HIP.: But the fitting, Socrates, makes things both be and appear beautiful when it is present.

SOC.: Is it impossible, then, that things which really are beautiful not appear to be beautiful, at least when that which makes them appear so is present?

HIP.: It is impossible.

SOC.: Then do we agree to this, Hippias, that all really beautiful things, both lawful things and pursuits, are both reputed to be beau- d tiful and always appear to be so to everyone, or, quite the contrary, aren't they unrecognized, and aren't strife and battle most of all about these things, both privately for individuals and publicly for cities?

HIP.: Rather the latter, Socrates. They are unrecognized.

SOC.: They wouldn't be unrecognized, at least if appearing beautiful were present in them. And it would be present if the fitting were in fact beautiful and made things not only be beautiful but also appear so. Consequently, the fitting, if it is that which makes things be beautiful, would be the beautiful that we are seeking, but not, how- ever, the one which makes them appear so. If, on the other hand, the

---

[34]Burnet's text, following Baumann, brackets Socrates' question, "Which of the two?" According to this reading Hippias says in answer to the preceding question of Socrates, "To me it seems that which makes them appear beautiful."

e fitting is that which makes them appear so, it would not be the beautiful which we are seeking. For that is what makes things *be* so, and the same thing would never have the power to make[35] things both appear and be either beautiful or anything else whatever. So let us choose which of the two the fitting seems to be, that which makes things appear beautiful or that which makes them be so.

HIP.: That which makes them appear so, it seems to me at least, Socrates.

SOC.: Oh, oh! There it goes, Hippias. It has fled from us, and we have failed to recognize whatever the beautiful is, now that the fitting has appeared as being something other than beautiful.

HIP.: Yes, by Zeus, Socrates, and very strangely so, to me at least!

295a SOC.: Nonetheless, comrade, let us not yet give it up. For I still have some hope that whatever the beautiful is will become completely apparent.

HIP.: By all means, of course, Socrates. For it is not difficult to find. I for my part know well that if I were to go into seclusion for a short time and consider it by myself, I could tell it to you more precisely than total precision.

SOC.: Ah, Hippias, don't talk big. You see how many troubles it[36] has already brought upon us. It may become angry at us and run away

b still more! And yet there is nothing in what I am saying. For you, I suppose, will find it easily when you are alone. But before the gods, find it in my presence. Or if you wish, seek it with me as we were doing just now, and if we find it, that will be most beautiful, but if not, I shall be content with my fortune, I suppose, and you will go away and find it easily. If we find it now, of course, I won't be an

[35]The MSS read *poiein einai,* which would probably dictate that one understand "make" only with "be" and not with "appear." This interpretation would then give the translation: "the same thing would never have the power to appear (as) beautiful things and to make things be beautiful." Most editors transpose the verbs and read *einai poiein,* which produces the translation given in the text. Burnet brackets *poiein.* Following him, one would translate: "the same thing would never have the power to appear (as) and to be beautiful things."

[36]The subject "it" refers to "the beautiful," as soon becomes apparent when Socrates speaks of "it" running away, but initially the reader would assume "it" refers to Hippias' talking big, which has indeed brought them troubles. Just how it does so becomes clearer if one translates Socrates' command, "don't talk big" as "don't say 'large' " or "don't speak a big speech." The Greek word for "large" or "big," *megas,* is characteristic of Hippias. See 281b (where it is translated as "important"), 294b, 301b, and 304b. Socrates, in contrast, is associated with little speeches.

annoyance to you by inquiring what it was that you found out by
c yourself. So contemplate now what the beautiful seems to you to be.
I say that it is—but be attentive to me and apply your mind completely so I won't babble. Let this be beautiful for us: whatever is
useful. And I said so because I was thinking this: we maintain that
eyes are beautiful, not those which seem to be such yet do not have
the power to see but those which do have that power and are useful
for seeing. Isn't that so?

HIP.: Yes.

SOC.: Then in this way we also say that the whole body is beautiful,
d one for running, another for wrestling, and so too all living things—a
beautiful horse and cock and quail, and all utensils and vehicles, those
on land and those on the sea, transport ships as well as triremes, and
all instruments, those in music and those in the other arts, and, if you
wish, pursuits and laws. We call almost all of these beautiful for the
same characteristic. Looking carefully at how each of them is by
nature, how it is made, how it is established, we say that the useful
e one, for how it is useful, and in relation to what it is useful, and
whenever it is useful, is beautiful, but the one that in all of these
respects is useless we say is ugly. Does it not also seem so to you,
Hippias?

HIP.: To me at least it does.

SOC.: Are we now correct in saying that the useful, more than anything else, happens to be beautiful?

HIP.: We are correct, to be sure, Socrates.

SOC.: Isn't a thing that has the power to produce something also
useful insofar as it has the power, and isn't a thing that doesn't have
the power useless?

HIP.: Certainly.

SOC.: Then power is beautiful, but lack of power is ugly?

296a HIP.: Extremely. Not only, Socrates, do other things bear witness for
us that this is so, but especially politics does. For in politics and in
one's own city, the powerful is most beautiful of all, but the powerless most ugly of all.

SOC.: You speak well. So then, before the gods, Hippias, because of
this isn't also wisdom most beautiful of all, and ignorance most ugly
of all?

HIP.: Yes, what else do you suppose, Socrates?

SOC.: Keep still, my dear comrade. How afraid I am again at what we
are saying.

b HIP.: Why are you afraid again, Socrates, since now at least the argument is advancing very beautifully for you?

SOC.: I wish it were, but consider this question with me. Could anyone do something that he did not know how to do or did not at all have the power to do?

HIP.: In no way. For how could he do what he did not have the power to do?

SOC.: Then those who make mistakes and produce bad things and do them involuntarily would never do these things if they did not have the power to do them?

HIP.: Clearly they wouldn't.

c SOC.: But nonetheless, by power the powerful have power. For surely not by lack of power.

HIP.: Of course not.

SOC.: But all those who do what they do have the power to do so?

HIP.: Yes.

SOC.: But all humans do many more bad things than good, starting from childhood, and they make mistakes involuntarily.

HIP.: This is so.

SOC.: What then? Shall we assert that this power and whichever useful things are useful for producing something bad, are beautiful, or far from it?

d HIP.: Far from it, it seems to me at least, Socrates.

SOC.: Then for us, Hippias, the powerful and the useful, as seems likely, are not the beautiful.

HIP.: Unless, Socrates, they have power to produce good things and are useful for such things.

SOC.: Then this much at any rate is gone, namely that the powerful and useful, simply, are beautiful. But was it this, Hippias, that our soul wanted to say, that this is the beautiful, namely, the useful and the powerful for doing something good?

e HIP.: It seems so to me at least.

SOC.: But this is helpful, or isn't it?

HIP.: Certainly.

SOC.: And so, both beautiful bodies and beautiful lawful things and wisdom and all the things that we were speaking of just now are beautiful because they are helpful.

HIP.: Clearly.

SOC.: So the helpful seems likely to us to be the beautiful, Hippias.

HIP.: By all means, surely, Socrates.

SOC.: But the helpful is that which does good.

HIP.: Yes, it is.

SOC.: And that which does something is nothing other than the cause, is it?

HIP.: Just so.

297a   SOC.: So the beautiful is a cause of the good.

HIP.: Yes, it is.

SOC.: But the cause, Hippias, and that of which the cause is a cause, are different. For presumably the cause would not be a cause of a cause. Consider it this way. Didn't it become apparent that the cause does something?

HIP.: Certainly.

SOC.: Then what is done by that which does something is nothing other than that which comes into being and is not that which does something?

HIP.: This is so.

SOC.: Then what comes into being is one thing, and what does something is another?

HIP.: Yes.

b   SOC.: So the cause is not a cause of a cause but of what comes into being because of it.

HIP.: Certainly.

SOC.: So if the beautiful is a cause of good, the good would come into being because of the beautiful. And for this reason, as seems likely, we are serious about prudence and about all the other beautiful things, because the product and the offspring of them—namely, the good—is worthy of seriousness. And probably, from what we are finding, the beautiful is in the form[37] of some sort of father of the good.

HIP.: Certainly. You're speaking beautifully, Socrates.

SOC.: Then am I also saying this beautifully, that the father is not a

c   son and the son is not a father?

HIP.: Beautifully indeed.

SOC.: And the cause is not what comes into being, nor in turn is what comes into being a cause.

HIP.: What you say is true.

SOC.: By Zeus, best of men, then the beautiful is not good, nor is the good beautiful! Or does it seem to you to be possible from what has been said previously?

HIP.: No, by Zeus, it doesn't appear so to me!

---

[37]"Form" here translates the Greek *idea*. See note on *eidos*, 289d.

SOC.: Then is it satisfactory to us, and would we be willing to say that the beautiful is not good and the good is not beautiful?

HIP.: No, by Zeus, it isn't satisfactory to me at all!

d SOC.: Yes, by Zeus, Hippias, to me it is the least satisfactory of all the arguments we have spoken!

HIP.: Yes, that seems likely.

SOC.: Then probably for us it isn't the case, as it just appeared to be, that the most beautiful of the arguments is that the helpful and the useful and the powerful to do some good are beautiful. Instead, if it is possible, this argument is more laughable than those first ones in which we were supposing that the maiden, and each one of those things mentioned earlier, was the beautiful.

HIP.: It seems likely.

SOC.: And I, at least, Hippias, no longer have anywhere to turn, and I am perplexed. But do you have anything to say?

e HIP.: Not at the present moment, but, as I was just saying, when I have considered it, I know well that I shall find it.

SOC.: Well, because of my desire to know I don't seem to myself to be able to wait for you while you are delaying. And in fact, I suppose that I have just now come up with something. Look. If we assert that whatever makes us delighted is beautiful—not all the pleasures, but that which comes through hearing and sight—how then would we

298a fare in the contest? Presumably, beautiful human beings, at least, Hippias, and all decorations and paintings and pieces of sculpture, whichever ones are beautiful, please us when we see them. And beautiful voices and music altogether and speeches and stories produce this same thing, so if we should give this answer to that bold fellow—"O noble one, the beautiful is the pleasant that comes through hearing and through sight"—don't you suppose we would check him in his boldness?

HIP.: It seems to me at any rate that now, at least, Socrates, you are

b saying well what the beautiful is.

SOC.: What then? Shall we indeed assert that beautiful pursuits and laws, Hippias, are beautiful by being pleasant through hearing or through sight, or do they have some other form?

HIP.: Perhaps they do, Socrates, even if the fellow is unaware of it.

SOC.: By the dog, Hippias, not he before whom I would be particularly ashamed to babble and to pretend to have something to say when I have nothing to say.

HIP.: Who is he?

SOC.: Socrates, the son of Sophroniscus,[38] who would no more
permit me to say these things easily without their being examined
than to say that I know what I do not know.

HIP.: Well, since you have said so, it seems to me too that this matter
concerning the laws is something different.

SOC.: Softly, Hippias. For though we have fallen into the same perplexity concerning the beautiful which we were in just recently, we
probably suppose that we have fallen into another solution.

HIP.: What do you mean by that, Socrates?

SOC.: I shall tell you what has become apparent to me, in case there is
something in what I say, because these things concerning laws and
pursuits might perhaps appear not to be outside the perception which
happens to come to us through hearing and sight. But let us be
patient with the argument that the pleasant that comes through these
is beautiful, without bringing the issue of the laws into the center.
But if this person whom I'm speaking of, or anyone else, should ask
us, "Why indeed, Hippias and Socrates, have you divided up the
pleasant, defining as beautiful the sort that is pleasant in the way that
you say but claiming that the pleasant with respect to the other
perceptions—of food and drink and sex and all the rest of this sort—
is not beautiful? Or do you assert that they are not even pleasant and
that pleasures do not exist at all in such things or in anything other
than in seeing and hearing?" What shall we assert, Hippias?

HIP.: By all means, Socrates, we shall surely assert that in the other
things too there are very great pleasures.

SOC.: "Then why," he will say, "although they too are pleasures no
less than those, are you taking away this name and depriving them of
being beautiful?" "Because," we shall say, "there is no one who
would not laugh at us if we should assert that it is not pleasant to eat
but beautiful and that it is not pleasant to smell something pleasant
but beautiful. And as for sex, presumably everyone would do battle
with us and maintain that it is most pleasant but that if someone
engages in it, he must do it in such a way that no one see, since it is
most ugly to be seen." If we say these things, Hippias, perhaps he
would say, "I too understand that for some time you have been
ashamed to assert that these pleasures are beautiful because they do

---

[38]Some MSS omit the name of Socrates. According to this reading, Socrates refers
to himself simply as "the son of Sophroniscus." For other references to Socrates as
son of Sophroniscus, see *Alcibiades I* 131e; *Laches* 180d, 181a; *Euthydemus* 297e, 298b.

b not seem so to human beings. But I was asking not what seems to the many to be beautiful but what is so." We shall say, I suppose, what we proposed. "That part of the pleasant which comes into being in relation to sight and hearing, we assert is beautiful." But can you make some further use of the argument, or shall we say something else, Hippias?

HIP.: Considering what has been said, Socrates, it is necessary to say nothing else but this.

c soc.: "You speak beautifully," he will say. "Then if the pleasant through sight and hearing is beautiful, isn't it clear that whatever pleasant thing does not happen to be this would not be beautiful?" Shall we agree?

HIP.: Yes.

soc.: "Then," he will say, "is the pleasant through sight pleasant through sight and hearing, or is the pleasant through hearing pleasant through hearing and through sight?" "In no way," we shall say, "would that which is through either one be through both. For you seem to us to be saying this. But we were saying that not only is each of these pleasant things itself by itself beautiful but also both are." Shall we not answer in this way?

HIP.: Certainly.

d soc.: "Then," he will say, "is any pleasant thing different from any other pleasant thing in being pleasant—not insofar as any pleasure is greater or smaller or more or less, but different in this very respect, that one of the pleasures is a pleasure and another not a pleasure?" It doesn't seem so to us at least, does it?

HIP.: No, it does not seem so.

soc.: "Then," he will say, "it is for some other reason than that they are pleasures, isn't it, that you preferred these pleasures to the other

e pleasures? You were seeing some such thing as this in the case of both—namely, that they have something different from the others—and this is what you are looking to when you say that they are beautiful, isn't it? For presumably the pleasure through sight is not beautiful because it is through sight, since if this were the cause of its being beautiful, the other, that through hearing, would never be beautiful. Surely the pleasure through hearing is not a pleasure through sight." Shall we say, "What you say is true"?

HIP.: Yes, we shall say so.

300a soc.: "Nor, on the other hand, does the pleasure through hearing happen to be beautiful because it is through hearing. For in that case, again, the pleasure through sight would never be beautiful. Surely the pleasure through sight is not a pleasure through hearing." Shall we assert, Hippias, that in saying this, the man says what is true?

HIP.: It's true.

SOC.: "Nonetheless, both are beautiful, as you assert." We do assert it, don't we?

HIP.: We do.

b SOC.: "So they have something the same which makes them be beautiful, something in common which exists for both of them in common and for each in particular.[39] For otherwise presumably they would not both and each be beautiful." Answer me as you would him.

HIP.: I answer, it seems to me too to hold as you say.

SOC.: If then both these pleasures are affected in some way, but each one is not, it would not be by this being affected at least that they are beautiful.

HIP.: How could it be, Socrates, that, though neither is affected by any one at all of the things that are, both are affected by that by which neither is affected?

c SOC.: It doesn't seem to you that this could be?

HIP.: If it could, I would be very inexperienced both in the nature of these things and in the speaking of the present arguments.

SOC.: Pleasantly spoken, Hippias. But I probably seem to see something that holds so in just the way that you assert is impossible, and yet I see nothing.

HIP.: It's not that you "probably" are seeing amiss, Socrates, but that you actually are.

SOC.: And yet many such things are appearing before my soul, but I
d distrust them because they make themselves apparent not to you, a man who has earned the most money for wisdom among our contemporaries, but rather to me, who have never earned anything. And I am pondering, my comrade, whether you are playing with me and intentionally deceiving me, because so many things are appearing so forcefully to me.

HIP.: No one, Socrates, will know more beautifully than you whether I am playing or not if you attempt to say what these things are that are appearing before you. For it will be apparent that there is nothing

[39]"In particular" translates the Greek adjective *idios,* which elsewhere is translated as "private," with the exception of the related adjective *idiōtikos;* see note on 287a.

in what you say, because you'll never find that we both are affected by that by which neither I nor you is affected.

e   SOC.: How do you mean, Hippias? Perhaps there is something in what you are saying, and I do not understand. But hear more plainly what I wish to say. For it appears to me to be possible for both of us to be affected in a way that I by myself neither undergo nor am and that you in turn are not either. But on the other hand, there are other states of being affected that both of us are, and yet neither of us is them.[40]

HIP.: Again, Socrates, you are like someone whose answers are even greater marvels than your earlier answers. For consider, if both of us are just, wouldn't each of us also be just? Or if each is unjust, wouldn't

301a   both be so too? Or if both are healthy, wouldn't each be so too? Or if each of us were at all weary or wounded or beaten or affected in any other way, wouldn't both of us also be affected in this way? Furthermore, if both of us happened to be golden or silver or ivory or, if you wish, noble or wise or honored or old or young or whatever else you wish that is found among human beings, wouldn't there be a great necessity that each of us also be this?

b   SOC.: By all means, of course.

HIP.: Yes, but you, Socrates, do not consider the wholes of things, and neither do those with whom you are accustomed to converse, but you test the beautiful by setting it apart and by cutting up in the arguments each of the things that are. Because of this you do not notice the naturally large and continuous bodies of being.[41] And you have failed now to notice this to such an extent that you suppose there is something, either being affected or being,[42] which exists in relation

---

[40]This passage involves an unusual Greek idiom, "to be affected by something so as to be that thing" (peponthenai einai; see also 302a and c). More literally translated, the passage reads, "For it appears to me to be possible for both of us to be affected by an affection that I am not affected by so as to be (it), nor am I (it), and neither are you. But on the other hand, there are other affections that both of us are affected by so as to be (them), and yet neither of us is (them)."

[41]In this sentence Hippias appears to be saying that, by nature, being is composed of large and indivisible bodies. The entire passage, however, is in dispute. For further comment, see the introduction. The word "you" in this sentence is plural, as it is in "you test" in the preceding sentence.

[42]The Greek for the state of being affected is pathos and for "being" is ousia. Pathos (except at 285c1) and ousia are so translated in all their occurrences in this dialogue. They could also be rendered by "accident" and "essence." They appear as a pair in one other place in the dialogues at Euthyphro 11a.

c to these "boths" together but not in relation to "each," or again, that exists in relation to "each" but not in relation to "both." So illogical is your condition, and so unreflective and naive and unintelligent!

SOC.: Our affairs, Hippias, accord not with what one wishes, as humans say on occasion, speaking proverbially, but with the power one has. But you help us by always admonishing us. Shall I show you still further how naive our condition was just now, before we were admonished by you about these things? Shall I tell you what our

d thoughts were concerning them or not?

HIP.: You will be speaking to one who knows, Socrates. For I know the condition of each person who is concerned with arguments. Nonetheless, if it is more pleasant to you in any way, speak.

SOC.: Well, it is indeed more pleasant. For before you said these things, best of men, we were so silly as to hold the opinion concerning me and you that each of us is one but that both of us are not what each of us is—for we are not one but two—so naive were we. But by

e now we have been retaught by you that, if both of us are two, it is also necessary that each of us be two, and if each is one, it is also necessary that both be one. For by the continuous account of being, according to Hippias, it cannot be otherwise: whatever both are, each is too, and what each is, both are. Now that I have been persuaded by you, this is my position. However, Hippias, remind me of something first. Are we one, I and you, or are you two and I two?

HIP.: What are you saying, Socrates?

SOC.: The very thing that I am saying. For I am afraid that you are

302a plainly saying that you are angry with me, since in your opinion there is something in what you are saying. Still, tell me something further. Isn't each of us one and affected so as to be one?

HIP.: Certainly.

SOC.: Then, if one, each of us would also be odd in number. Or don't you consider one to be an odd number?

HIP.: I do.

SOC.: So are both of us also odd, being two?

HIP.: That could not be, Socrates.

SOC.: Rather, both of us are even, aren't we?

HIP.: Certainly.

b SOC.: Then just because both of us are even, each of us is not also even for this reason, is he?

HIP.: Of course not.

SOC.: So there is not every necessity, as you were saying just now, that whatever both of us are, each also is, and whatever each is, both also are.

HIP.: Not in these respects, at least, but in those which I was speaking of earlier.

SOC.: These are enough, Hippias. For even these content me, since it is apparent that some things are so, while others are not so. For I was also saying, if you remember where this argument started, that plea-
c sures through sight and hearing were beautiful not by that thing by which each of them happened to be so affected as to be, but not both, or both but not each, but by that by which both and each were affected. I said so because you conceded that they both and each are beautiful. For this reason I was supposing that, if both are beautiful, they must be beautiful by that being which accompanies them both and not by that which is absent in them taken separately. And I still suppose so now. But tell me, as though from the beginning, if plea-
d sure through sight and that through hearing are both and each beautiful, does not that which makes them beautiful accompany not only both of them but also each?

HIP.: Certainly.

SOC.: Then would they be beautiful because each and both are pleasure? Or because of this would all the other pleasures also be beautiful no less than these? For it became apparent that they were pleasures no less, if you remember.

HIP.: I remember.

e SOC.: Instead, because they are through sight and hearing, it was said that they are beautiful.

HIP.: Yes, it was so said.

SOC.: Consider if what I am saying is true. For it was said, as I remember, that the pleasant is beautiful—not all of it but that which is through sight and hearing.

HIP.: True.

SOC.: Then does not this state of being affected accompany both of the senses but not each? For presumably each of them, as was said previously, is not through both, but both are through both, and each is not. Is this so?

HIP.: It is.

303a SOC.: Then, at any rate, it is not by that which does not accompany each that each of them is beautiful, for "both" does not accompany each, so that it is possible according to the hypothesis to assert that they both are beautiful, but it is not possible to assert that each is. Or how shall we say it? Isn't this necessary?

HIP.: It appears so.

SOC.: Then are we to assert that both are beautiful, and yet assert that each is not?

HIP.: Yes, for what prevents us?

SOC.: The following seems to me, my friend, to prevent us: that there were for us presumably some things that pertained to individual things in such a way that if they pertained to both, they also did to each, and if to each, also to both—all those things which you went through. Yes?

HIP.: Yes.

SOC.: But not those which I went through, among which were "each" itself and "both." Is this so?

HIP.: It is.

b SOC.: Then, Hippias, of which sort does the beautiful seem to you to be? Is it the sort which you were speaking about—if I am strong and you are, we both are too, and if I am just and you are, we both are too, and if both, also each, and similarly, if I am beautiful and you are, we both are too, and if both, also each? Or does nothing prevent the beautiful from being of the other sort, such as when certain composites are even in number, their components[43] are each perhaps odd, perhaps even, or again when the components are each irrational,

c the composites are perhaps rational, perhaps irrational, and countless other such things which I asserted were also appearing before me? Among which of these two sorts do you set the beautiful? Or is what has become apparent to me concerning it also apparent to you? For it seems to me to be very illogical that we both are beautiful but not each, or each is, but not both, or anything else of this sort. Do you choose in this way, as I do, or in that way?

HIP.: In this way, Socrates.

d SOC.: You do well, Hippias, so that we may also be released from more searching. For if the beautiful is among these things, the pleasant through sight and hearing would no longer be beautiful, because the expression "through sight and hearing" makes both beautiful but not each. But this was impossible, as I and you agree, Hippias.

HIP.: Yes, we agree.

---

[43]For "composites" the Greek literally reads "both's," i.e., the class of all pairs, and for "components" reads "each's," i.e., the class of all members of pairs.

SOC.: So it is impossible that the pleasant through sight and hearing be beautiful since, in becoming beautiful, it presents one of the things that are impossible.

HIP.: This is so.

SOC.: "Tell me, then, again," he will say, "from the beginning, since

e you have missed it entirely. What do you assert that this 'beautiful' is, the one that pertains to both of the pleasures and on account of which you honored these pleasures before the others and named them beautiful?" It seems to me to be necessary, Hippias, to say that these are the most harmless of the pleasures and the best, both and each. Or have you anything else to say by which they differ from the others?

HIP.: Not at all. For, really, they are best.

SOC.: "So this," he will say, "is what you say the beautiful is, helpful pleasure?" We seem likely to, I shall say. And you?

HIP.: I, too.

SOC.: "Then isn't that which does the good helpful," he will say, "but just now that which does and that which is done appeared different, and hasn't your argument arrived at the earlier argument?

304a For the good would not be beautiful nor the beautiful good, if each of them is something else than the other." By all means, we shall say, Hippias, if we think soundly. For presumably it is not sanctioned not to agree with one who speaks correctly.

HIP.: But, Socrates, what do you suppose all these things together are? They are scrapings and clippings of speeches, as I was just saying, divided up into bits. But the alternative is both beautiful and worth much—to be able to compose a speech well and beautifully in

b a law court or council chamber or in any other ruling group to which the speech is addressed and to go away having persuaded them and taking off not the littlest but the largest of the prizes, the salvation of oneself and one's money and friends. So one ought to cling to these things, bidding good-bye to those little speeches, in order that one not seem to be exceedingly unintelligent by engaging in babblings and drivel, as we were just now.

SOC.: Hippias, my friend, you are blessed because you know what a

c human being ought to pursue, and you have pursued it ably, as you assert. But some daemonic fate, as seems likely, has taken hold of me so that I vacillate[44] and am always in perplexity, and by exhibiting

---

[44]Compare the reference to "vacillation" at the end of the *Lesser Hippias,* and note 16 to the translation of that dialogue.

this perplexity of mine to you wise ones, I am in turn bespattered by you in speech whenever I exhibit it. For you people say of me the very things that you too are saying now, that I practice things that are silly and little and worth nothing. Yet whenever I have been persuaded by you people and say just what you do—that it is much the best to be able to succeed in the courtroom or in any other assembly by composing a speech well and beautifully—then I am called all sorts of bad things by some others here and by this fellow who always refutes me. For he happens to be very closely related and to live in the same house. Consequently, whenever I go home into my own house and he hears me saying these things, he asks me if I am not ashamed at daring to converse about beautiful pursuits when I am so manifestly refuted concerning the beautiful because I do not even know what it itself is. "And yet how will you know," he says, "whether anyone composes a speech beautifully or not, or any other activity whatsoever, if you do not recognize the beautiful? And when this is your condition, do you suppose it is better for you to live rather than to be dead?" The result indeed for me is, as I say, to be reproached and to be badly spoken of by you people and badly by him. Nonetheless, perhaps it is necessary to endure all these things, for it is not strange if it would help me. So, Hippias, I seem to myself to have been helped by my association with both of you. For I seem to myself to know what the proverb means that says, "The beautiful things are difficult."[45]

[45]This proverb appears elsewhere in Plato in the *Republic* (435c, 497d) and in the *Cratylus* (384a–b). According to a scholium on this passage in the *Greater Hippias,* the proverb was originally Solon's response to the reason that Pittacus gave for his not wishing to continue as tyrant of Mytilene. His reason was that "it is difficult to remain good." For a discussion of Pittacus' statement, see *Protagoras* 339–46.

Introduction to the
Greater Hippias

DAVID R. SWEET

Hippias of Elis was among the half dozen most influential Greek sophists, yet the surviving information about him comes principally from three Platonic dialogues, the *Protagoras,* the *Greater Hippias,* and the *Lesser Hippias,*[1] and from one passage in Xenophon's *Memorabilia.*[2] He was evidently a man who considered the aim of life to be self-sufficiency,[3] and to this end he accumulated as many skills as possible. The skill he seems to have prized above all, however, was his ability at speaking. Through it, he says in the *Greater Hippias* (282e), he made more money than any other two sophists, and as the dialogue begins, he claims that he is habitually chosen as envoy by his city and has now come again to Athens in this capacity because he is the most able of the Elians as a judge and reporter of speeches.

At the outset of the dialogue Socrates remarks that Hippias is visiting Athens after a long absence. During this absence he has frequently been to Elis' military ally, Sparta. Now he returns to Athens on public business for Elis, perhaps to negotiate the treaty of alliance with Athens that was concluded in 420. Thus the dialogue is set against the background of the Peloponnesian War and its diplomatic maneuverings.

The participants in the dialogue are Socrates and Hippias, and the principal subject of their conversation is "the beautiful," but this subject arises explicitly only after a rather long introduction (281a–

[1]Hippias is also mentioned in the *Apology* (19e) in association with Gorgias and Prodicus.
[2]IV 4.5–25. See also *Symposium* IV 62.
[3]See Diels-Kranz, *Die Fragmente der Vorsokratiker,* A.1.

286c). The rest of the dialogue is divided into six definitions, three by Hippias, then three by Socrates. Hippias and Socrates, however, are in a sense not alone. At the point that they raise the question of beauty, a third person joins them. This person is a part of Socrates himself but a part that he presents to Hippias as other than himself. He says that Hippias would not recognize this person's name (290e), and this person refers to Hippias as "stranger" (287d) or "stranger from Elis" (287c, 292e). The two speak to each other entirely through Socrates. As strangers to each other they are potential enemies, and in fact hostility does develop between them during the conversation, but it does so through Socrates, who plays the role of mediator as well as that of messenger. The difference between Hippias and the unnamed person can be understood as a difference between opinion and truth. When Hippias comes to giving his definitions, he supports them by saying that they will "seem so" to everyone (288a) or are what "we all know" (289e) or apply "always, for everyone and everywhere" (291d). The other person, however, is concerned with nothing but the truth (288d). He tells Socrates and Hippias not to be ashamed to say that pleasures are "beautiful because they do not seem so to human beings" (299a), and he reminds them that they are not being asked "what seems to the many to be beautiful, but what is so" (299b). The difference between the two also concerns being or the difference between appearing and being.

These issues of opinion and truth, and the apparent and the real, are closely associated in the Platonic dialogues with the question of the relation between sophistic and philosophic inquiry. It is therefore understandable that Socrates should discuss such issues with a sophist. Because of the kind of sophist that Hippias is, however—one who is so inextricably located among appearances—the *Greater Hippias* deals with these issues rather indirectly and for more explicit treatment of them points to other dialogues, especially the *Theaetetus* and the *Sophist*. Hippias' attributes, however, in conjunction with those of the unnamed person, reveal dramatically and dialectically various ways in which one may understand these issues in relation to beauty.

Dramatically, Hippias is characterized by beautiful "looks," specifically his beautiful shoes (291a) and his garb in general (see *Lesser Hippias* 368b–c), and by beautiful speeches, both his exhibition speech on beautiful pursuits and his beautifully composed judicial and probouleutic speeches, which he mentions at the end of the dialogue

(304a–b). And he is characterized by the very way Socrates first addresses him, in the nominative rather than in the much more usual vocative, as if he were a name and a title himself, "Hippias, the beautiful and wise."[4] But the person with the unknown name has no looks at all, or at least he is invisible to Hippias, and his speech— which is difficult and outlandish (292c) and heavily abusive—seems finally to Hippias to be so fragmentary as to be worthless (300d). Temperamentally, also, they differ in that Hippias is facile and full of answers (286e, 287b), certain that on his own he could easily find beauty (295a, 297e), and willing to say something that seems false to him in the hope that it will not be noticed (298b).[5] In contrast, the nameless person accepts nothing easily (289e). He is captious (290e), unyielding (289e), and not elegant but vulgar (288d), and therefore to Hippias he seems uneducated (288d) and ignorant (290e).

Dialectically, the differences in character are reflected in the course of the conversation, a course that proceeds from the easy to the difficult, from speaking beautifully to speaking precisely, from the visible, or from the looks of things, to the invisible, or to the forms of things, that is to say, from three accounts of beautiful things to three accounts of the beautiful. This sequence, however, does not lead to any clear reconciliation of the opposed parties. At the end there has been no apparent change in the positions of Hippias and the unnamed person. The only apparent change is in Socrates who maintains that he has been helped by his association with the two other participants and that he now seems to himself to know in what sense "the beautiful things are difficult." What connections there are between the disparate elements of the dialogue must therefore be within him. He imitates Hippias in that he represents Hippias' arguments to that nameless side of himself (292d–e), and he imitates that side of himself in presenting it to Hippias (287a, 292c). In the terms developed later in the dialogue, Socrates is a composite, neither one nor the other but both together.

The introduction is in two sections. The first (281a–283b) discusses the activity of sophists and compares them with the men of the past

---

[4]No other dialogue begins with a proper name in the nominative, and no person addressed in the first sentence of any dialogue is described as fully or as flatteringly as Hippias is. Contrast the rude beginning of the *Lesser Hippias* where Eudicus says, "You, why are you silent, Socrates?"

[5]See also 285b (he does not oppose arguments if he thinks they are in his interest) and 287e ("if the truth must be said").

who were famous for their wisdom. The second (283b–286c) discusses Hippias' activity as a sophist in general and at Sparta in particular. Socrates starts by proposing a definition of the wise and perfect man. Such a man combines the private and the public; on the one hand, he acts in his own interest, earning money by helping the youth (how he helps them is not said). On the other hand, he acts in the public interest by benefiting his city. How he does so, again, is not said, but in return he receives fame. Hippias assumes that modern sophists can effect this combination, although the men of the past could not.[6] Apparently, therefore, there has been progress, whether in power (281d), prudence (*phronesis,* 281d), or some form of wisdom (*sophia,* 281c, d) or, as Socrates suggests, in art or skill (*techne,* 282b). In gathering evidence that there has been such progress, Socrates describes the activities of Gorgias and Prodicus. Yet their activities are not said to be the same as those of the wise and perfect man. Gorgias and Prodicus make money privately by giving exhibition speeches and associating with the youth—not necessarily therefore by helping them. Publicly they win repute either by seeming to speak well (Gorgias) or by simply speaking before the Council (Prodicus)— not necessarily therefore by benefiting their cities. In contrast to them the ancients, as exemplified by Anaxagoras, were indifferent to money (283a), were unwilling to exhibit their wisdom before all sorts of people (282c–d), and apparently refrained from politics (281c). The ancients therefore avoided the general public and neglected their own private interests. They did not, however, neglect the public interest and avoid the private good. They were famous for their sagacity in giving advice to their cities,[7] and they cultivated the private good in the sense of knowledge of the sort that they would not or could not make public. The sophists, in contrast, convert the public into the private, they capitalize on their reputations and turn public sentiment into personal wealth, and they publish their knowledge. Money is a beautiful proof of this ability of theirs. It shows in what sense they can reduce the multiplicity of opinion to a single denomination that has value in any city, namely gold.[8] The second section of the intro-

[6]Hippias replaces Socrates' "public" with the word "common" (*koinon*). This is the term that figures in the later discussion of "the beautiful" as a common entity in relation to many beautiful things.

[7]For the political activities of Bias and Pittacus, see note 2 to the text of the dialogue.

[8]See Hippias' second definition of the beautiful.

344   David R. Sweet

duction is a demonstration that Hippias cannot always convert opinion into money. It therefore calls into question his ability to combine
the private and the public and does so by raising more explicitly the
questions of what sorts of knowledge and skills he possesses and what
sorts of help he gives, if any. The discussion develops a series of
contrasts that are part of the tension between the private and the
public and are based on the difference between precise speech and
customary speech. Those who know the truth speak precisely; those
who do not know it, and they are the many, are not accustomed to
use words precisely. This difference is reflected in the distinction
between precise or scientific knowledge and customary or traditional
knowledge. Examples of the former are astronomy, geometry, and
mathematical calculation. Examples of the latter are genealogy (that
of heroes and humans), archaeology (the ancient things, including the
founding of cities), and mythology (story telling). These two sorts of
knowledge imply that there is also a distinction between knowing
precisely and knowing beautifully.[9] What this list reveals, therefore,
is a possible conflict between the true and the beautiful. The claim to
be able to combine private and public must also involve the ability to
know and to speak both truly and beautifully. One might regard this
as the combination of mathematics and mythology. When Socrates
develops the two sides of the problem in relation to Hippias, however, he says that Hippias knows only one sort of thing precisely,
namely how to distinguish what pertains to the power of letters,
syllables, rhythms, and harmonies (285c–d). Hippias knows precisely
how to speak beautifully. Otherwise, even in the case of astronomy
(285b–c), Socrates speaks only of his knowing beautifully. The danger is that knowing beautifully will mean knowing how to say conventional or customary things beautifully. This Hippias does at Sparta. There the tension between the true and the beautiful appears as the
difference between the helpful, which is the lawful in the precise
sense, and the lawful in the customary sense. This latter kind of law
Hippias reinforces with his beautiful speech on "very many things
that are lawful and altogether beautiful" (286b). In the introduction,
then, "beautiful" appears as a kind of deception and as separate from
"helpful" in the precise sense. In what follows, one of the problems is
whether or not it can be connected with "true" and "good."

---

[9]See Socrates' responses at 282b ("You do beautifully in your use of terms and in
your thinking, it seems to me") and at 287d ("Well, to be sure, clearly you know
more beautifully").

When Hippias' speech on many lawful and beautiful pursuits has reminded Socrates of "beautiful," Socrates introduces the unnamed person, who asks a sequence of questions, regarding justice, wisdom, the good, and the beautiful, which have the form "aren't . . . all beautiful things beautiful by the beautiful . . . and by it as something that exists?" (287c–d). These questions raise three issues: whether or not many things can be understood in terms of one, what the causal relation between those many and the one is, and what the status of the one is with respect to being. Hippias shows that he thinks the one is simply one among many, that they are all alike beings, and that they could be nothing else but beings (287d). In response he points to one of them, and although he was asked about "the beautiful," his definition is simply that "a beautiful maiden is beautiful" (287e). What he is doing becomes somewhat clearer at the end of the dialogue when he chastises Socrates for not noticing "the naturally large and continuous bodies of being" (301b). Hippias is a materialist. For him the only things in being are bodies. Beauty is any beautiful thing.

The definition is tested by comparing beautiful maiden with beautiful mare, beautiful lyre, and beautiful pot. In each case Socrates imitates Hippias in that he too includes a form of the predicate in the subject. All cases are affirmed to be "beautiful" though very reluctantly by Hippias in the case of the pot. He thinks that as a whole it is not beautiful compared to other beautiful things. As he explains at the end of the dialogue, Socrates does not consider "the wholes of things" (301b). Hippias therefore is the first to raise the question of what "wholes" are, and he starts the process of comparing these wholes with each other. The difficulty for him arises when the gods are introduced. In comparison with them the most beautiful maiden will appear ugly (289b).

This first attempt at a definition presents "beautiful" as a quality that must be understood in close conjunction with an object. Within a class of objects that are all the same, whether all maidens, or pots, or gods, "beautiful" apparently does not present itself as a problem. When the classes of objects differ, however, comparisons among them must be made, and then even the superlative, "most beautiful," may appear "ugly." The quality itself seems to change as it changes class. These different classes are likely to be more significant "wholes" than the individual objects that Hippias identifies as wholes. Understanding classes will then be part of the problem of understanding beauty. In particular it will be necessary to understand the most beautiful class, in this case, the class of the gods. In the light of the gods, however, all lesser beautiful things will appear ugly. Lesser beautiful things will therefore appear beautiful only when the viewer of them looks away from what is above them. Knowledge of the most beautiful, the gods, works against seeing other less beautiful things. On the other hand, the power of a single beautiful thing tends to make the viewer forget other, more beautiful things. Beauty has the power to highlight the particular and to lend it a charm and an apparent perfection that works against seeing "the beautiful" beyond it. In this respect "beautiful" is false.

Hippias' second definition is set up for him by the nameless person who suggests that "the beautiful itself" is that "by which all other things are adorned and appear beautiful whenever this form becomes present to them" (or, more literally, "comes into being beside or on the surface of them," 289d). Hippias repeats this statement with several exceptions: he drops out "itself" and "form," he adds "made to" appear, and he specifies "beautiful objects" (or, more literally, "beautiful possessions"). Then he says that "the beautiful . . . is nothing other than gold," and his proof is that it will make a thing appear beautiful even if that thing appeared ugly before. Now it seems that only gold *is* beautiful; everything else only *appears* so when gold becomes present. Before, the attribute "beautiful" turned out to be less important than the substance (god, man, ape) in determining the quality of a thing's beauty. Now the attribute has become a kind of substance itself. It can even make other things change their appearance from ugly to beautiful, whereas, before, the beautiful gods only changed the appearance of other things from beautiful to ugly. Hippias therefore seems to be trying to compensate for the weaknesses of his previous definition.

Previously, he treated "the beautiful" as if it were "beautiful thing," and he ran into difficulties because of the relativity of adjectives to the nouns they qualify. Now, perhaps because of the notions implicit in the terms "become present beside" and "be adorned," he seems to be separating "beautiful" from "beautiful thing" in an effort to make "beautiful" a thing itself. If, before, it was an adjective, now it is a noun, "gold." Gold has the virtue of possessing a value and an existence independent of the things that are beautified by it. If, before, things as wholes (god, maidens, pots) determined the value of beauty, now beauty (gold) will determine the value of things. But it turns out that the value of things may be determined by the presence of nouns other than "gold" without their becoming any the less beautiful. Through the examples of ivory and stone, nouns are proven to be as relative as adjectives. If nouns are relative to adjectives and vice versa, if substance and attribute are interdependent, the possibility arises that beauty is the relationship between them. Hippias himself supplies the word for this relationship: "fitting." Thereupon, the unnamed person introduces the fig-wood ladle and, by the argument that "the fitting is more beautiful than the not fitting," proves that fig wood on occasion is fitting and more beautiful than gold. The definition has been overturned but not without advancing the inquiry into "the beautiful." Perhaps after all, "the beautiful" will be somewhat like gold insofar as gold is a substance that is not susceptible to deterioration and does not change its essential character no matter what it adorns. Furthermore, this definition has also raised the possibility that something could both *be* the beautiful itself and also make other things *appear* beautiful when it becomes present in them.

Hippias himself establishes the criteria for his third definition. His previous two have been refuted because "beautiful maiden" and "gold" have both been made to appear ugly under certain conditions. Therefore Hippias confronts the issue of appearance and relativity directly. He supposes that Socrates is asking about the beautiful "that will never appear ugly to anyone anywhere" (291d). Socrates tells him that he comprehends beautifully, and Hippias then proceeds to define "most beautiful" as a list of qualities characterizing human life. The qualities are described in Greek in a series of participles culminating in an infinitive, "to be beautifully and magnificently buried by one's own offspring" (291d–e). Whereas, before, he spoke first of "beautiful" as an attribute, then of "the beautiful" as a substance, now he speaks of "most beautiful" for a man in terms of verbs. Yet the description is of a peculiarly static beauty. The emphasis is on physical well-being, on honoring and being honored, but there is no mention of the soul or of what the virtues of such a man should be, neither that of courage, the most Spartan beauty, nor that of wisdom, the virtue Hippias prides himself on. And the only "beautiful pursuit" the man is said to engage in actively is the beautiful burial of his parents. The final act of his life, in which he is only passive, does indeed produce a "whole," namely an entire life, but it views the whole from the perspective of death, that is to say, from the perspective of not-being. Hippias' emphasis, however, upon the verb and upon this particular verb illuminates an aspect of the problem of beauty that the nameless person also emphasizes in his response. He restates as the aim of their search "the beautiful itself which *inheres* in everything to which it *becomes* present such that that thing *is* beautiful" (292c–d), and he constructs an argument that shows the difficulty of introducing the gods into time. The difficulty in part lies in how one is to understand the relation of the deathless beings to generation. How do they cause images of themselves to come into being? This question of causation arises again during Socrates' second definition. The discussion here, however, views the question from the opposite perspective. How is one to understand the relation of generated beings to the gods? This case may be regarded as an instance of the general problem of knowing. Is "knowing" in some sense the reverse of "becoming" (i.e., does knowing follow the images back upward into being)? These questions are suggested by the images brought forward by the argument. Introduction of the gods alone would have been enough to refute Hippias' definition. The nameless person, however, also adds the distinction between heroes born of gods and those not born of gods. This distinction and the reiteration of the problem of the coincidence of being and becoming (293c) occur just as the dialogue is about to proceed from Hippias' definitions to Socrates', from examples to principles, from a multiplicity of names of beautiful things to the unity of a class. Perhaps Socrates and Hippias are these two types of heroes, one with some divine component, the other wholly mortal.[10] Socrates, in any case, leads the way between the two realms, and as a sign that he is about to do so, the unnamed person now addresses him as "O daemonic Socrates" (293d).[11] And now for the first time the word "nature" appears (*physis,* 293e).

Hippias' three definitions have suggested the possibility of understanding "beautiful" as a relation, first, between attribute and substance, between "beautiful" and "maiden," such that she can both appear and not appear beautiful, and, second, between the phenomena and a form, between accidents and essence, such that "beautiful" can appear and "the beautiful" be. Among the forms themselves, one supposes that beauty may also exist as a relation in a third

---

[10]Hippias is likened by Socrates in the *Protagoras* (315b–c) to the mortal part of Heracles whom Odysseus sees in Hades (*Odyssey* XI 601). Seth Benardete makes this observation in an interpretation of the *Greater Hippias* that has influenced the present introduction at many points (*The Being of the Beautiful* [Chicago, 1984], p. xxiii).

[11]See the definition of a *daemon* in the *Symposium* (202e–203a).

sense. Socrates turns to this possibility in his last two definitions. Hippias' third definition, especially, also implied the problem of the relation between the knower and the thing known. Knowing seems to be a kind of heroic project connecting the world of appearances with the beings themselves. In the course of Socrates' second definition, wisdom is identified as a power and is said to be most beautiful (296a). The most beautiful life might then be that devoted to knowing the most beautiful things, the class of gods, as they seemed to be during Hippias' first definition. Hippias' wisdom, however, cannot encompass the high. His definitions are overturned by gods, a statue of a god, and heroes born of gods. Nor can his wisdom encompass the low. He is loath even to speak of pots and fig-wood ladles. He has difficulty with the useful and is more comfortable with the superficially or conventionally appealing, that is, with things that look beautiful. His wisdom is therefore suspect as to its utility and is confined to the middle. Nonetheless he reveals that beauty, too, is somehow intermediate between appeal and utility, and he is the one who first mentions the concept "fitting" (290c), which supplies the bridge between the two halves of the dialogue.

Socrates' first definition, that "the fitting . . . happens to be the beautiful" (293e), is examined in terms of whether the fitting makes each of the things in which it becomes present *appear* beautiful or *be* beautiful or neither (294a). Hippias wants it to be both, and repeatedly Socrates forces him to choose one or the other (294a, c, e). When pressed, Hippias opts for appearances, and therefore, insofar as Socrates insists on defining the beautiful in terms of being, the definition must fail. But when Socrates draws the conclusion to the argument, he suggests that the issue of being and appearing is still unresolved. He says that he and Hippias have "failed to recognize whatever the beautiful is now that the fitting has *appeared* as *being* something other than beautiful" (294e). The question remains of how one is to understand the appearance or the manifestation of being. Does beauty play a role in the way in which being comes to light? Socrates has defeated the definition by insisting on separating the powers that are responsible for appearing and for being. The possibility remains open, however, that there are situations in which this separation is overcome.

Hippias' contribution to the defeat of the definition again indicates how hard it is to disentangle beauty from appearances. Beauty may be different from "good" in this very respect. Men aim at the good in the sense of the real or the true good, and they do not wish to be deceived about what the real good is, although as Socrates points out in this dialogue, they are generally deceived about it (296c). Nonetheless, if they are corrected, they abandon their former opinions about the good and adopt those that they presume to be truer (see *Republic* 505d). But they do not act the same way in regard to beauty. They do not necessarily abandon their desire for beautiful things if these are shown to be only apparently beautiful. An example of such a thing would be poetry, which, despite Socrates' critique of it as "phantastic," continued to hold an attraction for him (*Republic*, particularly 598b, 599a). This first definition, then, is successful at least in that it suggests how elusive beauty is and how it constantly retreats into the attractiveness of the phenomena themselves.

The definition also captures what one may call the three-sided character of beauty because of the three senses contained within the Greek word for "fitting," *prepon*. It is originally a verb, "to be fitting," which in a participial form serves as an adjective or a noun, and it may refer, first, to the fact that two things are related to each other even to the point of resembling each other. Second, it refers to the adaptability of a thing to a purpose or function, that is, it suggests "useful." And third, it may refer to the looks, or occasionally to the sound, of a thing and mean "clear" or "conspicuous." All senses of the word are relevant to Socrates' definitions. The problem of resemblances is part of his third definition as well as of his first insofar as resemblances involve the question of appearing and being. He addresses the problem of the relation of beauty to utility in his second definition. In his third he examines beauty in terms of the pleasure that comes through the perceptions of sight and hearing. Perhaps the versatility of the "fitting" is responsible for Socrates' disappointment (294e) when Hippias prevents them from accepting it by associating it exclusively with "appears" and not with "is." Perhaps Socrates is disappointed because "the fitting" is a "common thing" (*koinon*), which suggests the composite nature of beauty as suspended between appearing and being, or between the good and the pleasant. "The fitting is the beautiful" is, in any case, the only definition in the dialogue that is left unrefuted.

Socrates begins his second definition by cautioning Hippias to apply his mind and then says that he was "thinking," or more literally, that he was "using the action of the mind in itself" (*ennooumenos*, 295c). What he was thinking is that eyes are beautiful if they have the power to see, and this thought leads him to enumerate a list of useful things on the basis of which he proposes that "the useful, more than anything else, happens to be beautiful" (295e). The example of eyes is curious in that the ordinary opinion about beautiful eyes is that they are beautiful to look at (290a–c). The example is perhaps designed to correct the self-centeredness of beauty and the opinion that beautiful things do not have to do anything but simply be there. Beautiful things may give the impression that they are perfect. Hippias seems susceptible to having this impression about himself, which no doubt accounts for his complacency. Therefore it is necessary to attach beauty to something beyond it. For this purpose Socrates suggests the useful. The length of his list of examples may indicate the difficulty involved in moving phenomenal beauty beyond itself. Certainly Hippias himself has been loath to associate beauty with mere instrumentality, and he replies to the definition based on that list simply that it is correct. But when Socrates relates use to power, Hippias heartily agrees as he supplies the proof that in politics and in one's own city the powerful is most beautiful of all (296a). For Hippias, however, this power is again directed to self-interest understood as "the salvation of oneself and one's money and friends" (304b). Therefore, Socrates first changes Hippias' proof by asserting that if power is beautiful, wisdom is most beautiful of all. This step can be drawn by inference from the fact that the definition started in the mind, but wisdom is especially difficult in that it combines interest in other with interest in self. Socrates' subsequent fear (296a) may be based on his recognition that Hippias' wisdom is finally wisdom for oneself. Therefore he completes his argument by attaching the beautiful as useful and powerful to helpful and good.

The argument connecting beautiful to good eventually fails because Socrates introduces efficient causation into it in such a way that the beautiful is made into a cause of the good. The emphasis given by the list of useful things to the instrumentality of beauty is in part responsible for beauty's being presented as a power in terms of efficient causation. But if beauty were only an efficient cause, then the sculptor might be beautiful but not his statue. The problem of causation is complicated in a second way by Socrates because of his argument that what is caused or done is what comes into being, namely a generated thing (*gignomenon*, 297a), and the result is the paradoxical conclusion that the beautiful has the form of a father of the good, the very opposite condition of that described in the *Republic* (508b) where the good is discussed as begetting an offspring.[12] The paradoxical conclusion is an offense to Zeus, as is indicated by the unusual profusion of oaths in his name, and reflects the path by which Hippias and Socrates have arrived at their present position. Socrates employs three terms, "a good thing," "good," and "the good," changing them frequently during the argument without Hippias' noticing the changes or at least without his objecting to them. The result is that the argument as presented can be used to support the conclusion that "the beautiful" is not and does not cause "the good," but it does not support the conclusion that Socrates and Hippias reach (297c).

The redefinition of beauty, however, as that which is useful and powerful for effecting something good, is a strong argument. When it is rejected, Socrates observes that, at the time they proposed it, it appeared to be the most beautiful of their arguments (297d). Perhaps the argument has failed because it has shown itself to lack a sufficient degree of "appearing." It is noticeably unadorned and logically complicated. Although the definition was the only one sufficiently comprehensive to embrace "beautiful bodies, beautiful lawful things and wisdom" (296e), and although it was the argument that the soul wished to speak (296d), it does not gratify. Except for one simile (see Hippias' responses at 297b–c), it lacks the cosmetic of surface beauty.

In his third definition Socrates attempts to supply the charm that his second definition lacked. Hippias cannot help him but through desire to know (297e), Socrates discovers a possible answer. He proposes to define as beautiful "whatever makes us delight—not all pleasures, but that which comes through hearing and sight" (297e), and he provides a list of examples of beautiful things that may be seen or heard.[13] The difficulty then becomes one of justifying the separation of these pleasures from others such as those of food, drink, and sex. The mention of sex and the fact that this definition has been prompted by desire remind one of the importance of eros for understanding the operation of beauty upon the human soul, yet the *Greater Hippias* avoids this question almost entirely. Despite the fact that Hippias begins his definitions with a beautiful body, just as Diotima begins her account of the ascent through stages of "beautiful" with

---

[12]See also the argument in the *Philebus* at 54a–c.

[13]The last two examples, beautiful pursuits and laws, are problematical. Silent thought about the principles of things is neither visible nor audible.

love of a beautiful body (*Symposium* 210a–b), Hippias has no eros himself. In this regard he is like beautiful things in general (see *Philebus* 53d–54a).

The next stage in the conversation indicates that his soul is also defective in another way. The unnamed person suggests that Hippias and Socrates differentiated sight and hearing from the other pleasurable senses because they looked away toward something that these two had that made them different from the others (299e). This something is "a common thing which exists for both of them in common and for each in particular" (300a–b). It is to be distinguished from a second type of "common thing" that characterizes both of two things together but not each of them separately (300b): for example, a couple is a couple together, but each of the partners is not a couple. Hippias cannot conceive of this possibility. Although many such things appear before Socrates' soul, none do before Hippias' (300c–d). The distinction between these two types of "common things" is clarified by a passage in the *Theaetetus* (184c–185e). There Socrates and Theaetetus decide that the soul is capable of having thoughts about objects of the several sense perceptions at once. Perception through any one sense alone cannot be responsible for such thoughts. Among the thoughts about the objects of sight and hearing, for instance, are, first, that both are, second, that each is different from the other and the same as itself, and, third, that both are two but each is one (as in the example of the couple). Theaetetus recognizes that no single "organ" is peculiar to these thoughts as there is a single organ for the objects of each of the senses but that, instead, the soul in itself reflects upon these "common things." But for Hippias such forms of commonness remain obscure despite the fact that he prides himself on his skill in mathematics (*Lesser Hippias* 366c–d), which is an area in which such "common things" abound.

When Socrates introduces this second type of "common thing" (e.g., the couple) into the conversation, Hippias objects. One of his arguments calling into doubt this type is a list of examples of "common things" that can be said of him and Socrates together as well as of them separately (300e–301a). But he shows that his understanding of these "common things" too is peculiar. Among the ways in which he and Socrates might be affected he includes the possibility that they might be golden or silver or ivory. One can imagine that statues of Hippias and Socrates might be so affected, but that they themselves should be so is a sign that Hippias treats "affection" and "being" indifferently, the very censure he makes of Socrates in a few moments (301b).[14] Confusion between them also caused difficulties for Hippias during his first two definitions. He now shows the reason for his earlier difficulties in this discussion about the two types of "common thing." He disregards both, yet they are the principles in terms of which classes of things become distinct from each other. In the same way, then, that Hippias converted public things into private, for him there are no "common things." All things are particular. There are apparently "wholes," yet they are inseparable from each other. Being is made up of large and continuous bodies. But as Socrates points out, Hippias' account of being is continuous, that is, indiscriminate (301e). Without classes and the ability to describe limits it is possible for Hippias to think that he is saying something when he maintains that he can speak "more precisely than total precision" (295a). This is a beautiful speech, not a precise speech.

The introduction of the two types of "common things" therefore helps reveal the nature of Hippias' position and accounts for his tendency to distort the arguments in the direction of the objects of sense. The introduction of the second type of commonness also advances the argument concerning the beautiful one further step. After Socrates fails in his attempt to define the beautiful in terms of the pleasant through sight and hearing, he suggests that the pleasures through these senses may be set apart from the others on the basis of their being the least harmful and best, and he therefore proposes that beauty is helpful pleasure (303e). His proposal combines his second and third definitions and makes a "common thing" of the second sort out of them according to which beauty is neither the helpful nor the pleasing but both (see *Gorgias* 474d–75a). As was the case with his first definition, this revision of his third one is aimed at understanding beauty as charming in itself and as leading to, or comprehensible in terms of, something beyond itself. The new definition cannot be tested, however, because it presupposes an understanding of pleasure and because, more immediately, it raises the same problem that stymied Hippias and Socrates earlier, the problem of the relation of "beautiful" and "helpful" to "good" (303e–304a). Therefore Socrates refutes the new definition himself, and Hippias in disgust deliv-

---

[14]Accordingly, for Hippias anything can be predicated of any other thing. See 300b, where he seems to use "one of the things that are" and "affection" interchangeably.

ers a closing attack upon Socrates' fragmentary and, by implication, ugly little speeches.

In his response, Socrates returns to the question of what is helpful and explains that, although Hippias and that unnamed person speak badly of him, he is helped by his associations with both of them. Specifically, he is helped to know what the proverb "the beautiful things are difficult" means. What the proverb might mean depends on what "the beautiful things" are. Insofar as they refer to the apparently beautiful things among the phenomena, those things that are exemplified by Hippias, they are difficult to know because they are so elusive. Yet in spite of their resistance to intelligence, they retain their charm. Their charm, however, acts as a deterrent to knowledge and prevents a man such as Hippias from seeing beneath the surfaces of things to the intelligible structure beneath. The beautiful things are in one sense those surfaces, the "looks" and "sounds" of things. The *Greater Hippias* therefore offers a chastening supplement to the *Symposium*. The *Symposium* describes how the beautiful things lead upward to the beautiful. The *Greater Hippias* suggests that they may do the opposite and tempt one to fix one's gaze upon the charming appearances.[15]

But on the level of things that are, the beautiful things may be, or at least include, the forms themselves. So, too, in the case of the forms, just as with the phenomena, their beauty may be in their "looks." Their looks are part of the problem of the relation of "beautiful" to "intelligible," to "being," and to "good." However the good is to be understood as a father and however it produces reflections of itself, beauty may be an aspect of the good that attracts intelligence. Beauty, then, would mediate between the knowable and knowing, between being and soul or mind.

[15]See the argument in the *Republic* at 475d–476c and 479a–480a.

ION

[or, On the *Iliad*]

Translated by ALLAN BLOOM

Socrates, Ion

530a SOCRATES: Ion, welcome. From where do you come to visit us now? From your home at Ephesus?

ION: Not at all, Socrates, but from the festival of Asclepius at Epidaurus.

SOC.: You don't mean to say that the Epidaureans dedicate a contest of rhapsodes to the god too?[1]

ION: Indeed they do, and also for the other parts of music.

SOC.: Tell me, did you compete for us? And how did you do in the competition?

b ION: We carried off first prize, Socrates.

SOC.: You speak well,[2] and see to it that we conquer at the Panathenaia[3] too.

ION: But it will be so, god willing.

SOC.: Well now, I have often envied you rhapsodes, Ion, for your art.

---

[1] Athletic and musical competitions were held in Epidaurus (a town in the Peloponnese not far from Athens) in honor of its patron Asclepius, god of healing. Ephesus was a Greek city in Asia Minor.

[2] Literally, "you speak well" (*eu legeis*). The idiom—"good" would be a more colloquial translation—is a common one, but the literal sense seems to acquire thematic importance in this dialogue; cf. 531c–532a, 536d. It is related to the expressions "you speak correctly or rightly" (*orthōs legeis*), "you speak truly" (*alēthē legeis*), and, above all, "you speak finely, nobly, or beautifully" (*kalōs legeis*), all of which occur frequently in the dialogue.

[3] The great Panathenaia was a festival celebrated every four years at Athens in honor of its patron goddess, Athena. There was also a small Panathenaia celebrated every year.

For that it befits your art for the body to be always adorned and for you to appear as beautiful as possible, and that, at the same time, it is necessary to be busy with many good poets and above all with Homer, the best and most divine of the poets, and to learn his thought

c thoroughly, not just his words, is enviable. Because one could never be a good rhapsode if he did not understand the things said by the poet. The rhapsode must be the interpreter of the thought of the poet to the listeners, but to do this finely is impossible for the one who does not recognize what the poet means. All these things, then, deserve to be envied.

ION: You speak truly, Socrates. For me, at any rate, this part of the art requires the most work, and I suppose that I speak most finely of all

d human beings about Homer—that neither Metrodorus of Lampsacus nor Stesimbrotus the Thasian nor Glaucon[4] nor anyone else who has ever lived has had so many fine thoughts to speak about Homer as I.

SOC.: You speak well, Ion. And it is evident that you won't begrudge me a display.

ION: It is surely worth hearing, Socrates, how well I have adorned Homer—so that I suppose I deserve to be crowned with a golden crown by the Homeridae.[5]

SOC.: And I shall surely yet find the leisure to listen to you. But now

531a answer me this much: are you clever[6] about Homer alone or about Hesiod and Archilochus too?[7]

ION: Not at all, but only about Homer, for that seems sufficient to me.

SOC.: And is there any matter about which both Hesiod and Homer say the same things?

ION: I suppose there are—many.

SOC.: About these matters, then, would you give a finer explanation of what Homer says than of what Hesiod says?

[4]Metrodorus of Lampsacus, a friend of the philosopher Anaxagoras, had interpreted Homer allegorically, understanding the various deities as representations of natural phenomena. Stesimbrotus of Thasos was another early practitioner of allegorical interpretation and apparently composed a book on Homer. Of Glaucon nothing is known.

[5]Originally a guild of poets claiming descent from Homer but generally applied to his admirers (cf. *Republic* 599e).

[6]*Deinos:* literally, "terrible." The word was commonly applied to an effective speaker.

[7]Hesiod's *Theogony* is an early systematization of Greek theology; it was considered only slightly less authoritative than the Homeric poems themselves. Archilochus was generally regarded as the originator of iambic or lyric poetry.

ION: A similar one, about those matters, at least, about which they say the same things.

b SOC.: But what about those matters about which they do not say the same things? For example, both Homer and Hesiod say something about divination.

ION: Certainly.

SOC.: Well then, of the things these two poets say about divination that are similar and those that are different, would you give a finer explanation or would one of the good diviners?

ION: One of the diviners.

SOC.: If you were a diviner would you not, if indeed you were able to explain the things said similarly, know also how to explain the things said differently?

ION: It's plain that I would.

c SOC.: Why, then, are you clever about Homer but not about Hesiod or any of the other poets? Or does Homer speak about other things than what all the other poets speak about? Didn't he tell about war for the most part, and about the associations with one another of good human beings and bad ones, and private ones and those in public works, and about gods' associating with one another and with human beings—how they associate—and about the events in the heavens

d and those in Hades and the begettings of both gods and heroes? Are not these the things about which Homer has made his poetry?

ION: You speak truly, Socrates.

SOC.: And what of the other poets? Don't they make poetry about these same things?

ION: Yes, but, Socrates, they have not made poetry in a way similar to Homer.

SOC.: How then? Worse?

ION: Very much.

SOC.: Homer is better?

ION: Better indeed, by Zeus!

SOC.: Dearest Ion, when there are many men speaking about number and someone speaks best, won't there be someone who recognizes the one who speaks well?

ION: I should say so.

e SOC.: Does this same man also know the one speaking badly, or is it someone else?

ION: The same one, surely.

SOC.: And isn't this the one who has the arithmetical art?

ION: Yes.

SOC.: What of this? In a situation where many are speaking about what sorts of foods are healthy and a single person speaks best, will it be one man who recognizes that the person speaking best does speak best while another recognizes that the person speaking worse does speak worse? Or will it be the same man?

ION: Plainly, to be sure, the same man.

SOC.: Who is he? What name is there for him?

ION: Doctor.

SOC.: Let us say then, in summary, that the same man will always recognize who speaks well and who speaks badly when there are
532a many speaking about the same things. Or if he does not recognize the one who speaks badly it is plain that he will not recognize the one who speaks well, at least about the same thing.

ION: That is so.

SOC.: Then the same man turns out to be clever about both?

ION: Yes.

SOC.: Don't you affirm that both Homer and the other poets, among whom are Hesiod and Archilochus, speak about the same things but not similarly, the former speaking well and the others worse?

ION: And I speak truly.

SOC.: Then if you really recognize the one who speaks well, you
b would also recognize that the ones who speak worse do speak worse.

ION: It's likely, at any rate.

SOC.: Then, my excellent fellow, we won't go wrong when we say that Ion is similarly clever about Homer and the other poets, too, since he himself agrees that the same man will be an adequate judge of all who speak about the same things and since very nearly all the poets make their poems about the same things.

ION: Then whatever is the cause of the fact that when someone speaks
c about another poet, I neither pay attention nor am able to contribute anything at all worthy of mention but simply[8] doze? But when someone makes mention of Homer, I wake up immediately, pay attention, and have plenty to say?

SOC.: That, at least, is not hard to guess, comrade, but it is entirely clear that you are unable to speak about Homer by art and knowledge. For if you were able to do so by art, you would also be able to

---

[8] *Atechnōs*: literally, "artlessly." The play on this idiom is almost certainly conscious; cf. 534d, 541e.

speak about all the other poets too. For presumably the poetic art is a whole, isn't it?

ION: Yes.

d   SOC.: Then when someone grasps any art whatsoever as a whole, for all the arts, the same manner of inquiry holds. Do you have any need to hear me explaining what I mean when I say this, Ion?

ION: Yes, by Zeus, Socrates, I, for one, do. I take pleasure in listening to you wise men.

SOC.: I only wish you spoke the truth, Ion. But presumably you are wise, you rhapsodes and actors and those men whose poems you sing. As for me, I speak nothing but the truth, as is fitting for a

e   private human being. Now see how what I asked you about just now is an ordinary and private thing and how it belongs to every man to recognize what I said—that, when somebody grasps an art as a whole, the inquiry is the same. Let us grasp this by speech: there is an art of painting as a whole, isn't there?

ION: Yes.

SOC.: And there are and have been many painters good and poor.

ION: Certainly.

SOC.: And did you ever know anyone who is clever at showing what Polygnotus the son of Aglaophon[9] paints well and what he does not

533a   but is incapable of doing so concerning the other painters—so that when someone makes a display of the works of other painters, he dozes, is at a loss, and has nothing to contribute but when he is required to give a judgment about Polygnotus, or any other single painter you please, he wakes up, pays attention, and finds plenty to say?

ION: No, by Zeus, surely not.

SOC.: What of this? In regard to sculpture, did you ever know anyone who is clever at explaining what was well made by Daedalus the son

b   of Metion, or Epeius the son of Panopeus, or Theodorus of Samos,[10] or some other single sculptor but before the works of other sculptors is at a loss, dozes, and has nothing to say?

ION: No, by Zeus, I haven't seen this either.

SOC.: Indeed not, as I for one suppose; nor in regard to aulos playing, cithara playing, singing to the cithara, or rhapsody, you never saw a

---

[9]Polygnotus was the most celebrated painter of the fifth century.

[10]Daedalus is the legendary inventor of carpentry, statues that walked, and wings for man; Epeius, the builder of the Trojan horse; Theodorus, a famous sculptor and architect of the sixth century.

man who is clever at explaining Olympus, or Thamyras, or Or-
c pheus, or Phemius the Ithacan rhapsode[11] but is at a loss about Ion
and has nothing to contribute about what in rhapsody he does well
and what not?

ION: I have nothing to say in response to you, Socrates, about this,
but I myself know well that I speak most finely of human beings
about Homer, and I have plenty to say, and everyone else affirms that
I speak well about him, but about the others this is not the case. Now
then, see what this is.

SOC.: I do see, Ion, and I am going to show you what it seems to me
d that this is. For it is not art in you that makes you able to speak well
about Homer, as I just said, but a divine power which moves you,
just as in the stone which Euripides named Magnesian[12] but which
the many call Heraclean. For this stone not only draws iron rings to
itself but puts a power in the rings as well to do the same thing the
e stone does—to draw other rings to them, so that sometimes a very
long chain of iron rings is strung hanging one from the other. But in
all of them the power depends on this stone. In this way also the
Muse makes some men inspired herself, and through these inspired
men, others are gripped with enthusiasm and form a chain. All the
good epic poets speak all their fine poems not from art but by being
inspired and possessed, and it is the same for the good lyric poets. Just
as those carried away by Corybantic frenzy[13] are not in their right
534a minds when they dance, so also the lyric poets are not in their right
minds when they make these fine songs of theirs. But when they
launch into melody and rhythm, they are frantic and possessed, like
Bacchic dancers who draw honey and milk from rivers when they are
possessed but cannot when they are in their right minds. And the soul
of the lyric poets works in this way, as they themselves say. For the

[11]Olympus is the legendary musician and aulos player, said to have been taught by
the satyr Marsias (see *Minos* 318b); Thamyras and Orpheus were celebrated in legend
for their abilities with the cithara; Phemius is Ion's counterpart in the Homeric poems
(*Odyssey* XXII 330ff.).

[12]From a district in Asia Minor where magnetized iron could readily be found:
Euripides, fr. 567.

[13]The words for "inspired" (*entheoi*) and "gripped by enthusiasm" (*enthousiazontes*)
are closely related, both suggesting the notion of "a god within." The Corybantic
rites were mystery rites that included frenzied dancing in which the worshipers were
guided and inspired by certain demons called Corybantes. There may have been some
connection between these Corybantic rites and similar ecstatic forms of worship
associated with the god Bacchus (Dionysus). Cf. *Laws* 790d; *Phaedrus* 228d and 234d.

poets tell us, don't they, that culling their songs from fountains flow-
b ing with honey and certain gardens and glens of the Muses they bear
them to us just like bees, flying as they do. And they speak the truth.
For the poet is a light thing, winged and sacred, unable to make
poetry before he is inspired and out of his mind and intelligence is no
longer in him. For as long as this is his possession every human being
is unable to make poetry or oracular utterance. Since they make
c poems and say much that is fine about things, just as you do about
Homer, not by art but by divine dispensation, each is able to do finely
only that to which the Muse has impelled him—one making dithyrambs, another encomia, another choral chants, another epics,
another iambic verses—while with regard to the rest, each of them is
ordinary. For they say these things not by art but by divine power.
For if they knew how to speak finely by art about one of them, they
would be able to do so about all the rest. On this account the god
takes away their intelligence and uses them as servitors along with
d soothsayers and diviners of the gods so that we hearers may know
that these men, who are without intelligence, are not the ones who
say things worth so much but that god himself is the speaker and
gives utterance to us through them. The greatest proof of the argument is Tynnichus, the Chalcidean, who never composed any poem
worth remembering other than the poem which everybody sings and
which is very nearly the finest of all songs, being simply, as he
e himself says, "a discovery of the Muses." In this man the god especially shows us, it seems to me, so that we need not be in doubt,
that these fine poems are not human nor belonging to human beings,
but divine and belonging to gods, and the poets are nothing but
interpreters of the gods, possessed by the one who holds each. To
show this, the god on purpose sang the finest lyric through the most
535a ordinary poet. Do I seem to you to speak the truth, Ion?

ION: Yes, by Zeus, to me you do. For somehow you lay hold of my
soul with these speeches, Socrates, and I believe that the good poets
are interpreters of these things from the gods through divine dispensation.

SOC.: Now, don't you rhapsodes, in turn, interpret the things of the
poets?

ION: You speak the truth in this too.

SOC.: Then are you interpreters of interpreters?

ION: Entirely so.

b SOC.: Wait now, and tell me this, Ion, and don't hide from me whatever I ask you about. When you are speaking epics well and most amusing the spectators, singing of Odysseus leaping on the threshold, revealing himself to the suitors and pouring out the arrows before his feet,[14] or of Achilles chasing Hector,[15] or of one of the pitiful stories about Andromache, or Hecuba, or Priam,[16] are you

c then in your right mind? Or do you become beside yourself, and does your soul think it is at the scene of the deeds of which you speak in your inspiration, either at Ithaca, or Troy, or wherever the epic takes place?

ION: How vivid is this proof of yours to me, Socrates! For I shall tell without hiding anything from you. When I speak of something pitiful, my eyes fill with tears, and when of something frightening or terrible, my hair stands on end from fear and my heart leaps.

d SOC.: What then, Ion? Shall we assert that this man is then in his right mind who, adorned with rich raiment and golden crowns, cries in the midst of sacrifices and festivals, although he has lost none of these things, or who is frightened while standing before twenty thousand friendly human beings, although no one is stripping or harming him?

ION: No, by Zeus, certainly not, Socrates, to tell the truth.

SOC.: Do you know then that you work these same effects on most of the spectators?

e ION: Indeed I do know it very finely. For I look down on them each time from the platform above as they are crying, casting terrible looks and following with astonishment the things said. I must pay the very closest attention to them, since, if I set them to crying, I shall laugh myself because I am making money, but if they laugh, then I shall cry because of the money I am losing.

SOC.: You know, then, that this spectator is the last of the rings which I said get their power from one another through the Heraclean stone?

536a And you the rhapsode and actor[17] are the middle, and the top is the poet himself, but the god through all these draws the soul of human beings wherever he wishes, transmitting the power from one to the other. And just as from this stone, a very great chain is formed of dancers, choral masters, assistant masters, suspended sideways from the rings hanging from the Muse. And one poet is suspended from one Muse, another from another. And we name this "being pos-

[14]*Odyssey* XXII 2ff.
[15]*Iliad* XXII 131ff.
[16]See particularly *Iliad* XXII 33ff., XXIV 477ff.
[17]Or "interpreter" (*hypokritēs*).

b sessed," and it is very nearly that, for he is held.[18] And from these first rings, the poets, other men are suspended—some from one, some from another—and gripped by enthusiasm. Some are suspended by Orpheus, some by Musaeus.[19] But the many are possessed and held by Homer. You are one of them, Ion, and are possessed by Homer, and when someone sings from another poet, you fall asleep and are at a loss for something to say, but when someone utters a song of this poet, you wake up immediately and your soul dances and

c you have plenty to say. For you say what you say about Homer neither by art nor by knowledge but by divine dispensation and possession. Just as those carried away by Corybantic frenzy perceive sharply only that song which belongs to the god by whom they are possessed and have plenty of figures and phrases for that song but pay no heed to others, so you too, Ion, have plenty to say when someone

d mentions Homer but are at a loss with the others. And the cause, for which you ask me, of your having plenty to say about Homer and not about the others is that you are a clever praiser of Homer not by art but by divine dispensation.

ION: You speak well, Socrates. But I should be surprised if you could speak so well as to persuade me that I am possessed and am mad when I praise Homer. Nor do I believe I would appear so to you if you heard me speaking about Homer.

SOC.: And I am certainly willing to hear you, though not before you

e answer me this: about which one of the things about which Homer speaks do you speak well? For surely you don't speak well about them all.

ION: Know well, Socrates, that I do about them all.

SOC.: But surely not about those things you don't happen to know and about which Homer speaks?

ION: And what sort of things are those that Homer speaks of and I do not know?

537a SOC.: Doesn't Homer in many places have many things to say about the arts—for example, about charioteering? If I can remember the verses, I'll tell them to you.

ION: I'll do it, for I remember.

---

[18]The word meaning "to be possessed" (*katechesthai*) is derived from *echein*, "to have or hold."

[19]Musaeus is the legendary inventor of poetry; oracular verses circulated under his name as well as under that of Orpheus (cf. *Protagoras* 316d, *Republic* 363c–64e).

SOC.: Tell me, then, what Nestor says to his son Antilochus when he urges him to be careful at the turn in the horse race in memory of Patroclus.

ION: "And lean yourself," he says, "in the well-polished chariot a little
b to the left of them. And calling aloud to the horse on the right, give him the goad; give him free rein with your hands, and let the left horse go near to the turning posts so that the nave of the well-wrought wheel seems to graze it, but beware of touching the stone."[20]

c SOC.: That's enough. And who would judge better whether Homer speaks these words rightly or not, Ion, the doctor or the charioteer?

ION: The charioteer, surely.

SOC.: Because this is his art or for some other reason?

ION: Because this is his art.

SOC.: Then each of the arts has been assigned by the god the power of knowing some work, has it not? For presumably we won't know by medicine what we know by piloting, will we?

ION: No indeed.

SOC.: Nor will we know by carpentering what we know by medicine.
d ION: No indeed.

SOC.: Isn't it so with all arts—that what we know by one art we do not know by another? But answer this for me first: do you affirm that one art differs from another?

ION: Yes.

SOC.: I find evidence of this in my calling one art different from another when one is knowledge of some things and the other knowledge of others. Do you also?

e ION: Yes.

SOC.: For if it were ever a knowledge of the same things, in what respect would we assert one to be different from the other, inasmuch as the same things could be known by both? Just as I know that these fingers here are five and you too know the same about them as I, and if I should ask you whether you and I know the same things by the same art—the art of arithmetic—or a different one, you would surely say by the same.

ION: Yes.

538a SOC.: Now, tell me what I was going to ask you a moment ago. Does it seem to you to hold for all the arts that the same things must of

[20]*Iliad* XXIII 335–40.

necessity be known by the same art and that by a different art the same things are not known but that, if it is really different, it is necessary that it also know different things?

ION: It seems so to me, Socrates.

SOC.: Then whoever does not have a certain art will not be able to know in a fine way the things of that art which are finely said or done, will he?

b ION: You speak truly.

SOC.: Would you or a charioteer, then, know in a finer way about whether the verses you just recited were finely said by Homer or not?

ION: A charioteer.

SOC.: For you, presumably, are a rhapsode but not a charioteer?

ION: Yes.

SOC.: And the rhapsode's art is different from the charioteer's?

ION: Yes.

SOC.: And if it is different, it is a knowledge of different things.

ION: Yes.

SOC.: And what about when Homer tells how Hecamede, Nestor's
c concubine, gives a potion to the wounded Machaon to drink. It goes something like this: "In Pramneian wine," he says, "she grated goat cheese with a bronze grater, and beside it set an onion as relish for the drink."[21] Is it for the doctor's art or the rhapsode's to ascertain in a fine way whether Homer says these things rightly or not?

ION: The doctor's.

d SOC.: And what about when Homer says: "She went down into the deep like a lead sinker which, set on the horn of a field-ox, comes in haste bearing woe to ravenous fishes,"[22]—would we assert it is for the fisherman's art rather than the rhapsode's to judge of what he is saying and whether he says it finely or not?

ION: Plainly, Socrates, it is for the fisherman's art.

SOC.: Consider, then. Suppose you were questioning and asked me:
e Socrates, since for these arts you find in Homer the things appropriate for each to judge, come now and find for me the sort of things with regard to which it is appropriate for the diviner and the diviner's art to be able to ascertain whether they are done well or badly— consider how easily and truly I shall answer you. For in many places in the Odyssey he speaks of it; for example, in what Theoclymenes,

[21]Ibid. XI 630, 639.
[22]Ibid. XXIV 80–82.

539a the diviner of the Melampid line, says to the suitors: "Wretches, what evil is this you suffer; covered over with night are your heads and faces and your limbs below; and wailing is kindled; your cheeks are bathed in tears. Full of ghosts is the porch, and full the hall, hastening

b to Erebus under the darkness. The sun has perished out of heaven and evil mist hovers over all."23 And he speaks of it many places also in the *Iliad,* for example in the Battle at the Wall where he says: "A bird came over them as they were eager to cross over, a high-flying eagle,

c skirting the host on the left, bearing in his claws a bloody red snake, a monstrous one, alive and still struggling, nor had it forgotten its battle joy. For it bent back and struck its captor on the breast by the neck; and the bird cast it from him to the ground, smarting with pain,

d and threw it in the midst of the throng. And he with a loud cry followed the windy blast."24 I assert that these things, and others like them, are appropriate for a diviner to consider and judge.

ION: And you speak truly, Socrates.

SOC.: And you, Ion, you speak truly in saying so. But come now, just as I have selected for you from the *Odyssey* and the *Iliad* the sort of things that belong to the diviner, the sort that belong to the doctor,

e and the sort that belong to the fisherman, since you are more experienced in Homer than I, so you select for me the sort of things that belong to the rhapsode and the rhapsode's art, those that it is appropriate for the rhapsode above all other human beings to consider and judge.

ION: I assert all things, Socrates.

SOC.: But you don't assert all, Ion—are you so forgetful? And yet it is not fitting for a man who is a rhapsode to be forgetful.

540a ION: What am I forgetting, then?

SOC.: Don't you remember that you asserted the rhapsode's art is different from the charioteer's?

ION: I remember.

SOC.: And since they are different, do you agree they will know different things?

ION: Yes.

SOC.: Then according to your account the rhapsode's art will not know everything, nor the rhapsode either.

ION: Everything, except, perhaps, such things, Socrates.

23*Odyssey* XX 351–57.
24*Iliad* XII 200–207.

b soc.: By "such things" you mean pretty much the things belonging to the other arts. But what sort of things will he know, if not everything?

ion: The things that are appropriate, I for one suppose, for a man to say, and the sort for a woman,[25] and the sort for a slave and the sort for a free man, and the sort for one who is ruled and the sort for one who is ruling.

soc.: Do you mean that the rhapsode will know in a finer way than the pilot what sort of things it is appropriate for a ruler of a ship caught in a storm at sea to say?

ion: No, the pilot will know that, at any rate.

c soc.: And does the rhapsode know in a finer way than the doctor what sorts of things it is appropriate for a ruler of a sick man to say?

ion: Not that either.

soc.: Then do you mean such as are appropriate for a slave?

ion: Yes.

soc.: Do you mean that the rhapsode will know, but not the cowherd, what things it is appropriate for a cowherd who is a slave to say to calm angry cattle?

ion: No, not at all.

soc.: Then, such as are appropriate for a spinning woman to say about the working of wool?

d ion: No.

soc.: Well then, will he know such things as are appropriate for a man who is a general to say when exhorting his troops?

ion: Yes, the rhapsode will know such things.

soc.: What? Is the art of rhapsody generalship?

ion: I would certainly know such things as are appropriate for a general to say.

soc.: For perhaps you are an expert at generalship too, Ion. And if you happened to be at once an expert at horsemanship and an expert at the playing of the cithara, you could know whether horses were

e being well or badly ridden. But if I asked you, "Through what art, Ion, do you know well-ridden horses? Is it the one by which you are a horseman or the one by which you are a citharist?" what would you answer me?

ion: The one by which I am a horseman, I would answer.

---

[25]Or "for a husband to say, and what sort for a wife."

SOC.: If, then, you are ascertaining those who played the cithara well, you would agree that you ascertain this through the art by which you are a citharist and not through the one by which you are a horseman.

ION: Yes.

SOC.: Since you know military matters, do you know them through the art by which you are an expert at generalship or the one by which you are a good rhapsode?

ION: For me, at least, there doesn't seem to be any difference.

541a SOC.: What? You say there is no difference? Do you say that the art of rhapsody and the art of generalship are one or two?

ION: To me, at least, it seems to be one.

SOC.: Whoever is a good rhapsode, therefore, happens also to be a good general?

ION: Surely, Socrates.

SOC.: And whoever happens to be a good general is also a good rhapsode?

ION: No, that doesn't seem so to me.

SOC.: But that does seem to you to be the case—whoever is a good rhapsode is also a good general?

b ION: Certainly.

SOC.: Aren't you the best rhapsode among the Greeks?

ION: By far, Socrates.

SOC.: Then are you also the best general among the Greeks, Ion?

ION: Know it well, Socrates, and these things I learned from Homer.

SOC.: Then why, by the gods, Ion, when you are the best at both among the Greeks—general and rhapsode—do you go about being a c rhapsode for the Greeks and not a general? Or does it seem to you that the Greeks have great need of a man crowned with a golden crown and none of a general?

ION: Socrates, our city is ruled by your people and commanded by your generals and needs no general. But neither your city nor that of the Lacedaemonians would choose me as general, for you suppose you are sufficient.

SOC.: Ion, my excellent fellow, don't you know Apollodorus of Cyzicus?

ION: What's he?

SOC.: A man whom the Athenians have chosen many times for their d general although he is a foreigner. And also Phanosthenes of Andros and Heracleides of Clazomenae,[26] for all that they were foreigners, were elevated to generalships and other offices by Athens when they had demonstrated that they were worthy of mention. Why, then, will she not choose Ion of Ephesus as general and honor him if he should appear worthy of mention? Weren't you Ephesians originally

e Athenians, and isn't Ephesus a city inferior to none? But Ion, if you speak truly when you say you are able to praise Homer by art and knowledge, you do me injustice. For you profess to have knowledge of many fine things about Homer and say you will make a display, but you are deceiving me. You are so far from making a display that you are not even willing to tell what things you are clever about, although I have been entreating you for a long time. You are simply like Proteus,[27] assuming all sorts of shapes, twisting this way and

542a that until finally you escape me in the guise of a general, in order not to display how clever you are in the wisdom concerning Homer. If, then, you are expert at the art, as I just said, you deceive me in promising to make a display about Homer, and you are hence unjust. But if you are not expert at the art but are by divine dispensation possessed by Homer and, knowing nothing, you say many fine things about the poet, you are not unjust. Choose, then, whether you want to be held by us to be an unjust man or a divine one.

b ION: There is a great difference, Socrates. For to be held to be divine is far finer.

SOC.: Then this finer thing you may have from us, Ion, to be a divine praiser of Homer, not one expert at the art.

[26]Phanosthenes was the commander of an expedition against Andros in 406–405 B.C. (Xenophon *Hellenica* I v 18); Heracleides raised the fee paid citizens attending the assembly, probably in about 393 B.C. (Aristotle *Athenian Constitution* XLI 3). Ephesus detached itself from Athenian hegemony in about 420–415 B.C. For a discussion of attempts to determine the dramatic date of the dialogue on the basis of these and other indications, see the Budé edition (Paris, 1920), pp. 23–24.

[27]*Odyssey* IV 455ff.

An Interpretation of
Plato's *Ion*

ALLAN BLOOM

In Xenophon's *Banquet* Antisthenes asks, "Do you know any tribe more stupid [or simple] than the rhapsodes?" This question, obviously rhetorical, leads the reader of the *Ion* to the further question, "Why in the world does Socrates choose to speak to a man like Ion, a typical member of the tribe of rhapsodes?" Even though Socrates claims that he investigates men with respect to their knowledge and ignorance, it is hard to see why he should think it important to test Ion. Moreover, their conversation is private, so that it cannot be Socrates' intention to show Ion off, or up, to others. Socrates in the dialogues exposes the important kinds of human souls and their characteristic errors. To make this particular discussion a worthwhile enterprise for him, the empty reciter of Homer's poems must represent something beyond himself.

30
-b
Socrates seems most anxious to have this conversation, since it is he who apparently stops Ion, who shows no particular interest in Socrates or desire to talk to him. Thus the first four exchanges occur entirely at Socrates' initiative, Ion responding in a way which would end the dialogue if Socrates did not return to the charge. Ion is a self-satisfied man who feels no need to render an account of himself or his activity; he knows who he is and what he does; and he knows both himself and his activity to be important. He is as far from the radical self-doubt of philosophy as a man can be. He is willing to talk about

himself and accept praise; he has, however, little curiosity about others, for he does not sense a pressing need to learn from them. In order to engage Ion and induce him to reveal himself, Socrates must attract him and become respectable for him. Ion is vain, and he is first attracted by flattery and then captured when his self-esteem is threatened.

Socrates begins by expressing the greatest interest in Ion's achievements, making it clear that he is one of Ion's admirers. We learn from Socrates' first questions about Ion's recent doings that Ion is a man who travels from city to city and is admired in the cities he visits. He is not bound by the ordinary limits of citizenship: he is a cosmopolitan (or more properly a Hellenapolitan, for his universality will prove to be counterfeit, based on Greek convention rather than anything universally human). His rhapsody is his passport, and he finds proof for his worth in the prizes the peoples award him. He knows himself in relation to the unquestionable acclaim he evokes from others. Above all, Ion is needed to partake in the festivals dedicated to the gods whom all Greeks honor. He is a servitor of the Greeks, and his authority is somehow connected with the gods of the Greeks; this is the ground of his pious vanity.

530
b–c
Socrates, who apparently knows Ion's character, prevents him from breaking off the conversation by praising him. Once Ion has taken Socrates' bait, he will soon be at his mercy—begging Socrates for a justification for his way of life. Socrates professes envy of the rhapsodes, and he goes on to specify what arouses that ugly but flattering passion in him. The rhapsodes are among the knowers; they possess an art—a skill or a kind of knowhow. That art is divided into two apparently unrelated parts of widely divergent dignity: its practitioners adorn their bodies so as to look most beautiful, and they occupy themselves with the thought of the good poets, especially the divine Homer, the teacher of the Greeks. Socrates has to explain what he means by the second part of the art, which is apparently not as clear as the first. To be a good rhapsode, one must understand what a given poet says, for the rhapsode is a spokesman or interpreter of the poet's thought to the listeners. Hence, the rhapsode must know what the poet means. Knowledge of what the poet thinks and fidelity in conveying his thought to an audience constitute the core of the rhapsode's art. He is an intermediary whose sole authority emanates from the poet.

530
Ion readily accepts this description of what he does, not consider-

c–d ing its broad implications. He has not reflected on art in general nor on the particular requirements of an art of Homeric thought. He does not see that the conversation has really moved from a discussion of himself and of rhapsody to a testing of the interpreters of Homer. Ion's adequacy as an interpreter is about to be put to the test, and thus the received interpretation of Homer, the interpretation by the most popular and typical of his interpreters, is to be called into question.

In response to Socrates' assertions about Ion's art, Ion avows that Socrates has hit the nail on the head and that it is precisely to understanding the thought of Homer that he devotes the greatest energy. He is delighted to participate in the prestige generally accorded to Homer, but he also covertly tries to strike out on his own; he puts the accent on his contribution to Homer, on what is his own rather than Homer's. His speech, not Homer's, is particularly beautiful; he has more fair thoughts about Homer than anyone. He is not simply Homer's faithful servant. Socrates recognizes that Ion would like to give a display of his talents; this is Ion's work, and he counts on charming his auditors, charming them in such a way that they ask no further questions. Ion insists that he is really worth hearing; he reminds us of the forgotten first part of the rhapsode's art: he has *adorned* Homer and for that he deserves to be adorned with a golden crown by the devotees of Homer. He uses Homer to his profit. Socrates, however, does not permit Ion's disloyalty to Homer; he has no interest in an Ion independent of Homer. The ever idle Socrates says he has no leisure to listen to the performance of Greece's greatest rhapsode; he wants the answer to only one question.

31a That question is as follows: is Ion clever only about Homer or about Hesiod and Archilochus too? This apparently naive query leads to the heart of the matter, for Socrates knows that Ion will respond that Homer is sufficient for him. And the fact that Ion has no curiosity about the teachings of the other poets is symptomatic of what he is—the most conventional agent of what is most conventional. It is a thing to be wondered at—though far from uncommon—that a man would be willing to live his life according to principles which are merely given to him, while he would not purchase so much as a cloak without investigating the alternatives. Socrates investigates such a man in this little conversation, one who accepts Homer's view of the gods, the heroes, and men without any need to see whether what the other poets say about these things is in any way useful. Even more, Ion is the one who transmits the Homeric view. In a word, he represents tradition. He accepts the orthodox view, and he teaches it. He does not seek reasons why this particular tradition should be accepted rather than any other. If there are a number of conflicting accounts of the world, men must make a choice between them. But Ion and his kind can give no reasons why their particular source should be preferred. They can merely assert the superiority of their text. In this respect, Homer's book resembles the Bible. It has adherents who rely on it utterly but who can provide no argument in its favor when confronted with other books. And if the book cannot be defended, neither can the way of life grounded in it. Ion relies on Homer, which would be sufficient if he had no competitors. But there are always other poets in addition to the official ones. The Greeks learn the poems of Hesiod and Archilochus as well as those of Homer, and any man who questions must wonder which of them he should follow, for his happiness depends on the right answer. For Ion, Homer is sufficient, but for the sole reason that it is for reciting Homer's poetry that golden crowns are awarded.

531
a–b Socrates presses the question about Ion's competence with the other poets in a comprehensive fashion; he does not leave it at Ion's insistence that the rhapsode need know only Homer. Where Homer and Hesiod say the same thing, Ion must be an equally competent exegete of both. So Ion turns out to be an expert on a part of Hesiod as well as on the whole of Homer. Now they must test Ion's expertise on the remainder—the part of Hesiod which is not the same as Homer. It is not so easy to determine this part as the other, and a new step must be introduced into the argument. Socrates begins to forge the link between what Homer and Hesiod say differently by pointing to a subject matter about which they both speak: divining. Now, divining plays a great role in the *Ion,* but here it is brought in innocuously as an example of a common theme of the poets. When the poets say the same thing, the poets' words are enough; when they say different things, one must turn away from the words to the things the words are about. Both Hesiod and Homer mention divining, and their words about it take on meaning from the object to which these words relate. And it is the diviner who can comment on what both Hesiod and Homer say about divining, not because he is a student of the words of Hesiod and Homer, but because he knows divining.

Knowers draw their knowledge from the great book of the world, and the poet, whether he is a knower or not, is dependent on and speaks about that world. No written book is sufficient unto itself;

every book is essentially related to something beyond itself which acts as a standard for it. Socrates has gradually narrowed the discussion and focused on the poet as a source of knowledge and on the rhapsode as a knower of that knowledge. Ion does not notice that it is the diviner, not the rhapsode, who is the expert on Homer in this case. The consequences of that fact will become clear to him later. Now the argument has established only that a man can speak well about Homer because he knows the subject matter about which Homer speaks. It thus becomes necessary to determine what Homer speaks about, since Ion must be a knower of that in order to be a competent interpreter of Homer. If Homer speaks about the same things as Hesiod, Ion's claim to be incompetent about Hesiod will not be able to stand, whether or not Homer and Hesiod agree about those things.

531c   What is it, then, that Homer speaks about and the knowledge of which Ion must be presumed to possess? The answer is, simply, everything—everything human and divine. Homer speaks about the whole, and if he speaks truly, he reveals to men those things which they most want and need to know if they are ·to live well. At this point Socrates reveals for the first time the reason for his choosing to speak to this slight man who is never himself aware of the import of the discussion. Homer presents the authoritative view of the whole according to which Greeks guide themselves: he is the primary source of knowledge or error about the most important things. Every group of men begins with some such view of the whole by which its members orient themselves and which acts as a framework for their experience. They are educated by and in it from earliest childhood. No one starts afresh, from nothing. In particular there is always an authoritative view belonging to the community, and it constitutes the deepest unity of that community. It purports to be the true view, and the man who accepts it is supposed to possess all the knowledge he needs for living rightly and well.

Socrates, then, is testing the Greek understanding of things, particularly of the gods. At least symbolically, he shows the beginning point of philosophic questioning. Every man starts from a more or less coherent view of the whole which has been instilled in him by a tradition. Somehow that rare individual who possesses a philosophic nature becomes aware that the tradition is not founded in authentic knowledge but is only an opinion, and he is compelled to seek beyond it. The philosophic quest implies a prior awareness of the inadequacy of traditional opinion, and the problems of philosophy come to light as a result of the investigation of that traditional opinion which appears unproblematic to most men. Socrates treats Ion as the purveyor of the Greek tradition which stems from Homer, and therefore he tries to ascertain whether what Ion says about Homer can be understood to have the authority of knowledge. If it does not, the man who seeks for knowledge must start all over again in the interpretation of Homer, unmoved by popular opinion. Ultimately, of course, the same question must be asked of Homer himself: is his speech about gods and men based on knowledge of them? And in the event that it is not, one would have to try to return to the beginnings and start a second time. In the *Ion,* Socrates confronts authority, the authority for the most decisive opinions. He does so with great delicacy, never stating the issue directly, for he knows that the community protects its sacred beliefs fanatically. In spite of his caution he was finally put to death by the community for investigating the things in the heavens and under the earth rather than accepting Homer's account of them. In the failure of Ion to meet the test Socrates puts to him we see the reason why Socrates was forced to undertake a private study of the things in the heavens and under the earth.

As the exegete of Homer, Ion must be the knower of the things of which Homer speaks if he is to be taken seriously. He must, it has been made clear, possess the art of the whole. According to the most famous of Socratic professions, Socrates is ignorant, ignorant about the whole, and his awareness of his ignorance causes him to make a quest for knowledge. He knows what it means to possess knowledge, and in the *Ion* he shows the kinds of things that men must think they know and why they are unable to see the inadequacy of their opinions. As the spokesman of the tradition, Ion has answers to the most important questions, but he does not know that those answers are themselves questionable. Socrates' contribution is only that of questioning the traditional answers and thereby elaborating the essential structure of human alternatives.

Socrates is, therefore, deeply indebted to the tradition, which is the only basis for the ascent to a higher level of consciousness, but he is forced to break with it. In the *Apology* Socrates reports that he examined three kinds of men who were supposed to know: statesmen, poets, and artisans. He chose the statesmen and the poets because they are men whose very activity implies knowledge of the whole. Thus the commands of statesmen imply that they know what the good life is, and the tales of poets tell of gods and men, death and life, peace and war. Socrates discovered that statesmen and poets knew nothing but that the artisans did in fact know something. They could actually do things such as making shoes or training horses, and by their ability to teach their skills to others they proved they possessed knowledge. Nevertheless Socrates preferred to remain ignorant in his own way rather than to become knowledgeable in the way of artisans, for the latters' knowledge was of partial things, and their pride of competence caused them to neglect the human situation as a whole. However, Socrates did learn from the artisans what knowledge is and hence was made aware that those who talk about the whole do not possess knowledge of it. The choice seems to be between men who talk about the whole but are both incompetent and unaware of their incompetence, and men who deal with insignificant parts of the whole competently but are as a consequence oblivious of the whole. Socrates adopts a moderate position; he is open to the whole but knows that he does not know the answers although he knows the questions. In the *Ion,* he applies the standard of knowledge drawn from the arts to the themes treated by poetry, thus showing wherein poetry and the tradition fail and what stands in the way of such knowledge.

31d–
32c   After determining what Homer talks about, Socrates asks whether all poets do not speak about the same things. Ion recognizes that an admission that they do would imply both that he is conversant with all the poets and that Homer is comparable to other poets. While agreeing that other poets do speak about the same things as Homer, Ion, therefore, adds that they do not do so in the same way. He means that Homer cannot be judged by the same standard as other poets, that they do not, as it were, inhabit the same world. Ion does not really accept or understand the position which Socrates has been developing; he wants to interpret the world by the book rather than the book by the world. He is quickly disarmed, however, when Socrates asks whether the difference consists in the others being worse than Homer. Ion cannot resist affirming this suggestion; its corollary, that Homer is better, he reinforces with an oath by Zeus.

"Better" and "worse," Socrates is quick to respond, are terms of relation, and the things to which they apply are comparable. Turning to the standard provided by the arts, the expert—the man who knows an art—is equally competent to judge all speeches that concern the objects of his specialty. To determine that one speech is better, a man must know that another is worse. When someone speaks about numbers, the arithmetician judges whether he speaks well or badly; when someone speaks about healthy foods, the doctor judges whether he speaks well or badly. The two are able to do so because they know numbers and health, respectively. Who is it, then, who can judge of the better and worse speeches of poets because he knows the object about which the poet speaks? The difficulty of responding to this question reveals the problem of the dialogue. The premise of the discussion with Ion is that the rhapsode is the competent judge of the poets' speeches, but rhapsodes are not even aware of the questions, let alone the answers. The very existence of the rhapsodes—these shallow replacements for knowers of the art of the whole—serves to initiate us into a new dimension of the quest for knowledge of the highest things. In investigating Ion, Socrates studies a kind of popular substitute for philosophy. When we reflect on who judges whether Ion speaks well or badly, we recognize that it is not an expert but the people at large. The issue has to do with the relation of knowledge and public opinion in civil society.

The iron-clad necessity of the argument based on the arts thus constrains Socrates and Ion to accept the conclusion that, if Ion is clever about Homer, he is also clever about Hesiod and Archilochus. Socrates urbanely maintains the unquestioned hypothesis of the dialogue, that Ion does in fact know Homer, and concludes from it that Ion is an expert on all poets. This conclusion is excellent and ineluctable except that it is not true. Ion recognizes that he is confronted by a mystery: reason forces him to be expert on all poets and he is not; he cannot give an account of himself. The tables are turned; his confidence is somewhat abated, and now he turns to Socrates, who has established some authority over him, for an explanation. With the poets other than Homer he dozes as do the people, according to Socrates' description in the *Apology,* when they have no gadfly to arouse them. It is this miracle that needs clarification.

532   Socrates has no difficulty in supplying the answer: he responds that
c–d   Ion is incapable of speaking about Homer by art and exact knowledge. Ion is not an expert as are other experts. Socrates pursues this result with further and more pointed comparisons to the other arts. At the same time, he takes advantage of his new prestige to make it quite clear to Ion that the latter is now in tutelage. He poses a question in an obscure way and forces Ion to ask for an explanation; Ion who wanted to be heard now must hear instead, and Socrates, by

engaging Ion's passions, will be a far more compelling performer for Ion than Ion would have been for him. But Ion, whose vanity is now involved, is not without his own wiles for preserving his self-esteem and humiliating Socrates. He gives gay assent to his instruction with the remark that he enjoys hearing "you wise men." For him, Socrates' argument is to be a display, such as any of the currently popular sophists might give, of technical virtuosity at confuting common sense, a display more notable for form than for substance. If one treats Socrates in this way, he need not be taken too seriously; one can observe him idly as one does any other performer. Socrates, however, does not grant Ion this protection for his vanity. He takes the offensive himself and accuses Ion of being wise along with actors and poets, whereas he, Socrates, speaks only the truth, as befits a private man. The opposition between what is here called wisdom and public men, on the one hand, and truth and private man, on the other, hints at the human situation which forces Ion to be ignorant without being aware of it and points to the precondition of the pursuit of the truth. In order to satisfy their public, the public men must pretend to wisdom, whereas only the private man, who appears to belong to a lower order of being, is free to doubt and free of the burden of public opinion. The private life seems to be essential to the philosophic state of mind. For example, the private man can think and speak of mean and contemptible things which are revealing but are beneath the exalted level expected of public men.

32d–
33e   After this skirmish for position, Socrates returns to tutoring his new pupil. Arts are wholes, Socrates argues, and the practitioners of an art are thus comparable; the man who can judge one practitioner of an art is in possession of the means to criticize all of its practitioners. He now provides Ion with examples of arts which are much more like rhapsody than either medicine or arithmetic are; he cites imitative painting, sculpture, and flute, harp, and cither playing. (He here covertly insults Ion by appearing to compare his grand art with the relatively trivial ones of flute, harp, and cither playing.) The ostensible purpose of this segment of the discussion is to prove to Ion that the grasp of an art implies competence to deal with all of it; Socrates succeeds in doing this and thus forces Ion to realize that he cannot pretend to the authority of art, as Socrates had first led him to believe he could. However, these examples implicitly raise a further problem that remains unexamined for the moment. What is it that constitutes the unity or wholeness of the arts of painting and sculpture? Two

possible answers suggest themselves: their subject matters or their use of materials. Obviously, the things represented are primary in one sense, but the medium is a more distinguishing and clearly separable aspect. The entire thrust of Socrates' argument is toward identifying poetry with its subject matter and not with its medium. He abstracts from the poetic in poetry, from what constitutes its characteristic charm, although in a hidden way he attempts to explain that charm. The duality of style and content, or medium and subject matter, in poetry calls to mind the two aspects of Ion's art mentioned by Socrates at the beginning: the rhapsodes are adorned and they understand the thought of the poet. Socrates seems to forget the beautiful in poetry, just as he has neglected to discuss the rhapsodes' adornment. But while apparently paying attention only to the poets' teaching, he is actually studying the relationship of the true to the beautiful, or the relationship of philosophy to poetry, from the point of view of philosophy or truth. Socrates is perfectly aware of the uniqueness of poetry, and he is examining the role poetry plays in establishing the false but authoritative opinions of the community. The need for poetry is one of the most revealing facts about the human soul, and that need and its effect on the citizens constitute a particular problem for Socrates' quest. Ion's total confusion about the difference between speaking *finely* and speaking *well,* between the charming and the true, is exemplary of the issue Socrates undertakes to clarify.

The examples of practitioners of arts used by Socrates, in the context of showing Ion that he must know all the poets, help to make an amusing, covert point. There is one painter, a contemporary; there are three sculptors, only one of whom is a contemporary, while the other two are mythical personages. Five rhapsodes are named; the only contemporary is Ion himself, and the others are all mythical. Of the mythical rhapsodes at least two of the first three met violent death as a result of their singing. The fourth, Phemius, served the mob of suitors running riot in Ithaca during the king's absence. He was saved from suffering death for it only by begging for mercy at the feet of the wise Odysseus. Perhaps there is a hidden threat in Socrates' speech; at least Ion asks for Socrates' succor, finally yielding completely. What does it mean that he who knows he speaks most *finely* or *beautifully* of all men about Homer and of whom all others assert that he speaks *well,* is unable to do so about other poets?

The dialogue has three major divisions. Ion's plea to Socrates ends the first, which has concluded that a knower of Homer must be a knower of the whole art of poetry and, implicitly, of the whole.

The central section of the *Ion* has, in turn, three parts, two long speeches on divine possession surrounding an interlude of discussion. The explicit intention of this section is to find some source of Ion's power other than art. This attempt at first succeeds but is finally rejected by Ion, and the final section of the dialogue is an effort to resuscitate his reputation as the possessor of an art. In this dramatic context Socrates' teaching about divine possession must be interpreted. It is presented as *the* alternative for giving dignity to Ion's speech about Homer; it proves unsatisfactory, but since the other alternative is no less unsatisfactory, it helps to reveal the nature of Ion's claim and appeal.

33c–
35a Ion insists that Socrates try to explain why Ion is so good about Homer and not about the other poets. In response, Socrates provides Ion with a respectable and flattering answer—divine possession. Moreover, he takes the opportunity to do what Ion himself had for so long wished to do; he offers a poetic display and gives a long speech, beautifully adorned, telling of gods and men and their relations. And the speech has the effect on Ion that poetry is supposed to have. "Yes, by Zeus . . . the speeches somehow lay hold of my soul." Socrates plays the poet, not to say the god. It remains to be seen whether he himself is divinely possessed or whether he self-consciously and rationally constructs a tale designed to appeal to Ion's needs and wishes.

The tale Socrates tells does satisfy Ion's demands. It explains why he can only interpret Homer and at the same time gives his interpretations a dignity perhaps greater than those based on an art would have, for there is no dignity greater than that of the gods. Socrates seemingly succeeds where Ion has failed: he establishes a special place for Homer, one that transcends the limits of rational comparison; the comparison between Homer and others would be akin to the comparison between the Bible and another book made by a believer rather than the comparison between two technical treatises. There is a source of wisdom which does not depend on the rational study of nature (a word which does not occur in the *Ion*), so that art is not the only road to wisdom. It must be stressed that art and divine possession are not merely two ways to arrive at the same result, alternative ways of understanding the same thing. They are exclusive, each implying a different and contrary view of the whole. An art requires a subject matter which is permanent and governed by intelligible rules.

Divine possession implies the existence of elusive and free gods who are not to be grasped by reason, who govern things and who can only be known if they choose to reveal themselves. In the latter case the highest and most decisive things are to be known only by the word rather than the word being judged by the thing. Ion, as the spokesman of a god, and not the artisan, would be the one who would know the truth. Socrates not only describes the well-known and undeniable phenomenon of passionate, frenzied insight but backs up the description by asserting that the source of that insight is really a god and that, hence, it is of the highest status. Reason (*noûs*) is delusive and must be denigrated.

Socrates takes *enthusiasm,* literally the presence of a god within, as the archetype of the poetic experience. The unreasoning and unreasonable movement of the soul which expresses itself in the orgiastic dances of the Corybantes is an example of the kind of condition in which this revelation is likely to be found. This is the state of soul in which men foretell the future, become diviners and oracles. Religious excitement and fanaticism constitute the ambiance in which Ion and his poetry move. Socrates compares the god to a lodestone which both moves and lends its power to move to other things. Reason, perhaps a source of rest or of self-motion, must be out of a man for him to be affected fully by this source of motion. Poetry, as presented here, ministers particularly to that part of the soul which longs for worship of the sacred, and Ion, who sings at the festivals dedicated to the gods, finds himself at home in this atmosphere of man's longing for the divine. Socrates, however, suggests that the stone can be understood in two different ways. One interpretation comes from Euripides, a poet, who calls it the Magnet, implying it is only a stone, and the other comes from the vulgar, who call it the Heraclean, implying that only the presence of the divine can account for its mysterious power. It might be suggested that in this speech Socrates adopts the account of the vulgar to explain Ion's mysterious attractiveness, lending to that attractiveness a significance commensurate with his and his audiences' wishes.

535
a–e   Upon Ion's enthusiastic reception of his speech, Socrates questions him. He does so ostensibly to tighten the links of his argument but with the real effect of revealing finally the nature of Ion's soul, this little Ion as opposed to the great interests he represents. At the same time Socrates elaborates the character of the religious experience which has been suggested. The poet is the spokesman of a god, and

the rhapsode is the spokesman of a poet and hence the spokesman of a spokesman. As a part of this great chain, Ion is asked to tell frankly of his experiences on the stage. Is he not possessed when he tells the fearful tales of the avenging Odysseus and Achilles, or the piteous ones of the sufferings of Hecuba and Priam? When he recites, is he not out of his mind and does he not suppose his soul transported to the place of these events? Ion confesses freely to this rapture, this total sympathy with his subject. When he tells of the piteous, his eyes fill with tears, and when he tells of the fearful, his hair stands on end and his heart jumps. Ion's world is that of the passions connected with tragedy; he arouses pity and fear, and he purveys that most curious of pleasures, the pleasure experienced in the tears shed for the imaginary sufferings of others. Men desire and need the satisfaction found in contemplating the mutilation and death of noble men. This satisfaction is provided in beautiful poetry and is presided over by fair gods. Socrates points out how unreasonable Ion's noble sentiments are in the real circumstances in which he finds himself—he, adorned with golden crowns, cries when he has not lost his crowns and is frightened when his friendly audience does not attack him. Ion's tears, Socrates implies, would be only for his golden crown, and his terror only for his life and comfort. He may be the spokesman for the grandest beings and sentiments, but he is a very ordinary mortal. His tragedy would be the loss of the means of display and self-preservation. He is, in the deepest sense, an actor. Ion readily accepts Socrates' characterization of his situation, without sensing his own vulgarity in doing so.

Finally, after establishing that the poet is possessed by a god, and Ion by the poet, Socrates completes his argument by asking Ion to confirm that the spectators are possessed by Ion. Thus the spectators would constitute the last link in a chain of attractions originating in the god. Ion asserts that the spectators do indeed share his experiences. He knows this because he is always looking at them and paying the closest attention to them. He reassures Socrates that this is so by explaining that he laughs when they cry, for he will get money, and he cries when they laugh, for he will lose money. This man possessed, living with the gods and the heroes, is at the same time counting the box-office receipts. He is at war with the spectators— when they cry, he laughs, and when they laugh, he cries—but there may be a deeper kinship in that Ion's low interest in the money which preserves life is not totally alien to the fear of death which is at the root of the spectator's interest in the tragic poems. At all events, we can see that the real magnet is the spectators and that Ion gives them what they want. He can best be understood by comparison to the Hollywood stars, who are nothing in themselves, are only fulfillments of the wishes of their fans, but who, in order to satisfy them, must appear to be independent, admirable, even "divine." The spectators must deceive themselves, absolutize their heroes, who exist only in terms of their tastes. It is a kind of self-praise; what the people love must be rooted in the best and highest; what appears to go from gods to men really goes in the other direction. Ion senses the vox dei in himself, but it is only the vox populi. He may think himself superior to the people, laugh at them, thinking he is duping them, but he is their flatterer and their creature; his self-esteem depends on their prizes; he does what he does at their bidding. The nature of the people and Ion's relation to them perhaps comes most clearly to light when we recognize that, if what the people most wanted were comedy, Ion would not have to deceive them and could be at one with them. He would laugh when they laugh. This may help to explain Socrates' earlier opposition between truth and public men and cast some light on his dictum that the city is the true tragedy.

535e–
536d   A second long speech is designed to complete the argument about divine possession and perfect the new view of Ion's calling designed for him by Socrates. But this speech, similar to the first one in its poetic qualities, is no longer successful, and Ion, far from being possessed, rejects it. The form is the same, so we must look elsewhere to account for the failure of this speech to persuade. The simple answer is that it no longer flatters Ion as did the first. Socrates gives with the first speech an example of successful poetry and with the second an example of unsuccessful poetry, slyly suggesting thereby that the essence of popular poetry is its capacity to flatter the aspiration of its audience. This second speech tells Ion that not only are the poet and the rhapsode possessed but the audience too is possessed. Everyone is possessed; possession is not a special honor or a title to wisdom; possession explains nothing. The story of divine possession is merely a description of the entire set of activities and attractions involved in poetry. Moreover, Socrates now stresses that the various poets are equally possessed, and Homer is in no sense superior in this decisive respect. It just happens that some men are more attracted to Homer than to any other poet. Divine possession provides no basis for believing what Homer says any more than what

Orpheus or Musaeus says. And Ion's speeches about Homer suffer correspondingly. As a matter of fact, each of the various conflicting sayings of the poets has equal divine sanction. Ion is now a helpless instrument of a blind power. Finally, Socrates implies not only that the poets and their votaries are at odds but that there are different gods revealing contrary ways. There is no cosmos, only a chaos; and the truth of Ion's and Homer's speech, which was the original theme, becomes impossible to determine. Such are the consequences of the teaching about divine possession when further elaborated.

536d   Ion, dimly aware of the unsatisfactory character of Socrates' explanation of his activity, refuses to admit that he is possessed and mad; he makes a last attempt to possess Socrates by making a display. Socrates, however, again puts him off, asking for an answer to yet another question. Ion is to be forced to support his claim that he possesses an art. He will, of course, fail in this attempt. The conclusion of the first section was that Ion knew all the poets; the conclusion of this one will be that he does not even know Homer. The first section shows the universality of Ion's proper concern, the third his incapacity to fulfill the requirements of that concern. Given the disproportion between the claim and the fulfilling of it, Ion will be forced back upon divine possession in order to salvage his reputation. But that divine possession will be nothing more than an idle, self-justificatory boast.

536e–   Socrates begins by asking Ion about what particular thing in Ho-
537c   mer he speaks well. Ion responds quite properly that there is nothing in Homer about which he does not speak well. But what about those things he does not know, that is, those arts of which Ion is not himself a practitioner? Without giving Ion time to respond, Socrates searches for a passage in Homer that is technical in character. Ion is caught up in the artifice and eagerly asks to recite the passage. At last he gets to perform, if only on a dull set of instructions for a chariot race. Socrates tells him what to recite and tells him when to stop. Socrates is now Ion's master and gives a demonstration of how he should be used. The passage recited belongs more to the domain of a charioteer than to that of a doctor. It deals with the details of a chariot race, but one might wonder whether such a poetic presentation could be properly interpreted by a charioteer either. Socrates relentlessly pursues the issue of expertise. Between doctor and charioteer Ion sees no choice, although he probably thinks he himself could best comment on the verses. But Socrates did not ask that; his goal is to get Ion

to admit that in this instance the charioteer is more competent than the rhapsode, but before he can compel Ion to do so, Socrates must come to a further agreement with him.

537c–
538a This agreement concerns the relation of arts to their subject matters. There is a variety of different kinds of things in the world, and to each of these kinds is assigned an art whose business it is to know that kind. One subject matter, one art, and what we know from one art we cannot know from another. The difference in names of arts comes from this difference in subject matter; there can be only one kind of expert for each kind of thing. Therefore, if the charioteer is expert on a passage in Homer, the rhapsode, as rhapsode, cannot be. Once this rule is accepted, Ion, who does not particularly care about this passage anyway, is prepared to admit that it is of the domain of the charioteer rather than the rhapsode. But this admission leads inevitably to the consequence that there is no passage in Homer about which Ion is competent, for the world is divided up among the well-known special arts. And even though there were some segment of Homer which dealt with rhapsody, Ion would be only one of many experts called in to interpret Homer; but, if rhapsody is anything at all, it must somehow be competent to deal with all of Homer. The helpless Ion, in order to be something, must look for some specific subject matter which he alone knows, and he finally emerges in the guise of a general.

This segment of the discussion is particularly offensive to anyone who loves poetry. Its consequence is not only that Ion is deprived of a claim to his profession but also that Homer is reduced to a mere compendium of technical information drawn from the arts. Nothing could be more antipoetic. After all, a poem is a whole, one which may use material drawn from the arts but which puts them together in a unique way which cannot be derived from the arts.

Socrates knows what poetry is; the argument is intended to be defective. The very verses cited prove this. For example, the passage assigned to the fisherman could not be interpreted by a fisherman as such, for it is a simile, comparing a fisherman's line falling through the water to the plunge of a goddess; the man who can understand this passage must know the gods as well as fishing tackle. Then, too, the verses about the healing of Machaon's wounds are more appropriately judged by the statesman who knows what kind of medicine is good for the character of citizens than the doctor (cf. *Rep.* 408). Even the first example, which on the surface looks like a straightforward account of the way to handle a chariot, is not unambiguously technical. Examination of the context of the passage reveals that Nestor is actually telling his son how to use somewhat unsportsman-like tactics in the race; the judgment of the propriety of such advice does not evidently fit too well into the charioteer's sphere of compe-tence. The insufficiency of this argument is clear; it does not do justice to the poem or to Ion. But Socrates wishes to compel us to see precisely wherein it fails and thereby to see a real and profound problem which Ion, and, for that matter, most men, do not suffi-ciently grasp. They, in their lives, are caught up in it unawares. This argument merely reflects a contradiction in the most common under-standing of things.

The problem would be most immediately perceived by modern men as that of specialization. If one looks around a modern univer-sity, for example, one sees a variety of independent, seemingly self-sufficient disciplines. Physics, astronomy, literature, and economics teach competences which are thought to be unquestionable. Now, where is the unity? They are parts of the university but there is no one who is expert about the knowledge present in the university as a whole. There is always a central administration, to be sure, but it does not have an intellectual discipline of its own; it merely provides the wherewithal of survival to the disciplines and accepts their intel-lectual authority. There are men who talk about the whole domain of knowledge and who are even applauded for doing so. But no one thinks of crediting them with knowledge of the same solidity or certitude as that of the specialists. One finds competent specialized speech or bloated, unconvincing general speech. It is this very prob-lem that Socrates is approaching here, the problem alluded to in the *Apology* when Socrates tells of his examination of the artisans as well as of the poets and statesmen. He does not deny that Homer con-stitutes a unity, which is more than the result of the mere addition of parts. The question is the status of that unity. Does Homer's general view have the character of knowledge, or is it an adorned deception which satisfies men's longings and which they can dupe themselves into taking seriously by calling "divinely inspired"? Men in Socrates' time, as at present, believed that the arts are the only sources of simply persuasive knowledge. But if that is the case, then men's general views can never be knowledge.

If one examines the principle of specialization posited by Socrates somewhat more carefully, one becomes aware that it is wrong. And

Ion's acceptance of that principle is the source of the dissolution of poetry's unity. Socrates asserted that each subject matter is dealt with by one art and that no other art can speak precisely about that subject matter. But this is not so. What is forgotten is the master arts. The horseman, for example, speaks of the saddle maker's art with great competence and precision. As a matter of fact, he may speak of it with even greater authority than the saddle maker himself, for he sets the latter in motion. He alone can judge the good and bad saddles, for he is their user, but he is surely not a saddle maker. The best model of the master artisan is the architect who rules the specialized artisans who build a house. Socrates' argument forgets that each of the arts treats of a subject matter which is part of a whole which is itself the subject of a more sovereign art. None of the specialties is really independent, although it may seem to be.

This leads us back to the art of the whole, the necessity of which emerged early in the discussion. The subject matter of poetry turned out to be the whole, and if poetry is to be based on knowledge, or to be discussed knowledgeably, there must be knowledge, or an art, of the whole. But somehow men do not see this art and do not see the whole presupposed in each of its divisions. They have a view of the whole, but it seems to stem from altogether different sources than their view of the parts. The helmet maker's art seems somehow altogether different from the statesman's art, which in war directs the wearers of the helmets. The parts seem rationally intelligible, but the whole of which they are parts does not seem to be so. The discovery of the possibility of a rationally intelligible whole may be called the discovery of nature, and that discovery is the origin of philosophy. It has already been remarked that the word *nature* does not occur in the *Ion;* it comes as no surprise, then, that the word *philosophy* is also nowhere to be found. In this dialogue Socrates examines the pre-philosophic soul which knows neither of nature nor of the master art which seeks the first principles of nature. This art is the quest for that universal and unifying knowledge which is neither special nor spurious, that knowledge of which Ion could not conceive and we can no longer conceive. Ion's world knows of special arts which are highly developed and even awe-inspiring; such arts are almost coeval with man, and reflection on them leads to the notion of a permanent and comprehensible order which is the cause of the intelligibility of the parts. But that reflection is not a part of Ion's world; instead there is a dazzling poetry telling of gods and heroes, a precursor of philosophy but its bitterest enemy. The *Ion* is a representation of the emergence of philosophy out of the world of myth.

538e–   It is not only ignorance that prevents the discovery of nature; man's
539   most powerful passion sides with poetry and is at war with his love of wisdom. Socrates reveals this in his final examples drawn from Homer. With great emphasis he recites passages from the *Iliad* and the *Odyssey* dealing with divining, presumably to show once again the kind of thing in Homer with which a specialist should deal. However, he has already amply made his point, and the peculiar solemnity of his presentation forces one to search further for his intention. It can be found in his desire to call particular attention to the art of divining. This art has been mentioned several times in the dialogue and has been connected with rhapsody throughout, suffering the same fate as it. In the first section, divining was treated as an art; indeed, it was the first example mentioned of an art. In the central section, it was one of the examples of divine possession, and now it has again become an art. Although not obviously similar to rhapsody or poetry, divining is used by Socrates to point up their character. By reflecting on divining we can penetrate what Socrates wishes to teach us about rhapsody and poetry.

Diviners exist because men wish to know the future, because they are worried about what will happen to them as individuals. There can be such knowledge only if there is providence; if the fate of individuals is but a matter of chance, this fond wish would have to remain unfulfilled. Providence implies the existence of gods who care for men. If divining is to be considered an art, it is strange in that it must profess to know the intentions of the gods; as an art, it would, in a sense, seem to presuppose that the free, elusive gods are shackled by the bonds of intelligible necessity. Divining partakes of the rational dignity of the arts while supposing a world ruled by divine beings who are beyond the grasp of the arts. It belongs somehow both to the realm of the arts and to the realm of divine possession. Moreover, divining is a most peculiar art in that it treats of the particular while other arts speak only of the general; the unique, the special, are the only concern of divining, while the particular is taken account of by other arts only to the extent that it partakes in the general rules. And finally, although divining is a pious art, the knowledge derived from it is to be used to avoid the bad things and gain the good ones. On the one hand, it presupposes a fixed providence; on the other hand, it ministers to man's desire to master his destiny rather than accept it.

Socrates' view of the proper use of divining has been preserved for us by Xenophon. In the context of defending Socrates' piety—he had been accused of impiety—Xenophon tells that Socrates

> advised them [his companions] to do necessary things in the way they thought they would be best done. As for things the consequences of which are unclear, he sent them to inquire of diviners whether they should be done. He said that those who are going to manage households and cities in a fine way had need, in addition, of the art of divining. With respect to becoming a carpenter, a smith, a farmer, an investigator or such deeds, a calculator, a household manager, or a general, he held that such studies can be acquired by human thought. However, he said that the gods reserved the most important parts of them for themselves and of these parts nothing is clear to human beings. For it is surely not clear to the man who plants a field in a fine way who will reap it; nor is it clear to the man who builds a house in a fine way who will live in it; nor is it clear to the general whether it is beneficial to exercise command; nor is it clear to the statesman whether presiding over the city is beneficial; nor is it clear to the man who marries a beautiful girl for his delight whether she will prove a misery to him; nor is it clear to the man who makes alliances of marriage with men powerful in the city whether he will as a result be driven from the city. He said that those who suppose that nothing of such things belongs to the domain of the divine but all are within the capacity of human thought are possessed by madness. But they are also possessed by madness who inquire of diviners concerning things that the gods have given to human beings to judge on the basis of study; for example, if someone were to ask whether it is better to get a charioteer for a chariot who has knowledge or one who does not have knowledge? Or whether it is better to get a pilot of a ship who has knowledge or one who does not have knowledge? Or to ask about what can be known by counting, measuring, or weighing. Those who inquire about such things from the gods he believed do what is forbidden. He said that what the gods have given human beings to accomplish by study must be studied; what is not clear to human beings should be inquired about from the gods by means of divining; for the gods give a sign to those who happen to be in their grace. [*Memorabilia* I i 6–9]

Art can tell a man how to sow, but whether he will reap what he sows is beyond the power of art to know, for chance is decisive in determining whether that man will live or die. But the man who sows does so only because *he* wants to reap. What he cares about most as a living, acting man is not guaranteed by art. Socrates reasonably prescribes that men should obey the rules of art where they apply, and, in what belongs to chance, consult the diviner. In other words, he urges men not to let what is out of their control affect their action. They should separate out their hopes and fears from their understanding and manfully follow the prescriptions of what true knowledge they possess. They must not let their passionate aspirations corrupt that knowledge.

But such a solution is not satisfactory to most men; they must see the world in such a way that their personal ambitions have a cosmic status. The fate of an individual man is no more significant to the knower of man than is the fate of a particular leaf to the botanist. The way of the knower is unacceptable for the life of men and cities. They must see a world governed by providence and the gods, a world in which art and science are inexplicable, a world which confuses general and particular, nature and chance. This is the world of poetry to which man clings so intensely, for it consoles and flatters him. As long as human wishes for the significance of particular existences dominate, it remains impossible to discover nature, the intelligible and permanent order, for nature cannot satisfy those wishes. Ion cannot imagine an art of the whole because, as rhapsode, he most of all serves the longing for individual immortality, and he uses his poetry to that end.

The effect of this longing for immortality on the soul is illuminated by Socrates' comparison of the enthusiastic diviners and rhapsodes with the Bacchic or Corybantic dancers (534a–b). In the *Laws* (790d–791b) the Athenian Stranger speaks of Corybantism as an illness resulting from excessive fear, which gets its relief and cure in the frantic dances. The hearts of the Corybantic dancers leap, just as does Ion's, and they dance wildly; carried away by powerful internal movements which they translate into frenzied external movements, they dedicate their dance, and themselves, to a protecting deity. The fear of death, the most profound kind of fear and the most powerful of passions, moves them until they are out of their minds, and they can be healed only in the fanatic religious practice. In the *Ion,* Socrates points to the most important source of religious fanaticism and suggests that the function of that kind of poetry which is taken most seriously is to heal this fear and console man in his awareness of his threatened existence. This poetry irrationally soothes the madness in all of us. It is a useful remedy but a dangerous one. Fanaticism is often its result. The man who most believes the poets' stories is likely to be most intolerant of those who do not. Socrates, the philosopher who tests the stories as well as those who tell them, is a menace to the sense of security provided by them. It is precisely overcoming this concern with oneself, in all its subtle and pervasive forms, that is *the* precondition of philosophy and a rational account of one's own life. Poetry, as Ion administers it to suffering man, gives a spurious sense of knowledge while really serving and watering the passions hostile to true knowledge.

539d–
540d Socrates, who has taken over from Ion and has himself been reciting from Homer, showing his own rhapsodic gifts, now demands that Ion select the passages that belong to the rhapsode. Ion must look for some special segment which speaks about rhapsody. But oxlike, he asserts that all of Homer belongs to him. He does not seem to have followed the argument. It is not only stupidity, however, but self-interest that makes him so dense. He loses his title to respect if he is not the interpreter of the whole, and besides, he clearly recites all of the *Iliad* and *Odyssey* and not just individual passages. Socrates forbids him, however, to say that he is an expert on all of Homer. Their earlier agreements about the practitioners of arts who can judge parts of Homer bind Ion. Socrates chides Ion for being forgetful. It is not appropriate for a rhapsode, of all people, to be forgetful. Socrates implies that the rhapsode is really only a memory mindlessly repeating the ancestral things. Ion believes he can abide by the agreements and emerge relatively intact. As he sees it, the parts of Homer dedicated to these petty, uninteresting arts are of no real importance to the whole. Ion can be the expert on what really counts: the human things. In particular he knows what it is fitting for men and women, slave and free, ruled and ruler, to say; he knows the proprieties of civil, as opposed to technical, man.

Socrates does not allow Ion to leave it at this general statement of his competence in what men should say. Homer never presents man in general; his personnages are always particular kinds of men doing particular kinds of things. There is a free man who is a ruler of a ship; he is the pilot; what he would say in a particular difficult situation is known to the practitioner of the pilot's art. The same is true of the man who is a doctor treating a sick patient. Ion must answer "no" when Socrates asks him whether he knows the proprieties of such speech. What about the things it is fitting for a slave to say? To this Ion answers "yes." But Socrates will not even let him remain a slave or be a woman. Both must be artisans too. Then Socrates asks whether Ion would know what it is fitting for a man who is a general to say in exhorting his troops. In a last desperate attempt, Ion seizes on this alternative, his final hope of salvaging his dignity. Socrates interprets Ion's assertion that he knows what a general should say to mean Ion possesses the general's art; he who knows the speech of a general must be a general. Socrates began by talking to a rhapsode and ends by commissioning him as a general. Socrates rejects the distinction between speech and deed which Ion suggests but cannot defend.

Now, there is clearly a possibility of discussing man in general without knowing all the particular activities which he can undertake. Similarly, there is a capacity to speak about deeds, and to understand them, without performing them. Ion is caught in a sophistic argument. But Socrates does not do him an injustice, for if he were able to present a defense of the dignity of speech, if he had any justification for his own life, which is devoted to speech alone, he could extricate himself from the difficulty. He makes a living from speech but does not really respect it or understand it. Ion, apparently following Homer, admires the heroes and their deeds; they are more important than the speeches which glorify them. Speech follows on deed, and the life of action is the best kind of life. Or rather, there is no theoretical life; for only if there is a theoretical life can speech be regarded as anything more than a means. Thus Ion sings the poems not for their own sake but for the sake of money.

Only in a world in which thought could be understood to be highest, in which there are universals—which means essentially intelligible beings—can there be significant general speech. Without such universals, only particulars exist. That is why Ion is unable to stop Socrates' progressing from the man in general Ion said he knew about to slaves guarding sheep, pilots in a storm, and so on. Only if he knew of human nature could he speak of man; but we have already seen why he cannot even conceive of nature. For him, all speeches are distillations of the deeds of doers, and the poets and rhapsodes are but incompetent imitators of the competent. The splendor and authority of poetry would seem to indicate that speech can be higher than deed, but the poets and rhapsodes do not explain how that can be. In order for that explanation to be given, there would have to be a total

revolution in their view, a revolution which can only be effected by
philosophy. When poetry can celebrate the speeches of Socrates, the
poet—in this case Plato—has found a ground for the life devoted to
speech.

540d–
541b
All of this becomes clearer in the further elaboration of Ion's generalship. Socrates permits Ion to masquerade in this comic garb, although he could easily have shown that this position cannot be defended either. This role for the actor is apparently too appropriate to
be denied him. Ion now knows what he must do to defend himself,
so he is willing to assert that there is no difference between the
rhapsode's and the general's art and that all rhapsodes are generals
(although he cannot bring himself to go so far as to argue that all
generals are rhapsodes). There is a hidden madness in all unselfcon-
scious human lives, and Socrates, in dissecting this soul, brings its
peculiar madness to light. Ion's choice of the general's art is appropriate for many reasons. It is a particular practical art, one which is
pervasive in Homer, one which is needed and admired beyond most
other arts.

But more profoundly one can see that the propriety of Ion's becoming a general has something to do with the whole view of the
world peculiar to Ion and his understanding of Homer. In the beginning, when Socrates listed the things the poets talk about, the first
item was war, and it was the only one which stood alone, not coupled
with an appropriate companion as were the others. The obvious
complement to war, peace, is missing in the poets. Superficially this
means that the great poems tell of warlike heroes and the struggles
between and within cities. In a deeper sense it means that they tell of a
world ruled by gods who also struggle and who refer back to an
ultimate chaos. The only harmony is to be found in the rational
cosmos, which is grasped not by the practical man but by the theoretical man.

541b–
542b
Socrates pursues this theme by asking Ion why he goes around
Greece being a rhapsode instead of a general. Adopting Ion's own
hidden prejudice, Socrates, who never does anything but talk,
ridicules the notion that the Greeks need a man wearing a golden
crown more than a general. Instead of arguing that the interpretation
of poetry is a better and nobler thing than leading men in war, Ion
offers an excuse for doing second best. He is a citizen of a subject city
and would not be used as a general by either Athens or Sparta. Ion
would apparently be willing to adapt himself to the service of either

of these warring cities. Perhaps this is also just what he does with his poetry: he adapts what is apparently universal to the needs of opposing heres and nows. His poetry provides the gods which Athenians and Spartans invoke as guarantors of their causes when they march out to slay each other. Ion's cosmopolitanism is only a sham with roots in nothing beyond the needs of the cities, giving particular and passing interests a universal significance. He is a servant who must appear to be master in order to satisfy his masters. While a philosopher is truly a citizen of the world, in that his pursuit is essentially independent of the opinions or consent of any group of men, the political man needs a country and a people to serve. Ion has no satisfactions which are not dependent on the approval of his spectators. He needs the cities as they need him. For political men the accident of where they are born is decisive in limiting their possibilities of fulfillment.

Socrates tries to act as though these limits of politics did not exist; he treats politics as though it were as cosmopolitan as any of the arts, for example, arithmetic. He abstracts from the peculiar atmosphere of chance and unreason surrounding political life, expressing astonishment at Ion's unwillingness to act like any other man of knowledge; he thereby provides a measure of the difference between the life of reason and that of cities. It is the city to which Ion belongs, and his irrationality only points to the city's. Socrates names a few obscure, not to say unknown, men, alleging that they were chosen as generals by Athens. On this rather dubious basis, he asserts that not being a citizen is no hindrance to politicial participation. Ion, Socrates concludes, must be insisting that it is a hindrance only in order to avoid giving that wondrous display which Socrates has been so eager to hear for so long. Ion, suggests Socrates, must be an unjust man, since he does not fulfill his promise. Or as an alternative, perhaps he is really divinely possessed. Socrates gives Ion a choice: he can be either divine or unjust. Perhaps the two are ultimately the same.

Socrates compares Ion to the slippery Proteus and thus implicitly compares himself to Menelaus, who sought for guidance about the gods from Proteus so he could save himself. But this Proteus cannot help the new Menelaus. So they part, Ion humiliated but wearing a new, divine crown, Socrates in search of more authoritative knowledge of the gods.

GLOSSARY

Aulos is our transliteration of the name of an ancient double-reeded wind instrument that bore some resemblance to the modern oboe. Though traditionally translated "flute," the aulos was in fact not at all like the flute as we know it today.

Beautiful, fine, and *noble* are words we have used in different contexts to translate the Greek *kalon*. The *kalon* is to be distinguished from, though in range it overlaps with, the "good," beneficial, or useful (*agathon, sumpheron*). Provisionally one may say that the *kalon* refers to that which is valued because of its splendor or because of its moral elevation, seriousness, and intrinsic excellence. The good is not necessarily noble or beautiful; whether the beautiful or noble is always good, or in what way it is good, is a pervasive Platonic question that goes to the heart of humanity's moral experience. This question is implicitly or explicitly raised, and new dimensions of its import come to sight, in every dialogue in this collection.

Cithara, citharist: see *Lyre.*

Convention, law, and *legal custom* are all used in different contexts to translate *nomos*, which means primarily written and unwritten law but also authoritative custom, tradition, and belief. The distinction between the legal and the customary is not as sharp in Greek as it is in English. *Nomos* may also refer to the realm of convention, in contradistinction to the realm of nature (see *Nature*). Finally, *nomos* can mean a type of song.

Courage, manliness: see *Human being.*

Draughts is a conventional translation for *petteia,* the generic name for several board names whose precise rules are unknown today but that evidently resembled our checkers.

Fine: see *Beautiful.*

Gentleman is a conventional translation for a phrase that means literally "a noble and good man" (*kaloskagathos*).

Harmoniae is our transliteration of the technical term for the patterns according to which musical instruments were tuned. The precise nature of these patterns is not known for certain today. Because certain of these *harmoniae* were usually used to tune instruments to accompany certain types of song, it came to be thought that some specific *harmoniae* befitted specific moods.

Hero is our quasi-transliteration of *heros*, the term for legendary individuals thought to be descended from the mating of a deity and a human or to have been raised from mortal to semidivine status as a reward for their exploits.

Human being, man, courage: Greek makes a distinction between "man" in the sense of human being or mankind (*anthrōpos*) and man the male (*anēr*). The latter term has the same root as the word for courage (*andreia*) and carries a more or less subtle connotation of manliness. We have not always been able to reproduce this important shade of meaning.

Law, legal custom: see *Convention.*

Lyre and *cithara* are names for two harplike musical instruments. The *cithara* had eight to ten strings stretched on a U-shaped frame with a tortoiseshell sounding board; it was usually played by professionals called *citharists.* The *lyre* was a smaller and simpler instrument with fewer strings and was often played by amateurs, but children learned to play the *lyre* by going to a *citharist.*

Man, manliness: see *Human being.*

Mina and *drachma* are transliterated names for monetary units, one *mina* equaling 100 silver *drachmas.* The precise value in contemporary money is difficult to gauge, but a day laborer would receive several *drachmas* in wages each day.

Music translates *mousikē*, a term with a wider range of meaning than the English word "music" usually has. The word denotes the crafts that are possessed and presided over by the goddesses called the Muses: primarily song but also the fine arts generally, history, and sometimes even philosophy.

Nature translates *physis* and means that which grows by itself and therefore does not owe its existence or its force and character to the will of the gods or to human making or belief. The root of the word for "nature" is the same as the root of the words for "growth" and "plants," and this common aspect should be borne in mind whenever these latter words appear.

Noble: see *Beautiful.*

INDEX OF NAMES

INDEX OF DISCUSSIONS OF
OTHER PLATONIC DIALOGUES

INDEX OF SUBJECTS

An asterisk indicates a sustained treatment of the subject.

Actions. *See* Deeds

Advantageous, *sumpheron,* 52, 114, 188–96, 227. *See also* Beneficial; Useful

Affection. See Experience (*pathos*)

Agreement, and knowledge, 31, 57–59, 71–73, 115, 127, 185–87, 247–49, 262–63

Ambition, 224–37

Arts: architectonic art, 84, 136–37, 156–58, 387–88; charioteering, 135, 154–57*, 364–65; cooking, 59–60, 73, 138, 160–62*; farming, 22, 40, 59, 60–61, 132–33, 136, 151, 156–57; gymnastic, 81–83, 96, 112, 124, 128–29*; medicine, 114–15, 124–25, 128–29, 135, 155–56, 182, 214, 220; music, 81, 112, 136, 155–57, 163, 180–82, 199, 205, 225, 238, 242, 252, 322, 327, 330, 361–63; shepherding, 61, 66, 73, 156–57

Astronomy, 107–8, 287. *See also* Heaven

Beautiful. *See* Noble

Being, or what is, 49, 58, 60, 66, 71, 77, 277–79, 332, 334–36, 341, 346–55

Beings, or the things that are, 28–29, 56–57, 59, 70, 101, 151, 216, 235, 264–66, 277–79, 305, 332–34, 388

Belongings, possessions, 113, 175, 200, 203, 209–18, 236–37, 243

Beneficial, helpful, *ōphelimon,* 24, 30–31 (advantageous), 46–47, 51, 81, 83, 95–96, 112, 113–21, 123–29, 141–45, 149, 164, 199, 244, 246, 289, 307, 311, 312, 328–30, 338–39, 343–44, 351, 354–55. *See also* Advantageous; Useful

Body, sōma, 29, 50, 61, 82–84, 95–96, 112–14, 116, 123, 209–15, 220, 235, 244, 280, 282, 288, 295, 327–28, 357

Capacity, power, *dunamis,* 284–88, 297–98, 302–6, 326–28, 335, 349–51

Care, trouble, concern, *epimeleia,* 37, 51, 65, 176, 221; for oneself, 43, 113, 116, 129, 197–209*, 210–19*, 232, 234, 241–45, 267, 289; for others, 41, 85, 98, 201–2, 241–42, 250, 311

Cause, *aition,* 73, 104–5, 329, 351–52, 359*, 361*, 364, 388

Chance, fortune, luck, *tuchē,* 75, 144, 145, 161, 314, 326, 389–91, 395

City, the, 55, 69–71, 118–21, 130, 154–55, 206–8, 232–34, 236–39, 271–72, 384, 391, 394–95

Clever, adept. *See* Terrible

Common, community, partnership, *koinon,* 40–41, 46–47, 50–51, 205–6, 272, 284, 296, 308–9, 333, 343, 350, 353–54, 375–76, 380; counsel, 138, 143, 197, 203, 241–42; investigation, inquiry, 57, 81, 194, 204, 237, 250, 261–67

Contradiction, 83, 113, 229, 247, 258, 263, 318, 321, 361; self-contradiction, 25, 37–39, 43, 69, 118, 194, 229, 261, 291

Corruption, destruction, *diaphthora,* 22 (harm), 43, 47, 92, 141, 144, 148, 152, 215, 220, 223, 235–36, 239, 249, 270, 272

Courage, manliness, *andreia,* 31, 149–50, 159–62, 201, 207, 240, 244, 246–66, 269–80

Craftsman, artisan, *dēmiourgos,* 23, 85–87,

.